Land of Big Rivers

Shawnee Books

LAND of BIG RIVERS

French & Indian Illinois, 1699–1778

‿

M. J. MORGAN

Southern Illinois University Press
Carbondale and Edwardsville

Printed in the United States of America
Chapter 2 in this volume is based on "The French in the Illinois Country, 1699–1735:
Using Historical Geography to Understand European-Indian History," in *Geography,
History, and the American Political Economy*, edited by Heppen and Otterstrom (Lanham,
Md.: Lexington, 2009). Chapter 5 is based on "Indians on Trial: Crime and Punishment
in French Louisiana on the Eve of the Seven Years War," in *Louisiana History* 50, no. 3
(summer 2009). Both essays were used with permission from the publishers.

13   4 3 2

Library of Congress Cataloging-in-Publication Data
Morgan, M. J., 1955–
Land of big rivers : French and Indian Illinois, 1699–1778 / M. J. Morgan.
    p. cm. — (Shawnee books)
Includes bibliographical references and index.
ISBN-13: 978-0-8093-2988-5 (paper : alk. paper)
ISBN-10: 0-8093-2988-3 (paper : alk. paper)
ISBN-13: 978-0-8093-8564-5 (ebook)
ISBN-10: 0-8093-8564-3 (ebook)
1. Illinois—History—To 1778. 2. Illinois—Environmental conditions. 3. Frontier
and pioneer life—Illinois. 4. Human ecology—Illinois—History—18th century.
5. Floodplains—Illinois—History—18th century. 6. Uplands—Illinois—History—
18th century. 7. Illinois—Ethnic relations—History—18th century. 8. French—
Illinois—History—18th century. 9. Indians of North America—Illinois—History—
18th century. 10. British—Illinois—History—18th century. I. Title.
F544.M86 2010
977.3'01—dc22   2009037935

To my parents, who brought me to the Country of the Illinois

Contents

Illustrations

Preface: A Word about *Buffalo*

Many readers will know that the correct term for the great herds of animals darkening the early Illinois prairies is *bison*. *Bison bison* is found in North America, while true buffalo are on other continents. *Buffalo* has become the common name and referent, however; and more important, the term *buffalo* is the one in almost all the sources used for this study. The French often wrote *wild cattle*, or *boeuf*; the British and Americans used *buffalo*. Sometimes I use *bison*; but mostly, I am choosing to use *buffalo*. This word was first recorded for the American mammal in 1635, while *bison* was first recorded in 1774.

Acknowledgments

The research for this study was made smoother because of the committed help of the following people: Valerie Berry of the Lewis Library, Vincennes University; James Cornelius and John Hoffman of the Illinois Historical Survey, University of Illinois at Urbana-Champaign; Tom Foti, State Ecologist and Chief of Research, Arkansas Natural Heritage Commission; John White, Ecologist and Nature Conservationist, Ecological Services, Urbana-Champaign; and Dr. William I. Woods, Contract Archaeology, Southern Illinois University, Edwardsville. I am also grateful to archivists at the Chicago Historical Society; Missouri Historical Society, St. Louis; the Filson Society, Louisville, Kentucky; the Lilly Library, Indiana University, Bloomington; the Glenn R. Black Laboratory of Archaeology, Bloomington; and the Newberry Library, Chicago. A special thank you for the careful editing and attention given my sources and terminology by an archaeologist reviewer.

In a separate category altogether is the contribution of Mr. Monty R. Baker, retired bibliographic librarian, University of Illinois. Mr. Baker worked tirelessly for over a year on his own time and often at his own expense to track down and procure hard-to-find source materials. His efforts allowed the completion of this study in probably half the time it would have taken otherwise.

I also thank Dr. David Stradling for important help in strengthening the ecological arguments; Dr. Willard Sunderland and Dr. John Mack Faragher for their reading of and useful commentary about a draft; Daryl Shadrick for many, many hours of listening, encouragement, and technical support; J. Kinsey Parkhe for being a willing audience for my speculations and stories; my husband, Tom Morgan, for scientific contributions to insect, buffalo, and plant ecology, as well as significant emotional strength; and my daughters Lila Walsh, Shelley, Kristina, and Adelle McFarland for living with much change and accepting it cheerfully. Thanks also to Melody Herr for early editorial suggestions and a vision of what this book could be; and thanks to Chassy Nichols for hours of detailed manuscript revising. Most of all I sincerely thank Dr. Geoffrey Plank, director of my research, for the hours he spent reading and commenting on drafts. His enthusiasm for my ideas and his careful, timely, and detailed suggestions have helped me time and again to think my way through a complicated story. Any errors or confusions in this narrative are entirely my own.

Introduction

Land of Big Rivers is an environmental history of a small, fertile niche along a great river. The French colonial settlements of southern Illinois lay right at an imaginary hinge point: here the Mississippi bows slightly to the west below the Big Rivers confluence of the Illinois and Missouri, the outermost point of the so-called French crescent—the curving French settlement line extending from Montreal to New Orleans. At the bow point, five French villages and at least four or five Illinois Indian villages coexisted from 1699 to 1765. Yet these clusters of homes, fences, barns, horse mills, tanneries, mission houses, and churches have been assigned a slight role in standard histories of Illinois. The real story begins, in many treatments, with the pouring in of American settlers into Illinois Territory after the War of 1812. Ferried over the Ohio River, 250 wagons a month rolled north into Illinois by 1820. Barely twenty-five years later, John Deere's plow bit into the prairies and began a formidable transformation. This is the story most consistently told and celebrated; and attached to it is a tenacious assumption about the emptiness of an untouched Illinois, an Illinois "opened" for settlement by President Madison. In truth, successive waves of interesting, innovative, and resourceful people had lived in the Country of the Illinois for thousands of years. They especially utilized the tripartite geographic division known today as the American Bottom; and it was on their history that the Americans followed.

Flooded and replenished for thousands of years, the black, fecund earth was well and intimately known along a sixty-mile stretch of floodplain between present-day Alton, Illinois, and old Fort Gage in Randolph County. Here was a theater for the prehistoric and historic meetings of many peoples. Each group who migrated and farmed there—middle and late Mississippian Indians, historic Illinois Indians, the French, the British, and finally, the

Americans—changed and were changed themselves by proximal relations of riverine earth and water. This study is anchored right in the fertile mud of that insular ecosystem and emphasizes the continuous relations between all peoples and the land. It especially examines the ways each successive group in the historic period moved into an environment already impacted by others.

Between 1699 and 1778, a peculiar, localized history evolved. The Europeans who arrived there were representatives of continental and international events and policies; their very coming—their deposition on the eastern shores of the Mississippi through ventures in exploration and trade—brought the "outside" into the Illinois. Yet inside the Illinois Country already lay a mobile, interactive world of diverse indigenous peoples. They were responding to distant events and catalysts within a wide-flung kinship and alliance system of their own. In truth, there never was—or only once was, very long ago in distant geologic time—a primeval, virgin Illinois. The power of European narratives, of European languages, the passionate evocation of the beauty of the Illinois, has created an enduring fable: pristine wilderness. In the "untouched" Illinois nestled an extraordinary, virile flora and fauna, a panoramic abundance often catalogued by first-time observers from floating river craft.

Yet even this view has become further textured over the centuries. As the fable goes, the Indian tribes who lived in the Illinois Country did not perceive its potential and cared little about its yield until the French arrived in 1699 to instruct them. The French alone among Europeans understood the country and inhabitants along the great river. They brought Old World peasant folkways and developed (primarily) illiterate, jovial relations with Indians that included much intermarriage, human contact, communication, and trade. Yet the French maintained a pronounced geographic isolation. Scant population growth and erratic influx of French settlers bespoke a failure to develop the rich Illinois lands. In 1765, following the cession of the Illinois Country after the Seven Years War, the British arrived. They came as military victors and commercial marketers and stirred up trouble, disrupting the French-Indian allegiances and prosperous—if desultory—trade-agricultural world. Focused on political and economic control, heavy-handed with French and Indians alike, and unprepared for distant frontier living, the British over ten years spurred an emptying out of the Illinois. The French migrated to the Missouri lands, while the Illinois Indians shrank away to impoverished remnants. Once more, a group of incoming people failed to correctly perceive or utilize the resources of the Illinois Country. Into the vacuum created by the British evacuation in 1775—into a waiting land—poured American settlers. Finally the wild prairie and woodland mosaic of the Illinois came of age. The right people had tenure.

A progression of local and regional histories of these diverse peoples has tended to produce this narrative, although late-twentieth-century studies by the Illinois Department of Natural Resources and the Historic Preservation Agency have begun to redress the focus on American settlement. However, in 2001, the state of Illinois reprinted a commissioned 1978 study by Richard Jensen, *Illinois: A History*. Jensen states that the French left no more impact on the land than place names. The fable of slight human impact before American settlement is enduring, created partially by a lack of broad synthesis studies for general readers. This study seeks to create such a synthesis, to discover and analyze exactly how prehistoric and historic Indians, French, and British peoples found ways to live on a sixty-mile stretch of water-dominated land. Their "failures" are construed here along two axes: what happened to their numbers, and why—the ebb and flow of population—and how did their ways of using natural resources contribute to those changes? In the past twenty years, other fine historical studies have begun to examine these questions. In particular, the work of Carl J. Ekberg and a host of archeologists, stimulated by the pioneering work of Margaret Kimball Brown in the 1980s, has focused right on the French and Indian settlements. Ekberg has studied French colonial Ste. Genevieve across the Mississippi River, as well as the agricultural practices of the French on the eastern shores. Archeologists have striven to determine locations of early Illinois Indian hunting camps and villages. Central questions involve the degree of contact between the Illinois tribes and the early French, the impact of European trade goods, and patterns of Indian movement. The dramatic drop in Illinois Indian population over the eighteenth century has attracted the interest of population geographers and anthropologists. Historians and archaeologists continue to reconstruct a fragmented, poorly documented story of decimation and eradication in a complex frontier habitat.[1]

Each history in its own way selects a specific group to follow, and while some interactions of groups are explored, these studies remain curiously incomplete: they take at face value the accounts of the Illinois land. The environment is treated as a backdrop for the stories of the people. Carl Ekberg does the best job of addressing differences in settlement and agriculture in each of the French villages along the Mississippi, pointing out the more saturate, watery lands of the Cahokia area to the north and highlighting the wheat-growing successes of Kaskaskia to the south. Yet in Ekberg's careful analysis of French agricultural practices, the Illinois Indians have a limited role. They remain for the most part domiciled in their villages near the French communal lands. Most studies of the Illinois Indians, are, in fact, anthropological; they do not re-create the ways these Indians were daily involved with French and British, the ways that all these people were using the land and resources of the Illinois Country, significantly altering the environment. This elision has to do with the persistence of the American settler narrative: the breaking of the prairies, the tapping of the dramatic agricultural potential of the American Bottom. The Government Land Office surveyor has appeared in the record as almost a kind of folk hero; it is in the early years of the nineteenth century that the story begins to be told about human interaction with the Illinois land itself.

This study argues that environmental changes in the Illinois Country were engendered not only by the Americans but also by the French and British and their relationship to both the riverine land and the Indians; and that the Illinois Indians in their particularized locale were caught in a matrix of forces based on resource competition among a variety of peoples. To reconstruct the eighteenth-century environment, an interdisciplinary approach has been used, culling longitudinal studies in botany, ecology, geology, and soil science. The cross-disciplinary fields of ethnohistory, anthropology, and archaeology have been critically important in reconstructing changes in the lives of Indians, French, and British. Another approach has been to make much more extensive use of French notarial records that contain invaluable property descriptions. These legal documents offer clues not only to how land was used but also to how it was perceived. To this point, historians have used the notarial documents to learn about inheritance practices and French material culture through estate listings. These records can also map out the floodplain settlements and establish patterns and changes.

Yet the eighty-year narrative of French occupation of the Illinois Country also includes a shift to the upland prairies after midcentury. Although the French never established a permanent village on the upland, the buildup of the Seven Years War across the late 1740s drew more people into the central prairies of the Illinois. French and British jockeyed for Indian loyalties and control of trade in both the Ohio and Mississippi Valleys. The upland till plain became more important as a meeting place, as well as a rich environment yielding timbers, thatch, herbs, nuts, game birds, buffalo, and deer. After a violent year, 1751–52, characterized by an eastern prairie Indian attack on French villages, a brutal northern Indian raid on the Illinois Indians, and a French march against the Miami-British trading post of Pickawillany in the Ohio Valley, more and more people began to appear on the upland prairies. The war itself drew men and foodstuffs out of French Illinois, across the Grand Prairie to points east. French bateaux ascended the Ohio River toward Fort Duquesne. Retreating French soldiers, driven south after the British took Fort Detroit, crossed winter prairies on snowshoes to reach Fort Chartres in 1760–61. During Pontiac's War in 1763 and after his murder in Cahokia in 1769, the Illinois Country became a land of rumor. Many people arrived with information, by foot, on horseback, by river craft. During the British occupation, scores of competing hunters, British, French, and Indian, fanned out across the uplands, and they reported on each other's movements, buffalo hauls, and camp locations regularly. European supply lines on the rivers began to reshape understandings of where foodstuffs came from. By 1778, when George Rogers Clark marched through the hardwood forests and then the prairies of southern Illinois to reach Kaskaskia, he was traversing land known, used, and frequently crossed by many peoples. The old tripartite division of the Illinois Country, used since antiquity for subsistence hunting and gathering and focused on three contiguous ecosystems, began to be perceived more commonly as the Uplands (prairies) and the floodplain riverine villages.

However, to tell this story, and especially, to re-create the nature of that upland stage, requires the analysis of a new set of data. While the floodplain French and Indian environment can be glimpsed in Jesuit French letters, French military correspondence, and notarial records, the upland prairies have been best documented by arriving American settlers, some at prairie stations as early as 1782. These people perceived, wrote about, and used land differently than French, British, or Indians. The ecology of that till plain, its complex bounty, is suggested through a careful examination and synthesis of observations from four groups of people. Yet the recording eye is most often American.

The persons who best knew both the floodplain and the uplands, of course, were the tribes who had occupied it since the early part of the seventeenth century. The history of the southern Illinois land and the history of the Illinois Indians are inextricable from each other. Therefore, this study has two purposes. First, it retells the history of European occupation of what would become the American Bottom—a tripartite environment—in terms of human relationships with the land. This approach embeds the French experience in a human continuum of life on an alluvial plain and upland corridor. An artificial periodization has been created by studying the French, or early American settlement, or prehistoric archaeological sites within set dates. The result is a curiously discontinuous history. The saturated, often-flooded plain to which the French came to begin farming shaped specific kinds of trade and settlement experience; yet those experiences were connected to the evolved history of the land itself, how other peoples had lived on it. At the village of Chartres and Fort Chartres, previously farmed Indian plots lying in scattered profusion over the bottomlands, as well as continual access to water routes, created a burgeoning agricultural and trade center. Farther north, at Cahokia, despite a one-hundred-square-mile grant, French agriculture failed to develop; the land was marshy and full of seeps. Over the course of the eighteenth century, French and Indians changed the sixty-mile riverine world that had previously known intermittent and migratory occupations (save the permanent prehistoric Indian city at Cahokia). Impinging international rivalries drew people out of the floodplain into the prairie uplands, where new kinds of relationships also began to change the land. How a shared European-Indian history altered the environment is a corollary theme to the French settlement studies and leads to a different interpretation of the 1760s and 1770s in the Illinois Country.

A second purpose is to tease out the role of the Illinois Indians in each of two case studies of French settlement and to continue to tell the story of these Indians across the eighteenth century. While there is scant information to reconstruct the ways Indian perception and use of land changed, histories to date have concentrated on Indian movements and the archaeology of village sites. There has been little analysis of relationships among Illinois subtribes and between the Illinois and other Indian nations historically occupying the area, especially the Miami, Potawatomi, and Osage. Close reexamination of French and British accounts can highlight survival strategies of the Illinois Indians in a changed natural environment. The Illinois Country sequesters a history of two broad human cultures intersecting in a powerful riverine habitat. Likewise, the Mississippi floodplain supporting five French and three Indian villages across eighty years was affected by the ways these populations met each other. Yet most of this interaction can be characterized as a culture of opportunism that left no enduring records. This is also true for the land itself. The fecund nature of the floodplain allowed for rapid successional growth and return to some presettlement characteristics once large numbers of people left the Illinois Country, as happened in the 1760s. Cessation of Indian burning practices, especially evident in the upland prairies, created the "heavy forests" described by American surveyors by 1806. At that date, very few buffalo were left in the Illinois Country.

While some tentative reknitting of old trade relationships began under British merchants, the hostility of northern Indian tribes to the British after Pontiac's War—and by extension, to the Illinois Indians who were depending on the British—prevented any enduring prosperity or renascence of Indian populations. The world these people were all living in was beginning to be depleted of animals, birds, and trees. Traces of those losses remain tantalizing in the record, a mixed report of "abundance" juxtaposed against stories of burning fort pickets for fuel and the trading of French rum for meat. Illinois Indians were selling their land to Anglo-American speculators in exchange for horses and flour. It was only toward the end of the 1770s that French traders began to establish new enterprises at Cahokia, for instance, and a fresh trade in French ponies developed. The study of this riverine world ends with the arrival of the Americans into the Illinois in 1778. They found a recovering landscape nonetheless permanently changed through losses of some animal populations and old-growth oaks. Then, under the aggressive agriculture of the settler wave from Kentucky lands, the Illinois earth began to dry out. The installation of ceramic drainage tiles in the nineteenth century became the last step in the two-hundred-year process of converting a complicated ecosystem. From a lush, arboreal prairie land, drenched with so much water it was seen through a shimmering lens by the first Europeans, the Illinois Country today is packed with monocultural fields that are only sometimes, down on the floodplain, glinting with that old, insidious moisture.

In two areas, this study has been delimited. The first concerns the Kaskaskia Indians. The experience of the Kaskaskia under the tutelage of the Jesuits is distinct and viewed by many (church historians in particular) as "the successful one." Especially after 1703, when the Kaskaskia relocated to the southern Illinois Country from the Starved Rock–Peoria area, they readily adopted European agricultural and religious practices, embracing wheat and maize farming, draft animals, the wheeled French plow, hogs, chickens, and Catholicism. Their story has been told by historians and archaeologists; and historical journal literature also contains some good studies of the Kaskaskia Indians. Because they were the most successfully converted tribe at the French Jesuit missions, there are many more extant church records of them, with references to marriages, baptisms, deaths, and witness roles. Jesuit priests left detailed accounts of ministering to the Kaskaskia. Europeans arriving at the French settlements almost always commented on their village, the largest, most thriving Illinois Indian settlement. Many left approving remarks about the progressive civilization of the Kaskaskia. While the Kaskaskia continued to maintain their winter and summer hunts, also living in traditional woven cattail lodges, their primary relationship with the land across the eighteenth century is documented as agricultural.[2]

In comparison, so little is known about or has been written about the Mechigamea that they are often referred to as "the mysterious Mechigamea." The history of the Cahokia and the French on the earliest 1699 grant is also sketchy, limited to French census data and the letters of the Seminarian priests who attempted an agricultural base there. For an environmental historian, establishing the nature of the *first* European-Indian land relationships is the most important. Patterns were set, animosities and allegiances arising predictably out of land use and control and resultant changes in the environment; cultural differences were sometimes forged into cultural similarities by the exigencies of survival. While studies of the Kaskaskia and their agriculture are important, the dominant symbol linking the rest of the Illinois nations with the French, the British, and the riverine environment is not an amber spring wheat stalk but a pelt. This study therefore omits the Kaskaskia Indians and French Kaskaskia as a chapter. Secondly, unlike other environmental histories that include all populations using a given land, this study does not investigate the slave population of French and Indian Illinois. The numbers of African slaves in the settlements were at first small, growing from an initial population of around two hundred brought in by the miner-entrepreneur Phillip Renault in 1724 to furnish labor for mining schemes. Most of these slaves ended up on Kaskaskia wheat farms. The slaves' increase across fifty years brought their numbers at Kaskaskia to nearly three hundred, while the total European population at Kaskaskia was just higher than six hundred (from a census conducted by the British in 1766); these slaves remained concentrated in the southernmost part of the French settlements. The French and Indians themselves also used Indian slaves, identified as *panis*, a term that may relate to the tribal designation *Padoucah* (Apache or Comanche)—the southwestern plains tribes from whom Missouri Indians in particular obtained slaves in raids and warfare. These Indian slaves, often arriving in the Illinois settlements as small children, remain some of the most shadowy, lost figures in the historical human occupancy of the area. Traces of them in documents are extremely rare. Names of both African and Indian slaves do appear in church records, especially in the early decades of the 1720s and 1730s. Slaves are listed in property inventories for French estates and willed away as property; during the French exodus in the early 1760s, many slaves crossed the river into Missouri, where their descendants, still enslaved, became central to the bloody conflict in that state one hundred years later. Historians such as Carl J. Ekberg have examined the black population of Ste. Genevieve in the 1790s, where artisanal and trade records can trace their ascendancy. A more recent work, also by Ekberg, focuses on enslaved Indian populations of this area. However, there is scant evidence relating to slaves on the eastern shore as fur trappers and hunters, or slaves interacting with Indian populations. The opaqueness of French church and notarial records, the unbendable, unchanging legal forms and language, and finally, the very low literacy level of the French population obscure fundamental relationships: slave to Indian, slave to land and river. *Land of Big Rivers* acknowledges the presence of slaves without even being able to detail whether they routinely used the Mississippi River to supplement the French diet with channel catfish or turtles, both of which were exploited by hungry British soldiers in the 1760s. The questions posed by environmental historian Timothy Silver in general guide this study: "How did these humans alter their environment? How did their environment change them? How did they change each other?" Yet for African slaves in the Illinois Country, the answers to most of these questions remain buried.[3]

"America has always been a land of rivers," writes Peter C. Mancall; yet it is also the riverine geography of continental North America that deserves the scrutiny of scholars. Only relatively recently has the Mississippi River become attractive to colonial historians. A plethora of cultures developed in unique ways all along this snaking waterway so densely peopled with aboriginals. The challenge of *Land of Big Rivers* has been to write a history both narrow and wide. Questions relating to repeated use of land in key locations, to fluctuation in animal and bird populations, and to the movement of rivers and people on rivers are explored in the context of external forces of empire and war. Here is a localized history, replete with small human dramas, with re-created visual pictures of the eighteenth-century environment, and with narratives of life: ascending trumpeter swans, raspy cordgrasses interspersed with waving, six-foot aster-like flowers, clouds of green-headed flies driving buffalo north, and French ponies trained to swim. It is above all a study of mobility, not only the ebb and flow of peoples in and out of the Illinois, but the ebb and flow of the Mississippi River and its tributaries. Yet the study is also tightly focused in time and place. What happened one day in the Illinois of the eighteenth century is as important as what happened there over the sweep of time in the eighteenth century. *Land of Big Rivers* is a history of the people on the ground, to borrow a phrase from Geoffrey Plank's study of French Acadia, *An Unsettled Conquest: the British Campaign against the Peoples of Acadia* (2001). It is also a study of the ground itself. In the signifying of land formations and settlements with joint Indian-French place names, in the way the French and Algonquin languages combined to inscribe a small area with familiarity and recognition, and in the shared culture of both the horse and the boat, the Indians and the French of the Illinois Country occupied a common landscape for eighty years. Their lives were what they were, neither failed experiments nor disorderly and indefinite fragments of larger empires. They changed the land they lived on and were in turn changed by it, and therein lies a tale.[4]

I

Illinois Country Ecology

Along the Mississippi River in the eighteenth century, sandhill cranes rose ponderously from a morass of shore vegetation, scrub willow and bulrushes trembling with clouds of biting insects. At times of flood, backwater sloughs trapped catfish described in the late 1790s as "monstrous" and of "uncommon size." Sometimes, especially at high water, snakes such as water moccasin ribboned palely around submerged trunks, churning against the current. At times of low water, in the hot midsummer seasons, sounds carried: terrapins hitting the current in splashing waves from half-submerged logs, or the startled liftoff of waterfowl—teal, swans, and pelicans—through the heavy air. These waterbirds, "such as are seen in the sea-coast colonies," impressed visitors with their variety and abundance. Yet this aquatic habitat was not the lower bayou country of southern Louisiana but the Illinois Country far to the north, an essentially unbounded riverine world. Often, specifically, the Illinois Country was taken to mean the stretch of fecund, alluvial river plain along the Mississippi that would eventually be known as part of the American Bottom. This land was transformed through settlement processes into a high-yielding agricultural basin claimed by vigorous row crops. Beginning in the 1880s, a system of drainage ditches, levees, and subsoil tile subdued and managed the water. Today, Illinois is part of the breadbasket of the Midwest. Across her rolling, central prairies march hybrid corn species, shoulder to shoulder in immense waves. Down on the floodplain of the Mississippi, between Kaskaskia and Cahokia, the corn continues, coating the old French common fields, filling in the soil to the last inch between the levees and the river bluffs with a virile green. At mid–eighteenth century, however, this land inhabited by successive waves of humans across eight thousand years, and most recently by French colonists, was a watery world.[1]

Across this prairie state, in fact, water was the persistent, visible, and lush reality of the landscape. Between the Mississippi and the Wabash, deep, timbered rivers carved up the land into drainage basins: the Kaskaskia, the Embarras, the Vermilion, the Kankakee, the Fox, and the Illinois. Each river corridor was distinct, a riparian wetland channel often memorialized by incoming settlers in images of Edenic abundance. Early accounts of the Wabash, for instance, employ the phrase "wagonloads of fish," fish teeming in startlingly clear waters; in a single night, using a weir, settlers caught nine hundred pike, bass, and perch. Other early observations are more interesting, mentioning the interplay between streamside tree species and great schools of fish swimming close to the banks, mouths breaking the surface to catch falling redbud and plum blossoms.[2]

Yet these accounts are also paired with dismissive characterizations of presettlement Illinois as wilderness or wasteland. It is the single most remarkable dichotomy in all European and American characterizations of the Country of the Illinois: preternatural abundance that was also somehow untamed, inaccessible wilderness. "The entire State was then a 'waste, howling wilderness,' peopled by Indians, wolves, panthers, bears and other wild and savage animals," states an 1879 history of Edgar County.[3]

To sift through the changing perceptions of this land and, especially, to find evidential strands that characterize human relationships evolving with the environment here, it is necessary to move beyond historic accounts. In a way, we must embark on the rivers themselves, to follow them into tributaries and feeder streams, then the tiny creeks and trickles the French termed *rigolets*. Moving into the area that would become the American Bottom, a tripartite environment of floodplain, talus bluffs, and upland till plain, often broken with both wet and dry prairies, we discern a particular prehistoric environment that shaded into the historic. The description that follows often moves back into geologic and prehistoric time, as well as forward; it also relies on many written postsettlement accounts and even present-day analyses, for the goal is to suggest a continuum, a core reality of earth, water, and living organisms that transcends artificial boundaries set by the writers of history.

The story of the Country of the Illinois concerns large numbers of diverse people who began to change their ways of living across the eighteenth century. The key factors in this change were mobility and encounter: arrivals and departures, trading forays, transient camps, forts and churches built and abandoned, villages moved, Indian groups traveling between floodplain and upland prairies, crossing rivers into allied or enemy territory and then returning. And at the level of the soil itself, human passage, as important as human settlement, produced change; greater numbers of grazing animals, such as horses, pushed back the watery fringe of prairie sloughs. Hunting parties navigated the overflow of the great boundary rivers of the Illinois Country, using horses trained to swim, and pursued buffalo northward. And all across the uplands, human trails dating from antiquity, long following the edges of streams, began to lose their edges as water levels changed. They "sank away to nothing" across the bottoms of prairie sloughs filled with marly, clay-laden soil.

We can trace these disappearing trails, talisman of encounter and change long before Americans moved into the "waste, the howling wilderness." In doing so, we acknowledge continuums as strong and significant as cultural artifacts left behind: whelk shells depicting Birdman of the Cahokia mound builders, the protohistoric calumet wrapped in silky duck skin, the blue-rimmed French faience plate, American bone buttons and glassware. We acknowledge a powerful, watery ecosystem that shaped and continued to shape human history but also one that itself was changed by the people who were long part of it. The following maps introduce this riverine world.

In the Country of the Illinois, water rushed through the biome. Marshlands, sloughs filled with standing water, and crescent lakes formed by the cut-through action of the Mississippi released significant amounts of moisture into the atmosphere. The first histories of St. Clair, Randolph, and Monroe Counties, early formed from the Illinois Territory in the 1780s and 1790s, are filled with references to lakes. The upland regions contained hundred-acre sloughs and marshes. An account of the great hurricane of 1805 describes how the winds sucked all the water from a portion of the Mississippi and lakes in the American Bottom. While some sloughs and marshes were wet year-round, the hot, sometimes arid summers of the Illinois Country more often produced a drying-out effect. Historical atlases refer to "periodical marshes" appearing after severe rains on the upland inundated the sandy soil. In these initial counties, early mills erected by American settlers after 1785 were known as wet-weather mills, suspending operation after the summer droughts. In 1804 surveyors working to lay Thomas Jefferson's rectilinear imprint on the Illinois Country began marking off range and section on the upland and central prairies of the Illinois Territory. They left descriptions of the land: "A very large portion of this land is prairie," they wrote, "and it is a fact yielded by all observers, that the interior or middle regions of the larger prairies are always low and covered with lakes and ponds of water."[4]

The hydrologic cycle here must have been remarkable. As late as mid–nineteenth century, there are accounts of torrential rainstorms on the upland ridge country that sent waterfalls bursting from the rocky faces of the bluffs. In the 1790s, the British traveler Gilbert Imlay described the pocking and channeling of the limestone bluffs. These bluffs, he noted, shot up from 100 to 130 feet high and were divided in several places by "deep cavities," through which gushed many small rivulets. One spectacular waterfall in what would become St. Clair County was early used by French missionaries

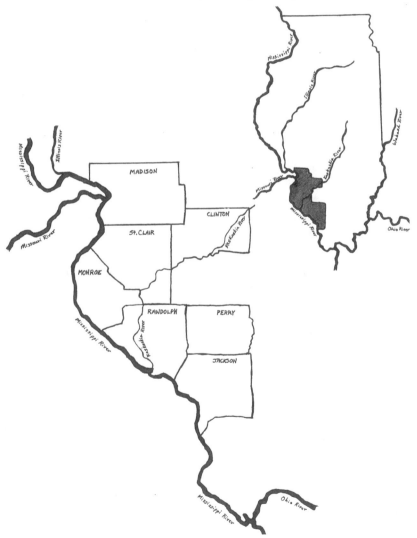

The French Illinois Country, with modern counties identified. Map: Sandra Reddish.

for communal baptism of Indians. Christened L'eau Tomb by the French, it later became Falling Springs for the Americans. The water table on both the upland and river floodplain was much higher than that of today, yielding a rich tributary system of creeks and streams; in addition, the quality of natural springs and wells is described in early historical accounts as "cool, sweet, generally hard water." The first American upland settlements in the 1780s clustered near the large, clear, gushing spring the French named La

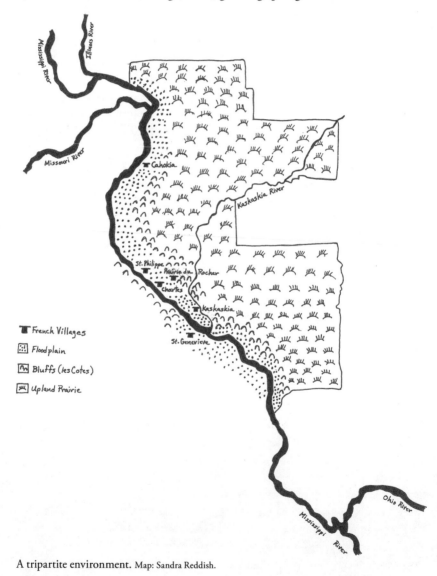

A tripartite environment. Map: Sandra Reddish.

Belle Fontaine; although they did not settle there, the French knew of these higher-country springs, for they named both the spring and its surrounding open land: the Prairie of Apacois. This word may have been borrowed from the Illinois Indians, who, according to the Frenchman Deliette in 1678, called the reeds used to cover their cabins *apacoya.* The Prairie of Apacois may thus have had a marshy area where cattails and bulrushes once grew. So important was La Belle Fontaine spring to American settlement that by 1800, a third of the 960 recorded settlers in the area lived in its vicinity. Wells on the upland were sunk from ten to eighty feet, and the nineteenth-century geographer who recorded these observations perceived that the water was "inexhaustible."[5]

The rough quadrilateral of southern Illinois enclosed by the Mississippi, Wabash, and Ohio Rivers was often a saturated country. Bisected also by the Kaskaskia River, it was interspersed with semi-mesic (moderately wet) prairies where undulant, higher ground allowed for better drainage and thus for intermittent burning of the vegetation by humans. The first history of St. Clair County estimated that the relative proportion of open land to woodland was six to one. It is likely that the "open" described in such accounts included a number of hill prairies, a particular kind of small prairie found only on the south or southwestward slopes of hills. This may account for the use of the word *dotted* in early descriptions of the uplands of Randolph and Monroe Counties. Early settlers also wrote and spoke of oak openings and barrens in terms that at times seem synonymous. Larger, more level openings such as the Twelve Mile or Horse Prairie attracted bands of wild horses or were used by the French for the grazing of black cattle. These level mesic prairies often became the periodical marshes of wet seasons. The Illinois Country in the late eighteenth century was a diverse and changeable ecosystem.[6]

Yet the first histories, valuable as they are, record the area one hundred years after the period addressed in this study. It is striking that travelers' accounts and military correspondence of the French, British, and Americans—who crisscrossed the Illinois Country between 1763 and the 1790s—mention the presence of water almost always in extremes. The major floods of the Mississippi, those inundated years of 1725, 1772, and 1785, are dramatically recorded. The flood of 1785, remembered by many French and Americans alike as the "greatest of the last century," forced the French of Kaskaskia and Cahokia up to bluffs and swept away the western walls of stone Fort Chartres near Prairie du Rocher. To the French, 1785 was the Year of the Great Waters. Accounts abound of George Rogers Clark's 1779 march to Vincennes, when he and his men waded thigh-, waist-, and

Falling Springs near Cahokia in the nineteenth century.
In J. C. Wild, *Valley of the Mississippi, Illustrated* (1845).

shoulder-deep in icy water much of the way. Yet little appears in routine military and political correspondence about the daily role of water in this common riverine world. The action of the Mississippi, fed not only by swollen tributary flow from the Missouri but by consistent hydrologic cycles of great rains and waterfalls, routinely affected the lives of humans. In 1765, for instance, notarial records for Kaskaskia list an auction of a house and lot at New Chartres, soon to be washed away by the Mississippi.[7]

Water affected health, travel, roads, soil fertility and annual yields. From early American settlement records are accounts of the sickening of the water in wells, even on the upland ridges. Drought was as real to these communities as flood. Despite glowing affidavits to the deeper well water in the Illinois Country, early geographers also spoke of "indifferent water . . . obtained from shallow wells and stagnant pools." They described an air "laden with malaria" emanating from exuberant, rotting vegetation. Great fevers often raged through the floodplain. Father Gibault, arriving in Illinois Country in the fall of 1768, became almost immediately ill with a fever that plagued him on and off until 1770. Earlier, in 1752, the French commander Macarty Mactigue wrote of the inadvisability of building barracks next to the ramparts of a fort on the Kaskaskia River. The humidity of the ground would make them dungeons rather than barracks, he felt. In times of low water or ice plating on the river surfaces, pirogues and military supply flotilla could not progress smoothly up rivers, and the fluctuant nature of the major rivers used for such transport—the Mississippi, Kaskaskia, Ohio, and Wabash—specifically affected the outcome of military operations in the Illinois Country. In 1768 Major Butricke completed a tedious and exhausting cordelling of his military keelboats between the mouth of the Ohio River and Kaskaskia. He remembered a navigation "fatiguing and dangerous" in which he rowed for four hours without gaining a mile. Sixteen years earlier, the French commandant at Fort Chartres had similar complaints about the Kaskaskia River: Some of his boats "failed" or grounded daily. Yet traveler accounts, military journals, and political correspondence concerning settlement often stress only the positives: soil fertility, the open parkland of the (burned-off) upland prairies, the diversity of plants and animals, and the beauty of the land. In 1698 Father Hennepin inaugurated a long line of glowing impressionistic accounts of the Illinois Country by writing, "The Country beyond those Hills is so fine and pleasant, that according to the Account I have had, one might justly call it the *Delight of America*."[8]

These were ancient glacial lands, scoured by ice, rock, water, and wind, molded by a giant river in a diverse floodplain. The Mississippi in fact had occupied at least one other valley, a wide bed to the southwest of its present course. Ninety percent of Illinois was covered by glaciers in the late Pleistocene; the effect of so much funneled water pouring into the glacier-scoured depressions during withdrawal and melting created an enormous embayment there. Drainage from the Missouri and Illinois Rivers in this American Bottom creates a wide basin of converging waters from a significant portion of North America. Most important, glaciation created many lake ridges lying between broad curved channels. Headwaters of tributaries lay so close to each other that only brief overland portages were necessary to cross from one massive river system, the St. Lawrence, to another—the Mississippi. Indian nations engaged in far-flung trade networks knew of these portages long before they were discovered and named by Europeans: the Fox-Wisconsin Portage, the Chicago Portage, the Fort Wayne Portage, the Oneida-Mohawk Portage. Although created by ancient ice, these channels, crossings, and lakes were—and still are—forming and changing.[9]

The Mississippi itself continues to scour, dredge, and mold the lands around it. The excavating power of this river, built up on both banks by extensive comminuted materials, makes it dynamic and changeable, violently capricious in the era before hydrologic engineering and flood control. The first geologic studies of the Mississippi documented that in flood, it could cover thirty miles, its channel marked by a fringe of woods. Sedimentation studies conducted in the early twentieth century showed that at times of high water, the Mississippi between Ste. Genevieve, Missouri, and Cape Girardeau could roll boulders as large as a man's head along the bottom of the main channel. Writers describing the river silt deposited on the lowlands after the spring "overflows" of the Mississippi have continuously made comparisons to the Nile. Gilbert Imlay saw the flood slime as comparable to a similar manure left by the Nile. An early geographer wrote that as the Mississippi receded, its sediment deposited on the bottomlands was "as fine and fertilizing as the Nile mud." American settlers in the early nineteenth century noted that at times, the level of silt and spring mud left by receding waters could be marked at ten feet on the cottonwood trunks of the floodplain. These references to the Nile, to manure and fertilization, probably reflected an understanding of the replenishment processes of the floods; yet they were also likely referring to smell. During the great Mississippi flood of the late twentieth century, 1993, the overflow waters rose to create silver-surfaced lakes behind levees and sandbagged walls around Prairie du Rocher. Descending from the bluffs, anyone approaching the half-submerged town met the smell before seeing the water: decaying vegetation and organic remains—sometimes farm animals as well as many small, drowned mammal species—rotting in the trapped runoff.[10]

Yet the Illinois Country was not defined solely by the Mississippi, great trade artery that it was. Eighteenth-century observers of the Ohio and Wabash Rivers have also testified to the overflow appearance of flooded lands. Near the junction of the Ohio and Mississippi, in Massac County, in fact, the land was known as the Black Bottoms, a veritable den of ponds and swamps. Advancing into the Illinois Country in 1765, Captain Thomas Stirling noted that the land on either side of the Ohio River was "full of aquaticks." In 1788 General Harmar wrote to the Secretary of War that land cornered between Fort Massac, on the Ohio, and the Mississippi had so much overflow, it was not habitable. Gilbert Imlay estimated that the land at the confluence of the Ohio and Mississippi had been built up at least twenty feet, yet the spring floods overflowed this embankment at least twenty miles inland. As late as 1816, a traveler to the Wabash Country wrote about having to "swim a horse" to cross Union Prairie. Up north along the Illinois River, observers in 1790 also noticed just how much water marked the land. They described small lakes and gullies of black water that could not be distinguished from the rivers themselves.[11]

A pattern emerges in reading these kinds of comments about the Illinois Country: the contrast between low and high ground, between wet and dry seasons. The action of glaciers and abrading rivers chopped the earth into a configuration of uplands and river bottom that very early created a dual subsistence pattern. This pattern was determined by the marching back of highly differentiated land and water habitats. The American Bottom drifts downward toward the Mississippi in a three-part succession. The uplands, or till plain, often described in accounts as rolling, was laid over bedrock by the shoveling edge of the glaciers. The loess here is glacier outwash. When Europeans settled the area, they found it intermittently forested by Southern hardwoods, stands of oak and hickory varieties often standing "fair and apart" from each other in sunny groves, bespeaking a long-standing practice of prairie burning that created a parklike atmosphere. The presence of so many oaks was incredible natural bounty for white-tailed deer, who gorged on acorns; oaks would also play a part in the roaming hog herds encouraged by the early French and later by the Americans, those drifts of half-wild pigs who feasted on the acorn and nut mast of these shadowed groves. Till plain ran to the edge of limestone bluffs. These bluffs are most dramatic between Alton, Illinois, and the mouth of the Illinois River; yet, especially between Prairie du Rocher and Kaskaskia in Randolph County, they also jut straight up in a rocky escarpment. It is an absolutely vertical and dramatic rise, contributing a strong sense of isolation and seclusion to the villages on the floodplain.

Most important, these bluffs function as a severe demarcation between the lowlands and the uplands.[12]

The French of Prairie du Rocher who settled on the floodplain below the bluffs used both lowlands and uplands, choosing to locate their grazing lands on top of the bluffs after an original common grazing land along the Mississippi proved inadequate. The initial commons was on a marsh called the Marais Gossiaux. So patchily wet was the floodplain between Cahokia and Kaskaskia, in fact, that the French farming lands, those longlot strips so ubiquitous to French settlements everywhere in North America, were run in long arpents straight back to the base of the bluffs. They often defined marshes between them. The historian of French agriculture in the American Bottom, Carl J. Ekberg, describes notable portions of plow land near Cahokia as waste acreage in coppices, ponds, and marshes. The initial French settlements, depicted in a 1734 map by Ignace-Francoise Broutin, engineer, lay wholly on the river floodplain, and no settlements appear on the bluffs. The road, however, that connected these necklace villages ran on the floodplain at the base of the bluffs (and still does) between Prairie du Rocher and Kaskaskia. It ascends to the bluff level between Fort Chartres and Cahokia near the present-day village of Fults. This road follows a natural declivity in the bluffs identified in the late eighteenth century as Le Grande Passe. It is significant that the road rises through Le Grande

Mount Vernon Bluff at Elsah, Jersey County, Illinois. Jutting cliffs and bluffs enclosed most of the French floodplain settlements along the Mississippi. Lithograph in *Geological Survey of Illinois*, vol. 3, by A. H. Worthen (1868).

Passe just here: the flooding around the Fort Chartres area was extensive and relentless. Settlement, agriculture, and transportation adapted to the amount of water in a flux and flow environment.[13]

The social and political history of the period between 1699 and the 1780s constitutes a small segment of interaction and occupation in the American Bottom. These years saw arrivals of different groups intent on invasive and opportunistic uses of resources. For more than sixty years, the French occupied five small villages and drew from the Illinois lands an agrarian gold: French wheat. They also harvested a glut of furs. The British control of the Illinois Country, lasting for only ten years, followed by the period of Virginian Anarchy (a term used conveniently by Clarence Alvord), blew apart an intricately functioning natural economy already in the process of change. That world had been built by humans who had learned to glean from three different natural environments and whose patterns of mobility effectively linked those environments through food production, trade, hunting, and the gathering of aquatic and upland resources. These humans were first a series of prehistoric aboriginal groups, followed by the Illinois Confederate Tribes of the seventeenth and eighteenth centuries, and last, the Illinois French. With the entrance of the occupying British, environmental change, always ongoing, accelerated. As just one instance, archaeological analysis of latrine pit remains at Fort Chartres, dating from the British occupation, reveals the presence of great numbers (a marked increase) of red-eared turtle or "slider" shells. Also found were remains indicating the high use of domesticated animals, as well as white-tailed deer. Clearly the British were attempting to hold onto the diet they were familiar with, including, possibly, turtle soup! The effect of the British occupation on the French and the Indians in the American Bottom is the content of later chapters.[14]

At the same time, it is important to establish the connections between how Indians used and imprinted land and how the incoming French (after 1699) may have profited from those patterns. Humans living in the American Bottom from the Late Woodland (circa 400 A.D.) and emergent Mississippian cultures onward utilized its tripartite ecological divisions. On the loess hill-prairies of the bluffs grew spurge and stiff bedstraw, adapted by Indians as medicinal herbs. Archaeological excavations of numerous American Bottom sites have revealed a broad tool inventory including projectile points, knives, scrapers, gouges, gravers, choppers, anvil stones, metates, and celts. Archaeologists posit that Indians occupied the uplands on a year-round basis by the beginning of the Mississippian phase (circa 1000 A.D.). They were growing tobacco and, later, maize. The broad tool inventory, along with faunal remains, suggests a strong diversity in diet and subsistence patterns.

Upland sites reveal the importance of deer, turkey, and grouse. Such upland bird species, especially, thrive in open, grassy environments.[15]

Ecologists have identified the maintenance and probably enlargement of prairie lands through the practice of annual or periodic burning. The burning of prairies by both Indians and early American settlers is documented in accounts ranging from Father Hennepin (1683) and Father Vivier (1750)—both of whom wrote about the burning practices of Illinois Indians specifically—to explicit descriptions of mid-nineteenth-century agricultural fires set by settlers on prairie margins. There is a vast literature on the role of burning in environmental change. Central debates no longer revolve around indigenous firing practices as evidence of complex agricultural adaptation. The questions concern the degree of change perpetuated by routine prairie and woodland burnings, and how the tongues of black prairie extruding into the upland woodlands in, for instance, the Illinois Country, may or may not have been "created" by aboriginal practices. Some of the earliest accounts by white observers of prairie burning occur only a few miles from the American Bottom. For instance, in 1796 Victor Collot, a French spy sent to America after the French Revolution, traveled on the Prairie du Rocher–Cahokia Road. He observed a grassy meadow, known in later years as the Storment property, that had clearly been recently burned. Another observer, the Philadelphia businessman George Hunter, wrote that the trees on the Storment property were mainly oaks stunted by annual burning of grass. Although by that year, 1796, American settlement of the upland prairies on the bluffs above the old French colonies had proceeded apace, spurred on by the 1795 Treaty of Greenville, some Indians were still burning land. That they had done so as well across the years of French occupation is a strong conclusion. Omer Stewart's insistence that fire was a multipurpose tool has import for historical studies. Why and how were Indians in the protohistoric and historic periods using fire? Leaving aside the use of fire in agriculture, some interesting trends can be identified.[16]

Evidence of aboriginal burning of prairies on these bluffs has suggested to some researchers that they were used as lookout points. Surely anyone who has ever stood on the bluffs above old Fort Gage at Kaskaskia can attest to the view. The Mississippi Valley lies below with a consummate clarity: the river in its sinuous curves could be assessed immediately for the presence of any kind of approaching pirogue, canoe, or keelboat. Smoke rising from even a single campfire deep in the floodplain forests would be visible. Ecologists today researching the changes in ridge-top prairies use early accounts spread over three centuries to trace the changes in the land. In discussing the view described by Timothy Flint in 1828, for instance, one researcher has commented on Flint's "long clear view from atop the Dividing Ridge of Calhoun County" (farther north, above the American Bottom, near the confluence of the Illinois and Mississippi Rivers). Flint's account suggests he had come to stand in a ridge-top prairie. The openness there was maintained by fire, keeping the view clear against ambush.[17]

In addition, the burning of prairie lands was a way to manage game, either in creating the best possible habitat or to make it possible to hunt certain species more easily. Such burning practices have a direct bearing on food supply. In 1712 Father Gabriel Marest wrote a lengthy letter to a fellow Jesuit, Father Germon. He described his return to the Illinois missions after a trip up to Michilimackinac. His small party had traveled—as usual—by way of the portage between the St. Joseph River and the Kankakee (the *Huakika*), followed by a navigation down the Illinois River, past the Peoria Mission. As his canoe approached the lower Illinois River, he wrote, "At last we perceived our own dear welcome Country; the wild oxen and the herds of deer were roving along the bank of the river, and from the canoe we shot some, now and then, which served for our repasts." These herds of buffalo and deer were roving on a river floodplain. The transition that Marest observed, between the lower Illinois River Country and Michilimackinac, may have reflected an environment manipulated by fire. In 1863 a scientific article noted that forests were invading Illinois prairies, a clear result of cessation of regular burning. The author, Henry Engelmann, identified hunting as the primary motivation for burning but noted it also would have removed dry stalks, killed snakes and insects, and created a better pasture. Ungulates like elk and buffalo eagerly sought the bright green growth appearing on burned earth. Yet those roving herds of 1712, healthy and abundant, that allowed canoe parties to select a choice animal for a repast—such options had disappeared by the mid 1760s. As explained later in this study, by the time of the War of 1812, the buffalo herds were gone. They had been hunted nearly to extirpation on the uplands.[18]

The Upland Prairies and Passers Through

The prairies of the glacier till plain, stretching east from the bluffs, were unique enough in character to be named by Indians, as well as French and American settlers, and the list of such specified prairies includes hundreds of names. In the uplands above the French settlements, Round and Horse Prairies especially show up in early American accounts, and there may have been as many as three Six Mile Prairies. The old French Prairie du Rond lay to the northeast of the first American settlements on the till plain, near present-day Waterloo. The number of these open grasslands interspersed among riparian forests, often noted as gallery forests, had long created a dynamic hunting and gathering environment on the uplands. Archaeology of sites in the till plain has established a consistent usage of the area, especially important for the introduction of maize agriculture by 1000 A.D. However, the most complete written records begin with the record keepers: the Americans who began to settle the uplands as early as 1782. As in many accounts of this land, reports contain contradictions. The first Government Land Office (GLO) surveyors in southern Illinois described inland prairies always covered with lakes and ponds, but later surveys showed "heavy" forests and did not often record the presence of sloughs or marshes. Randolph County, in fact, was described in an 1806 GLO map as being predominantly forested, containing few marshy areas.[19]

The surveyed portrait of the Illinois Country (old French and Indian Illinois) suggests an environment in the process of fairly rapid change, including afforestation after the cessation of Indian burning practices and shifts in the relationships among plants and animals engendered by the fur trade and by increased numbers of people. To understand these processes, many connected to traffic across the uplands, it is important to re-create the environment there as Indians and the French knew it. Because those groups did not leave precise observations of the land above the floodplain, the detective story must use a variety of sources from many disciplines; and the memories and experiences of American settlers become important. With the use of historical geography, archaeology, botanical science, and impressions from Americans, French, British, and where possible, Indians, it is possible to answer the question, What was the upland till plain like across the eighteenth century?

After the mid 1700s, these uplands saw intensified movement and meetings of peoples as the theater of history opened eastward and up. Political intrigue, involving increasingly diverse peoples, entered the till plain and brought these lands more emphatically into the historical record. Often glossed in earlier French accounts as simply the upland prairies, blufflands, or hunting grounds, these interesting, idiosyncratic locales had long been understood and utilized. One of the prevailing interpretations of this till plain land is that it was important primarily for American settlement; that under the French and Indians, it remained underutilized and vacant, crisscrossed only by hunters and travelers to points east on the Wabash, such as Ouiatanon and Vincennes. In truth, the upland till plains were a vital corridor, even a stage. The year 1751–52 saw the beginning of new forms of human interaction, and those patterns escalated toward the year 1778. The arrival of George Rogers Clark in Kaskaskia involved a crossing of the upland till plain portentous for the Illinois Country. Yet the uplands had been a country of passers through for perhaps eight thousand years.

Many recorded observations contain references to the ocean or seas, the common analogue in the minds of observers. Travelers rode out of the timber fringe along creeks, streams, and rivers into the wide, green undulating grasses that stretched in "limitless waves" to the horizon. Lying south of the Grand Prairie that covered most of the upper two-thirds of the present-day state, these smaller, individual prairies were microhabitats well known to indigenous peoples. Because so many incoming Europeans and Americans left precise accounts of the prairies of Illinois, these tend to overshadow earlier perceptions of the upland corridor. Many kinds of prairie blended or shaded into each other to form a mosaic of small, named places. Early observers noted vegetational shifts as small habitats flowed, one to another, across this belt. The perception of blending or "arising" land formations was still strong in the 1830s, when the Swiss settling on Looking Glass Prairie in eastern Madison County used language like "a change of scene on a stage," or land that "made way for a meadow." Hills took "strange forms," they wrote. Without any change in elevation, for instance, prairies broke out at the edges of the Post Oak Flats in Jackson and Perry Counties. On the other side of such prairies, sometimes also termed *barrens* or *savannas*, the post oaks began again. Sometimes long spikes of woodland sharpened out into prairies; these spikes were known as "points." Observers were mystified and termed the land "broken," seeking language to convey the differences: scattered prairies, pure stands of oak varieties in clustered wedges, seams of timber following myriad streams and draws, and extrusions of limestone pushing up through the thin, calcareous soils toward the western borders. Massive limestone underlying the thinner soils on the blufflands produced the myriad sinks and seeps recorded by the first geographers. Striking caves formed over eons through the action of seeping water. The karst formations of the Illinois Caverns spread beneath the old French uplands spring of La Belle Fontaine in Monroe County. And the well water itself in this corridor left strong impressions. Round Prairie in southern Monroe County, about three miles south of present-day Hecker, was described as late as the 1920s as being an "open space" spreading almost four miles in all directions, drained by three different creeks. Such was the nature of the wells in this upland prairie that one was yet remembered, a hundred years after settlement, as having "splendid water."[20]

Investigations have established the importance of upland prairie, bluff, and floodplain for human occupancy of the area. From as early as 8000 B.C., Modoc Rock Shelter near Prairie du Rocher was visited consistently by many peoples. The alluvial record left by the flooding of the Mississippi has enabled archaeologists to carve through twenty-eight layers of deposits, reading a well-preserved record. On the uplands, archaeology of scattered sites has established transient human residency as well. Yet archaeology only suggests the level of human occupation. While hoofed bison, usually referred to in this study as buffalo, have left evidence in trails, traces, and wallows, the movement of people through the uplands has been primarily on foot, not on horseback. It was only in the eighteenth century that large numbers of persons rode horses across this broken land, and when they did, they used the existing buffalo trails or the few earliest French roads, the Chemin du Roi running between Kaskaskia and Cahokia and the east-west prairie trail across to Vincennes. In the latter half of the century, a meandering north-south trail emerged, labeled on a French map used by Lewis and Clark as "quickapoux" (Kickapoo). With the advent of horses, new and interesting relationships began to develop among plants and animals. The horses themselves would play a role in creating distinct human history of specific locales, notably Horse Prairie on the uplands directly above the French floodplain settlements. The acceleration of environmental changes in this corridor can be seen as a fascinating corollary record blending with key historical events of the times. Just as the floodplain settlements of the French can be shown to be different, one to the other, neither were the uplands homogenous.[21]

Many distinct prairies originally lay in the present-day counties of Madison, Monroe, St. Clair, Randolph, and Jackson, all having the Mississippi River as their western boundaries. Parts of Perry County, a bit farther east, were also known to till plain users. This upland region formed a mosaic landform buffer between the broad, central-eastern Grand Prairie of the Illinois Country and the floodplain. In this territory proliferated a variety of smaller prairies—mesic, xeric, sand or hill prairies, prairies named for water-loving reeds and claimed by strident waterfowl each spring, prairies preferred by wild horses, and prairies inviting to sandhill cranes because they were both wet and dry. Twelve Mile Prairie in St. Clair County is one of the few Illinois prairies for which the Native American name is known: a large prairie, described as "undulating," it was called *Tay-mar-waus*. This was likely a variant of *Tamaroa*.[22]

On such prairies, migrating waterfowl found marshes to support their numbers. Waterfowl settled both below the bluffs, on the inundated floodplain, and high above the Mississippi on the till plain. The choices made by waterfowl for nesting were evolved choices. Birds like snow geese preferred to settle in large ragged flocks on lakes and wetlands, using safety in numbers to protect their nests. Other waterfowl, like mallards, nested on upland sloughs, using protective coloration or the shelter afforded by tall, saturated grasses. In times of spring runoff and heavy, equinoctial rains, pools of water rose through vibrant stands of cordgrass and switch-grass to reflect the sky to ancient populations of sandhill cranes who had learned to look for the glimmering flash of such waters interspersed in heavy grasses below. Archaeology of the uplands has established the presence of sandhill cranes, *Grus canadensis*, in prehistoric and historic sites; and two Algonquian tribes of the inland prairies have specifically identified with the crane (the Illinois and Miami Indians). Sandhill cranes were also hunted and consumed by the French. The upland mesic prairies of the till plain, frequently moist, would offer cranes the feeding habitat they preferred: two side-by-side microsystems, one wet, one dry, for these birds like adjacent food sources and have, like white-tailed deer, an exceptionally broad, omnivorous diet. From the "periodical" marshes, they gleaned roots and tubers and other riparian vegetation, wading confidently on long pole legs; they scooped up insects, nutritious seeds, and even fish. In the drier margins, they could locate earthworms as much as five inches underground, using their long pointed bills to stab into the moist soils. Cranes have even been noted in large flocks in pecan "orchards." Since these were migratory and summer resident birds, they fit into patterns evolving over eons in the uplands: their presence at specific times of the year determined the presence of people. Moving with food supplies, following the availability of cranes, mallards, Canada and snow geese—and consuming eggs as well as fledgling and mature birds—groups of prehistoric and protohistoric Indians moved through the prairies and up from the floodplain. They were precise, inveterate consumers whose survival depended on key movements of many life forms. The inundation of the bottomlands in the spring drew people to the drier uplands; and people who had permanent winter camps to the east, across the prairies, would move west toward the wetter lands as millions of migrating mallards settled in. From as early as 800 A.D., Woodland Indians were migrating seasonally. Archaeology of early sites in west-central Illinois, for example, has shown abandonment of farm sites coinciding with peaks in waterfowl migrations.[23]

The pattern of moving through microenvironments to locate resources has been established for many native cultures along the Mississippi. Farther south, in the lower Mississippi Valley, floodwaters created natural levees, a midsection ridge of deposited soils. These marked a change from the higher, inland habitat, drawing Indians to a new set of resources, available to them when the more fecund bottomlands were flooded. Although separated by only a few miles, the lowlands, natural levees, and uplands of southern Arkansas and Louisiana were each distinct storehouses. People long knew this; seasonal use of the three microenvironments has been established from 1500 B.C., with humans using the cycles of animal and plant availability in floodplain forest, levee, and uplands. For instance, on the levees in summer, gatherers could find persimmon and southern crab apple. By fall, they could gather mulberry, pawpaw, and three prized nuts: black walnut, hickory, and pecan.[24]

Although these inland levees did not often form in the upper Mississippi Valley, peoples did consistently move up onto the prairie uplands. These high grounds were temporary home to the great passers-through of the land: migrating buffalo, migrating waterfowl, and migrating humans. In precise ways, the flora of the prairies, both the expansive watery prairies and the much smaller hill or sand prairies nearer the bluffs, had evolved to support the cycles of life arriving and departing and to depend on those arrivals. One example is prairie cordgrass, *Spartina pectinata*. A lover of wet prairies and so found extensively on the floodplain as well, cordgrass was utilized heavily by Indians and early French for thatch. Also called slough grass, *Spartina* grows in places too wet for other prairie grasses like big bluestem and Indian grass. Across the Mississippi on the floodplain of both the Mississippi and Missouri Rivers, it was observed growing in hundreds of square miles, often appearing in pure stands. An early history of Madison County, Illinois, described a "kind of bottom prairie" on which flourished "an enormous growth of wild grasses." This was likely cordgrass, which, when mature, was called ripgut by American settlers for its sharp-toothed leaves. Grazing herbivores—deer, buffalo, and domesticated stock such as the black French cattle—could only safely eat it in the spring, when young and tender shoots could easily soften in the mouth. This grass evolved to become dangerous to animal consumers at the exact time waterfowl would need its sheltering stands for nesting. On the other hand, greater prairie chickens, *Tympanuchus cupido*, habitually nested in knee-high grasses. Studies have shown that if grass clumps are not present, prairie chickens cannot substitute other options for nesting. They may have relied on large herbivores, such as elk and buffalo, to crop prairie grasses for them. While buffalo have dominated many early accounts north of the till plain corridor, along the Des Plaines and Kankakee Rivers, elk specimens were found to be much more numerous than buffalo in archaeological sites dating from as late as 1600. Along with white-tailed deer, they formed a substantial portion of the diet of prairie Indians for millennia.[25]

A few scattered elk, *Cervus elaphus*, were still seen in Madison County in 1806, reported as giants with antler spreads of over twelve feet. These were probably remnant animals, for like the buffalo, elk rapidly disappeared from the Illinois Country. Around 1750, however, they were still important in maintenance of nesting habitat of upland bird species. Laying as many as twelve olive-colored eggs in a clutch, prairie chickens furnished a prime food for many small, fur-bearing animals, especially red foxes. Other fur-bearing mammals, such as mink, weasel, and raccoon, ate the eggs of upland-nesting birds routinely as well. The successful nesting of prairie chickens—and the availability of their eggs in the food chain—was connected to an evolved relationship with powerful grazers like elk and buffalo, who contributed to their best habitat. Conservationists and naturalists have focused on reconstructing such habitats. Yet the fluid mobility of the upland corridor, in which many animals, birds, insects, and people arrived and left in giant patterns, bespeaks a truly complex biome. Grazers moved over clumps of nutritive grasses, also cropping weedy growth. They fed and roamed on, allowing native grasses to rebound after the passing of a herd. Bluejoint grass, in fact, has been shown to especially tolerate heavy grazing and rebound quickly. The eighteenth-century uplands, that "broken" land corridor, that prairie mosaic, was an integrated world of moving and adapted life forms.[26]

When migrating buffalo crossed through the mosaic of prairies, traveling north in early summer to wide, windy expanses of open land, their calving grounds, they left trails through the grasses. Over millennia, the surface of the earth was molded by such ungulates. Emerging shoots were repeatedly trampled and cut by hooves, grazed and torn up by powerful jaws. Moving steadily abreast in columns of four or five, buffalo stamped arid, packed, and rutted trails swerving through and bisecting the grasses for hundreds of miles. From the air, this grassland would have looked tunneled through by massive life forms—and it was. So many buffalo and Indian trails "laced" northeastern Illinois, in fact, that many of the roads of present-day Chicago follow these ways through the grasses laid down by millennia of moving life forms. On the Kaskaskia River, researchers and observers have located buffalo crossings, noting that the wide swath cut through prairies by bison would narrow to efficient crossing sites in Moultrie and Shelby Counties. Southeast of Sullivan, Illinois, lies a remnant of the old Kaskaskia-Detroit Road known by French and Indians for years before American settlers found it useful. At the river crossing, a portion of a sunken road leads down to the water, in autumn covered by drifts of yellowing leaves and hickory nuts. These crossing sites are gouged with ruts, a possible testament to centuries of animal fording. Americans arriving in the 1820s found many smaller trails leading to salt licks and springs, as well as buffalo skulls and picked-clean bones scattered across Shelby and Moultrie Counties. An early county history of the northern till plain area (present day Madison County) records "heads, horns, and bones" of buffalo still numerous and visible in 1820.[27]

Despite descriptions of sterility and barrenness by arriving Europeans and, later, Americans, buffalo trails and wallows developed their own microenvironments. Invited by the hot, dry, packed soils, a particular vegetation moved in and found a niche: fleshy, ground-hugging purslane. One of the few recorded French observations of buffalo trails across the Illinois prairies mentions this plant. *Portulaca oleracea*, in Old French *pourcelaine*, is a succulent, highly nutritious conserver of moisture. A large mat of the reddish, fleshy, coiled purslane stems could be scraped or cut repeatedly by buffalo hooves and then sprout adventitious roots, connecting it once again to the earth. In addition, under periods of drought either cyclical or prolonged, purslane sacrifices its leaves and resorbs water into its stems. These adaptations connect it to waxing and waning levels of moisture and buffalo migration, both of which were unpredictable in the Illinois Country. The French stewed and consumed purslane, as well, and perhaps had learned to gather it from the uplands. It has shown up in their records as a resource of the drier, packed soils where buffalo repeatedly crossed.[28]

The rhythms and ecological connections among buffalo, plants, birds, and the earth itself have only been teased out in the last fifty years of burgeoning prairie studies. Churning buffalo hooves aerated the dense, tightly sodded prairie earth as perhaps nothing else could; buffalo dung enriched and fertilized the land near fords and crossings, contributing to a healthy streamside environment; and buffalo hair itself was a prime carrier of tiny grass seeds, redistributing key species over land ranges that spread from the Ohio River to the present-day Wisconsin border. It is not only the rich ecological diversity of upland prairies that must be noted; equally important are the relationships among life forms. And many of these relationships had everything to do with the seasonal flux and flow of water. In keeping with an overall argument of this study, that the tripartite environment of French Illinois—the Illinois Country—was neither homogenous nor static, an analysis of specific upland prairies can offer understanding of how diverse peoples came to rely on them. Prehistoric, protohistoric, and historic Indian tribes moved through them, down to the floodplain, back up through the rocky escarpment of the bluffs, fanning out onto the uplands—in a blended rhythm of procurement. The French continued that pattern, making forays to the uplands repeatedly to harvest prized white oak and other timber;

seeking seasonal harvests of hickory nuts, pecans, and walnuts, upland herbs and medicinal plants, wild strawberries, prairie "hay," and migrating waterfowl; they also hunted white-tailed deer and passenger pigeons that came seeking the great acorn harvests of the upland prairie oaks.

The resident French and Indians therefore belong to a time of fluid mobility in the ecosystem, a time—spanning perhaps eight thousand years—when boundaries were nebulous and shifting, and forays, hunting and gathering trips, created an out-and-back rhythm. Neither the British nor the Americans participated in this way of life. Their manner of thinking about land was cartographic and property-oriented, arising from a strong sense of dominion. Early accounts from American settlers described how they simply chopped down immense old pecan trees, felling giants weighted with nuts to strip the branches. The loss of these trees, described as "large in trunk, and of great height," some producing for more than three hundred years, necessitated the replanting of pecan groves on bottomland farms especially. In a nineteenth-century sketch of the farms of J. Gant in Randolph County, for instance, the bottomland acreage is captioned as "the long field" lying next to uniform rows of young pecan trees. Incoming permanent settlers to the uplands thought about land in terms of boundaries and markers. A British traveler out on Looking Glass Prairie in eastern Madison County once observed the degree of specificity with which American settlers could give directions: "Not the slightest peculiarity in the surface of the ground, not an old log, or singular-looking tree, is omitted," wrote William Oliver. He was rarely lost and could navigate all over the Looking Glass Prairie using such directions. In reading through fifty years of French military correspondence and Jesuit accounts, it is striking how no such references to upland land markers occur. In the notarial records of French Illinois (floodplain settlements) are found precise property descriptions; and named places, the designated prairies of the French, also appear. The specificity seems to be confined to the bottomlands, however. For the till plain of the uplands, locations and boundaries are rarely given. "Out on the prairie" is a commonly appearing phrase.[29]

Hill Prairies and the Horse Prairie

The few remaining loess hill prairies in Illinois may very well function as the "last living windows" of the original prairie biome and thus are invaluable to scientists and historians. Several of these are on the bluffs above the French settlements. Such small, isolated hill prairies, one near Fults in Randolph County (the American Bottom), nonetheless reveal a striking diversity of plants. Steeply sloped and difficult to reach, these hill prairies lie at the very edge of the river bluffs. While they may have been used for grazing, it is more likely that the French drove their black cattle farther back to richer prairie commons. There, cows and "half-wild" French ponies fed on the little and big bluestem grasses, as well as purple prairie clover, that form the most frequently occurring ground covers. Most important, these mature bluff and tiny hill prairies can be distinguished from wet or mesic prairies lying farther inland. Indians and French knew the difference. For instance, species of wild indigo and wild quinine (feverfew) are noted for their absence in hill prairies but occur in mesic prairies. Nineteenth-century botanical inventories of the upland prairies contain identifications of herbs such as horehound, boneset, horsemint, catnip, and pennyroyal. These are medicinal and cottage industry plants. That American settlers also distinguished hill prairies is seen in the other names given them: bluff prairies and goat prairies. Even small hill prairies, however, are liable to contain a wide variety of flora. Assessment projects carried out by the Illinois Department of Natural Resources have produced careful and exhaustive studies of remnant prairie communities. One such study, the Kaskaskia River Area Assessment, identifies an extraordinary species density in small prairie remnants, typically five to six acres. Such areas may contain as many as 100 to 130 species of vascular plants. Over and over, botanists and ecologists studying the uplands of the American Bottom stress ecological diversity. Such diversity contributed in similar ways to both Indian and French resource use and habitat.[30]

One of the most interesting continuous uses of an upland prairie occurred in an expanse of semimesic prairie in Randolph County known as Horse Prairie. Lying between the Kaskaskia River, snaking its way to the northeast, and Horse Creek, a tributary, the prairie long held a reputation for attracting horses. Every discussion of it states the origin of the name came from herds of wild horses that had escaped from the French settlements. Such observations were made by many incoming settlers after 1780, yet the question has not been answered: why did horses choose that prairie among many available grasslands on the till plain? This mystery becomes even more intriguing when examining the first territorial newspaper published in the area, the *Western Intelligencer*, later the *Illinois Intelligencer*. Between 1814 and 1819, this newspaper repeatedly recorded the presence of "found" horses in the area. Of forty-six such reports, twenty-two locate stray or wild horses in the vicinity of Horse Prairie. One explanation could be the presence of water, a flow that fed a particular, nutritious grass that might stay green late into the winter. In addition to a considerable number and variety of sedges, several cool-season native grasses might in fact have thrived there. Possibly Canada Wildrye was one, a grass liking river banks and retaining its above-ground protein levels well into November. Another cool-season grass, bluejoint, often appears as a bridge plant between drier prairies and marshy areas. These grasses may retain nutrition longer, streaking the late autumn prairies with bands of green. Early American settlers in the till plain corridor used a particular term to describe such prairies: "slashy." A memoir about Horse Prairie records the presence of "a sort of slash" running south between Richland Creek bluff and the Kaskaskia River. The slash widened to the south and formed a basin or walls of unusually fertile earth. This was exceptionally rich grazing land, the moist slash encouraging timber growth for shelter and the grass staying green "even during the winter." Indians apparently had also used it to graze their ponies and horses. In fact, it may have been known as Indian Prairie before it was Horse Prairie. Thus a single rich, partially wet prairie on the uplands, fairly close to the great limestone bluff demarcation, can be established to have been part of the livelihood of Americans, French, and Indians, and likely long before that for proto- and prehistoric peoples. Despite GLO survey observations of the heavily wooded and dry nature of the uplands, portions of the old mesic prairies remained, slashed with a virile green that enticed runaway and feral horses.[31]

When Indians were routinely burning upland (and floodplain) prairies, the land in the till plain corridor maintained its rolling, parkland look. Streams and creeks flooded in spring, saturating surrounding prairie lands. Large upland sloughs remained year-round, and old-growth oaks, especially magnificent, fire-resistant white oaks, dotted the prairies. It was a landscape affording shelter, cover, and point-to-point access for movement. French and Illinois Indians had been travelers through rather than residents, choosing to use the uplands as hunting and gathering sites, as a throughway east and north. The preferred site for permanent villages, however, was the floodplain.

The Floodplain

The Mississippi River floodplain, site of all French and Illinois Indian villages in the eighteenth century, is a mercurial, highly complex environment just beginning to be fully understood by naturalists. Studies of the role of flooding—small, yearly spring floods and floods labeled five-year, ten-year, fifty-year, hundred-year—have established critical life-form connections. These relationships involve the role of water in both scouring out and depositing sand and rich alluvium. Riverine ecologists have given the name *flood pulse* to the phenomenon on which a host of organisms depend, from fish to insects to rare plant species. During the flood pulse, waters swirl out over the floodplain, water temperatures rise, and the floodplain becomes connected to adjacent habitats via watery corridors. Miniature migrations occur. Many plant species become submerged; consequently the survivors, given a greater chance for light, thrive on the flood. These are ancient adaptations evolving along an ancient river. The diversity of such floodplain species once included the six-foot tall false aster, *Boltonia decurrens*, today threatened with extinction. The earliest descriptions of floodplain grasses and other vegetation often mention "tall, waving plants" so thick they could obscure people and livestock. One of those plants may have been this giant, flowering stalk, now found mainly on the floodplain of the Illinois River but noted historically on the Mississippi floodplain near the old French settlements. This immensely tall, elegant, asterlike flower, blooming pale purple and white, appears to thrive after muddy inundation. With the changes to the river floodplains engendered through levee building and agriculture, *Boltonia decurrens* has become extremely rare. The watery world of riverine wetlands was its natural home. The floodplain of the eighteenth century was so rich an environment, in fact, that many of the historic French accounts repeatedly mention both size of vegetation and sheer, exuberant abundance.[32]

However, the floodplain is also a differentiated environment. Botanists distinguish two types of forest on the lowlands: the floodplain forest and the lowland depressional forest. Floodplain forests occur where flooding often and strikingly alters the shorelines of rivers. Here grow the water-loving cottonwood, sycamore, hackberry, and elm. Elm was important to Mississippi Valley Indians, who removed entire sheets of bark and treated it like plywood to construct canoes and sometimes houses. The French also constructed bark canoes but preferred birch, thus pinpointing the point of origin for such canoes—farther north than the Illinois Country. (These lighter birch canoes were known as "north canoes"). Although Indians and the French shared resource use of tree bark to cover light river craft, such overlap seems to have occurred in initial contact years of French settlement, between 1700 and 1720. The French rapidly came to prefer the larger, sturdier pirogue, or hollowed-out boat, which in the Illinois Country was usually made from a single black walnut or cottonwood trunk. Like the Indians, the French also used buffalo skins stretched over willow frames: the bullboat. Light, strapped-together boats made only of cane were called *cajeu* and used for quick river crossings, such as the back-and-forth traffic between Kaskaskia in the Illinois Country and Ste. Genevieve across the Mississippi. Willow was an important tree for both Indians and French, as its light, pliable branches could be easily woven. Unlike elm, which would die once large sheets of bark were removed, especially if the bark had completely girdled the tree, willows grow quickly. They take fast root in newly formed sandbars to create miniature islands from year to year. These are the water-logged and insect-filled trees that hang over the soggy marshlands along the river shores. It took the firmer soils farther inland to attract beech and hickory. Also along the shorelines grew an abundance of cattails and bulrushes, both used by Illinois Indians in the construction of woven mats. Such mats had multiple uses, both functional (laid over frames for dwellings) and symbolic, as a form of communication. References to Indian mats are consistent in the letters of French military personnel engaged in negotiations; they recognized them as important.[33]

In staggered years, the oaks most common on the floodplain—pin, black, and bur oak—could produce an immense acorn crop. While black oak acorns are the least palatable to animals, foraging hogs and some venture-some deer would eagerly seek out bur oak acorns. However, the main nut harvesters were human. It was on the floodplain of the Illinois Country that pecan, persimmon, and mulberry grew most profusely. *Carya illinoinensis* even takes its name from the giant, twisted, and gnarled old-growth

Prairie du Rocher in the American Period. The giant willow hangs over Prairie du Rocher Creek, today a one- to two-foot-wide, mostly dry streambed. Engraving published by Herman J. Meyer, New York, circa 1843. Courtesy of the Abraham Lincoln Presidential Library and Museum.

pecans observed on the drier ridges of ground, on islands in the river, and on the upland bluffs of Illinois. Hickory and pecan have been identified in the strata of the Modoc Rock Shelter near the Mississippi River as far back as the Early Archaic Period of 8900–8700 B.C. For precontact and early historic times, nut yields for the floodplain forest have been estimated at 2,207 bushels per square mile for hickory and 3,395 bushels per square mile for pecan. On islands in the Mississippi, pecan harvest could amount to fourteen thousand bushels of nuts. It is likely that both the French and Illinois Indians were harvesting these nuts, especially, perhaps, the Mechigamea, who lived close to the shore in two villages.[34]

Their familiarity with the river and its food yield was documented in the early 1700s. The "walnut-tree" dugout of the Illinois Indian was described by both Father Charlevoix and Deliette, who noted that there were as many as three dugouts in each cabin. Narrow, swift, and deep, these whole-tree craft could circle around nut-laden islands, moving easily under the thickety overhang of willow and elm. In addition to pecan, black walnut (*Juglans nigra*) was a profuse producers of nuts, but the black walnut giants of the bottomlands were also coveted for the making of river craft. Walnut wood does not warp or shrink; it holds its shape with a tensile strength and never splinters. The longer it is touched by human hands, the more smooth, soft, and glossy the wood becomes. (Such qualities must have been perceived rapidly by Europeans, for the first colonists in Virginia were shipping walnut to England as early as 1610). The wood of these early walnut harvests, taken from virgin hardwood stands, was heavy, dark, and straight-grained. Illinois Indians looked for another characteristic of floodplain walnut: these trees could reach heights of 150 feet, and often, the first fifty feet shot straight to the sky without branching. Standing in the deep, fertile, loamy soils of the river margins, mature black walnut trees would appear as dugouts upended to a trained eye. The French rapidly learned the advantages of walnut as well, for early building contracts in notarial records specify that barns and furniture be built of "walnut or sassafras." They chose walnut and oak for construction, but entrepreneuring French also sold pecans in New Orleans, thus competing with the Illinois Indians as traditional harvesters.[35]

Lowland-depressional forests supported more oak, hickory, and sweet gum as well as red and silver maples. Red mulberry, *Morus rubra*, often grew to immense heights near the base of the cliffs; the French rapidly learned about its rot-resistant qualities and used it in homes and barns. Because the soils typically contained clay, they did not drain as well, and "ponding" occurred among these trees. In marshes flourished the roots and tubers that could be gathered for diet supplementation, including the yellow water lily root (the macoupin), wild sweet potatoes, Indian turnips, arrowleaves, and cattails. Fruits were also plentiful: the indigenous pawpaw and persimmon, wild grapes, elderberries, gooseberries, blackberries, and strawberries. The aquatic environment of the lowlands furnished a wide variety of fish, mussels, turtles, and waterfowl. Lowland forests attracted some fur-bearing terrestrial animals, such as deer, elk, opossum, raccoon, foxes, wolves, and tree squirrels, but the greater availability of these species in the forested uplands gave rise to hunting trips. Initially, however, commons left intact on the floodplain furnished wood for fuel and small game for consumption. A description of Cahokia common land in the 1720s, scattered in various places across the Mississippi lowlands, indicates that these commons were places for pasturing animals, gathering wood, and hunting small mammals and prairie chickens. Over the course of the nearly seventy-year French occupation, clearing of the lowland scrub vegetation, such as hazel and rough-leaved dogwood, gradually resulted in the parklike lands that travelers described rhapsodically in the late eighteenth century. By midcentury, hunting for meat began to require trips up to the bluffs or across the Mississippi. The buffalo herds of the prairie uplands were pursued so extensively by Indians and the French, and then the British, that by the late 1760s, French hunting parties were ranging down into Kentucky.[36]

A Tripartite Environment

While the French settlers along the Mississippi became productive agriculturists, they also adapted to a diverse and fluctuant environment. That they knew the topography and geography of the floodplain and the upland till plain is evidenced in French place names scattered across the American Bottom and in their footpaths and roads. Commander Macarty at Fort Chartres mentions "the trail in the woods du Rocher" in an account of an Indian ambush in 1752. (The original letter, in French, capitalizes the name of this trail). The same letter refers to the blufflands above the villages as "the heights." The intrigue among Indian tribes, French, and British that characterizes the decades of the 1750s and 1760s takes place in geographic interaction among the upland prairies, the heights, and the floodplain. The French used prairies for grazing and running their horses and built what Daniel H. Usner Jr. has called an "exchange economy" of trade and travel both to Indian villages and across the prairies to Vincennes on the Wabash and north to Peoria on the Illinois River. From the Illinois, boatmen could reach the Kankakee and Des Plaines, then the Chicago Mission, Lake Michigan, and Detroit. By using the rivers running into the Mississippi from the east—the Illinois and the Kaskaskia, the Ohio further south—

as well as footpath and trail approaches down over the bluffs, the French in the five riverine settlements along the Mississippi were mobile people. After the founding of St. Louis in 1764, the traffic back and forth across the Mississippi increased. There had been early river crossings between Kaskaskia and Ste. Genevieve in present-day Missouri, a French community built around lead mining, salt works, and wheat. The burgeoning fur trade center of St. Louis provided other incentives for people to cross the river. Well before the influx of independent fur traders in the 1760s (often described as an onslaught by contemporary writers), the French were using their rivers in casual, personal ways. In 1737, for example, a French woman from the Illinois Country, the Widow Lefevre, pushed off in a canoe with trade merchandise, headed for the Iowa River on a fur-trading expedition.[37]

Despite the evidence of a well-traveled and precisely named environment, Canadian French, British, and American accounts of the Illinois French consistently stress their indifference to "pushing out" into the open uplands, their lack of ambition, their unhurried, peasant world, epitomized by long, indolent summers playing cards in the shadows of their veranda porches. In 1761 a Frenchman at Kaskaskia, Joseph Labuxierre, petitioned the commandant Neyon de Villiers for a grant of land at La Belle Fontaine on the uplands. While the land was granted, actual French settlement there never seems to have occurred. These images of the unambitious and simplistic French help to cement a view of the inhabitants as hugging the shores of their watery world and staying there. In fact, as evidenced especially by the Kaskaskia Manuscript records of land sales and exchanges, as well as the notarial records of Fort Chartres, the French were mobile and enterprising. They established extractive industries such as lead mining and saltworks; they built windmills and grain mills. Most especially, they developed an array of specialized river craft ("bateaux") for fur trade and downriver trade with New Orleans; and they became master builders, joiners, roofers, and coopers. Yet despite the sense of enclosure and isolation created by the massive limestone bluffs, this busy, interknit world of surplus wheat marketing, livestock sales, construction, and hunting was not self-sustaining. The agents to the outside world were numerous and diverse peoples, drawn from Canadian voyageurs and traders, at least ten Indian tribes, New Orleans merchant firms and factors, Philadelphia merchant firms, land company scouts, frontier hunters of all nationalities, and the Catholic priest network between French Illinois and Quebec. Most of the French families living along the Mississippi had come out from Canada. Through trade and the river systems, they maintained contact across half a continent. Young French soldiers posted to Fort Chartres often married local girls. Notarial records from the 1740s reveal incidents of Canadian heirs to Illinois property. Although declared part of Louisiana in 1731, the Illinois Country was still leashed to the French settlements along the St. Lawrence. At least three water and land routes led to La Nouvelle France. Indians also traveled these routes to Montreal. Although the country of the Illinois had been visited by Europeans for the first time in the 1670s, it took only fifty years for the river systems of the Mississippi, Great Lakes, and St. Lawrence to become common knowledge. Travelers to the Illinois set out and arrived regularly; people knew where the rivers would take them.[38]

In the past two decades, historians have enthusiastically explored and characterized the diverse nature of frontier zone populations, while new military histories have focused on social relations and political and economic change. The approach of this study is to continue that focus while emphasizing the natural environment. Later chapters will describe the processes through which this complex, watery ecosystem and natural trade economy were profoundly altered. Long used as a north-south corridor by Kickapoo Indians, who raided deep into the southern Chickasaw country south of the Ohio, the upland prairies saw accelerating change in the decades of the 1750s and 1760s especially. The impact on upland mammal species directly affected relations of people on the floodplain. One small incident in 1767 illustrates this change. During the British occupation, Commander Reed fined a French woman in Kaskaskia 250 livres for selling a pint of rum in exchange "for a piece of meat from an Indian." The author of the letter, the agent George Morgan writing to his employers Baynton and Wharton in Philadelphia, expresses outrage; it is clear he considered this transaction to be normative and everyday and the fine tyrannical. Morgan points out that the woman had not had any meat for several days. Why was an Indian peddling a piece of meat normative? Why was the woman in need of meat? Why was the fine imposed? Answering these questions requires understanding the changing relations among diverse groups of people.[39]

It is important to take into account the Illinois French and Indian way of life, dictated by the riverine world they inhabited and built on ancient patterns of land use, patterns of movement between lowlands and uplands. The physical environment of the Illinois Country in the last half of the eighteenth century especially can help to clarify themes of conquest, adjustment, political and social upheaval, vacillating loyalties, and relations among diverse groups of Europeans, French Creoles, and Indians. The ways in which many peoples adapted to living in a dual world of aquatic resources and upland prairies affected political alliance and trade loyalty. The long, bitter Seven Years War, beginning to build in the Illinois Country as early as 1750, the arrival of the British (1765), and the decades leading up to the American invasion (1778) disturbed patterns of resource usage, trade, and livelihood among an increasingly diverse population. The chaotic adjustments that make up the record of these years were intimately woven with changes in the way inhabitants—the Indians and the French—were using the land on which they lived, the Country of the Illinois.

PART ONE

The Flourishing Floodplain,
1699–1750

2

Cahokia: French and Indian Struggles

The story of slow, inexorable changes in the land of big rivers, and thus by extension, to the lives of people in it, begins with migrating life forms, human and avian. In the lush, saturate lands immediately south of the Big Rivers confluence—the Illinois, the Mississippi, and the Missouri—Cahokia and Tamaroa Indians had been living on and off since Marquette and Joliet glided by in 1673; they had occupied the lands along the Illinois River long before that, emigrating as Algonquian-speaking peoples from the southern Michigan area perhaps early in the sixteenth century. This was their country, gashed with openings of black, fertile earth and glimmering with water that ebbed and flowed in response to both climate and the action of rivers. Many peoples, prehistoric and protohistoric, had moved in and out of this rich, alluvial confluence area. While occupancy of the land may have been continuous across several thousand years, it is not certain at all that one culture gave rise to the next. Archaeologists had assumed recovered material culture would be linked directly to prehistoric sites, but studies beginning in the 1980s showed that establishing this connection is difficult. Both Caddoan and Siouxan peoples may have moved through the area. The mounds of prehistoric Cahokia, counted by Henry Brackenridge in 1811 as numbering over 150, and the immense terraced Monks Mound rising dramatically from the floodplain, dominated the environment. Trails and paths crisscrossed the earth as animals and peoples, at least since 1000 A.D., moved around the earthworks. It is not clear how the mounds were used by groups of people who moved into the Big Rivers area after the decline of Cahokia. Many American settlers, for instance, saw the earthworks as natural features of the land, and earlier protohistoric Indians may have done so as well. Monks Mound in particular, named for a Trappist monk community occupying it in the 1830s, is depicted in most archaeological reconstructions as having steep sets of steps and terraces. A strong inference is that people living in or moving through the area would have climbed this monument. Men and women reaching the top of Monks Mound could watch the setting sun turn pools of standing water, ponds, and the Mississippi itself blood-red. Against such a backdrop, they watched the skies roar and tremble with immense flocks of waterfowl, likely in the millions; in the case of migrating passenger pigeons, the estimates are in the billions.[1]

Much has been written of the sky-darkening migrations of the extinct passenger pigeon, *Ectopistes migratorius*. Larger than mourning doves, slate gray with cherry-red breasts, these birds settled into trees along the Mississippi in such numbers that they snapped off limbs and bowed saplings to the ground. They provided food for hundreds of species of life along the river: their eggs, droppings, carcasses, and live bodies fed a range of organisms from voracious soil bacteria to humans. Archaeological work at the Modoc Rock Shelter in the American Bottom has established that prehistoric Indians simply clubbed sleeping pigeons out of the trees at night, where they thudded thickly to earth. Passenger pigeon migration was directly linked to bountiful acorn harvests. In 1737, the botanist John Bartram noted, "The pigeons always frequent the most fruitfull part of the Country; there being the greatest variety of Vegetables produced for their Support." The appearance of these birds along the Mississippi floodplain, termed a "large-scale phenomenon" covering hundreds of thousands of acres, would have affected the environment, including concepts like patch dynamics, nutrient status, and habitat diversity. One naturalist believes the birds altered light regimens and microclimates wherever they settled in to feed.[2]

Similar bounty would have been present in the Cahokia area: there, waterfowl replenished the earth and its life forms. While the numbers and variety of waterbirds in the eighteenth century cannot be accurately assessed, the migration and mobility of many life forms, including human, formed a complex, interactive ecosystem. Cahokia-Tamaroa Indians were included in these natural processes as hunters and gatherers. However, they were also activists. Their maize farming techniques, a keenly selective agriculture, had already changed the earth of the floodplain. These proto-historic Indians were a mobile people, using the rivers and tributaries to reach hunting areas or to visit; the Cahokia, for example, often visited the Peoria along the Illinois River. Indians also decamped and moved up to the bluff-top prairies on seasonal hunts. The availability of myriad waterways and superior, straight-trunked walnut and cottonwood for dugouts insured travel. It was not only the lower Mississippi bayou country that gave rise to aquatic cultures. The inland waterways of the middle Mississippi Valley created a moving human panoply, a rich social network whose true scope is perhaps yet unrealized. And the numbers of waterfowl on the Cahokia grant, long attracted by aquatic plants in a saturated earth, helped to determine the experience of the first French settlers in the floodplain area. Cahokia Indian spiritual fidelity to waterfowl, as well as the problems created by wet soils, shaped the settlement narrative here.[3]

The lives of prehistoric and historic Indians were filled with coming and going, and that habit persisted after the arrival of the French in 1699. While the Cahokia readily adopted some European practices, especially the raising of hogs and the use of iron farming implements, their relations with the Seminarian missionaries on the Cahokia grant remained tense. Agriculture developed very slowly here; the Indians had no economic role as provisioners of Europeans, and the French themselves did not settle the area as the early missionaries had anticipated. Uneven ratios of people, Europeans to Indians, and a lackluster farming record created a climate of dissatisfaction. The wet, marshy earth—more wet, more marshy than the bottomlands farther south—can be accounted a major factor in the early settlement history of the confluence area. Cahokia was a wet place. While the extensive agriculture of the mound builders may have created firmer earth during their tenure, by the time the French arrived 150 years later, the streams, creeks, rigolets, and marshes were brimming.

A Country of Birds

In 1698–99, a completely new people became part of the migration into Illinois lands. French Catholic missionaries descended the Illinois River into the area known today in Illinois as Big Rivers. The waters of the Mississippi, the Illinois, and the Missouri meet in a commingling of colors and flow rates. Pouring into the Mississippi from the west and east are rivers that redefine its character right at this point, where the Missouri churns a muddy froth. Father Zenobius Membre, a member of La Salle's expedition, created a succinct word picture in 1682, writing that the Ozage River (the Missouri) poured in a slimy stream of mud, "troubling" the great River Colbert (the Mississippi). In contrast, the Illinois River is usually described in first-impression accounts as calm or peaceful. Macoupin Creek, descending from the east across present-day Macoupin, Jersey, and Greene Counties, is the largest tributary into the Illinois in the region; farther down the western border of the state, Piasa Creek empties into the Mississippi above present-day Alton. This major confluence area saw continuous human occupation for at least eight thousand years. Archaeologists have found that consistently, the faunal and floral remains excavated from the (prehistoric) Mississippian Indian sites here are aquatic. Even today, the Mississippi River is the home of one-third of the six hundred freshwater fish species in North America and most of the freshwater mussel species (nearly 297); and this long, north-south river is the main migratory corridor for eels. For millennia, the river was feeding the people.[4]

The Big Rivers area also includes the north end of the American Bottom where the Cahokia and Tamaroa tribes lived and where the French Seminarians established their first mission. Naturalists today describe this part of the Illinois Country as a mosaic of rivers, bottoms, bluffs, broken lands and plains. The Cahokia area is only about thirty miles to the south and is still part of the region. Descriptions of the land here by journeying French in the late seventeenth century characterize it as lush, variegated, and filled with water—"the valley between . . . a Marshey Ground." In 1698 such observers as Louis Hennepin and St. Cosme found striking land forms, "ridges of mountains," and great meadows "cover'd with an infinite number of wild Bulls [bison]." St. Cosme, arriving with the first party of Seminarian missionaries, wrote of the Illinois River that "during that time" there was an abundance of swans, bustards (geese), and ducks. The time was actually winter on the Illinois River below Peoria: the waters were plated with ice. The bark canoes used by the party were too fragile to withstand the capricious movement of sharp, jagged floes, and so they waited out the freezing weeks. Yet swans, geese, and ducks flocked in abundance on open patches of river water. Through such suggestive clues, the slight, offhand words of a missionary in 1698, the Big Rivers area emerges as a country of birds.[5]

It is the presence of swans especially that reveals the intensity of birds, especially waterfowl. Illinois has lost resident populations of trumpeter swans, *Cygnus buccinator*, extirpated from the state by the 1880s. But swans have an ancient history in the Illinois Country. Trumpeters were casual winterers on major rivers of southern Illinois. Swan bones, as many as 375 specimens, have been found in archaeological digs at Cahokia, and along the Fox River, they show up in layers dating from the Pleistocene. Mature trumpeter swans have a wingspread of eight to ten feet. Thus a single wing would have perhaps been just slightly less tall than the average Indian man. Trumpeters are heavy, snow-white birds whose call sounds like the note of a French horn. In their slow, ungainly liftoffs, their wings ply and churn the surface of the water; they fly among the slowest of any of the North American waterfowl. A flock of "wing-loading" trumpeter swans ascending to flight on the Illinois River would be no insignificant event;

and those swans were intermixed with snow geese, Canada geese, migrant grebes of several varieties, bitterns, herons, egrets, wood ducks, teal, mallards, wigeons, pintails, and cranes. Each bird has a distinctive call; en masse they would have produced a cacophony, particularly in the areas of the Illinois River where immense, rocky bluffs trap and magnify sound. Not all of these water birds were resident in the winter in the Big Rivers area; some were summer breeders or merely passers-through. But the Mississippi River is one of the great flyways of the world. As late as the year 1955, after at least seventy-five years of hunting and drastic habitat erosion, observers estimated as many as six million mallards alone in the Illinois River migratory corridor. And just as ethnohistorical studies of the eastern and northern Woodland Indians have linked their spiritual and self-created identities to fur-bearing animals, what little is known about Illinois Indian tribes links them to this kingdom of birds.[6]

The journal of the Frenchman Deliette who encountered and lived among the Peoria before 1700 (and continued as a resident trader in the area well past that year) is the single most authoritative source on the Illinois Indians. Most of what is known about these tribes as they were living when they met the French comes from the period between 1673 and 1700. Such information describes the Peoria and the Kaskaskia, dwelling then on the northern Illinois River at the Mission of the Immaculate Conception (Starved Rock). For smaller tribes such as the Cahokia, Tamaroa, and the Mechigamea, very little is known at all. Because these five tribes had become the dominant members of the Illinois Confederacy, however, and especially because of the geographic proximity of the Cahokia and Peoria, it is possible to use accounts of the Peoria as careful representations. The Peoria and Kaskaskia lived in seasonal subsistence patterns. Winter and summer hunts were separated by a spring planting season beginning in March, when maize was hilled in previously readied plots. Observers noticed that the women prepared to plant corn by first gathering firewood, as they would not have time or energy to undertake this once they began to work in the fields. The verb in use here, "gathering," stems directly from the anthropological usage of "hunter-gatherer" and, unfortunately, can imply that women walked around the land picking up limbs, small branches, and twigs. Such ease of gathering can only occur in areas heavily timbered with a thriving understory of young trees and brushy growth. However, the habitat of the American Bottom was managed by fire. Annual burning off of the underbrush and small tree growth—usually in the autumn—directly shaped the many tallgrass prairies so in evidence when the French arrived.[7]

Some evidence exists about the difficulty of obtaining firewood. In 1698 one of the *engagés* hired to accompany the Seminarians down to the Cahokia area, M. De la Source, observed of the Tamaroa tribe encamped at the Cahokia area that there were as many people "at the Tamarois as at Kebeq." At the time there were about three hundred Tamaroa cabins. Later in the same year, St. Cosme observed that the Tamaroa had moved to an island in the Mississippi "to get wood more easily." The initial populations of the five Illinois tribes at the time of French settlement in 1700 range from estimates of 5,400 people up at Peoria to 2,000 people at the Cahokia-Tamaroa village. Historians estimating the numbers of people in Indian villages use the formula of twenty people to a cabin, based on estimates that four warriors lived in each cabin, and that each warrior would represent a family population of five individuals. The Indian settlement with the same number of people "as at Kebeq" would require considerable outlays of firewood. Even at one fire per cabin or lodge, the need for wood fuel would have been high. Some archaeologists have estimated that early housing practices of the Illinois Indians may have included large cabins with vaulted roofs erected on low mounds (two feet high) to avoid ground flooding. These larger cabins had four fires, warming one or two families per fire. Given the numbers of home fires to supply, Indian women may well have had to use axes to chop off limbs and fell smaller trees such as mulberry. In 1678, Deliette described Peoria women "run[ning], each with an axe, into the woods to cut poles and peel bark for their summer hunting cabins." By 1691, however, the Peoria had relocated down the Illinois River from Starved Rock to Lake Pimiteoui due to firewood depletion. The Seminarian priests mentioned the usefulness of the heavily forested islands in the Mississippi. Father Jean-Baptiste Mercier described the Island of the Holy Family as being completely coated with a forest of mature trees, specifying poplar, walnut, and mulberry. The prize heating wood, evidenced by ash pit remains, was hickory. But hickory and oak are not consistent floodplain varieties; in general, they like sunny, open, and well-drained upland soils. Seminarian letters from the Cahokia grant in the early 1730s indicate the priests were hauling white oak from the top of the bluffs. Like the Indian tribes who had long utilized the three-part geography of the American Bottom lands, the French eventually learned to take wood from the mature groves of the upland till plain.[8]

After gathering firewood, the Illinois Indian women planted maize, beans, squash and melons (melon was an introduced plant, observed by Deliette among the Peoria as early as 1678). The hunts for buffalo were launched from camps set up on the edges of the prairie, right at the timber margin, or along streams and rivers. In winter, Indians erected portable sapling-frame lodges covered in woven cattail mats. Winter camps tended to be tightly clustered, perhaps for warmth. The only known winter camp site of the Illinois to be excavated archaeologically is Woman Chief's Camp, along the Illinois River near Naples. Ash pits at this camp have yielded carbonized hickory bark; faunal remains recovered included bison, cottontail, beaver, muskrat, domestic dog, black bear, raccoon, white-tailed deer, turkey, waterfowl, turtle, fish, and mussels. Floral elements were hickory, little barley, maize, and common bean. A second pit excavated and carbondated to a somewhat later period, possibly 1706 (after the French Cahokia settlement), includes among the faunal remains evidence of pig. While at summer and winter camps, Illinois Indians hunted initially on foot, organizing communally. They surrounded a herd and drove the buffalo into ambush where the rest of the hunting party waited. Deliette, who recorded these details, participated in a summer hunt in which twelve hundred buffalo were killed, as well as "deer, bears, turkeys, lynxes, and mountain lions." This number of animals was taken over a period of approximately five weeks. While twelve hundred buffalo seems high for humans hunting on foot, Deliette also records that on a single hunting day, Indians killed 120 animals, culling them from a "great herd" and running them down. The hunters used both firearms and bow and arrow on this hunt; Deliette states they shot off "an extraordinary number of arrows," after which he observed large numbers of buffalo on the ground. Before the Illinois Indians obtained horses, they relied on their speed on foot. Baron LaHontan, writing "Discourse on the Savages of North America" in 1689 observed that "the Illinese" were of an indifferent size but could run like greyhounds. Deliette also admired the Illinois as being "trained runners" and described them, too, as having "lynx-eyes."[9]

Summer villages of the Illinois were strung out along the river banks and could contain many lodges; observers have counted 300 to 351 at different times before 1700. Summer lodges were covered with lighter bark sheets (elm) to admit air and light. Yet before either summer or winter camps were set up, Illinois Indians launched a month of raiding and warfare in February. It is here, in their warfare rituals, that the connection with the immense natural bird population of the Mississippi floodplain can be found. Birds were part of the rituals of war; for the Illinois, birds were emblems of supernatural power. Warriors chose a personal bird or birds and collected their skins in a colored reed mat. Before departing for the raid, warriors participated in night-long rituals in which the bird skins were displayed. This was to ensure the cooperation and aid of their personal bird spirits.

Deliette mentions the warriors "pay[ing] homage . . . to their birds." Later, during the raid itself, warriors skillfully imitated the cries of their birds. Captives brought back to the Illinois camps sang their death chants while holding long sticks adorned with feathers of birds killed by raiders. Thus the metaphor of the bird of prey was woven into the chronology of war raids.[10]

Descriptions of Illinois Indians by modern writers employ the terms "semipermanent villages," "seminomadic lifestyle," or "subsistence based on farming, hunting, and gathering." The circannual rhythms of these Indians involved a coming and going between river bottom summer camps, upland winter camps, buffalo herds roaming on the larger prairies farther inland, enemy Indian camps to the north and south, as well as across the Mississippi into the lands of the Missouria and Osage. The Mechigamea "continuously journeyed" as far down the Mississippi as Arkansas and the Quapaw tribes. The world of the Illinois Indians, before the French arrived and during the French occupation, was a traveling one. In a 1750 letter written by Father Vivier at the Kaskaskia mission, he states that the Kaskaskia were continuing to hunt seasonally. "From the beginning of October to the middle of March, they hunt at a distance of forty to fifty leagues from their village; and, in the middle of March, they return to their village. Then the women sow the maize." In 1750 the Kaskaskia had been living in a permanent village near the French for almost thirty years. They had learned to use the French plow, the charrue, and were considered to be the most highly Christianized of any of the Illinois Indian tribes. Yet they still kept to the rhythms of their hunts; they still decamped in masse. Despite the five French settlements devoted to agriculture, lead mining, and milling, the traditions of the Illinois Indians and trade relations among tribes and with the French and British created a highly mobile environment. The movement of people across the American Bottom was continuous. In their subsistence patterns, Indians occupying the American Bottom were migrants and summer/winter residents themselves. They were part of a diverse ecosystem dominated by prodigious numbers of migrating and resident waterfowl. The topography of this area was also highly attractive to scavengers and birds of prey like the bluff-loving turkey vultures, river-loving bald eagles, red-shouldered and red-tailed hawks, and many species of owls. It is not too remarkable that birds should have become spiritually important to the Indians who lived and moved with them.[11]

Into this structured world built around migratory patterns arrived a group of Jesuit and Seminarian Catholic missionaries. They found an animistic cosmology based on the reading of extremely specific, unmistakable, and dependable signs and codes from the natural world; Catholic missionaries sought to replace this with a hierarchical faith in which the concepts of "the unknown" and "the unknowable" reigned supreme. Perhaps the least-explored aspect of Catholic conversion efforts among American Indians has to do with the role of knowledge, not belief, in both Indian religions and Catholic Christianity. Yet the story of the French missionaries in the Illinois Country is not only about religion, about the introduction of an alien theology; it is also about property. Property came to play a central role in the French Catholic penetration into Indian lands. Jesuit and Seminarian possessions, whether sacred or secular, were sources of keen interest to Indians. More than movable property, however, mission lands came to stand as symbols for French presence. The presence was permanent and agricultural, as well as spiritual. Catholic missionaries to the Illinois Country—Seminarian as well as Jesuit—methodically developed and improved their holdings as corollary activities to converting the Illinois Indian tribes. It was at the southernmost colony of Kaskaskia that a donné on a Jesuit mission first cultivated wheat in 1718. Sixty miles north in Cahokia, the Seminarians developed an extensive grant; their letters reveal excited plans for the establishment of grist mills, water mills, forts, and farms for incoming Canadian settlers. The letters of the Jesuit missionaries and of the Seminarians over time, from 1699 through to the Seven Years War, reveal a shift away from the priority of converting Indians to the priority of establishing French colonies with centrally located chapels and churches and enough priests to minister to French souls. Of the five French settlements on the Mississippi, two are particularly instructive as case studies. Cahokia, settled in 1699, and the village of Chartres, growing up in the prairie next to Fort Chartres, offer avenues for comparative analysis that can trace differing profiles of land and resource usage and, hence, different patterns of interaction with Indian tribes as well.[12]

The natural and human environments of these two settlements determined trajectories of settlement growth. It has been all too easy to lump the French settlements together; they were different. In Cahokia, the river bluffs ran to the northeast fifty arpents (about one and a half miles) away from the settlement residences, and the French concession meandered across sixteen square leagues of soggy land occupied intermittently by Cahokia, Tamaroa, and Peoria Indians. The river bluffs on the Cahokia grant are not uniformly "clifty"—that is, there are gentle, intermittent slopes toward the higher ridge ground. Access to the Cahokia concession from the upland till plain is easier and probably facilitated human traffic. In addition, the Cahokia grant contained the great Cahokia mounds, a land form entirely anthropogenic (humanly derived); the mounds distinguish the Cahokia lands from all other French grants along the Mississippi. At Chartres, severe, vertical bluffs protected the village within walking distance; French and Indian settlement and interaction took place in a sheltered land cove lying between the Mississippi River and the limestone bluffs, and the only Indians living in the vicinity were a small group of domiciled Mechigamea (also spelled Metchigamea or Michigamea) who occupied a village a league and a half north of the fort. The contrasting development of Cahokia and Chartres is marked. At each place, differing habitats and settling populations combined to create distinct frontier worlds, separated by only thirty miles.[13]

In the Illinois Country, in the early years after the establishment of the Cahokia mission, letters and records detail competition between the Jesuits and the Seminary of the Foreign Missions for control of mission property and neophytes. Seminarians ended up in Cahokia, and their experiences with Cahokia-Tamaroa Indians in an often-flooded ecosystem stand in counterpoint to the Jesuit experiences farther south. Exceptionally large territories in New France—and myriad Indian groups who occupied those territories—were assigned to missionaries in dramatic proclamations; French Catholic officials in Montreal and Paris manipulated immense tracts of North America. Indian tribes of the interior were viewed as resources comparable to land itself, both as potential converts to Catholicism and as fur gatherers for the monarchy. In the late seventeenth century, officials in New France began issuing letters-patent for the opening of the Illinois Country. A recounting of the arrival of Jesuit missionaries along the Mississippi River, however, must begin with a historical error. The failure of Bishop Monsignor St. Vallier, second Bishop of Quebec, to distinguish between land and peoples in a series of letters-patent created a jurisdictional confusion in the Illinois Country that would still be ongoing as late as the 1790s, when lawsuits over property rights were finally settled. In 1690, Bishop St. Vallier gave a commission to the Jesuits to "preach the Gospel to the Ottawa, Miami, Sioux, and Illinois Indians." Then in 1698 he gave permission for another Catholic group, the Seminarians of Quebec (the Seminary of Foreign Missions) to penetrate the Illinois Country for the purpose of setting up missions on either side of the Mississippi: "en deca et au dela du Mississippi." In both cases, these grants, directly conflicting as they were, bespoke a rather naive—or untutored—sense of the numbers of peoples and the leagues of land involved. Between 1699 and 1703, then, both the Seminarians and the Jesuits, charged with evangelizing the Illinois Indians, journeyed down the Illinois River past Lake Pimiteoui (Peoria) to the lands of the Tamaroa Indians near Cahokia. Henri de Tonti, usually described as a "soldier of fortune," had recommended to the bishop that the Tamaroa Indians were likely candidates for conversion. One of the first actions of the Seminarians was the baptism of a son born to a French soldier, La Violette, and an Indian mother, Catherine Ekipakinoua, with Henri de Tonti standing in as godfather. The baptism took place in La Violette's small cabin and was recorded in the old parish registers of the Immaculate Conception of Kaskaskia. In November 1698, when the cabin Mass and baptism occurred, the Kaskaskia mission was north of Cahokia, on the Illinois River at Fort Pimiteoui (Peoria). In a "Memoir Concernant le Pays Illinois," the author describes Peoria as being populated by six of the eight Illinois nations living in 260 cabins, with a "fighting population" of nearly eight hundred warriors. The baptism of the La Violette son at the Kaskaskia Mission introduced the Seminarians to the kinds of relationships already flourishing in the Illinois Country.[14]

These members of the Seminaire des Missions Etrangeres, described as "a new group of Frenchmen," were guided down the Illinois River to the Cahokia site by the knowledgeable Henri de Tonti himself. The Seminarians were just in the process of learning about the Illinois Indians. In two important ways, arriving Seminarians differed from the Jesuits, who also claimed the right to mission territory in Illinois. These differences reflect powerful psychological conceptualizations that had developed in Jesuit understanding of Indians over the nearly seventy years they had been laboring in North America. The differences also shaped patterns of Jesuit-Indian interaction in the Illinois Country.[15]

The first difference is linguistic. None of the Seminarians spoke any of the Illinewek Algonquin language, used by all the tribes. These tribes originally numbered as many as seventeen and included the five most consistently appearing in French-Indian relations of the eighteenth century: the Peoria, Kaskaskia, Cahokia, Tamaroa, and Mechigamea. Father Gabriel Marest would describe the Seminarians, using the term "gentlemen," stating that the Jesuits helped the gentlemen Seminarians by giving them a translation of the catechism and prayers. These translations were the result of years of intricate, arduous work on the part of Jesuit priests across a wide band of North America. Facility in Indian languages was connected intimately with a second important principle of Jesuit work: constant presence among Indians, even to the point of accompanying them on winter hunts, trading trips, and difficult journeys from village to village across the prairies. Missionaries shared Indian cabins or crude shelters at night, suffering from scorched feet and smoke inhalation. These early accounts are full of references to hunger. Sometimes priests were forced to chew old moose skins for sustenance. Father Rasle described his hunger as "the most cruel torture," and mentioned the only resource in times of lack of game: "a sort of leaf which the savages call Kenghessanach and the French Tripes des Roches." He likened it to the French herb chervil. Priests took with them a bag that contained articles for the Holy Communion but also an assortment of small gift items: needles, fishhooks, glass trinkets. Instructions to these early priests stressed the "embellishment" of religious ceremonies. Priests were to use decorations gleaned from nature, such as leaves, bouquets, and garlands, to attract Indian eyes and keep them interested.[16]

Gradually, Jesuits laboring in New France set up permanent mission complexes and ventured out to nearby villages on short trips to preach, evangelize, and minister. Jesuits believed that they could make more progress with the early Huron converts, for instance, by encouraging them to remain isolated from other French, especially coureurs de bois, whose lives were rife with the two excesses most detested by priests: drink and licentiousness. Teams of preaching missionaries fanned out from the mission into nearby native towns. Jesuits continued to maintain their policy of keeping Indians separate from the French and teaching them in their own languages. When the fur trade pushed west into the upper Mississippi Valley, the Jesuits followed the furs. And they brought with them an ingrained idea about permanent mission settlements attracting "domiciled" Indians who would live near to but separate from the French. The pattern was already established for the location of Illinois Indian villages near French missions.[17]

The Illinois Country, though, would challenge these conceptions in dramatic ways: its sheer size, its daunting remoteness. Here lay immense, variegated land, a rich mosaic of tallgrass prairie, riparian forest, blufflands, ravines, and barrens. This variety spanned the North American continent between Fort Pontchartrain (Detroit), built in 1701, and the southernmost (transient) settlement in the Illinois Country, the Juchereau Tannery established between 1702 and 1705 near the confluence of the Mississippi and Ohio Rivers. When in 1699 the French priests sailed down the Illinois River past the late seventeenth-century fort of Pimiteoui (and also past short-lived forts such as St. Louis and Crevecoeur), there were no French settlements or missions; an assortment of Illinois tribes—perhaps as many as eight distinct nations—lived and roamed along the Illinois, Mississippi, and Kaskaskia Rivers. Above Pimiteoui (Peoria) lived the Fox, Sauk, and Potawatomi; to the east lived Kickapoo and Miami Indians such as the Wea and Piankeshaw. The Jesuits soon realized that the Illinois Country would demand of them an intense mobility. As late as 1780, letters from the Jesuit Pierre Gibault discuss the exhaustive demands of his traveling, although Gibault was covering territory to minister to French inhabitants by that time. The theme of distance is instinct in the Jesuit letters from the Illinois Country. Nicolas de Finiels, who explored Upper Louisiana in the late 1790s, wrote about the travels from Quebec and Montreal of traders and priests: "You must comprehend the geography of North America to comprehend such a journey."[18]

In 1712 Father Marest, writing from the (relocated) Kaskaskia Mission, sent an extensive account to Father Barthelemi Germon, a professor at Orleans, France. This letter is not only about the country, Indian groups, missions, spiritual ministries, and the problems and procedures in conversion activities; it is also Father Marest's testament to the Jesuit missionary's exhausting and painful peripatetic life. The extremes of distance and weather, the physical punishment inflicted on toiling, dedicated missionaries, and their looping trips across prairies, down spring-flooded rivers and up ice-bound rivers—such accounts stand forth conspicuously. At the Tamaroa Mission, Jesuit priests ministered to Illinois Indians, speaking in both French and Algonquian. It is clearly the Jesuits, not the Seminarians, who were traveling, embarking on lengthy and life-threatening trips down the Mississippi in pirogues or northward across the prairies on ancient trails. An account of the Holy Family Mission at Cahokia stresses the permanency of the Seminarians there, tracing the continuous site of the mission church of the Holy Family. "The present old mission church of the Holy Family, Cahokia, built in 1775, certainly stands on the site of the mission of 1737. And the church of 1737, with the same certainty, stood on the site of the Tamarois village and first mission church of 1699."[19]

This description of the permanency of the Cahokia mission stands in counterpoint to all other French missions and churches in the Illinois Country. At the French villages of St. Philippe, Prairie du Rocher, Chartres, and Kaskaskia, the Jesuit churches disintegrated, were moved, were rebuilt, were occupied by farm animals, stood roofless, and became barracks for British soldiers and then Virginian (American) despots. Even the 1735 satellite mission established by the Seminarians at the River L'Abbe, headed by Father Mercier, was abandoned in 1752 as the Cahokia Indians fled south, away from Fox attacks. The stability of the Holy Family Mission at Cahokia can perhaps be explained by the work of the Seminarians, who stayed put, preferring to minister to the incoming French settlers who very slowly began to arrive and till a small amount of land around the mission sites. In 1702 the Jesuits were directed to give up their claim at the Cahokia Mission in favor of the Seminarians. Father Pinet then left and crossed the Mississippi River to the relocated Kaskaskia Mission, joining two other Jesuit priests in their work there. The Seminarians stayed on. By the 1720s records indicate that the Cahokia tribe had become dominant at the Cahokia mission, and three groups—Seminarian priests, a few French habitants, and the Cahokia Indians—created a distinct settlement narrative. Just as archaeologists have stressed differences in frontier outposts that reflect access to rivers, proximities to Indian nations, and availability of certain game and plants for specific diets, the same analysis holds true for French settlements occurring across only sixty miles.[20]

Cahokia rapidly became not an agricultural settlement but a fur trading entrepôt, advantaged by its location near the confluence of the Mississippi and Missouri (and across from the future village of St. Louis). Patterns of land and resource use began to develop in the area: farming (although limited), fur trading, and the commercial services necessary to sustain a fluctuating population of river traders, voyageurs for hire, and the permanent mission populations. The furs passing through Cahokia in the early decades were not primarily beaver. The beaver of the Illinois Country were described as very light, "almost a straw color," with thin fur of little value. However, other peltries were shipped down the Mississippi to New Orleans "in great quantities." By 1720 officials of the Company of the Indies in Illinois were even planning to ship large numbers of buffalo skins from the Wabash country. Although some historians have posited that French settlers arriving at Cahokia inaugurated a "thriving agriculture," there are suggestions that this was not the case. On a 1735 map prepared by Father Superieur Jean-Baptiste Mercier, the Cahokia lands reveal longlot holdings as a cluster of alluvial fields. Two points about this map and census interpretation are important, not only for establishing comparisons between Cahokia and the other French settlements, but because they highlight the importance of a specific environment in determining the kind of community that would develop, in this case a transportation-trade nucleus with the largest, most enduring Catholic mission settlement in the Illinois Country to anchor it.[21]

First, several historians have drawn a distinction between the activities of Jesuits and the activities of the Seminarians. Joseph Schlarman's 1929 study of New France asserts that the missionaries were characterized by a "restless craving" for exploration, that they too often felt "the lure of the forest." Footnote evidence for this, however, reveals remarks leveled at Seminarians, by Seminarian authorities, in the very earliest years at Cahokia. Seminarian authorities thought that several of the original missionaries, including St. Cosme and Davion, "loved too much to roam about and make new discoveries." The Seminarians may have been directed, therefore, to remain more centralized and to develop their property holdings. Carl Ekberg points out that the Jesuits demonstrated a much stronger proselytizing fervor. For whatever reasons, the Seminarians began assiduously to develop their vast holdings at Cahokia; in the early 1720s they held a tract of land encompassing a full sixteen square leagues (approximately one hundred square miles)! In 1722 French commanders in the Illinois Country, De Boisbriant and des Ursins, representing the Company of the Indies, granted the Seminarians this extensive tract. The Seminarian concession was termed "unique" in the Illinois Country and held within it all forms of French settlement, including military garrison, mission house, both French village and Indian (Cahokia-Tamaroa) village, and agricultural lands. While an exceptionally large concession incorporating a variety of land features, Cahokia shares in common with St. Philippe and Prairie du Rocher the extension of its lands up to the top of the bluffs. St. Philippe, in fact, was a tiny, marshy settlement on a concession having a single league of river frontage. The present-day bluff village of Renault is still viable, hugging the southeast corner of the original Renault tract that contained St. Philippe. All the farmed longlots ended at the bluffs, a consistent practice in the St. Lawrence River Valley, the Illinois Country, and the lower Mississippi Valley above New Orleans: longlots were run from one specific land formation to another. The giant limestone bluffs, topped with scrub trees in summit profusion, provided a natural demarcation. From the sheltering rock walls of the bluff line on Mercier's map, the Cahokia concession drifted toward the Mississippi River across approximately fifty arpents. It did so in a series of bogs, marshes, and saturated wetlands. On the Mercier map, goose-egg-shaped droplets dot the land, identified as "marais" (swamp). This reality is all too evident in the distribution of Cahokian common lands, and, along with the Seminarian dedication to permanency, must be accounted a factor in Cahokia's small population and lesser agricultural status. Seminarian missionaries, frustrated not only by the lack of French settlers and subsequent agricultural development but also by their lack of success in converting Indians, especially the proud and recalcitrant Peoria, began to think about mills.[22]

At French settlements such as Chartres, Prairie du Rocher, and Ste. Genevieve (in Missouri), the commons were apportioned in large tracts. Le Grande Champ at Ste. Genevieve, in fact, is such an extensive, alluvial spread that it may still be viewed today from the high land above it. Cahokia's commons farther north were scattered in bits and pieces: across the Riviere du Pont, on the Isle de la Famille, and between Cahokia Creek and the Mississippi. The French mission and Indian villages at Cahokia lay in an area fingered with lakes, small streams, tributaries, and inlets to the Mississippi. The Prairie du Pont river or creek was especially fluctuant. As described in an early history of southern Illinois, it occupied a new bed every few years. The presence of so many small feeder streams would likely result in the phenomenon known as backflooding. When the great rivers were at flood stage, overflow waters would pour into the tributaries, over the banks, and into the already sodden earth. When Yankee settlers first encountered the French living around the Detroit area, they coined the term "Muskrat Frenchmen" for these people who "lived almost in the water of [their] favorite stream or marsh." Such a sense of the French would cling to

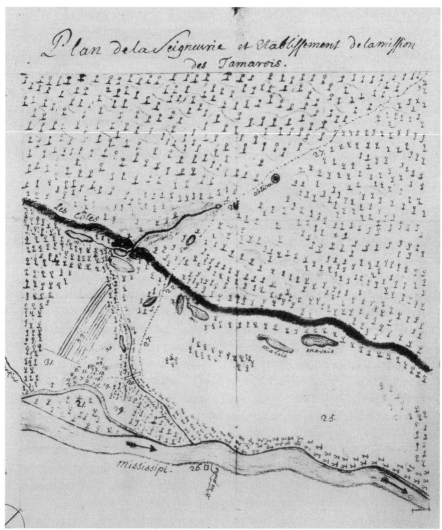

Detail from a 1732 map by Father Mercier depicting the Cahokia Mission complex. Goose-egg lakes and ponds denote a marshy environment.

them, reinforced by settlement patterns in watery areas like Cahokia. Agriculture was not developing at the rate it was farther down the French coast, especially at Kaskaskia, a settlement on an alluvial floodplain that proved nearly perfect for cereal-grain farming. The tiny settlement of St. Philippe, about seven miles north of Fort Chartres, was also described as marshy or swampy; it is sometimes referred to as "St. Philippe du Grand Marais." Some habitants at St. Philippe did negotiate wheat-supplying contracts; the La Croix family entered into what has been called a "small agribusiness" of wheat production and supply in the 1730s, as did the original owner of the St. Philippe concession, Phillip Renault. These records seem somewhat exceptional, however, in St. Philippe's history. La Croix and Renault very likely owned the largest number of arpents at St. Philippe. In 1765 the arriving British commander Thomas Stirling would describe St. Philippe as having only "some good farms."[23]

Given the greater agricultural success of the more southern French settlements—Prairie du Rocher, Kaskaskia, and Ste. Genevieve across the river—Cahokia and St. Philippe were noteworthy as two settlements of greater commercial and trade activity. Both maize and wheat suffer in wet soils, where the roots easily rot. The aboriginal transition to maize and tobacco growing has been documented archaeologically as occurring up on the high ground above the American Bottom floodplain. The import of ground saturation for Cahokia lies in its failure to attract French settlers and, therefore, its growth as a trade rather than agricultural center. As with all the French settlements, there were good years for wheat and maize and bad, but French settlers were slow to arrive in Cahokia, despite a conventional interpretation that the Seminarians developed their large holdings and ministered "chiefly to the French settlers." In the first thirty years of settlement, the number of French settlers never approached that at Kaskaskia, sixty miles to the south. In 1700 there were only seven Frenchmen at Cahokia. The 1732 census lists only four French priests and helpers living at the Cahokia mission complex, as well as three *habitants*; but it also itemizes African slaves and domestic animals, both in such small numbers as to imply little growth in French settlement. In 1732 Kaskaskia had 102 slaves; St. Anne de Fort Chartres, 37; St. Philippe, 22; and Cahokia, 4. This is clear evidence of a lack of agricultural growth. In 1731 the priest at the Seminarian Cahokia Mission, Father (Monsignor) Mercier, began to purchase land from the Indians in an effort to lure French immigrants down to the Illinois Country. The Seminarians were in contact with the Cahokia and Tamaroa tribes, yet still felt themselves to be isolated. Father Mercier exclaims wistfully, "If only twenty families would come down from Canada

. . . more than two hundred habitants could be wonderfully placed." This view was perhaps colored by an exceptional wheat harvest that year, 1732; Mercier described it as "3500 bundles of the best wheat in the world." By 1743, however, he was complaining to Vaudreuil, Governor of Louisiana, "We do not grind enough grain to pay the miller."[24]

Father Mercier was full of plans for how the Cahokia Mission could be developed, especially in the building of mills. The granting of land in French North America carried an implicit responsibility for development, for the improvements that would lure other settlers and foster agriculture and industries that would in time repay the crown. Such responsibilities were also felt by priests, who have been described as primary undertakers of territorial settlement. The 1735 letter by Fathers Mercier and Courier is interesting because their development ideas clearly focus on discussions of water and mills. The letter contains at least ten specific references to mills, the placing of mills, the problems of high and low water, the seasonal droughts:

> The rivier du pont [river of the bridge] also issues from a swamp and flows quite gently into the mississippi, almost directly across from the former village of the Kaskaskias. The mississippi never backwaters it to such an extent that it would not turn a mill a short distance above the place where a bridge is indicated. It is the cost of the dam and the lack of water in the long droughts which have kept us from building one there rather than in the hills.

Father Mercier also compares the efforts of the Seminarians in building mills to the efforts of the Jesuits sixty miles to the south, in Kaskaskia. Priests at both establishments obviously knew what the others were doing. Kaskaskia, however, was shipping rich wheat harvests to New Orleans as the principal supplier in annual convoys beginning in the 1720s. By 1732 Kaskaskia had fourteen gristmills, whereas St. Philippe had only two. Also at Kaskaskia, the Kaskaskian Indians had moved two leagues north of the settlement, relocated by the incoming French commander De Boisbriant in 1721. They lived on a prairie that became named for them. Unless Kaskaskian Indians journeyed to French Kaskaskia, they were out of sight of the French residents. At Cahokia, the village of the Tamaroa was near both the Mission of the Holy Family (on the Isle de la Famille in the Mississippi) and the Mississippi shore; Father Mercier's 1735 letter clearly states this adjacency. In simple terms, what this meant for the French living near the mission on the Cahokia grant was daily sight of Indians. The Peoria tribe to the north frequently came to stay with the Cahokia and Tamaroa Indians; they especially did so under pressure from Fox raids. Historians have speculated that as the French priests acquired more land from the Illinois tribes near Cahokia, Indians reacted with hostility. The so-called Cahokia revolt is credited to Cahokian dissatisfaction with incursions of the French onto their hunting and agricultural grounds. This explanation—that white settlement invaded and disturbed hunting territories of Indians—so often appears in historical interpretations that it must be both questioned and expanded.[25]

On the Cahokia grant that included much watery ground and a series of named marshes, it is likely as well that the amount of prairie in these bottomlands was as high as 50 percent. The references to prairies in letters from Seminarians (as well as the named prairies, both small and large, occurring around Fort Chartres and the Village of Chartres) support this conclusion. Thick with long, sharp-edged indigenous grasses growing as high as a man's head, obstructing riders on horses, filled with noxious insects and a humid, choking heat in high summer, these tallgrass prairies were not the home of myriad animal populations capable of providing a sustained protein base for Indian populations as large as two thousand. Tallgrass prairies and wetlands attract small mammals and birds like rabbits, prairie chickens, squirrels, and mice, all of which were hunted and consumed by both Indians and French. The roving herds of deer and buffalo on the floodplain described by seventeenth-century French rapidly disappeared as a consistent food source. From the time of the permanent French settlements, a major protein source for Indians and, frequently, for French themselves came from buffalo tenderloins, carried back to villages by Indians in massive packs after days of smoking and drying on the prairie uplands. Pork became important as well, especially for the inhabitants of agricultural communities like the village of Chartres and Kaskaskia. Notarial records as early as 1724 detailing land and home sales and transfers for the village of Chartres mention hogs; in 1726 hams "of fifteen or sixteen pounds in weight" were listed as part of a selling price.[26]

Although the Illinois Indians living in domiciled villages were still going on summer and winter hunts, their more permanent occupation of lands would have accelerated environmental change. The abundant waterfowl described by Hennepin and St. Cosme in 1698 were sharing the Cahokia grant not only with Indian villages undergoing many changes of population but also with a large French mission complex; the Seminarians were involved with land clearing, mill building, and orchard planting. Gradually across thirty years, despite the lesser French population, the Cahokia grant became a peopled world. The impression of human activity at Cahokia is strong, conveyed by a sense of arrival and departure, of the coming and going of tribes and traders. Its location near the confluence area of Big Rivers attracted the downriver trade traffic. While there is little direct evidence of a severe decline in resident and migratory bird populations on the Cahokia grant, archaeologists who have excavated an eighteenth-century French colonial site called the Cahokia Wedge site have found a lacuna in faunal remains: very low numbers of waterfowl. Ducks, shorebirds, and marsh birds were underrepresented at the Cahokia Wedge site. Additional findings from this site indicate low numbers of domestic animals in comparison with other French sites in the Illinois Country; however, trumpeter swan wing bones were represented, as well as large blue catfish. The Cahokia French consumption pattern may have been quite similar to Indian consumption patterns, that is, it was based on the availability and ready location of food-stuffs and was highly seasonal in nature. Questions can be raised about what this may have meant—did the French settlers simply prefer certain sources of protein, or was the waterfowl population being affected by the mobility and trade culture around Cahokia?[27]

The Cahokia Indians, like the Peoria to the north, had used bird popu-lations in ritualistic and adornment practices. The trumpeter swan, for instance, becomes flightless during the molting season over the summer. At this time, they can be captured without need of weapons. Swansdown and swan skin, cut from a mature trumpeter swan, would furnish a delicately warm clothing layer and glorious feathers. The same can be inferred for an extinct species, the Carolina paroquet (parakeet), whose long, brilliant green feathers were seen sailing among and drooping from river trees in the American Bottom. These parakeets typically flocked ten to twelve at a time and were easy to hunt. Deliette's description of the calumet he saw among the Peoria in 1678 is specific for the incorporation of feathers, men-tioning bright red, yellow, and black feathers, as well as a handle covered in duck neck skin. Additional descriptions of the calumet of the Illinois Indians are found in *Jesuit Relations*, where priests writing of the feathery calumet termed it "beautiful." In addition to the role of birds, bird skins, and bird spirits in raiding and cosmology, birds were important in Indian adornment. The few representations of Illinois Indians drawn from the eighteenth century show them brilliantly adorned with feathers. The men have rippling sprays of upright feathers on their (roached) hair. Illinois men wore a long, pendant hair ornament suspended from the crown of the head with a woven thong. A photograph of such an ornament, collected before 1845, shows wrapped quillwork and pendants made of feathers. In a rare 1735 painting of Illinois Indians taken to New Orleans, the chief is shown standing with his hand on the head of a crane. Later portraits of Peoria men by George Catlin in the 1830s also reveal masses of feathers used in original ways, although these Peoria were living in Kansas at the time. Traces of the role of (especially) waterfowl and raptors can be found consistently in the historical accounts of the Illinois Indians.[28]

Sketch of Illinois Indian by De Granville, circa 1700. The Illinois nation identified strongly with birds and used their feathers in ritual and adornment.

From the Collections of The New York Public Library, Astor, Lenox, and Tilden Foundations.

The Cahokia tribe living on the mission lands had long used the floodplain and cliffs as sources of waterfowl feathers, eggs, skins, and flesh. By the 1730s, however, the Cahokia grant was almost certainly a more altered habitat. Indians living adjacent to the French faced issues of deforestation and wetland reclamation (affecting firewood availability and nesting bird populations); scarcity of small game; and possible soil exhaustion on overworked and constantly-used Indian plots. Accounts of bird populations on the Mississippi River below Cahokia continued, however. In 1751 the Frenchman Bossu wrote a description of the St. Francis River in present-day Arkansas. Bossu was an officer in the party ascending the Mississippi, led by the incoming Commander Macarty. He observed the (undisturbed) bird populations near the mouth of the St. Francis, an unsettled area; and he complained about the noise of the birds at night, describing a multitude of swans, cranes, geese, bustards, and ducks. In 1765 the British commander Thomas Stirling described the Illinois Country as containing "millions of waterfowl." Stirling listed waterfowl species and even described the adornment of the calumet with waterfowl feathers. However, Stirling's destination was Fort Chartres, and there is little direct evidence that he journeyed on up to Cahokia, an additional thirty plus miles. His journal account of Cahokia contains virtually no description, merely enumerated information. In general, except for strong impressions of Kaskaskia as a resplendent agricultural community, observers tended to gloss the entire Illinois Country as one environment.[29]

It is not possible to compare the numbers of waterfowl observed in the 1790s with original bird populations in the Big Rivers area at the time the French arrived. Such values must be taken from descriptions such as the one by Father Marest in 1712, noting that waterfowl stuffed themselves on wild oats growing "freely" on the plains, often eating so much they suffocated. He also identified many wild turkeys, perhaps lured to the area by prodigious stands of protein-rich Illinois bundleflower (prairie mimosa), a preferred turkey food source once found growing rampantly on mesic prairies. In November of 1750, Father Vivier described the environment along the Mississippi River well below Kaskaskia, specifically mentioning immense numbers of ducks, bustards, geese, swans, and snipe. When he writes of the French settlements, perhaps specifically Kaskaskia where he was working, he mentions only the abundant ox (buffalo) and white-tailed deer, *Odocoileus virginianus*, the mainstay protein sources for Indians and the French alike. He does not write of birds. Yet in another letter he does mention waterfowl. The pattern is tentative.[30]

However, changes in the natural habitat of the Cahokia, changes that may have affected waterfowl populations, comprise only one possible factor in events leading to the Cahokia revolt of the early 1730s. The Cahokia and Peoria Indians were also proving difficult spiritual subjects. There is evidence from the letters of Father Mercier in 1732 that successful conversion of the Cahokia and, especially, the Peoria was eluding priests. The Peoria, often described as "arch-traditional," in fact were perceived as impediments to the conversion of the more "tractable" Cahokia. By the early 1730s, the relations between the French settling around the Cahokia mission and the Cahokia and Peoria Indians worsened. The dynamic of population must be accorded a role in escalating tensions. An important study by Joseph Zitomersky focusing on the population geography of the Illinois Indians stresses the importance of mutually supportive relationships existing between Indians and Europeans in these earliest years. Zitomersky believes that Indians had a state-sanctioned role as food suppliers, their productivity enhanced because they had adapted French draft animals and mills. The ratio of Illinois Indians living on the Cahokia grant to the actual numbers of French creates questions about that food-supplier role. Conventional interpretations stressing Indian hostility over invasion of traditional lifeways and subsistence patterns overlook hostility created by inadequate and vacillating opportunities for trade. Where there are high and growing numbers of incoming colonists in a frontier region, the role of Indians as initial food suppliers is important. When the number of inhabitants is small enough to rapidly develop a self-sustaining economic world, as on the Cahokia grant, the shift in relations of power and dependence between colonists and Indians is ominous. The irritation the Cahokia felt when French pigs and cattle roamed into their fields was perhaps exacerbated by the reality that this livestock was owned by only eleven Frenchmen. In 1732 the estimated village population for the Cahokia Indians was 1,480. Although there would have been some French soldiers, French voyageurs and traders, and occasionally, other Europeans at the Cahokia settlement, the difference between the French and the Indian population on this grant is striking. No other Illinois tribes supported the Cahokia in their so-called revolt. The explanation for this is not political but demographic and economic. Other Illinois tribes had too much to lose. In the Kaskaskia village, fifty miles to the south, Indians produced maize and wheat and had a thriving French population downriver to sell it to; because of the garrison of soldiers at Fort Chartres, they also furnished game regularly for the troops. Kaskaskian chiefs even journeyed up to Cahokia to try to restore order and security between the French and the Cahokia.[31]

In May 1733 resident priests and several inhabitants of the French village "fled at night" after a warning that the Cahokia might rise up and massacre them. Such fears had been exacerbated by the 1729 Natchez Revolt on the lower Mississippi. In the environs of Fort Rosalie, the Natchez Indians laid careful plans to entrap French settlers. Using what one historian has noted as a typical pattern of frontier exchange, the Natchez welcomed French visitors with tribute and promises of food and furs. They then massacred 145 men, 36 women, and 56 children, as well as capturing "nearly 300 Negro slaves and some 50 white women and children." Despite major differences in population between French Fort Rosalie and French Illinois, the story of the Natchez Revolt has particular parallels with the settlement history in Cahokia. Like the declining numbers of the Illinois Indians to the north, the Natchez had been decimated by contagious diseases and compressed by French land grants. From initial population estimates of perhaps thirty-five hundred before the advent of the French, the Natchez numbered barely half that, scattered among five villages. Also like the Natchez, the Illinois used livestock and food-theft raids against white settlers as a prime weapon. (In 1722, in a single week, the Natchez killed eleven cattle and stole horses, pigs, and vital stores of flour and grains). The French in Illinois had heard all about the Natchez revolt and the bloody massacre of innocent French men, women, and children. The restiveness of the Cahokia and their depredations against livestock seemed harbingers of disaster. In 1733 the commandant at Fort Chartres, St. Ange, wrote to France to request additional troops, mentioning "the wrong which they [the Cahokia] have done the inhabitants [settlers] by killing their animals." In 1732 a letter from Father Mercier refers to the "trouble we have had with them [the Cahokia]." As a result of the (bloodless) Cahokia Revolt in the early 1730s, the French insisted on the tribe removing from the French mission area. The Cahokia eventually settled near the Cahokia mounds, specifically the great terraced Monks Mound, nine miles away from the French. There the River L'Abbe mission was established for their benefit, and the French assisted the Cahokia in the plowing of fresh fields for their corn. In addition, the new Commander D'Artaguiette posted French soldiers to the small French fort at Cahokia and issued a punitive message to the Cahokia: they would receive no French presents until "they repair the wrongs which they have done." Estimated population figures for the Illinois Indian tribes between 1723 and 1733 reveal a dramatic drop in the population of the Cahokia village: from 1,800 to 473. The sharp drop after 1732 can perhaps be explained by the relocation of some Cahokia to the River L'Abbe Mission; yet by comparison, the Kaskaskia in their village to the south fell only from 1,000 to 930.[32]

While the Cahokia had been attacked repeatedly by the northern raiding Fox prior to the Fox defeat of 1730, the drop in population cannot be explained just through tribal warfare. Other theories advanced for population decline among the Illinois include monogamy introduced by Christianity, thus affecting the birth rate; epidemics; and the use made of Illinois Indians by the French who recruited them for military campaigns. The Cahokia and Peoria had contributed large numbers of warriors to the French campaign against the Fox Indians in 1730. St. Ange, the French commander from Fort Chartres, appeared at the battle site—the Grand Prairie of north-central Illinois—with one hundred French and at least four hundred Indians. In 1736 Indians from the Illinois Confederacy would march south under D'Artaguiette in an ill-fated expedition against the Chickasaw; and by the 1740s Illinois Indians were participating in French-directed raids against English settlements in the Ohio Valley. Indian losses in these expeditions are not concretely known. In addressing the radical drop in population of Indians living in traditional village sites on the Cahokia grant, Joseph Zitomersky suggests that the Cahokia eventually embraced out-migration to the north, back into the region of the Peoria on the Illinois River. The northward movement of the Cahokia Indians is actually accounted a factor in the relative stability of the Peoria tribe between 1733 and 1763. After 1733 it was the French-Indian nuclei of Kaskaskia and Fort Chartres that attained importance militarily and agriculturally. Significantly, following the relocation of the Cahokia, the French colonial population at the mission settlement of Cahokia jumped from 11 to 113 individuals.[33]

The history of the French Catholic efforts in the Illinois Country can be seen as a stream of small, localized, and initial successes at long-lasting ministries like Cahokia and Kaskaskia and at on-the-spot encounters out in Indian villages. Such history is punctuated with thefts, depredations, regression of Indian converts, and the destruction of property. By the early 1750s, the French at Fort Chartres were desperately trying to keep the loyalty of the Illinois Indians as tensions escalated toward the Seven Years War. French-Indian interaction had shifted along a trajectory that had begun with the Indians' proposed conversion to Catholicism and French ways; then to their peaceful cohabitation with the French on French concessions; then to their removal to independent villages two to six leagues distant from the French; and finally to an international political struggle in which the Illinois tribes were traded with, used as intermittent food suppliers, gifted, proselytized, and eventually denied French aid relative to their loyalty. This record is clearest on the Cahokia grant. A marshy, creek-dominated concession allowed for only clusters of arable French fields near the mission. Large floodplain prairies swept south, filled with heavy "miasmic" grasses. Not enough French settlers arrived to clear those lands. Because French agriculture was extremely slow to take hold, Cahokia Indians had little opportunity to profit in a frontier exchange environment. Nonetheless, the Cahokia settlement history is also about changes in the ecosystem in which permanency of settlement created new ways of relating to land and habitat. In the village of Chartres, near the French bastion of Fort Chartres, a different tale unfolded between 1721 and 1752. Despite little documentary evidence available for the Illinois tribe living near the fort, the Mechigamea, the survival of the Chartres notarial records and archaeological data allow a reconstruction that may be contrasted with what happened on the Cahokia grant.[34]

3

Chartres: French and Indian Successes

Farther south down the Mississippi coast lay the settlement of Chartres, growing up around Fort Chartres twenty years after the Seminarians founded Cahokia. As with all the French villages, intriguing questions can be asked about sites and locations. Unlike the English in their settlement history, the French did not often envision towns on paper. There were few intricately drawn projections, town squares, and home lots that would be pasted onto an alien landscape. Yet sifting through the remaining accounts of the founding of Fort Chartres and its village, it is possible to discern human and environmental characteristics that may have prompted French officials to settle there. The nature of this site led to high productivity quickly, a bounty of rich, cereal-grain agriculture. Factors leading to the success of the Chartres settlement near the fort must include a linkage into the human continuum, connections with thousands of years of agriculture there.

The reconnaissance party sent north from Kaskaskia to find a fort site likely had no helpful maps, despite French presence along the Mississippi for almost fifty years. One of the tragic mysteries of the French discovery of the Mississippi occurred when the canoe of Louis Joliet capsized on his return trip to Quebec in 1674. Joliet was likely "the most expert map maker" in New France at that time; he had visited France and may have spent time in cartographic workshops learning the use of the astrolabe. With his training and careful documentation, he and Father Marquette charted over one thousand miles of the Mississippi, and Joliet may well have noted in detail the area that would become the heart of the French settlements in southern Illinois. The loss of all of Joliet's notes, journals, sketches, and maps in the Ottawa River capsizing may well be one of the accidents of history that changed history. The locating of French Fort Chartres across from what would become the St. Louis area was not based on informed cartography, and the question remains: why did the French, seeking to establish a garrison in the Illinois Country, build the first (wooden) Fort Chartres exactly where they did?[1]

Today, high levees running parallel to the Mississippi have created a quarter mile swamp between the levee and the Illinois shore; in addition to dense vegetation and standing water, the levee itself obstructs any view of the floodplain from the river. But in 1718, when the French arrived to establish a fort midway between New Orleans and their Wisconsin outposts, the bottomland would have rolled back from the shore, as much as 50 percent open prairie. When Fort Chartres was constructed and fledgling agriculture begun around it, the prairie-woodland mosaic was a fire-managed environment sculpted by Indians for centuries. Both prehistoric and historic Indians had identified specific soils with highest fertility. Contrary to sweeping European accounts, the earth here was not uniformly alluvial and rich. Indian farmers had carefully located patches of exceptionally fertile, black soil. The success of agriculture in the Chartres area led directly to a flourishing trade matrix and involved the Mechigamea tribe especially as provisioners. Located between the wheat-farming settlement of Kaskaskia to the south and the large, watery Cahokia grant to the north, the villages of Chartres, Prairie du Rocher, and St. Philippe drew Indians from all directions, including the Missouri lands across the Mississippi. French censuses give numbers for French inhabitants, African and Indian slaves, and Illinois Indians living in these locations and in their own, sequestered villages; and all traditional histories of the area stress the small number of persons, the lack of burgeoning growth. But these French farmers and military and their slaves, both black and Indian (*panis*), were like islands in a river of human traffic whose power and flow never got into official censuses. The success story of agriculture here, usually credited to annual flooding of the Mississippi and to the French, must begin with human perception, selection, and management practices much older than those of the relocating French. The Chartres settlement fit into a continuum of human occupancy. The prairies of the bottomlands and the oak-hickory savanna on the upland till plain were both products of perhaps millennia of human burning practices. That careful management, in addition to a selective agriculture, had built upon and enlarged a tripartite ecosystem of great richness. In virtually all European accounts, however, the fertility of the earth is accounted a product of "nature."

Reconstructions and accounts describe the arrival of the Company of the Indies in 1718, the granting of concessions to habitants, military elite, and Jesuits, and the building of a small wooden fort surrounded by palings in 1720. A typical description appears in Mary Borgias Palm's *The Jesuit Missions of the Illinois Country*: "He [De Boisbriant] chose a site near the east bank of the Mississippi on flat alluvial bottom land, sixteen miles above Kaskaskia." Relying on company correspondence, letters to New France and the governor, and impressions and journals kept by the French in the 1720s, historians tell the story of Fort Chartres and the village of Chartres in the same way. Pierre DuGue Sieur De Boisbriant apparently sailed up the Mississippi from the mouth of the Kaskaskia, or traveled seventeen miles overland across wet, bottomland prairies before deciding on the spot.[2]

Although the mission at Cahokia had been founded in 1699, until the 1718 arrival of "young" De Boisbriant (he was forty-seven at the time), French Illinois had no fort, no government, and no official French presence other than the Seminarians and Jesuits. Lieutenant De Boisbriant, described as a "young French Canadian officer . . . the King's military representative in Louisiana," reached the Kaskaskia mission in December 1718, where he stayed for eighteen months. De Boisbriant was to find and select a site for a French fort that would command the Mississippi Valley. It is clear that the building of Fort Chartres was conceived within the ambit of French empire in the North America. At least one historian has posited that the incessant raids of the Fox necessitated erecting a garrison to protect the Mechigamea Indians who lived a half league north of the fort. While this may have been an ancillary consideration, De Boisbriant established a firm military presence in upper Louisiana under the auspices of the Company of the Indies (also known as the Company of the West). He rowed up the Mississippi from New Orleans in a canoe flotilla. In his ten craft were packed government officials, laborers, and a hundred soldiers. Arriving at the confluence of the Kaskaskia and the Mississippi Rivers, he found at the mission a conglomerate of French farmers, voyageurs, and both Kaskaskia and Mechigamea Indians. De Boisbriant set about reorganizing this settlement. He first built a fort, and then about the same time, he divided the Kaskaskia mission population into three groups, effectively purifying the French settlement. He relocated the Kaskaskia Indians north onto the upland plains above French Kaskaskia and the Mechigamea Indians north of the new fort. Peoples who had been living together in such proximity as to encourage Indian-French marriages and births were wholly separated; the Mechigamea village would lie eighteen miles away.[3]

The same frontier population mosaic existed at Cahokia as at Kaskaskia: French missionaries, French farmers (although many fewer in number), travelers, and traders—and at least three Indian tribes. The question of why De Boisbriant acted to divide the Kaskaskia and the Mechigamia from the French at Kaskaskia has never been answered clearly. According to Father Charlevoix, who passed through Kaskaskia in 1721, "it was thought proper to form two villages of savages instead of one." A possible explanation may lie in the presence of the Jesuits, who quickly built a small house in the Mechigamea village. Perhaps Jesuit missionaries discerned the need to minister to tribes exclusively; if so, this suggests the tempering and shaping of Jesuit interaction with specific Illinois Indian tribes—a pattern evident in their translation and linguistic work. The long-term Jesuit preference for separating resident Indian tribes from French populations may also have been a factor. One clear result of proximate Indian and French populations was the blending of French and Indian families. Limited records exist from the 1720s for St. Anne's Parish Church, founded to serve the population of the village of Chartres near the new fort. Between 1721 and 1726—the only years before 1743 for which records survive—priests recorded marriages, baptisms, births, and the names of godparents on twenty-nine occasions. In eight of these entries, an Indian woman is listed as the wife, mother, baptismal recipient, or godparent. Sometimes the women are identified as "an Illinois," or "a free Padoucah"; in other cases, the word *Indian* is used, as in this poignant entry: "This same year 1721 . . . was born a daughter of Brigitte, an Indian girl, known as 'The Lame One'; the father is unknown." In three of the records, the actual name is recorded, as in the 1725 marriage of Jean Baptiste Lalande and Catherine 8abana Kie8e. This evidence is for the village of Chartres after the French were separated from the Mechigamea and Kaskaskia. Despite distances, French soldiers especially were continuing to form long-lasting liaisons with Indian women. On the Cahokia grant, the Seminarians did not seek to divide the Tamaroa from the Cahokia, although priests were relieved when the visiting Peoria returned north to the Illinois River. Perhaps the very low numbers of resident French did not produce the number of French-Indian liaisons—or the level of administrative concern—as happened farther south. The combined military, economic, and religious vision of France for colonies in the Illinois Country found its most synthetic expression south of Cahokia.[4]

Soon after arriving in Kaskaskia, De Boisbriant set out to select a fort site. From descriptions of property bought and sold in the village of Chartres, growing up in the prairie next to the fort, certain features of the original terrain can be gleaned. There was a fairly substantial ash grove lying between the site of the fort and the Mississippi River; a small feeder inlet of the Mississippi, which became the Coulee Deneau, ran to the northwest, becoming a convenient separator of the French lands from those of the Mechigamea Indians; the bottomlands held a considerable number of red mulberry trees that soon proved excellent wood for the posts and palings used by the French to surround their homes and lots; and the land between French Kaskaskia and the newly erected fort likely contained tallgrass prairie (meadows), marshes, and stands or groves of elm, hackberry, cottonwood, and sycamore. The early American Government Land Office (GLO) survey plats recorded pecan trees on the floodplain, while back toward the bluffs on the denser soils grew towering, old-growth walnut, oak, and hickory, the important fuel and construction woods for both the Indians and the French. The marshes, forming near the ponds closer to the bluffs, were filled with prairie cordgrass. On the floodplain near Fort Chartres, cordgrass would have furnished dense protective cover for waterfowl nests; it was also used for thatching and, occasionally, for fuel. Waving in the humid air in pure, gray-green stands as high as ten feet, cordgrass would have defined the marshy areas. Clearer lands in the bottomland mosaic—the true prairies, the broad and coveted "meadows" of the French—had almost certainly been managed by fire.[5]

Yet the prairie was not uniform. Some of the land supported a dense shrub growth, such as hazel, which grew into coppices and thickets. Other areas had been burned clean of vegetation. Still others held the mixed grasses of the true prairie—big bluestem, Indian, and switchgrass, growing in clumps with deep root systems. Prairie plants such as the tough, rhizomatous leadplant bound the earth (it was leadplant that so resisted the early wooden plows of the American upland farmers and that was effectively uprooted only by the large, wheeled, iron plow). The grasses dried out by late summer and were easy to burn. The smoky pall of smoldering, autumnal grasses continued to be an observable phenomenon as late as 1803, when William Clark on his way to the Missouri River with the Corps of Discovery tried to take a reading with his sextant. He recorded the dimness of the air at the mouth of the Kaskaskia River on November 28, writing that the smoky air prevented him being entirely accurate.[6]

The site of the three future Fort Chartres was watery but not as lake-filled and stream-crossed as the Cahokia grant. Flowing across the land selected by De Boisbriant in 1719 was the east-west stream that eventually became known as Prairie du Rocher Creek. Notarial records indicate the building of mills on or near this stream; and its course down from the bluffs—much more vigorous in 1720 than the deeply eroded, sluggish trickle visible today—was likely the route that cattle initially followed up to the common grazing lands on the till plain. Whether De Boisbriant surveyed this area by water or by land in 1719, he would have been struck by the level, pancake-flatness of the earth on the site that eventually held the first fort. One imagines the soldiers in canoes and pirogues approaching the eastern shore of the Mississippi and noting a large island lying parallel to the banks, land likely detached from the original shore through a cut-off action of the river. Although there are no descriptions of this island, it was probably heavily wooded, as was the Isle of the Holy Family where the Seminarians settled at Cahokia; it would have offered protection for a landing. De Boisbriant was likely able to gaze straight back from the river, through scattered, old-growth cottonwoods standing upon the floodplain. There he may have noted a level, recently burned, and relatively vegetation-free meadow (prairie). Archaeological excavations of the Laurens Site, the first wooden fort built by the French, have located it approximately one-half to one mile inland from the river shoreline near a small stream, perhaps the Coulee Deneau of later accounts. The Mississippi ran calmly here. On still, humid summer days, it seemed to stretch tight as a drum skin to the western shore. In the distance De Boisbriant and his men would have noted the great rocky cliffs offering protection from surprise attack. Were there signs on this initial exploring mission that De Boisbriant's men would construct the first Fort Chartres on Illinois Indian village sites?[7]

Anecdotal, undocumented evidence presented in one early Illinois history suggests that the first fort was built on the site of an old fur warehouse or "blockhouse," the crude storage facility erected by the French merchant Crozat, who had held developmental rights to the Illinois Country prior to 1718, when his venture failed. Observations made in 1927 noted tall forest trees growing on the ridge of alluvial land where the old fort stood, suggesting that the site was indeed on higher ground. Behind this ridge lay a "bayou" paralleling the foot of the bluffs for two or three miles. A footpath, likely originally an Indian trail, may have run along the base of the bluffs to the Kaskaskia settlement. This trail would expand through use to become the Chemin du Roi, rising to the top of the bluffs beyond Fort Chartres and running all the way on the uplands to Cahokia. Thus the site De Boisbriant selected was already impacted and altered by human occupation. If he were drawn to build on ground revealing evidence of a prior structure, then it is also true that Crozat—if he did build a warehouse here—may have been drawn to land imprinted through many generations of human use. The significance of this for French agriculture around Fort

Chartres is often overlooked. Equally important are the pacific nature and downriver trading history of the Mechigamea Indians.[8]

The Fort Chartres Prairies

One of the most strikingly consistent themes in all early accounts of the American Bottom, especially in the lands lying between Fort Chartres and Kaskaskia, is the fertility of the soil, also sometimes conflated with ease of working the soil. From Father Louis Hennepin in 1698 (who appended Joliet's observations of 1674 to his own account) to Timothy Flint in 1828, observers have written of the soils of the Illinois country often in near-hyperbolic terms. Hennepin (citing Joliet) felt that settlers need not "bestow" ten years of labor clearing land, for the ground lay waiting, ready for the plow. The French observer Le Page du Pratz at mid-eighteenth century praised French grain-growing in the Illinois, writing that they "need only to turn the earth in the slightest manner." A remarkable observation also came from the British soldier Robert Kirk, ascending the Mississippi in 1765, who wrote that the Indians here, although "poor agriculturists," could harvest a hundred bushels from one sown. In 1812 the observer Timothy Flint maintained that despite a continuous raising of maize, in some parts for more than a hundred years, the soil showed no exhaustion. He spoke of the "power of the vegetation" growing on a "plain of exhaustless fertility." These early observers were no doubt thinking of the worn-out soils of Europe as they viewed the rich black alluvial floodplain along the Mississippi. So black was the earth, in fact, that Hennepin noted "it looks as if it had been already manur'd." Even modern historians writing about the Illinois colonies have accepted these views. For instance, the historian of French Louisiana Marcel Giraud wrote in 1958, "The soil, flat and fertile, could produce crops without preliminary clearance." Yet it is misleading to view the soils of all the French settlements as the same.[9]

By 1723, only four years after the construction of Fort Chartres was begun, Diron D'Artaguiette made an inspection journey of French Illinois for the Company of the Indies. In the southern villages, he described rich and fertile soil that "never failed" to produce anything sown in it. In describing the relationships of dwellings in the Fort Chartres area, D'Artaguiette mentions a church outside the fort and homes built a half league below the church and a half a league above. The French farmers around the fort produced what has been termed a more "diffuse" and strung-out settlement pattern than at Kaskaskia. There may have been good reasons for that. By 1723 the land around the fort had been granted to French settlers and soldiers, homes had been constructed, and agriculture was under way. Homes were also being threatened by the river. Notarial records from the Parish of St. Anne's, adjacent to the fort, confirm this. By 1724 a house "situated about fifteen feet from the wake" [of the Mississippi River] and about to be carried off, was inventoried for its heirs. Located on two arpents of land that began at the shore of the river, this property by 1724 already supported eight hogs, twenty hens, and twenty chicks. Home and lot sales in the vicinity of the fort for the years 1724–25 specify "uncultivated lands" and "the crop," or payment of "seven hundred pounds of flour" as an asking price. One property in 1725 sold for the exchange price of a cottonwood canoe and four hundred pounds of flour. The earliest extant notarial document from the Fort Chartres area is possibly from 1718–1719. Extensively damaged, it appears to be an agreement for a tenant to rent out and farm a tract of land near a "Fort." The lease period is for three years, and expected returns are such that the rent is listed as "thirty-six minots of wheat" and "forty minots of maize." While there is no direct account of agriculture in the prairie lands around Fort Chartres, De Boisbriant's 1720 description of taking up the prairie at the Kaskaskia settlement is illuminating. He writes that clearing the land using slave labor was easy. "The prairie sod is taken up with a mattock, after which the land is easy to work. Several inhabitants plow it with one horse."[10]

The historian of French agriculture in the American Bottom Carl J. Ekberg points out that the mattock [*pinoche*] could not have been that exceptionally easy to use, since some observers at Kaskaskia noted that only a fourth of a French league of fields was being cultivated. The slight evidence for early agricultural practices around Fort Chartres suggests the planting of wheat and maize occurred fairly rapidly. One key aspect is that despite the mention of cleared land, crops, flour, and domestic animals in the notarial records, it is unlikely there were African slaves in the Chartres area until after the arrival of Phillip Renault in 1722–23. Renault, a Parisian banker who led a contingent of miners and the first Caribbean slaves to the Illinois country to establish lead mining, received a land grant from De Boisbriant in 1723. This concession became the small, marshy settlement of St. Philippe. Without slave labor to clear densely rooted prairie lands around Fort Chartres, agriculture should have been fledgling for at least the first few years. In addition, a severe flood of the Mississippi River in 1722, exacerbated by a violent hurricane in the Gulf of Mexico, created much feverish sickness all along the river. In New Orleans, a "malignant fever carried off scores of inhabitants," while to the north in the Illinois Country, the flood also caused fever and sickness. Yet despite the absence of slaves in the initial years and this epidemic, the land around Fort Chartres was being improved: crops were in. One inference is that the French were plowing on previously farmed lands. The "strung out" nature of the French longlot farms suggests a discretionary selection of land that looked the easiest to put under cultivation. The mosaic of land around the fort, with some arpents fully plowed and producing, intermixed with scrub land and woods, is reminiscent of protohistoric Indian farming practices. Productive maize fields lay scattered among abandoned, exhausted fields in a calculated rotation.[11]

French farming practices in the bottomlands offer clues to the early success of cereal-grain agriculture. The French plow, the heavy, wheeled charrue, was in use at Kaskaskia by 1711, because André Penicaut remarked on its use by the Kaskaskia Indians. Even in the embryonic agricultural settlement growing up around Fort Chartres, the charrue and a few oxen would have been necessary. Such was the value of oxen on these earliest grants that a lease agreement lays out specific terms for recompense should an ox die by any means but "war or lightning." Descriptions of the French working their land emphasize the holdover of Old World peasant and French Canadian practices. One archaeologist specializing in French Kaskaskia has characterized French farming tools as "primitive." Both the charrue and the harrow were made of wood, the harrow an improvement over the first scratch plows, antlers or limbs from trees dragged over the ground upside down to break up the heavy surface clods. Harrows manufactured in the Illinois Country were likely made of seasoned hickory, the hardest wood. Historians and archaeologists have drawn connections between the French Illinois farming implements and those in use for centuries in early modern Europe. Canadian historians have linked the charrue to the kind of soil found in northwest France, which was deep and wet. It required a heavier, wheeled plow that could create ridges in the fields; these would help the soil drain and dry. The charrue had a fixed moldboard that created a ridged field—"a rise of one foot in a width of about nine." Just-plowed French fields would have looked corrugated, heavily textured, and there is evidence archaeologically that in the prehistoric farms of the upper Mississippi Valley, Indian farmers were also ridging their fields, using several different ridge patterns.[12]

The ridging created by the charrue in the soil of Illinois bottomlands contributed to the success of French agriculture there, but it was not the only factor. Nor is the periodic flooding and enrichment of the fields by the Mississippi to answer for how quickly the area around Fort Chartres yielded surplus crops—an explanation offered by virtually all observers. Archaeologists and geologists specializing in Indian subsistence have discussed Indian farming practices from the Middle Mississippian (approximately 1000–1300 A.D.) onward in terms of a highly selective and informed agriculture. Because Indian groups farming the bottomlands as part of a subsistence mosaic used only hand tools to work the soil, they increased their crop yields by other means. Three of the most important were the creation of ridges for drainage, field rotation and a combination of outfield-infield agriculture, and expert knowledge of kinds of soils. Archaeology of the American Bottom focusing on the botanical record identifies both commonalties and variability in the kinds of crops grown by prehistoric and protohistoric Indians. The diversity alone of cultigens routinely planted by Mississippian peoples suggests that soils and growing conditions in this single strip of alluvial soil in the American Bottom encouraged experimentation. Site explorations have shown an exciting, diverse range of domesticated and semidomesticated crops. The list includes maize, common bean, squash, gourd, sunflower, sumpweed, tobacco, and many small starchy seeds such as chenopod, maygrass, erect knotweed, and little barley. Grain amaranth may also have been included as a late-introduced cultigen. These crops were cultivated and harvested on specifically selected soils, with preference given to a rare soil type identified as Wakeland. Occurring in isolated patches, this single type of silt loam has all essential requirements for incomparable plant growth. Wakeland is but one of twelve kinds of soils identified as occurring in the American Bottom, with varying combinations of certain critical variables: texture, chemical reaction, nutrient content, and drainage—including flooding and high water tables. Where this soil patched the landscape, it was possible to grow high-yield nutritive crops.[13]

While archaeologists have completed most site studies in the northern area of the American Bottom, similar conditions for placement of large Indian fields occur in the Fort Chartres area. Indian agriculturists selected rich bottomland soils for their fields, and they practiced outfield-infield agriculture, in which field selection and development were neither haphazard nor automatic. The best soils were not contiguous and actually have been characterized by archaeologists as "circumscribed." It is important to recognize the highly selective quality of Indian agriculture, because historic accounts imply that all soils in the bottomlands were fertile and accessible, scarcely needing to be turned over. In actuality, the indications are strong for a consistently careful selection and improvement of scattered fields. Indian farmers mixed ashes into their cleared earth; they practiced field rotation; and they lived in villages on the higher ridges of sandy soil back from the floodplain. Infield gardens surrounded their farmsteads, while large, dispersed, carefully identified and chosen fields were worked as common land for crops. Most important, however, was the continuous use of such discretely selected land. Historic Indian farmers in the Midwest knew that crops grew better in the fields long identified and worked by prehistoric farmers. Through a chain of human use, as well as river flooding, the soil of the American Bottom developed its alluvial vigor. Researchers have found indications that prehistoric farmers also had learned to recognize what is termed "culturally enriched soils."[14]

Despite the abandonment of the fields in the American Bottom area by late Mississippian Indians—a confirmed out-migration to upland fields by 1550 likely caused by erosion, soil exhaustion, and deforestation—evidence has shown that historic Indians reoccupied the Fort Chartres area. A detailed 1697 map by Louis de la Porte de Louvigny, based on a memoir and accounts of explorations to the Illinois Country, shows two Tamaroa Indian villages side by side in the area of the future Fort Chartres. Mechigamea Indians are depicted living in a village across the Mississippi. It is likely that Tamaroa and perhaps Mechigamea Indians were farming maize fields in the Fort Chartres area floodplain. Long-term human occupation of the Chartres floodplain would result in culturally enriched soils there, soils containing chemicals like lime and salt from butchering, food preparation and disposal, human waste, calcium from burial of animals and humans, sharpening flakes, and ashes and carbonized wood from fires. The first successful effort to locate the original Fort Chartres, for instance, was made by a soil scientist who identified increased levels of calcium, phosphorous, and hydronium in the perimeters of the original fort site. A patch of inland earth yielded distinct evidence of human occupancy; this particular human structure, the first fort, had existed for only five years before being abandoned and rebuilt. Yet significant soil changes had occurred, traces clear enough to be identified 270 years later![15]

What are the implications for soil selection and enrichment on the Fort Chartres concession? Arriving French settlers in 1719–20, whose first priority was the building of a wooden fort and chapel, would have found it onerous and probably dangerously physically debilitating to have worked and improved earth on which no domestic crops had ever been grown. A description of using a wooden breaking plow on freshly cleared land in western Indiana, taken from oral interviews with pioneers who used such plows, reveals a formidable toll on both animals and humans. Witnesses from the early part of the nineteenth century describe the opening of never-before-cultivated earth with a team of powerful horses, Clydesdales and Percherons. Despite the straining strength of these enormous draft animals, the team "could only pull a plow once acrossed the field before they needed to rest." The ease with which the French farmers around Fort Chartres with a single team of oxen (or often, a single animal) could put a considerable amount of common field land into cultivation within the first few years is suggestive. These farmers were employing oxen, "fastened

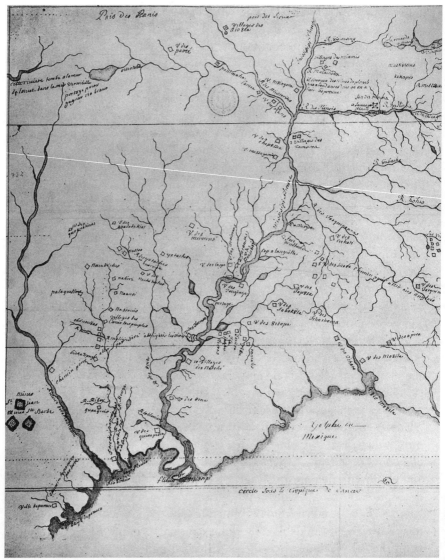

Portion of 1797 Louis de la Porte de Louvigny map, "Carte de Fleuve Misisipi," showing Tamaroa Indian villages on the site of future French settlements.

together by the horns," a piece of flat wood bridging the wide expanse of shoulder. They did not use the familiar yoke of English farmers. French agriculturists, drawing on European tradition, likely used the hard, durable heartwood of hop hornbeam to fashion these flat yokes. Varieties of hop hornbeam were so preferred in Europe that the wood acquired the name "yoke-elm." Hop hornbeam was used in French Canada for sled runners and tool handles of all kinds. Master carpenters of the Illinois Country, working at first out of French Kaskaskia and then Fort Chartres, knew the value and use of a variety of woods; notarial records specify, for instance, "planks" and "boards" of white oak or walnut as portions of selling prices. A 1726 contract for building a barn specifies the frame to be built "of walnut, of sassafras, or of mulberry." Naturally abundant in the Illinois Country, the small, sturdy hop hornbeam was also a source of food for white-tailed deer, who peeled off its feathery bark; the drooping clusters of hop hornbeam seed cases furnished winter food for ruffed grouse and gray squirrels.

As the French population grew, settlers began to draw upon the diverse resources of the bottomlands and also, the upland till plain, hauling some of their wood from "the hills." Before switching to shingling, they thatched their barns with "straw" (likely dried cordgrass), burned shagbark hickory for fuel, and planed "sawn boards" of red mulberry for posts, pickets, and palings, hop hornbeam for tool handles and yokes, and most often, cottonwood and walnut for river craft and furniture. Diron D'Artaguiette noted in 1723 that wood planks sawn from mulberry lasted thirty years in the ground without rotting. The expansion into artisanal crafts and specializations by carpenters, joiners, and mill builders is a key result of early, successful wheat and maize yields. Increased hunting and trapping forays followed.[16]

Taking apart a settlement history that has become standardized in published narratives helps to embed it in a continuum of occupancy in the area. It is true that the alluvial silt of the floodplain was enriched through annual flooding downstream from the mud-laden Missouri; but that unicausal explanation of French agricultural success obscures an intricate history. Indians who had the eye for the best soils, who worked the black, heavy, redolent silt in ragged-edged fields, may also have been using their unfenced and unprotected lands as a form of bait. Field margins drifted into the understory of tangled brush and woods. From that adjacency streamed small mammal populations eager for grain. Indians hunted the margins, gleaning mice, rabbits, squirrels, and voles. They had made calculated decisions to locate maize fields in a fringe of timber margin and woods—leading to a European perception of haphazard, random usage. In subtle and often oblique ways, the prehistoric and historic Indian cultures of the bottomlands were working the ecological system. Even when settlement spread up onto the bluffs and upland till plains, those settlements, while never becoming as plentiful as those in the American Bottom, continued to be significantly correlated with Wakeland soils. The predilection of arriving European and then American settlers to plant in what is commonly phrased as "old Indian fields" links settlement choices across thousands of years.[17]

The deliberate, patchwork field mosaic of the Chartres floodplain, then, initially attracted French farmers in certain patterns. Increases in population resulted in the clearing of more land, the use of common fields, the drying out of wet surface soils, and a different kind of selective use of resources. At least one ecologist has made connections between the hop hornbeam and beaver colonies. Scores of songbird populations feasted annually on red mulberry fruit. Environmental studies of colonial resource use in the eastern seaboard often focus on the theme of overexploitation and wanton waste, of the impact of sheer abundance on incoming Europeans whose pinched lives in cities or on exhausted rural lands drove them west. These themes are tied to other themes of the "unstoppable tide" of settlement. Because the numbers of French along the Mississippi floodplain remained low, historians have not focused on immediate and ongoing changes in the tripartite ecosystem of their world. However, ecology also describes the introduction of new species and invasives, as well as the depletion and extirpation of native ones. These twin processes were set in motion with the arrival in the Illinois of livestock, particularly hogs.[18]

Domestic pigs may have arrived in the Illinois via Catholic missions as early as the 1690s (the missions on the Illinois River, for instance). In 1712 Father Marest described Indians raising chickens and pigs at the Kaskaskia Mission. By accompanying settlers, hogs, chickens, and horned cattle naturally migrated to the Chartres establishment, and by 1725 hogs are showing up in notarial records. One property included "three pigsties fenced with posts and thatched . . . four sows, eighteen medium pigs, twenty hens and roosters." Another entry, also in 1725, included twenty-two male and female pigs and at least forty hens. Evidence taken from the listing of animals on French censuses shows that swine increased faster than any other domestic animal. Between 1732 and 1752 for French Illinois as a whole, they increased from 563 to 1,682. These counts do not include hogs raised by Indians. It is likely that before maize (Indian corn) production became steady enough to ensure a supplemental food base, hogs were turned loose to forage in the floodplain. (Indians who owned hogs probably rarely fed them with reserves of corn but let them forage.) Hogs particularly consumed amaranth (pigweed), wild onions, the water lily root called *macoupin*, and perhaps some varieties of root plants that have now disappeared from the Illinois country. The variety in hog diet—and the abundance—was certainly a factor in hog fertility. Hogs also ate many kinds of acorns and nuts raining down from old-growth, prolifically producing trees. The natural oils in the abundant nuts of the southern Illinois region, especially sweet pignut hickory, were prized by Indians, French, and hogs alike. These oils imparted to freshly butchered and smoked hog meat a memorable, oily sweetness. Yet ripe nuts coat the ground only during a precise interval each year, and rich mast years alternate with sparse years. The lure of milky, developing corn ears over an entire growing season was much greater.[19]

To keep animals out of their fields, the French in the Chartres area resorted to fencing in a long riverine strip of common pasture land that also included some wooded areas. Eventually, once the population grew large enough, fences and gates were built around the arable fields. After the harvests, the gates were opened and animals permitted in to graze the stubble. French owners of livestock used both ear cropping and branding as ways to identify their animals. There is no evidence for what Mechigamea Indians living close to Fort Chartres did with their livestock. Since they were occupying a shoreline grant that included a prairie named for them, their pigs may have been permitted to roam freely. Unlike the documented history of colonist-Indian conflict over roaming animals on the eastern seaboard, there is no clear record of continuing French-Indian squabbles over food resources for foraging livestock or animals invading and destroying planted fields. One reason for this is French adherence to the Coutume de Paris, the operant legal system transported from France. The Coutume was not often changed by exigencies in the New World. No new laws, rulings, or court-established precedents could easily evolve in a colonial outpost. Thus there are few records illuminating changes to the social and legal structure and none showing how Indians may have affected laws to their own advantage. Early English laws in the Virginia colony, for example, stated, "Any Englishman taking up land near Indian fields must help build fences around the fields to protect Indian crops from the settlers' hogs and cattle." Such rulings facilitated the adaptation of hogs by Virginia Indian tribes; by the 1660s the Weacock, Meherrin, and Nottoway Indians were all raising hogs, and by 1692 the Nottoway were selling them. Other studies of hog penetration into Indian lands point to conflicts. Not all Indians readily adapted to the hog, seeing the animals as both fecund and destructive; some half-wild hogs routinely destroyed Indian crops. The Shawomets and Pawtuxents began fencing their corn fields, but hogs took to the woods. The spread of hogs through the rich eastern forests is actually counted by some historians as a "dynamic force of territorial expansion." Hogs are described as "funnel[ing] out" in an advance guard to the English colonies. These patterns were not replicated in the Illinois Country. The tripartite environment of floodplain, bluffs, and upland prairies did not allow hogs, either French or Indian, to "funnel out" expansively. Nor could Indians use an existing legal system to protect their fields.[20]

The impact of free-roaming hogs and other domestic stock on the environment must be traced through slight references from observers and through long-enduring cultural knowledge. Such references begin as far back as the initial Cahokia settlement years. The trouble on the Cahokia grant with French livestock, contributing to the Cahokia revolt in the early 1730s, is revealed in letters of the Seminarian priests. In those instances, French livestock invaded Indian land. Indian animals mingling with domesticated French stock or foraging in French fields comprises a different pattern, one not well documented. Oblique references to friction do occur, however. In 1733 the colonizer and governor of Louisiana Jean Baptiste le Moyne, the Sieur de Bienville, wrote of the French-Indian relations in Louisiana as a whole that proximity of Indian villages to French villages often caused dangerous disputes. In the 1750s Commander Macarty at Fort Chartres makes reference to Indians killing French pigs and horned cattle, but the French living at Chartres complained much more vocally about Indian dogs. In the early 1750s the traveler Bossu told some departing Mechigamea and Cahokia Indians, "It is good you are leaving. Consider the damage that the dogs of your village have done to the livestock belonging to the French settlers." Bossu mentions that hungry dogs killed livestock during food shortages and describes the "dogs of the Illinois" as being half wolf. A few years later when he was visiting the Peoria, he shared a feast with them that included maple sap, persimmon bread, bear paws, and beaver tails, as well as corn meal, maple syrup—and dog. Indians raised dogs, used primarily as feast meat, as a form of livestock. French perceptions that Indians killed and ate dogs when provisions were low, in an opportunistic and random fashion, is probably incorrect. Yet dogs and hogs did apparently roam freely in many areas of the floodplain, while French black horned cattle and horses grazed on common land on both the floodplain and up on the bluffs. The grazing of horses there may have helped to shape the evolution of Horse Prairie, perhaps eight miles out on the till plain, a rich, green, wet prairie named for escaped French horses. (See discussion of Horse Prairie in chapter 1).

The grazing of Kaskaskia cattle and horses on islands and a peninsula in the Mississippi echoes the Eastern seaboard practice of hogreeves, where hogs were let loose on islands and "reeves" (reefs). The ability of hogs to become feral in a short period contributed to the problems with resource exploitation in the bottomlands. While Indians and the French alike prized hogs because of their independence, hog behavior in the wild seriously impacted the environment. Descriptions of feral hogs from observations made as early as 1830 include large droves of animals acting in concert to "shake down" hazel nuts; some animals climbed and bent trees, breaking them. Hogs also left deep, rutted trails in the earth. Hazel thickets on the prairies were often threaded by numerous trails. In cold months hogs created large nests from fallen oak leaves, seemingly preferring the oldest, broadest-leafed trees. High mounds of piled, sleeping animals lay under a blanket of oak leaves actually fetched by a series of hogs each carrying a mouthful. The churning, pawing, and rooting activity in building these oak-leaf nests, described as twenty inches high and twelve to twenty feet across disturbed the root systems of trees. Finally, hog consumption of acorns deprived oak trees of their reproductive means. The loss of future oak trees to voracious hog appetite is discussed particularly in studies of the disappearance of white oak, *Quercus alba*, the most prevalent and successful oak of presettlement Illinois.[21]

Livestock depleted natural vegetation; yet in a reverse process, French and, especially, American landowners spread rich grazing grasses like *Poa pratensis* (Kentucky bluegrass), timothy, and tall and meadow fescue. The French wheat strains were also new to the area, introduced by Jesuits at Kaskaskia in the early 1700s. These processes resulted in ecological shifts that may not have shown up as observable changes for years. For instance, waterfowl, land bird, and white-tailed deer populations were affected by changes in native vegetation. The abundance and variety of native floodplain plants developed as a result of alluvial flooding, of having to spread into disturbed and marginal habitats. To combat annual, relentless inundation with mud, these varieties compensated through the production of immense amounts of seed. The preference of migrating waterfowl for the Mississippi flyway was partially built around the copious, heavily laden seed heads. Rich, stem-clustered, so bursting with seeds they dragged low to the muddy earth, stands of common arrowhead or smartweed fed the millions of waterfowl described so consistently by observers along the Mississippi.[22]

Bird and small mammal populations would have been affected as well when the floodplain became firmer and drier and when new less bountiful and productive species crept into the grazed and mown wetlands. Land not under cultivation in the floodplain was often wet in a distinctive way: full of appearing and disappearing springs, seeps, sinkholes, and mud puddles.

Earth could glisten and then dry out rapidly under conditions often described as "droughty." Land birds also depend in some instances on a high moisture content in soils, a level correlated with areas of standing water. In the bottomlands of Arkansas, forming with Illinois the Mississippi Alluvial Valley (MAV), moist forest habitats and soils have been shown to support high numbers of insects and invertebrate species. These form significant percentages of some songbird diets, especially warblers, whose food source was reduced when bottomlands began to dry out. Conversely, when white-tailed deer learned to browse corn and other row crops, foraging in the wider and wider cropland margins, their overall body weight probably increased. Deer become larger, sometimes considerably larger, where cultivated crops add significant nutrients to their diets. White-tailed deer spend more time feeding than in any other activity, and they would have eventually begun to incorporate seasonal crop availability into their forage patterns. There are implications of this (gradual) increase in size for the deerskin trade, for deer agility and migration, and for deer reproduction. Thus, despite the low numbers of French and Indians living along the floodplain in the first fifty years of the eighteenth century, they had begun a process of measurable ecological change. And although such change occurs in any environment, the shifts in the floodplain ecology were ones that would facilitate the massive wave of American settlement after 1790. In the lands around Fort Chartres, French and Indian men and women set trajectories of resource use that would eventually impact all peoples in the decades of keenest political unrest.[23]

On initial grants of land, two to four arpents, in dispersed areas around the fort, French farmers began to produce grain. The first convoy to New Orleans loaded with wheat and produce left the Illinois Country in 1721, although most of the grain likely came from the Kaskaskia grant. The wheat was noted as "being of a very fine quality." Convoys arrived in 1725 and 1729 as well, with the 1729 convoy reflecting a bumper crop year. Large shipments of wheat and salted meat were soon supplying the lower Louisiana colonies. French farmers were but the latest in a long line of agriculturists who had discovered the fecundity of certain soils of the floodplain. The importance of early agricultural success in the Illinois Country is twofold: first, the record stands in stark contrast to other attempted French settlements on the lower Mississippi; and second, crop productivity in turn drew more people to the area, much more rapidly than had occurred on the Cahokia grant twenty years before. The presence of a fort with two companies of soldiers provided a local market for wheat, Indian corn, and garden produce. Networks of supply and demand began to grow naturally out of cultigen surplus. The connection between successful agriculture and its corollary—burgeoning trade—is clearly demonstrated in the settlement pattern around Fort Chartres. This connection has been recognized by Canadian historians of the French fur trade, who have written of the deeply entwined relationship between agriculture and trade. The relationship has not always been emphasized in the Illinois Country, where French farmers have been studied as one specific socioeconomic group and French traders, voyageurs, and coureurs de bois as another. But the two livelihoods were inextricably meshed. Interestingly, an amateur local historian in the mid-nineteenth century suggested this same connection: "A post established at Kaskaskia, was the means of creating a lively trade in deer, buffalo, and bear meat, which were purchased for the transportation to New Orleans and Mobile. This also stimulated the erection of Mills for the manufacture of flour." By the late 1740s some traders and voyageurs had established permanent farming bases in the French communities. An inventory of a trader/voyageur who died in 1747, for example, describes both porcelain and glass trade goods for Indians and "1486 livres of wheat."[24]

Such a reciprocity did not occur in French settlements to the south of the Illinois Country. Historians who have examined the dismal record of the attempted French agricultural settlement at Arkansas Post on the Arkansas River sketch a poignant picture of the decimation of the French there. The Company of the Indies under the speculator John Law had recruited and sent groups of French and Germans to lower Louisiana (the same company was administering the upper Illinois). In late summer 1721, as many as eighty French *engagés* (indentured servants) arrived to settle a small piece of open land called Little Prairie, twenty-seven miles inland from the Mississippi on the Arkansas River. Here was the site of an abandoned French trading post. Just as had happened two years earlier in the Chartres settlement of Illinois, incoming French settlers chose land that showed traces of European impact; some initial clearing of land had apparently already begun. This area of Arkansas, fed by two major rivers but far enough inland to avoid the relentless flooding of the Mississippi, would have been a morass of rampant vegetation, including some varieties of trees that had become flood-adapted: water tupelo, water hickory, and water oak, for example. In this area, the MAV (Mississippi Alluvial Valley) supported truly extensive high-quality timber stands punctuated by some open prairie land. The prairies, however, may not have been the same type as those found in southern Illinois. Arkansas in particular has distinctive Pleistocene sand dune barrens, formations that were once endemic on the Mississippi Alluvial Plain. Such barrens are not the same as grassland prairies managed through regular burning and would not have supported agriculture as easily. Yet early observers, most especially the GLO surveyors of the early nineteenth century, often named all open, grassy areas "prairies." Perhaps the land the French tilled at Little Prairie along the Arkansas River had not been opened to agriculture before, or had been unsuccessfully tilled and then abandoned hundreds of years before. There is no clear way to know. The environment of this area, however, would have been a factor in French colonization.[25]

At a more southern latitude than the Illinois Country, insect and animal populations differed: tortuous clouds of mosquitoes and biting flies shimmered in willow thickets and hummed in stands of giant cane. Alligators likely hunted the steaming swamplands. (Audubon recorded alligators at the mouth of the Arkansas River in 1810.) The southern, heat-saturated latitudes here did not host thick fur-bearing mammals. In 1673 Marquette noted of the Arkansas Indians (Quapaw), "They do not know what a beaver is." French accounts of the first contact with the Quapaw stress their usual attire as near nudity in the humid Mississippi country as the river plunged south. Quapaw women wore a single deerskin around their waist, while Quapaw men wore nothing. The intense heat of these river lowlands was likely a factor in failed attempts at agriculture. Between 1727 and 1729, for instance, a priest assisting Father Paul du Poisson at the Quapaw Mission died of sunstroke.[26]

A comparative glance at the twin French efforts at farming in the Illinois Country and Arkansas Post can establish long lines of impact. Both Morris S. Arnold, who has extensively studied colonial Arkansas, and the French historian Giraud have documented the miserable lives and fate of the first French settlers at Arkansas Post. Of the eighty who arrived, only fifty remained by the following spring, with a single surviving woman. Father Charlevoix, touring Arkansas Little Prairie in 1722, called the French there *"triste debris."* They were living in twenty rude cabins, had cleared only three arpents of land, and had produced a meager harvest. The French response was to release twenty of the *engagés* from service and give them their own land to cultivate in wheat and corn. The ability to raise grain was now seen as critical, since no French supply ships were sailing up the Mississippi. Sadly, a year later, the population was down to thirty, with no surviving women. The settlement also suffered flooding from the Arkansas River, but the floods were not annual and did not require immediate protective measures.[27]

From the beginning, efforts to make the Arkansas Post settlement a sturdy agricultural community had completely failed. The Louisiana census of 1726 reported that French *habitants* were very poor and survived only from trade with Indians. By 1746 only twelve French families lived at Arkansas Post, engaging in hunting, curing meat, and trading tallow and bear oil. This pattern of falling into trade with Indian villagers living near French outposts and forts is confirmed by Daniel H. Usner Jr. in his study of lower Mississippi trade networks. The neglect of these settlers by the French government resulted in desperate settlers "left to their own designs." Those designs were based exclusively on livelihood and seemingly did not involve much participation in the fur trade. Survival and subsistence determined how Arkansas French settlers, unable to support themselves with agriculture, would interact with Indians in their area. The trouble between the French and Indians on the lower Mississippi comprises a clear and escalating record, best explored in Usner's study of a deteriorating economic system pressured from the east by English deerskin hunters and traders. For a variety of complex reasons, the Indian tribes of the lower Mississippi Valley—with the exception of the strongly French-allied Tunica and Quapaw—created a dangerous environment on the Mississippi River for Europeans. One of those complex factors has to do with the absence of agricultural surplus and its core relationship to successful and equitable trade. Up in the Illinois Country, as a result of productive French agriculture, the fur trade was burgeoning. Just as important was the provisioning trade that engaged the local Mechigamea Indians.[28]

4

Trade Matrix at Fort Chartres:
Farmers, Traders, and Provisioners

From the first 1673 trade encounters between Father Marquette and the Illinois Indians, the Illinois drove a hard bargain. Marquette noted they would "give hardly any more than do the French," seeming in fact like seasoned traders. In one of these first exchanges, Marquette obtained from the Illinois three fine buffalo hides in return for tobacco, but he felt pressured by their bartering and saw the need to hold Mass immediately after they left. The Illinois, in fact, had at least a century of trade experience with European and indigenous peoples living as far north as Michilimackinac and as far south as Arkansas; and in this north-south corridor, nests of riverine exchange locales had developed, particularly around portages. What has been termed both the Great Lakes Heartland and the Algonquian Heartland included at least fifteen critical portages on the Michigan peninsula and at least five in northern Illinois. Because of seasonal inundation of these portages and heavy rains creating new, rapid river course ways, portages could disappear, even those less than a mile across seeming suddenly unfamiliar and inaccessible. This phenomenon made it hard for any single community of people to emerge as dominant in the fur trade, and nations like the Illinois, much farther south, could travel north, to participate in the Great Lakes fur exchange. The human trade network in the Mississippi watershed, in fact, developed a vigor and endurance that outlasted the commercial structures built to sustain it. But this trade network also included Indians who hunted solely for the provision trade. How such peoples, especially the Mechigamea Indians living around Fort Chartres, became drawn into the trade, is a story that has import for the land itself.[1]

If a bountiful agriculture around the fort and south in Kaskaskia grew from a blend of factors, including Indian farming practices, alluvial flooding, and French animal husbandry, the same kind of analysis holds true for the growth of trade here. Historians like Richard White have emphasized the importance of French-Indian alliances built on gifts, trade privileges, and political-judicial sanctions. The natural environment of French-Indian Illinois was also critical, in that water routes allowed for the meetings of many diverse tribes. The French river settlements nestled in a geographic and geopolitical intersection where Eastern Woodland, Great Lakes, and Plains Indian cultures began to shade into each other and overlap. Illinois Indians, riverine people, were related through trade and marriage alliances to the Miami across the Grand Prairie in what would become Indiana and Ohio—a nation who never became canoe men. In fact, studies of the Miami emphasize that although they routinely located villages at river confluences and springs, they did so to exploit the alluvial floodplain soils and cultivate superior varieties of corn, including a noted "soft white corn." Consummate agriculturalists, the Miami are described as "turning increasingly to the rivers" only after the War of 1812. In the early part of the eighteenth century, Indian nations all around the riverine Illinois tribes had developed distinct and diverse subsistence practices. The Osage of the Missouri highlands across the Mississippi to the west were skilled and fearless horsemen and horse traders; they were visiting the fort very early, as were other Missouri lands tribes, the Missouria and Omaha, for example. The Fort Chartres matrix attracted Indians who traveled by horse, by boat, and on foot; the differing lifeways of these tribes would have created demands for specific material trade items, thus shaping a complex mercantile hub that influenced European settlements as far away as New Orleans and Montreal.[2]

In the middle of a vigorous traffic in trade, legal and illegal trade, fur, hide, and provisioning trade, the Mechigamea Indians adapted to become suppliers of oil and meat. Domiciled and living separately in their villages—and continually described that way in French and European travel accounts—these Indians did not stay isolated. Their level of daily interaction with French people and with other arriving Indians was likely very high. New ways are needed to detect their traces in a landscape where maps, notarial records, and French correspondence routinely establish separatism. Today, although Fort Chartres has been fully restored and does include detailed dioramas of Indian village life, a roadside plaque marks the site of St. Anne's chapel in the long-gone village of Chartres, and Prairie du Rocher retains French homes and iron crosses in the cemetery, no marker identifies the probable site of the Mechigamea villages. This is a fairly striking omission when compared with the amount of public information available on the prehistoric Cahokia mound builders, barely thirty miles to the north. Research suggests that the Mechigamea were in fact a critical factor in the success of Fort Chartres, more important than their depiction as an adjacent community implies. While their population continued to decline precipitously over the century, Mechigamea are often identified in French correspondence—the "mechy"—and are specifically denoted as allies of the British at Fort Chartres in the late 1760s. The ways the Mechigamea used the natural resources of the upper Mississippi Valley and their traces in the eighteenth-century localized topography establish them as far more present in the history of this area than traditional documents reveal.[3]

It is possible to trace the evolution of local Indian interest in the provision trade. One of the most valuable and incisive overviews of the trade networks among the Indians and French in the Illinois Country appears in the journal of Diron D'Artaguiette in 1722-23. D'Artaguiette noted the three Illinois Indian villages located next to French settlements. The Illinois, he writes, "are scattered about in three villages—the Cascakias, the Mekchiquamias and the Cahokias." He gives population estimates for two of the three villages: the Kaskaskia and Mechigamea each had about two hundred warriors. Of the Cahokia he gives no specific number, yet he judges the entire Illinois nation to be "at present not more than 700 warriors." (As noted in chapter 2, historians interpret a single warrior as representing five persons). Between 1699 and D'Artaguiette's observations in 1722-23, a pattern of human interaction became established among French farmers, French soldiers, Jesuit priests, resident Indians in villages, traders and suppliers journeying downriver from Canada and upriver from fledgling New Orleans, and constantly appearing members of many other tribes—Missouria, Wea, Miami, Potawatomi, and the Peoria from up on the Illinois River above Cahokia. D'Artaguiette perceived that the French settlers had rapidly become middlemen in the provision trade between French troops stationed at Fort Chartres and the Indians who both lived in the area and passed through it. D'Artaguiette's perceptions about trade relations are remarkably concrete and concise. The exchange relations among myriad peoples are detailed:

> The trade of the inhabitants of the Illinois, who are Canadians, French, or discharged soldiers, consists in selling their wheat and other products to the company [Company of the Indies] for the subsistence of the troops, in exchange for merchandise (which they are obliged to fetch from New Orleans) which they trade to the Indians for quarters

of buffalo, bear oil, and other meats, which serve them for food or which they sell in exchange for merchandise.[4]

In this description, the interesting and undifferentiated phrase "which serve them for food or which they sell in exchange for merchandise" raises an important question: to whom were the inhabitants of the Illinois selling buffalo quarters and bear oil? Since they were getting merchandise in return, the implication is that they sold salt meat and bear oil downriver or to members of the French garrison with access to the official *magasin* (warehouse). D'Artaguiette clearly states that inhabitants sold maize to the soldiers; his journal entry for June 9, 1723, describes setting out for Kaskaskia to load a boat with maize for the troops. The *magasin* at Fort Chartres became central to the French settlements in terms of amount and variety of merchandise stored and dispersed and its general social role. Originally the *magasin* serving the Company of the Indies, the fort warehouse continued its role as supplier when the Company of the Indies returned the French colonies to royal charter in 1731. A study of the role of the *magasin* in the French communities of the floodplain concludes the warehouse early on evolved into a central collection point for export items, "a buyer as well as consignee-agent and forwarder." The Fort Chartres *magasin* served the villages of Chartres, St. Anne's, St. Philippe, Prairie du Rocher, and, seven leagues south, Kaskaskia.[5]

D'Artaguiette's perceptions about the trade relations among diverse groups in the Illinois Country are all the more compelling given the incessant warfare between the Fox and the Illinois Indians, despite a French-negotiated truce in 1716. The truce did not last, leading to the historic defeat of the Fox by the French in 1730, for which some estimates place the number of massacred Fox at one thousand or twelve hundred. Even after this defeat, the Fox continued to attack the Illinois, and the Illinois sporadically killed Fox hunters they encountered, especially in the forested area along the Illinois River. Prior to both the Iroquois penetration into the northern Illinois Country and the evolving relations with the French, the Illinois and Miami Indians had participated in what Daniel K. Richter and Margaret Kimball Brown term the "mourning war." Other historians have described this kind of warfare by using the words 'localized, limited, and personal." The mourning war was a form of ritualized revenge for long-remembered and recounted losses. It could be sporadic and spontaneous. However, the localized nature of the mourning war disintegrated when Fox hunters moving south and Illinois hunters moving north on seasonal hunts both became dependent on the prairies of northern Illinois and southern Wisconsin. Into these areas buffalo were accustomed to migrate in the summer to escape the torment of green-headed flies and other deer flies. Competition for peltries and European trade, often cited as driving the Fox-Illinois warfare, was complicated by a hunting war involving buffalo. The size of these Illinois herds never approached that of the western Great Plains herds. Nor did the Fox and the Illinois have horses during the time they were first observed hunting on the prairies. In fact, R. David Edmunds's depiction of the Fox lifeways, the hunting-gathering-horticultural subsistence mosaic, is indistinguishable from descriptions of the Illinois subsistence style: "Large numbers of waterfowl were taken on a seasonal basis, and during the summer Fox hunting parties left their villages to travel to the prairies of Illinois or Iowa where they killed buffalo." The nature of the Fox-Illinois animosity changed over the course of the eighteenth-century as the Illinois became domiciled Indians and the Fox did not. Many factors enter into the periodic outbreaks of violence between these two nations. In 1719, for example, a party of hunting Illinois surprised a camp of mixed Fox, Kickapoo, and Mascouten near Rock River, Illinois. They killed twenty people, including some women and children, and took at least twenty prisoners back to Illinois. Such raids, already beyond the scope of the mourning war, escalated right up until the Fox defeat in 1730 and continued beyond it. Each time a significant number of persons died, the event became encapsulated in the oral history of the tribe and was recounted in an additive and vehement litany. In 1724 Mechigamea and Kaskaskia Indian chiefs recited to White Cat (a traveling chief down from Michilimackinac) a long, bitter list of Fox attacks and killings that had occurred over the years at Illinois villages.[6]

The century of French occupation of the Illinois included consistent and sometimes horrific violence between the Fox and the Illinois. In 1752 the Cahokia were driven permanently from their mission settlement on the River L'Abbe near Monks Mound, south to the Fort Chartres area, by an attack of Fox, Sauk, Potawatomi, and Sioux. This war party had also wiped out the Mechigamea village near the fort. Fox raided the Kaskaskia Indians steadily through the 1760s and 1770s. As late as 1778, George Rogers Clark was negotiating yet another treaty with the Fox at Cahokia to bring about a cessation of Fox-Sauk-Illinois hostilities and raids. The brief overview here does not begin to document the spiking, retaliatory, ambush-laden nature of the Fox-Illinois relations across the eighteenth century. The river systems played an important role in haphazard and unplanned attacks, and in cases where French traders happened to be accompanying Illinois Indians on upriver forays, they were often killed. Even at Fort Chartres, French soldiers remained vigilant. The threat of a Renard (Fox) attack on the fort in 1723 caused the soldiers to "cut down the large bushes . . . which would favor an approach to Fort Chartres."[7]

Yet despite Fox raids on their fields and on Indian villages, the French continued to trade with Indians on both sides of the Mississippi. Middlemen French farmers were receptive to the Indian provision trade. At the settlement around Fort Chartres, they encouraged—and gradually adopted for themselves—hunting and trapping trips across the Mississippi River into the Missouria and Osage country, a practice bitterly resented by the Fox. Using the rivers that made western Illinois so accessible and such a natural point of departure for lands north, west, and south, Illinois Indians allied with French voyageurs drew on an abundant natural wilderness storehouse. French officials in New Orleans had clearly perceived the possibilities of the Missouri lands as early as 1719. In that year, the Council of Commerce meeting on Dauphine Island awarded gifts to two groups of Indian chiefs in the hopes of establishing amicable trade relations with them. Two chiefs were "Kaskaskias who have come down here to sing the calumet," but the other were four Missouria chiefs. Both Kaskaskia and Missouria Indians received a great abundance of gifts, including eight dozen large knives and over two hundred pounds of powder for each group. Hunting and trapping merchandise weighed large in these early gift inventories. The council directed the gifts to be dispersed among village warriors.[8]

Studies of extant Indian gift lists in the decade before the Seven Years War—for both the French and British—indicate blurred distinctions in the meaning of merchandise. Gifts were to impart a civilizing influence, yet offerings of munitions, war paint, scalping knives, and even cutlasses appear to have promoted tribal warfare, as well as Indian-white hostilities. Given the amount of fervent writing in early French memorials about the rich possibilities of the Illinois and Missouri lands, it is more likely that these 1719 gifts were meant to encourage large-scale hunting and trapping. In fact, the scale of fur harvesting from the upper Mississippi Valley continued to be staggering through the 1740s. A peltry inventory of a single trader-trapper from 1745, for example, contained "1,156 cats large and small" and "1,160 bear large and small," as well as otter, 134 fox skins, wolf, beaver, and five packets of deerskins. These were the halcyon days of French-Indian interaction, an inaugural period in which gifts encouraged the development of a trade matrix at a new fort. By 1747 Governor Vaudreuil of New Orleans would write threatening letters about withholding gifts to the Illinois Indians if they continued "inactive" (possibly meaning, refusing to garner furs). In the same letter Vaudreuil says of the Quapaw in Arkansas that he had difficulty "stirring them out of their lethargy." The theme of Indian service to the French via a highly industrious fur-collecting commitment remains clear in the letters of French officials all the way through to the collapse of the regime.[9]

It didn't take long for Indians across the Mississippi to note the possibilities of a midcontinent trade warehouse. In late May of 1723, D'Artaguiette reported the arrival at Fort Chartres of four Missouria Indians. The fort these Indians were visiting was not the imposing, wide-winged limestone structure with an impressive enceinte and ornate gate (constructed in the early 1750s as the third Fort Chartres). Surrounded by crude palings already decaying in the soggy earth, the 1723 Fort Chartres was a log rectangle, smoke-stained and palisaded, with two bastions at diagonal corners. Two other bastions may have been added to a second fort. On the scaffolding of each bastion was a bell, and the bastions themselves eventually held a prison, a henhouse, and a stable. The strikingly level lands around the fort would have enabled arriving visitors to take in the extent of French settlement: scattered houses made of "pickets," partially cleared land in black gashes of seeded earth, and unfenced, foraging domestic animals. Archaeological investigations at this first Fort Chartres site confirm high numbers of domesticated and large-mammal bones, a trend supported by documents describing the early florescence of agriculture and cattle-and-pig husbandry; bison bones are also well represented. Despite the presence of numerous wooden structures, pigs and chickens, garden plots and grain outfields, the Fort Chartres prairies in the spring of 1723 would have still been very wet. The French had encountered spring flooding of streams and the Coulee Deneau. In addition, the great marsh overflowed as rains and river saturated the floodplain. Notarial records from years later indicate the building of ditches into natural runs to direct the "discharge" from the marsh toward the river. Myriad ponds of all sizes dotted the land, forming overnight in small depressions and dry runs as the water table rose unchecked. On brimming surfaces were already breeding the malarial-laden mosquitoes. Retreating spring floodwaters—an annual inundation that all who lived along the river would get used to—laid down a shining, tacky surface and filled the air with alluvial stench. Fort Chartres, the future pride of the French Empire in western North America, sat on a plain of black mud.[10]

Nonetheless, the fort and its surroundings impressed Indian tribes, especially those living to the west and north. In 1723 the Missouria Indians who came to pay their respects would have encountered an altered landscape, where only four years before browsing deer brushed through tallgrass prairies and raucous waterfowl nested in the wide marsh near the cliffs. Word was out among Missouri tribes about change, about settlement and a permanent trade center. Missouria Indians had evidently come to open up trade relations with the French, for on June 6 they recrossed the Mississippi with some Frenchmen who wanted to trade for horses and buy skins. By 1725 the lure of the Missouri lands was consistently drawing French and Indians across the river. Reports to France in 1725 by French observers Longuiel and Begon mention the French traders being attacked by Kickapoo and Fox as they attempted to cross into Sioux lands. The Fox wished to keep the trade in these more northern parts for themselves. Longuiel adds that both the Fox and Sioux had attacked French and Illinois Indians living along the Mississippi and that these tribes, Fox and Sioux, were "enraged" with the Illinois Indians. The mourning war was showing signs of escalating into trade and provision wars.[11]

The spread of French hunting and fur-gathering efforts across the Mississippi into the plentiful game country of the Missouri lands is clearly indicated in commercial records. In 1724 the Osage Indians had sent a message to French authorities in Louisiana that they had amassed a quantity of peltry, including much beaver, that they wished to trade for French merchandise. The Illinois colonies lay directly across from the Osage lands; and the garrison of Fort Chartres was stocked with both merchandise and gifts for Indians willing to trade with and stay loyal to the French (such loyalty often meant serving in French armies, attacking other tribes and British outposts). In 1735, for example, despite renewed hostilities between the Fox and the Illinois, French traders were able to purchase from the Sioux "100,000 beautiful beaver skins." Approximately nine years later, at the outbreak of King George's War, such was the lure of deerskin and peltry profits that one estimate put sixteen hundred Frenchmen engaged in the trade. Commercial figures from the Archives Nationales, Colonies, Paris, indicate a large number of furs going down the Mississippi to New Orleans each year; in 1745 the value was given as 9,621 livres.[12]

While agricultural studies such as those of Carl Ekberg have stressed the production of cereal grains and the shipping of surplus wheat and flour south to New Orleans, neither these studies nor analyses based on French government economic figures and regulations take into account the clandestine activities of individuals in a fluid frontier trade environment. The number of beaver pelts reported to have floated down the Mississippi—one hundred thousand—is likely not even close to the entire number of animals killed. In the first decade of French occupation, there must have been many opportunities for exchange among French and Indians. In the first years of the Chartres settlement, in 1727, for instance, a series of notarial records details an inquiry into a trading mission carried out by the Sieur Poudret into the Pawnee and Osage territory across the Mississippi. In an inquiry that spanned two months, a voyageur Poudret hired to accompany him, Jean Jacques Desmanets, gave a deposition about Poudret's activities. There was evidently some question about whether Poudret's words to the Osage had incited them to make war on the Pawnee. As revealed in the long, tangled narrative involving the stealing of Indian slaves and Spanish trade horses, Poudret's dealings with these trans-Mississippi Indians took him into three different camps: the Missouria, the Osage, and the Pawnee. The efforts of the French to keep peace among the warring tribes to facilitate their own trading success were often ineffectual. Desmanets' testimony, for example, indicates how Poudret's diplomacy was received: "We told them [the Pawnee] to live in peace with the Osage and other nations, that this was the word of the French chief. But they replied that they had eaten the Osage and that they would always eat them." These early records suggest a fast-developing trade center acting on tribes across the Mississippi as well as to the north, south, and east.[13]

Through the formal establishment of Fort Chartres, France sought to control French-Indian trade in the Illinois Country. The Provincial Council in Illinois, the governing body authorized by the Company of the Indies, had instructed French traders and military going into the Missouri Country not to interfere in the traffic in Paducah (Apache) slaves or horses. The Missouri tribes involved in these trades might become "alienated" and begin to sell peltries to Fox Indians or rogue British traders. Official accounts of expeditions, or notarial depositions such as that of the Poudret trip, detail only isolated cases. Other kinds of records provide interesting measures of the degree of casual, opportunistic trade contact between French and Indians developing out of the Chartres trade matrix. Ten years after the Poudret trip, a Frenchman living at Fort Michilimackinac compiled a census of Indian tribes. While French censuses were usually taken by arriving military commanders or by officially appointed engineers and cartographers, this time the numbers of tribal warriors, ranging from Kickapoo and Mascouten to the Illinois Confederacy, were based on the on-site estimates of French voyageurs and fur trappers. There were enough Frenchmen present in Indian villages to take head counts. One historian studying the contracts drawn up among French Canadian voyageurs and employers, as well as the numbers of *billets* (due bills) for trade goods has concluded that by 1736, French traders were "regularly" ascending the Missouri. In the next year, for instance, four pairs of French traders planned to penetrate the Missouri lands via this river.[14]

The river systems in which major waterways drained into the Mississippi from the east and west left the trappers and traders of French Illinois uniquely poised: once on the rivers and streams, they became fundamentally unaccountable. In light bark canoes or heavier pirogues designed to ferry specific weights and amounts of furs and goods, trappers, hunters, and seasonal traders could fan out over hundreds of miles of feeder streams, smaller rivers, many unnamed and appearing on no maps until the late eighteenth century. Both the Company of the Indies and the French government sought to regulate trade activity through the licensing of traders, the leasing out of fur posts, and gifts dispensed from Fort Chartres and other forts to secure and monitor tribal loyalties. Yet the slippery, spontaneous trade of riverine traffic remained impossible to monitor. Surviving narratives of escapes from Indian attacks on the rivers—contained mainly in the detailed letters of Commander Macarty at Fort Chartres—often describe how French traders, slaves, and Illinois Indians hid in bulrushes, laid low on islands, crawled through canebrakes, or secreted their canoes in tangled willow copses. The Mississippi River offered concealment and escape, but it also played a strangely undefined role as a boundary. Part of the amorphous nature of the trade west and north of Fort Chartres had to do with the unspecified nature of the Illinois Country. The official boundaries between French Canada and French Louisiana were never crisply set out anywhere. After it was made part of the province of Louisiana in 1731, the Illinois Country was thought to extend to "the headwaters of the Mississippi." Although this was disputed by both French Canada and Louisiana, French Canadians, French Illinoisans, and myriad Indians continued to hunt, trap, and trade on the tributaries and inlets of the Mississippi River System, indicating a generally-held belief that trade law and trade boundaries were unenforceable.[15]

River trade was facilitated by the presence of master boat builders at the French villages of Kaskaskia and Chartres. The deep, sturdy pirogues hewn of whole cottonwood trees or, sometimes, black walnut were used for the New Orleans convoy. Private individuals, as well as the French government, contracted for such craft, and commercial agreements provide official specifications and descriptions. Yet these few surviving records barely sketch in the outlines of river transport. A 1726 estate inventory in the Chartres notarial records includes "Half of one Indian pirogue of walnut," suggesting Indians were also builders of river craft, and that some French traded for or otherwise obtained these boats. Analysis of contracts for voyageurs has shown that some Illinois Indians signed on as voyageurs for the French, including one Penchirois, "said to be from the Xavier mission located on the Mechigamea reserve." Voyageurs are identified in some contracts as "upriver," yet the historian who has analyzed these contracts in depth,

Margaret Kimball Brown, indicates how entwined the official network of traders/voyageurs was: their names form an "interconnected network" of different and occurring associations. Brown points out that it is impossible to know just how many persons ever participated in the river trade; the only specific indication lies in the 1732 census that lists "transients who come and go, about fifty men." And of course, French inventories of furs held by successfully returning traders do not detail how those furs were obtained. Behind entries like "448 livres of beaver in five packets," or "120 livres of dry beaver at 30 sols the livre," there may have been a complicated trading history involving Indians from as many as ten upriver tribes. These packets of beaver pelts and hundreds of cat and bear skins represent a drainage harvest of a formidable amount of land; and they may have been obtained in a myriad of casual trade transactions ranging from the exchange of a single raccoon pelt that would net a "small knife for a woman" to a man's ruffled shirt priced at "2 Bucks or 2 middleing D[eer] or 2 otters or 7 raccoons."[16]

The number of light, easily carried canoes on the feeder streams and rivers of the upper Mississippi Valley—the unofficial record—was likely legion. While most interpretations of the Ojibway word for the Mississippi settle on "father of waters" or "great river," at least one river historian believes the real meaning to be closer to "river of waters from all sides." The French, as well as the Indians, had grasped this. At the end of King George's War, in 1749, a curious document appeared called "Instructions for the Exploration of Louisiana." An objective, even scientific assessment of the entire Mississippi River Valley was to be undertaken by M. Riday, also known as Bosseron. Bosseron's instructions are extremely precise. In the area of the Illinois, he was to state exactly how many leagues the rivers would carry canoes without a portage, as well as the amount of land over which canoes would be portaged. He was also to determine the origins of the rivers, whether they "come from various lakes, marshes, or prairies." Finally, Bosseron was also to determine the relationship between the Ohio River and every one of its tributaries, as well as investigating the Illinois and Mississippi Rivers. All aspects of Bosseron's instructions, in fact, stress the riverine geography of the French Empire south of the Great Lakes, revealing some realistic understanding of the French and Indian trade networks. Bosseron was also to undertake an anthropological assessment of Indian tribes living in the lands drained by the rivers. The trade behaviors of these Indians were of particular importance, along with their propensities for alcohol, their populations, and curiously, the exact numbers of men and women in tribal estimates. The fruits of this expedition, if it ever took place, are not recorded. Included among a host of documents from the period before the

Seven Years War, this set of instructions says a great deal about the role of water and river transport in the French Empire along the Mississippi.[17]

An additional factor in the growth of such riverine exchange contacts was the long cultural trading history of the Mechigamea Indians, living in a village only a mile north of Fort Chartres. It is important to factor in the skilled trade history of these Indians, because as one archaeologist-historian of the French fur trade in the central subarctic (Hudson Bay region) has noted, Indians were in fact "shrewd consumers." Studies of Indians as consumers in the eighteenth century have shown discriminating trade behaviors of a complexity far beyond the earliest European-Indian contact patterns, in which, for instance, all Jesuit priests ventured into the Canadian wilderness with supplies of small trinkets. While historians have been able to reconstruct trading patterns of northern Indians, good evidence for trade behaviors of the Illinois Indians is not manifest across the French regime. And because of the distressingly real deleterious effects of French brandy on Illinois tribes, historians have sometimes concentrated on the problems of the liquor exchange and glossed the role of the provision trade. An emphasis on agriculture as the best measure of industriousness has also contributed to perceptions of Indians living near the fort as dependent and opportunistic. Yet it is clear from a 1726 memorial written by the Sieur de Bienville that Indians in the Illinois Country were molding the kind of trade that developed there. Bienville noted that "the voyageurs of Canada formerly obtained from them [the Illinois] a large number of beaver and racoon skins." He then stated that the French, for six or seven years, "had been obliging" the Illinois to produce bear oil and meat for trade purposes. This is an oblique way of saying that Illinois Indians learned to furnish the provisional items that would net them the kind of trade goods they wanted.

It may also suggest that the Illinois Indians were finding it difficult to hunt and trap beaver. As early as 1725, Illinois chiefs made a speech accusing the Fox of dominating the beaver trade with the Canadians, from whom they could easily secure guns and ammunition; the Canadian traders, said the Illinois chiefs, were interested only in beaver skins. Most significant, one chief added, "I admit we do not kill as many beavers as the People of the Lakes."[18] This somewhat elliptical statement is perhaps the only evidence attesting to the decline of Illinois beaver, rapidly trapped out along the rivers and wetlands of the interior and occurring more plentifully in forested streamsides of the north, in Wisconsin, Minnesota, and Michigan especially. It was from these areas that the Sioux would take the one hundred thousand "beautiful" beaver skins of 1735. Studies of aboriginal hunters in southern Wisconsin have shown that all tribal hunters, including those coming in from neighboring areas, favored wetlands occurring in the ecotone, the transition zone between prairie and forest. Exact numbers of beaver in presettlement Illinois cannot be known, but the count for the upper Mississippi Valley before European contact is estimated at 10 million to 40 million. That number of active, constructing animals in a watery world had a critical role in maintaining it.[19]

Beaver Tales

Because of limited records on the fur trade out of French Illinois and, especially, the lack of information on the origin (location) of animals trapped and shot, discussion of beaver in Illinois must focus on suggestive changes in the land. Through removal of this key species, we can trace a cascade effect. The rich brown rodent with a pelt of silky softness, *Castor canadensis*, is recognized today as a formidable ecological engineer. In a watery world like presettlement Illinois Country, beaver probably controlled the flow of hundreds of smaller streams. In the year 1600 natural ponding created by beaver dams spread over an estimated 51.1 million acres of surface area in Illinois; by 1990 beavers were creating only 511,000 acres of wetlands. The long-buried, remaining hydric soils that lie beneath Illinois farmland drainage systems are in fact the "footprint" of past beaver ponds and wetlands. Some researchers who have delved deep into this black, fecund, watery earth believe a most dramatic and profound alteration in the hydrologic cycle occurred as a direct result of the fur trade. In addition to the effect on all living creatures who have evolved an exchange relationship with wetlands, especially migrating waterfowl and spawning fish, the loss of these 50 million acres of saturated, spongy earth contributed to catastrophic flooding along the Mississippi. Indians and French experienced dramatic floods, it is true, some so devastating there were reports of waters sloshing up the cliffs between Fort Chartres and Kaskaskia, of people rowing between homes and villages in canoes for weeks. These great floods were rare, however, one perhaps occurring in 1725 and another in the 1740s; the year 1785 entered history as the Year of the Great Waters. Between these hallmark years, Illinois wetlands, in large part created and maintained by beaver ponding, were doing their job. The original hydric landscape could have stored floodwaters to a depth of three feet. In dispersing such overflow over vast acres, wetlands accommodated waters that could amount to more than three times the floodwaters of the great 1993 Mississippi flood![20]

There are few figures available for the decimation of Illinois beaver across the eighteenth century. Yet in addition to the removal of the animals themselves, their trapped-out dams often disintegrated or were destroyed by farmers. In addition, beavers will not often choose to build their dams on stream slopes showing evidence of grazing. They like the natural vegetative cover of a tangled, diverse stream bank; one study identifies herbaceous wetland as very important for their survival. Beaver dams, built four hundred to five hundred feet apart, pooled sediments and organic matter in the many streams of the Illinois Country, creating wetlands. The high water table as a result kept streams dynamic and flowing at certain times of the year, in turn preventing the choking of channels by heavy green algae growth in late summer. These intricate ecological relationships—too often termed a "delicate" ecological balance—have been disturbed not only through ditching and draining of Illinois farmlands; the fur trade of the eighteenth century with its initial, insatiable demand for beaver was a powerful factor as well, emptying out the gallery forests of the Illinois Country. Wrenching changes to Illinois prairies occurring through rapid settlement in the nineteenth century hastened processes set in motion in the eighteenth. By 1843 a visitor to the Illinois upland prairies noted that beaver were considered nearly extinct there. This was long before the 1879 Illinois Farm Drainage Act and must be accounted the first formidable factor in permanent land change. One hydraulic engineer has noted, "Wetlands disappeared by the acre," as all across North America, beaver populations plummeted from 200 million to 10 million.[21]

As many historians have demonstrated, the fur trade was not one economic and extractive process that gave way to another, market agriculture. The overlap in the two livelihoods was long and drawn out, and it involved incoming peoples participating in and using variations of both economies. Very often trading peltries supplemented a farm; and trappers and traders had agricultural home bases. In 1827, for instance, long after the national fur trade had shifted to the trans-Mississippi and transmontane West, pioneer accounts note a trading establishment a mile south of present-day Sparta on the upland prairies. There, a frontier entrepreneur operated Sherron's Store out of a rough log hut. He sold cast-iron skillets, pots, knives, and dry goods to American farmers and scattered Indians, accepting hides and furs in exchange. The same kinds of exchanges were occurring in the Chartres area all through the eighteenth century, despite an emphasis in French histories on the Illinois Country as a breadbasket. The history of French wheat convoys leaving Kaskaskia each spring—the multitude of embarking pirogues, heavy with concentrated grain, furs, skins, salted meat, and oils—inscribes a cultural, as well as economic, upriver ritual. This emphasis obscures the reality of hundreds of such riverine trading voyages each year by Indians, French voyageurs, and even some enterprising women. By 1741 the governor of Louisiana was noting the arrival in New Orleans of "a rather large quantity of peltries." Some of the furs had come from the Missouri Indians and other Indians living west of the Mississippi. Although many different tribes relied on the Mississippi, from the Sioux near the Falls of St. Anthony all the way down to the Alibamon and the Taensas near the Gulf, the French at midcontinent had particularly observed the Illinois Indians. In 1729 one M. Perier declared in a letter that the "Illini were masters of the Mississippi River and must be kept from joining the English." And this broad, sinuous, chimerical river was especially important to the Mechigamea Indians.[22]

The Mysterious Mechigamea

The Mechigamea emerge in the history of French Illinois as one of the most interesting and least-studied tribes; there is a dearth of documentary history concerning them, but archaeological evidence and their histori- cal association with the Quapaw in Arkansas suggest a strongly riverine people. In reviewing the French-Indian interaction across approximately seventy years, on a strip of riparian land sixty miles long, one fact stands out: among the four Illinois Confederacy tribes, the Mechigamea avoided open conflict with the French. They lived the closest to them, a mile above the village of Chartres; yet unlike the events at the Cahokia grant, in which the Cahokia-Tamaroa were removed to a village nine miles away after a bloodless "revolt," the Mechigamea stayed in their village in fairly intimate contact with French inhabitants and the fort. By 1721, in fact, it seems there were actually two Mechigamea villages above Fort Chartres, strung out along the river bank. Archaeological excavations have not been conducted at these former villages, due to their being entirely on private land. Researchers, however, have analyzed surface finds, especially ceramic shard collections turned up through cultivation. Both pottery and glazed earthenware, as well as the incised geometries and concentric swirls dis- tinctive to lower river tribes like the Tunica and Natchez, reveal an ex- tensive trading history. Use of ceramic vessels by the Mechigamea—and the poignant, scattered overlay of French faience plates, platter shards, and pitchers—bespeak a process of acculturation and change. At certain key points of transition in kinds of pottery sought, traded for, and used, it is possible to infer shifts in trade and subsistence behaviors. These trade patterns in turn were linked to the French settlements on the lower river, to French mercantilism and trade policies, and to seemingly peripheral developments such as animal husbandry on an island peninsula between Kaskaskia and Fort Chartres. While ceramics were "traded widely" among

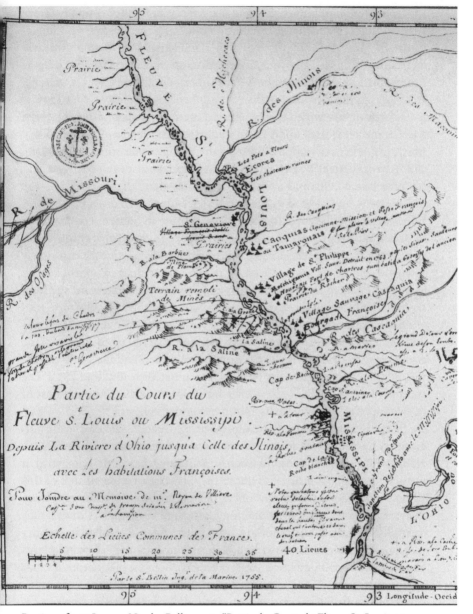

Portion of 1755 Jacques Nicolas Bellin map, "Partie du Cours du Fleuve St. Louis ou Mississipi." On this map, all the Illinois Indian villages are indicated in relation to the French settlements.

Indian nations and groups living in the Mississippi Valley region between 1680 and 1750, after that date, aboriginal ceramic vessels were no longer in use in Mechigamea villages. Partly due to heavy extraction of beaver from Illinois lands—and the traveling distance now necessary to compete in the northern fur trade—the Mechigamea had shifted early on, possibly by 1719, into the provision trade.[23]

Before contact with the French became fairly steady, after 1680, the Mechigamea had been middleman traders for the Quapaw Indian tribes of northeast Arkansas and possibly as many as nine other tribes living along the Arkansas River before 1700. They likely had a summer village near the present-day Arkansas town of Pocahontas along the Black River. The Grigsby site, investigated in 1988 by the Arkansas Archaeological Survey, is believed to be the Mechigamea village written in on two separate maps by Joliet and Marquette. At this central location, accessible through the river systems, the Mechigamea came to secure ceramics in the distinctive Quapaw tradition (characterized by the so-called Quapaw swirl), as well as horses obtained from the Spanish and driven overland toward the Mississippi. Arabian horses were herded along a (possibly) paleohistoric trail winding northeast between San Antonio and St. Louis. In return for horses and pottery, the Mechigamea were the purveyors of prized French trade goods, readily available in the protohistoric period and certainly in rich metallic flow across the Great Lakes region between 1610 and 1670. The trading loop regularly brought the Mechigamea downstream in a host of transport craft extensive enough to move entire villages.[24]

This role changed dramatically when the French settled the Illinois Country. While some artistic re-creations of Mechigamea villages show women engaged in agriculture (such as pounding corn or flailing grain), it is more likely that a prime activity in the Chartres riverine villages of this Illinois tribe was the making of bear oil. Omnivorous black bears, *Ursus americanus*, ranged densely along the Mississippi River and its woodlands, eating constantly as they moved across miles of terrain, following white-tailed deer herds, fish runs in inland streams, insect and grub populations, and seasonal berries and nuts. The shooting of shoreline black bears, including mothers and cubs, by Europeans in river craft is documented many times, especially before 1720. Europeans rapidly developed a taste for bear oil; an often-cited comment is that black bear oil was as good in salads as the best grade of olive oil. Such imported oils were not arriving at French settlements with any regularity at all; in the early years the supply ships from the Company of the Indies were erratic, sparse, and sometimes lost at sea. Animal fat from game became an important source of calories and was necessary in the care of guns and the few metal implements available in the Illinois Country. Indians living south of the Illinois were observed at midcentury making a "deer of oil," using an entire, peeled-off deerskin with orifices plugged with a lime-and-salt paste to hold rendered bear oil. Choctaw Indians used deer heads with plugged orifices as containers. The deer of oil, filled heads, and filled bladders were treated as units of exchange in the trade. An "Illustration of Illinois Indians in New Orleans in 1732" depicts Indians and trade goods waiting for exchange on the banks of the Mississippi. The goods are labeled *plat cote* (buffalo ribs), *suif* (tallow), and *huille dourse* (bear oil). The bear oil appears to be in some kind of flexible skin container. This drawing may be the single depiction of a trade container that was once ubiquitous in the Mississippi Valley. In Alabama, southern Indians even managed natural bear ranges devoted to the increase of black bear populations; one such range lay near the Chattahoochee River. Indians themselves prohibited villages and hunting in these areas. In the French bear oil trade, Indian hunters obtained much of the meat and oil along the St. Francis River in northern Arkansas; Arkansas Indians could furnish as much as three thousand pots of oil annually.[25]

These Indian hunters would have had to develop astute knowledge of black bear movements and ranges. A single foraging black bear may need more than three thousand acres, and individual bears of the same sex do not roam overlapping ranges. In addition, the notion of a bear's home range varies considerably with sex, time of year, and geographic location. Male black bears need a much larger range than females. Did Arkansas hunters like the Quapaw share their knowledge of bear ranges with the Mechigamea? It was with the Arkansas Indians that the Mechigamea had sustained trade and living contacts. The St. Francis River and the Black River, summer camp to the Mechigamea, are both in the same northeastern quadrant of Arkansas.[26]

It is likely the Mechigamea were drawn into the bear oil trade through their Quapaw connections, although it may also have been the other way around. In 1740 a free black in the Illinois Country, Jacques Duverger, also a surgeon and trader, acquired 150 pots of bear oil. Surviving records include a contract with another voyageur to transport the pots of oil south to New Orleans. How did Duverger acquire the substantial number of 150 pots of bear oil? While in rare instances, a very fat black bear might be rendered to produce as much as 120 pots of oil, this was likely not a common outcome. The misleading aspect of surviving trade and commercial records is the way they commodify large amounts of organic trade material to suggest a single source. Bear oil, like salted meat, smoked buffalo tongue, hides, furs, and smaller peltries, was a trade item of incremental as well as gross value. A French trapper-trader or an Indian could exchange one pot or one hundred pots, and such transactions could occur literally anywhere—on river banks, at midstream from canoe to pirogue, between mounted hunting parties on the bluffs of the Missouri River, at the mouth of the Illinois River in the shade of the towering rock formations there, on an island south of Kaskaskia—or at Fort Chartres. Contracts with voyageurs to accompany traders on hunting expeditions were usually made in late summer, for the party to leave in the fall. In particular, autumn bears were fat from their summer feeding and produced the greatest amount of oil. Yet the sheer amount of oil being convoyed downriver to New Orleans suggests strongly that many Indians were regular producers, and that they traded oil in both small and large amounts.[27]

The oil production process highlights the connection between bear and deer. To kill a black bear and butcher it using heavy knives; to boil the meat down in large kettles, rendering the fat slowly through hours of tended wood fires kept at a steady heat; to procure a freshly killed deer and skillfully butcher it to keep the skin entire and uncut, or skin and boil a deer skull, then fill and caulk orifices—this process required the skilled, joint handling of both bear and deer and an established work site. The size of both mammals, black bear and deer, and the cauldrons necessary to render the oil as a commodity make it unlikely that Indians could produce good-quality bear oil in an opportunistic fashion. It also mandates the use of large kettles. Indian demand for both iron and copper kettles remained consistently high in the Illinois Country. The French government had taken on an increasingly active role in provisioning, transporting, selling, and dispersing goods as part of a mercantile economic system; that system depended on the fur trade, in which peltries flowed both north and south, and on the sale of surplus wheat to the New Orleans colony, in which foodstuffs flowed south. Surviving in the Macarty correspondence collection at Huntington Library is a single undated French government requisition for supplies sent to the Illinois Country by convoy up the Mississippi. Best estimates at dating this manifest would place it in 1751 or 1752. Lists of goods are identified for various parties: "For the Indians," "For the French in Payment for Jobs," "For the Barracks," "For the Hospital," "For the Magasin," and "For the Office." This inventory is revealing of trade trends, both sanctioned and perhaps unsanctioned. At a time, 1752, when the number of French troops defending the Illinois Country was not over three hundred, the goods designated "For the Barracks," included fifty large cooking pots for the troops. Yet these troops were living not in a fort but with the townspeople in French Kaskaskia. Plans were under way for the building of a new fort on either the Kaskaskia River or farther inland from the existent Fort Chartres; the second wooden fort, erected between 1725 and 1728, was so decayed it could not lodge or support a garrison of troops. French commander Macarty hoped that construction could be completed on the new barracks by 1753, but in the meantime, soldiers were eating and sleeping in private French homes. The fifty iron cooking pots for the troops, shipped upriver from New Orleans, may not have made it to the new barracks at all. An inventory of the material goods at Fort Chartres, conducted by both the French and the British in 1765, reveals less than ten iron kettles scattered throughout the various structures of the fort.[28]

This trade manifest also profiles Indian trade good preference. In the list of goods designated "For the Indians" appears an entry for "400 pounds of copper cauldrons, all sizes, like those in Canada." This entry for cauldrons is one of the largest on the list of trade and gift items for Indians. Anthropological and archaeological studies have consistently stressed the high preference of Indians in many North American locations for iron and, especially, brass and copper cooking pots. Excavations at Osage village sites in Missouri, for example, reveal that almost all brass artifacts were made of scrap from brass kettles. A comparison of goods traded to the Illinois Indians at three different points in time—1688, 1710, and 1765—shows the escalation in demand for pots. In 1710 Father Marest, writing from the Cahokia Mission, did not include any requests for pots on his list of requested items. By 1765 entries appear on trade lists for "brass kettles as they weigh at the rate of 1 lb. Beaver a pound" and "tin or camp kettles of a Gallon 1 Bever or 1 Buck and Doe." In that year, 1765, Captain Thomas Stirling described an incident on the Ohio River on his way to the Illinois Country. One of his party tried to buy a kettle from a Mingo woman; she insisted on twenty-five buckskins and eventually got the equivalent in rum, for which she immediately traded and received twenty buckskins. Stirling thought the kettle "old" but noted that the woman effectively sold it for four and a half guineas. The use of these large pots as rendering implements is one way of measuring the importance of the provision trade among upper Mississippi Valley Indians. The shift into provisioning is also highlighted archaeologically. Sites along the Mississippi River, such as the Waterman Site, the Mechigamea village occupied between 1753 and 1765, reveal an equal concentration in ornamental goods—glass beads and tinkling cones, for instance—and artifacts connected with hunting: brass projectile points, flint knives, iron fleshers, gun flints. European ceramic vessel shards are also prevalent. Of some significance in this later Mechigamea site is the relative scarcity of agricultural implements. The record can be read as a story of shifting economic activity.[29]

Once French trade goods became available on the lower river, after the settlement of New Orleans, the Mechigamea's role as middleman traders collapsed. They abandoned their permanent village in Arkansas, and although they made trips up and down the Mississippi to visit and hunt, they substituted a trade in foodstuffs and furs for the pottery-horse-slave-French-merchandise trade of the protohistoric period. Their role as hunters and meat-and-oil procurers may have affected their subsistence agriculture as well. One indication of this in the Chartres notarial records is a gradual increase in sales of Mechigamea Indian land to the French, land granted to them by De Boisbriant in 1719. In this year the French had been expressly forbidden to settle on and farm lands given to the Mechigamea. Yet challenges to this ruling resulted in conflicts. A Jesuit priest, Father de Ville, had even traveled down to Mobile to talk to Governor Bienville about French incursions into Indian farmlands. Records of the Company of the Indies show the missionaries requesting that the French be kept out of Indian villages. This proximity is phrased as "the French living *pesle mesle* with the Indians" (the source of the evolved English phrase *pell mell*). The Company complied by giving the Mechigamea their own grant. However, since the edges of some French grants abutted the edges of the Mechigamea Prairie, there soon began to be haggling over the addition of small bits of Mechigamea land. As early as 1724 one Charles Naut, a Frenchman married to an Indian woman, began farming land in the prairie of the Mechigamea. The Indians enlisted the help of Father de Kereben to plead their cause, but Naut was not stopped. The historian of the Jesuit missions in Illinois, Mary Borgias Palm, points out that the Mechigamea grant yet existed in the early 1800s, described in the first surveys by Americans. It was bounded by the Coulee de Nau (Deneau), the Mississippi, and the lower line (southern edge) of St. Philippe. This tract, Palm states, was "never conceded away, either by the French or English government."[30]

However much the Mechigamea resented Charles Naut's incursions into their prairie, they eventually began to use their land as a source of revenue. In 1737, for instance, a notarial record refers to the sale of land owned by Jean Francois Becquet and his wife, Marianne Fafart, to Hubert Finet. This piece of land had originally been purchased from "Joachim the Indian" and lay "in the prairie of said Metchigamia Indians." The entry endeavors to clarify the terms of the sale and refers also to earlier transactions in which Mechigamea sold land. "As long as the Indians do not take it back by some caprice," the record reads. In 1741 mention is made of land acquired from "one Chikagou Chief of the Indians," land situated in the low part of the Mechigamea Prairie.[31]

Four years later another record presents a petition by some Chartres villagers to acquire four arpents of land through a concession rather than a sale. An Indian "with pretension to be the heir" claimed ownership of the land. The Indian is fully identified in the record as Etienne Miaching8ia, "son of Joachim, formerly a chief of the Moinguenas [an early, small, and quickly absorbed Illinois tribe]." One revealing point about this petition is the reason stated by the commissioners for granting the land to the French and not permitting Miaching8ia to sell it: the land had been abandoned for a number of years. Four arpents of untilled and abandoned land sitting next to their own farms may have grated on French landowners. They continued to acquire very small pieces of the Mechigamea Prairie. In 1746 Chief Chikagou again sold land, this time a parcel "measuring 220 paces" in the Mechigamea Prairie. For these 220 paces, he received two hundred livres. While French landowners were neatening out the corners of their grants by edging into the Mechigamea common fields, it is also true that the Mechigamea were using this land as a commodity to raise cash.[32]

The loss of agricultural land may not have seemed a problem to them, given their declining numbers. The estimated population for their village fell from 1,000 in 1723 to only 295 in 1752. For this decline, historians have proposed factors of disease, alcohol, nutritional changes, subsistence shifts, and especially in the case of the Illinois Indians and the French, the recruitment of warriors for European wars. (To this list for the Mechigamea must be added a decimating attack on their village by the Fox, Sauk, and Sioux in 1752). Concrete factors such as subsistence and food resource changes and natural environment degradation become part of more abstract and complex variables; causal relationships likely existed among all kinds of change encountered by Indians across the eighteenth century. The much lower numbers of the Mechigamea—and their willingness to sell their land—can be understood also in terms of acreage productivity. According to studies of maize farming by the Iroquois and Eastern Woodland Indians, an acre of corn could likely support one to five people. An early English observer and explorer, Martin Pring, noted that each Indian family worked about an acre of ground. The American Public Lands survey states that the Mechigamea grant eventually spanned 50 arpents, an amount of land that would just about support an Indian village population of three hundred (an arpent is equal to approximately 0.84 English acre). As a broad generalization, the declining numbers of Mechigamea may have also paralleled the erosion of their land, despite the statement in *American State Papers*,

Public Lands that the grant was never "conceded away." It was, however, sold away. Yet the Mechigamea were not affected in a vacuum. On the eve of the Seven Years War in Illinois and on through the 1760s, both these Indians and the French villages in the Chartres area were losing people.[33]

By the 1750s, records are describing the selling (and abandonment) of entire French farmsteads in the village of St. Philippe. Located north of the Mechigamea village and the fort, St. Philippe suffered from marshy earth and periodic inundation. Records detail the washing away of farmsteads there by the Mississippi. Property descriptions of sold and abandoned farms consistently refer to land owned "in the prairie of the Mechigamea," making it clear that the Indians continued to own the land that lay between the Coulee Deneau and the river. Over the years, however, they had sold pieces of their land in the prairie to French farmers. A re-created map, the "Common Fields and Villages of Chartres," circa 1752, clearly shows the "Mitchegamia Village" lying northwest, across the Coulee Deneau. This village may or may not represent the new village the Indians constructed in 1752, after their original village was decimated in a Fox attack. The land to the northeast of the village is not labeled "the prairie of the Mechigamia." Yet bounded by the great river and a coulee, the "Indian prairie" continued to support Mechigamea, French farmers from St. Philippe, and, after 1752, some itinerant Peoria.[34]

The relationship of French and Indians to their land must be discerned through a close, investigative reading of notarial records, since there is little else to suggest patterns. All across their concessions in the bottomland, the French labeled natural land formations. Some are toponyms, referring to surnames, such as the Prairie Chassin or the Plains of Lafabut. Others seem to identify populations or even distinguishing trees: "the Butte of the Cherakee" or "Prairie L'Orme," Meadow of the Elm. Some mark historical events, as in Prairie L'Heurt, Meadow of the Clash. One inlet of the Mississippi is often called "the Rigolet." These French-language terms appear to mean different things in different places and times; "the Rigolet" also shows up in writing about Cahokia from the nineteenth century, identified by one amateur historian as a little stream known as Cahokia Creek. In the eighteenth-century Fort Chartres area, the Coulee Deneau and the Rigolet and the ash grove, early described in notarial records, perhaps functioned as a means of demarcation between the French and Indian villages. A grove of untouched ash trees suggests this. In fact, the ash grove near Fort Chartres is one of the spatial markers of the floodplain across most of the century.

This is somewhat of a mystery, since for both the French and the Mechigamea, firewood was becoming a premium by the 1750s. The correspondence of Commander Macarty at Fort Chartres makes reference to the lack of fuel and wood along the Kaskaskia River by 1752. Wood is noted as being hauled in for lumber and construction, and property inventories from as early as 1741 begin to assert that sellers of homes will be taking with them their boards, doorsills, windowsills, and fences. It is surprising, therefore, that the ash grove appears so consistently in the records across forty years: "the hill of the ash grove," "from the ash grove to the hills," or "the coulee of the ash grove." Both white and green ash are trees of the Illinois bottomlands. Ash is a fairly hard wood and burns with a Btu of 20 per cord; this number places it seventh out of sixteen on a list of practical fuel woods (shagbark hickory burns with the highest Btu—24.6—while basswood and aspen burn at only 12.6 and 12.5, respectively). Additionally, white ash is recorded as having a high ease of splitting, as opposed to oak, beech, or elm, for instance, which are very hard to split. To the north of the Illinois settlements, the Fox Indians used the bark of white ash, *Fraxinus americana*, in an infusion to relieve skin ailments such as sores and itching; such knowledge may have been available to Illinois Indians as well. These qualities of ash would have been attractive to both the French and Indians. Finally, green ash, *Fraxinus pennsylvanica*, has been identified by botanists as having tenacious and spreading root systems, forming groves that secure and maintain riverine banks against soil erosion. An interesting inference is that Illinois Indians recognized the role of the ash grove in flood control and had passed that knowledge on to the French.[35]

For the presence of the ash grove is distinctive in the records. The Mechigamea Prairie was sold off; the settlement of Chartres gradually filled in the lands around the fort; and its sister settlement, Prairie du Rocher, established by a nephew of De Boisbriant on a generous grant in 1720, also attracted many French. Yet the ash grove apparently was not cut down— or utilized to an extent that it could not reseed itself—by any of these peoples living in three French villages, a fort, and two Indian villages. The heavy-crowned, golden-leaved autumn trees of a mature ash grove would have made a striking natural boundary. Despite the arguments from the French historian Giraud that the Mechigamea Indians resented being isolated and separated in their riverine villages, the actual geography of the French settlements suggests that natural markers like groves and coulees (feeder streams) were comfortably used by both peoples. Perhaps the ash grove and the Coulee Deneau somewhat prevented the intermixing of roaming livestock from both villages. A winding path designated in the notarial records as "the path to the Mechy village" led northwest across the Coulee Deneau to the Mechigamea. There, along the riverbanks, these trading peoples moored many river craft. They also had likely imparted their knowledge of the Missouri-Arkansas lands across the Mississippi to the French. Their ties with the Quapaw, for instance, are particularly important because the Quapaw were a Siouxan-speaking tribe related to the Osage, Kansa, Omaha, and Ponca. Through the Mechigamea, knowledge of trans-Mississippi geography, trading options with other tribes, and possibly other Indian languages would have been available to the French attracted to the fur-and-provisioning trade. There is some evidence in the letters of Commander Macarty from Fort Chartres in 1752 that the Mechigamea maintained a particularly close connection with the Missouri Great Osage. It was to the Mechigamea that the Osage "gave much in horses and peltries." Macarty felt that the Illinois Indians (Mechigamea and Kaskaskia) tried to get the Osage "to come closer to the French." The population growth of the Chartres area, permanent and peripatetic, can be linked to the twin acceleration of agriculture and skin-and-meat trade. This in turn was due at least as much to the proximity of particular Indian tribes—prehistoric and historic—as to the presence of the fort.[36]

The decades between the setting up of the Mechigamea village and its destruction by a party of Fox, Sauk, and Sioux in 1752 saw exchange, barter, and trade networks between the French and the Mechigamea and the French and the trans-Mississippi Indians become enmeshed in the livelihoods—and lives—of both peoples. Although the Jesuits had abandoned their mission and chapel at the village in 1735, after the death of the resident priest, Father Guymonneau, the Mechigamea were ministered to by the priest at the fort. The contact with the French through the institutions of trade and religion affected native Indian crafts and shifted the emphasis. By 1750 none of the Illinois tribes was producing any pottery of their own, preferring to trade downriver with the Arkansas and Natchez Indians for ceramic vessels and with the French for blue-and-white patterned faience. Along the shores of the Mississippi, in a village established for over thirty years, Mechigamea Indians ate domestic dog on French faience plates. Their homes, lodges of cattail mats draped over willow frames, dotted a long, rambling shoreline clearing. While they farmed some maize fields in their northeastern prairie, keeping to rituals of March planting before the summer hunt, they also likely manufactured bear oil. On the path that wound over the coulee and through the ash grove, they passed daily to the village of Chartres and were often at the fort. A good many of them continued in the Catholic faith as "praying Indians." Mechigamea daughters lived with Frenchmen, in sanctioned marriages and in unmarried liaisons, and bore them children. Between 1726 and 1751, in the parish records of St. Anne in

TRADE MATRIX AT FORT CHARTRES

the village of Chartres, steady reference occurs to children born to Indian mothers and French fathers. The Mechigamea are sometimes named specifically: on September 26, 1747, for instance, the missionary priest Gagnon baptized a child born "of the lawful marriage of Hiasin Kepechinga and Elisabeth Nereton M8koe . . . of the mission of the Metchigamea." Other entries in 1751 and 1745 identify Frenchmen as widowers "of Dorothy, an Illinois woman," and "of the late Marie de Cheka8ita, an Illinois woman, inhabitant of this parish." These records use both the phrases "a natural child" and "an illegitimate child" to describe births to unmarried French, African, and Indian women. Often the father is listed as unknown.[37]

One of the distinctive patterns in French documents from the Chartres area is how often Indians are mentioned, how much a part of life on the floodplain they were: they appear in reference to trade interactions, land sales, visits to the fort, church sacraments, and casual wilderness encounters. They frequently came as messengers taking letters between priests, the Jesuits down in Kaskaskia, the Seminarians up in Cahokia; they also carried warnings, information, and requests to the fort from both priests and resident military in other villages. Their roles as emissaries and spokesmen for many tribes, including nations bound by kinship and alliances to the north and east, brought them to Fort Chartres almost daily by the late 1740s. We find them continually referenced in the French language of 250 years ago, these domiciled Indians of the Illinois: the *metchy*, the *peor*, the *cohos*, and the *cusquskia*. Coming and going, members of these individual tribes would have been distinctly known, traveling on the Chemin du Roi south to Kaskaskia or north to Cahokia. Given the small numbers of both the Mechigamea and the French villagers of Chartres, it is likely these people knew each other by face and name. Yet familiarity and daily interaction do not automatically translate into harmonies of adjustment and loyalty. By the early 1750s the trade matrix at Fort Chartres was severely threatened, pressured from the east through a Miami-British trade alliance and from the north by a resurgence of Fox-Sauk hostilities. French soldiers often deserted or traded rations for alcohol. Governor Vaudreuil in New Orleans cautioned the incoming Commander Macarty Mactigue that the garrison of the Illinois had frequent opportunities to "get into bad ways." The fall of 1751 and on through 1752 was an explosive year in the Illinois Country, and this interlude resulted in a shift in action and numbers of people to the prairie uplands.[38]

INTERLUDE

5

Prairie Invasions, 1751–52

From the vantage point of more than 250 years later, the 1751 Indian conspiracy to massacre French inhabitants along the Mississippi reads like
fiction: two children accosted on a footpath through the Prairie du Rocher
woods . . . Indians up on the bluffs ("the heights") leaving messages marked
on certain trees . . . a tomahawk "newly made and reddened" found along
the trail . . . an interpreter from Fort Chartres coming upon a bloody corpse
. . . the alarm tocsin beating through the night . . . parties of French militia
"taking to horse" and galloping down the Chemin du Roi after the criminals
. . . and the eventual, triumphant capture of the Piankeshaw Indian chief
Le Loup, a purported leader. French commander Macarty Mactigue, newly
arrived in the Illinois Country, detailed the outrage of the foiled Indian
conspiracy to Governor Vaudreuil in New Orleans, and Vaudreuil then
relayed it to Antoine-Louis Rouille, Comte de Jouy, French Minister of the
Marine. Their letters flew across the months between December 1751 and
June 1752. The distance of Vaudreuil and Jouy from the Illinois Country,
yet their grasp of the implications of the plot, highlight the intensity of the
Anglo-French hostilities out on the western prairies two years before the
outbreak of war in the Ohio Valley.[1]

The events of December 7, 1751, also underscore the importance of Illinois Indians in the rising territorial competition, a role often overlooked
by historical treatments focusing almost entirely on the Ohio Valley. Most
interpretations have not emphasized the Illinois Country in the years leading up to the Seven Years War; consistently low numbers of people and
a reputation as a far-flung or distant colony have consigned that rich and
interesting land a peripheral status. Because of this bias, historians have

often failed to examine patterns of local history as indicators of continental conflict. The impact of the year 1751–52 lies also in the way it introduced new patterns of human contact, a shift in action to the upland prairies. As part of this shift, varied splinter populations began to frequent the central prairies. How they affected the Illinois Country—its settlements, land, resources—has not been explored.

In general, the history of the Illinois Country has been told in strands, with historians concentrating on single populations. Primary accounts for much of this history include a reliance on the observations of passers-through. Many travelers toured through the Illinois, from Charlevoix and André Penicaut in 1721 to Bossu at midcentury; the British military, engineers, and merchants in the 1760s; and Victor Collot and Nicolas de Finiels in the 1790s; the records of Lewis and Clark begin in 1804. One clear pattern emerges from these accounts, repeated in popular histories: the French are frequently treated as a single population, the Illinois Indians remain the domiciled Indians of the French, and changes in the relations between the two peoples—as well as among other tribes in the Illinois Country—are glossed. Most ingrained are the American observations of the early nineteenth century, in which the French of the Illinois emerge as indolent and childlike people who danced away their cares and played cards on their shaded porches in the sultry summer months. Language describing French villagers often includes the words "merry" and "simple." As late as 1976 the illustrations in a special edition of the *Journal of the Illinois State Historical Society* include "Summer Evening in a French Village," a pencil sketch depicting heel-kicking French, metis, and a group of watching Indians encircling a seated fiddler.[2]

British and Americans alike were also contemptuous of French agricultural efforts. Carl J. Ekberg cites many instances of American disdain for French agriculture, in which the *habitant* farmers are labeled "nonprogressive," "stationary and retrograding," or "defective." In general, as the eighteenth century progressed, these characterizations of the French and of the "degraded" Illinois Indians become more pervasive in the literature. Long buried and ignored are the remarkable proposals of early French officials in the 1730s: French soldiers stationed in the Illinois should learn more about the Illinois Indians' farming practices in hopes that these soldiers would stay on in the area after their tour of duty. In contrast, studies of the French military, the colonial population who had been posted to the remote Illinois and were trying to advance their careers, stress the industriousness, labor, efforts, and service to the crown of these faithful officers. To weave all of these population strands together in a single narrative is daunting, yet it is critical to emphasize that a myriad of populations was meeting every day in the Illinois Country, especially in the vicinity of Fort Chartres, and that their interactions forged a potent—if shadowy—history. The complexity of human populations there began to increase at midcentury.[3]

How did the people actually living along the Mississippi—who had lived there for many generations—perceive and react to startling events? In a single year, two invasive attacks occurred, one on the French villagers and one on the Illinois Indians. The French commander Macarty spent six months unraveling a complicated Indian conspiracy. In that same year, French and Indian farmers faced a devastating drought. Despite the effect on French wheat, the French military was asked to oversee the first shipments of supplies and foodstuffs to other French forts, especially Detroit. This pattern—of military supply convoys leaving Fort Chartres to provision French forces to the east—would be the hallmark of Illinois French participation in the Seven Years War. Meanwhile, emigration from Canada was continuing: also in 1752 Commander Macarty received a petition from a Kaskaskia *habitant* who wished to settle his Canadian stepsons in the area but had not enough land left to apportion out. Finally, among the ordinary French people living around the fort, the buying and selling of property continued. People arrived and people left. The rhythms of an agrarian community strongly meshed with natural cycles of autumnal yield and fur harvesting can provide a counterpoint to the dramatic events that make their way into the histories. There is so little extant evidence of what the French—or Indian—people thought of the changes in their lives. An examination of a single year can illuminate the experience of many diverse peoples in the Illinois, a year in the ominous shadow of an approaching war.[4]

The conflicts of 1752 signify an escalation in intertribal friction. The analysis of these conflicts has been primarily political, yet by 1752 the Illinois Country was beginning to show evidence of fur and wood depletion, as well as thinning of game animals used for food. Histories detailing the 1752 Fox attack often use phrases like "traditional enmity" or "age-old hostility." There was certainly this; yet the presence of a British trade post in the Ohio-Wabash River Valley, an intrusion far into traditional French territory, was creating new opportunity for Indian-European trade. At the growing center of Pickawillany, British traders offered generous, high-quality goods; the post had drawn a large number of encamped Miami Indians and was acting as a stimulus on Ohio and Mississippi Valley Indians who previously may not have hunted aggressively in the fur trade. In 1750 Governor Hamilton of Pennsylvania had noted the movement of eastern Indians into the Wabash lands. He described "Numbers of the Six Nations" (the Iroquois

Confederacy) settling on branches of the Mississippi, observing that they were becoming very numerous. Calling them "these Refugees," Hamilton also described Shawnee, Delaware, Wyandot, and Twightwee (Miami) massing to form camps of as many as two thousand men. Another source also mentions Ottawa Indians. What game reserves were feeding these newly arrived peoples? Drawn by the trade opportunities at Pickawillany, the mixture of Ohio Valley tribes would likely have had to hunt not only across Indiana but on the Grand Prairie between the Wabash and the Mississippi. On the Wabash itself, the French trade posts of Fort Ouiatanon and Vincennes were also luring large numbers of encamped Indians. These two posts formed the Wabash-Maumee link in the French system of river transport. In the early 1740s there may have been as many as three thousand encamped Indians from three different tribes, Ouiatanon (Wea), Kickapoo, and Mascouten, living outside Fort Ouiatanon. As had often happened all across the French empire in North America, ratios of Indians to Europeans were greatly imbalanced: the number of resident French at the fort may have been no more than twenty-five. As eastern Indians like the Shawnee moved into the valley, competition for natural and trade resources escalated. By the early 1750s groups traveling "on the prairies" were often ambushed. For instance, a group of French deserters accompanied by some Illinois Indians and a few Shawnee were crossing from the Illinois settlements when they were attacked by a party of Ouiatanon; one Shawnee was killed. Two of the French and Illinois managed to return to the Mississippi settlements, but the rest were never heard from again. This open prairie corridor was also frequently used by mounted Kickapoo to raid south, across the Ohio River, into Chickasaw lands. They employed fast-moving, guerrilla-style ambush to harass and terrorize Chickasaw towns; and their presence north of the Ohio and east toward the Wabash was an effective deterrent to British infiltration from the south.[5]

There is also evidence that the lure of British trade goods reached across the prairies to the Illinois Country. About this time, Peoria Indians began to cross over the Mississippi to hunt in the Missouri lands, seeking better and more plentiful furs to trade. Some Illinois Indians, including the Kaskaskia and possibly the Peoria, had tried out the British market at Pickawillany. Parties of hunting Kaskaskia, for instance, were far out on the north-central Illinois prairies when they were approached by pro-British Miami Indians. Traditional analyses of Indians in the fur trade sometimes imply that Europeans simply tapped into ongoing patterns of hunting and trapping. In the Illinois Country in the 1750s, European markets engendered competitive hunting among tribes in a corridor of prairie and timbered river lands that was already thinning out. While Richard White attributes a "wave of murders and attacks" on French traders in these years to Indian frustration with French supply, the outbreak of violence may also have had another cause. Tribes, factions, and remnant hunting parties were all using the Illinois prairies; their chance meetings increased because of both hunting competition and the market polarity of Pickawillany and Fort Chartres.

Once that broad prairie corridor opened up to more and more Indian and European traffic, trails and routes were etched more firmly and camp locations grew into semipermanent meeting places, especially on inland rivers like the Illinois, the Kaskaskia, the Vermilion, and the Embarrass. Historians of the Kickapoo, for instance, have described a network of rutted prairie trails created by the use of laden travois dragged through the sea of grasses. Some of these ancient Indian trails eventually became routes used by Europeans. Crossing from the Illinois settlements, meandering through one upland prairie after another, the old Kaskaskia-Vincennes "road" cut through 150 miles of Indian and big bluestem grasses, switchgrass, and the heavy slough grass of wetter lands. A single rider could cross the upland prairies in five days on this trail. A well-used route also ran from Kaskaskia north through present-day Danville, Illinois, heading for old French Detroit. The uplands were laced with myriad Indian trails and paths long used for trade, hunting, and war. Paths could snake away over

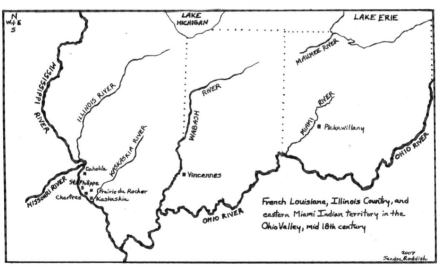

Map showing both the Illinois Country and the Ohio Valley. The British-Indian trading center of Pickawillany lay far to the east of Fort Chartres yet created trade and loyalty divisions among the nations of the rivers and the prairies. Map: Sandra Reddish; reprinted by permission from Louisiana History (2009).

oak savannas, carefully maintained by burning, and were known and used by specific tribes exclusively. Described as "well-beaten," these paths also typically ran along streams and creeks, where they sank away into swampy, weedy underbrush. At various points, especially on upland swells, these human paths were crossed and intersected by buffalo roads. Long-lasting impressions have been created by American settlers after the War of 1812; they described unbroken, grass-choked prairies—vast expanses of land that had in truth been emptied out of both buffalo and Indians who had long used them. Yet at mid-eighteenth century, these prairie uplands were becoming a stage for diverse Indian peoples, French and English traders, French military, and then British soldiers. Centuries of human use had etched many access points and approaches into old French Illinois. While the attack on Illinois Indians by a raiding party of northern tribes was carried out in a giant canoe flotilla descending the Mississippi, the infiltration of French settlements by eastern Indians came as a wave over the upland prairies. Down into the floodplain settlements slipped British-allied Indians, descending the great limestone bluffs on foot.[6]

Year of Intrigue

In mid-January of 1751, on the frozen ground of the floodplain, a group of Frenchmen stood looking at a property in need of considerable work. Described as "a house of posts stuck in the ground," with outbuildings "badly constructed," the little homestead crouched low to the earth. It had no upper story. While fenced almost clear around, this property in the village of Chartres appears to have had little appeal. It sold for just 200 livres, payable in a customary way with "bills, bonds, or flour." The owner was a billiard keeper in Kaskaskia, selling his small, indifferent house to a resident of St. Philippe du Grand Marais. A few months later, some Canadian heirs in the village of Chartres sold off an arpent of ground filled with marshes and ditches. While the French were selling and trading property, Illinois Indians were becoming increasingly anxious. As the winter progressed and the Mississippi lay plated with ice, a group of Peoria visited Fort Chartres with worries. They feared an attack by their northern enemies, the Fox and the Sioux. Some time before, the Illinois had carried out a successful raid against these tribes, killing seven important members of both enemies. The Sioux later stated to a group of voyageurs that they were out to avenge the death of their "great chiefs."[7]

From that time in early 1751 until almost the same time a year later, no property changed hands in the French villages; and the Indian villages lay in an uneasy peace. The summer passed without incident, a strange, unnerving time in which fort inhabitants heard escalating rumors of Fox raids from the north and anti-French activities to the east, among the Miami. The Cahokia and some Peoria moved south to live at the Mechigamea villages for protection. French farmers continued to tend their wheat and maize fields. In the fall the land slowly began to yield its natural fruit and nut bounty.

As equinoctial winds began to blow, the oaks most common on the floodplain, black and bur oak, rained down an immense acorn crop. In addition to natural nut and fruit crops that autumn in 1751, Indians and the French alike were harvesting squash and beans from their summer gardens; the French had planted and dried peas as well. The air held a slightly smoky quality from the smokehouses where hams were curing, from the village tanneries, and from the burning of the tallgrass prairies. On the bluff talus, as well as the edgy fringe of forest clinging to the uplands, white walnut (butternut) and black walnut formed groves of ragged yellow-green. Here and there among them, sassafras flashed crimson, and liquidambar (sweet gum) spread its wine-colored, star-shaped leaves. The autumn foliage of the bluff crown was not dramatic, yet the deciduous trees clinging intermittently among hill prairies slowly lost the virile green of deep summer. An amber pall set in, streaked by the dark green of cedars. And overhead, the southern migration of waterfowl was common: the skies rang with cries and calls of trumpeter swans, snow geese, Canada geese, and migrant grebes, as well as booming bitterns and many varieties of duck.

On December 8, 1751, the Jesuits would normally have been celebrating the Feast of the Immaculate Conception of Mary with a special Mass. Whether this Mass was actually held is not known, for the evening before, the French villages were attacked by a group of Miami Indians and a few Kaskaskia, acting under the orders of the pro-British chieftain, La Demoiselle. In a happenstance of ironic timing, the new French commander, Macarty, arrived to assume his command of the Illinois Country on December 8 as well. As his convoy reached Kaskaskia, he stepped out into a crowd of distraught townspeople, many from Prairie du Rocher. When Macarty debarked, he was fatigued; the rivers were low and had been difficult to ascend. As the boatmen and soldiers alternately hauled and rowed the heavy pirogues up the Mississippi toward the French settlements, Macarty certainly was not expecting to find the inhabitants in a high state of alarm, only one day past an attack in which a soldier lay scalped and Miami and Piankeshaw Indians, boarding in French homes, had planned to murder their hosts. Macarty no sooner set foot on the landing at Kaskaskia than he had to organize pursuit militia to fan out through the bottomlands. He sent a detachment of one hundred men, both regulars and militia, hoping to overtake wounded Indians. The day of the attack, two of Macarty's boats had landed in an advance guard. It is not clear from Macarty's account whether the soldiers in these boats participated in the initial exchange of fire with escaping Indians, but Macarty reports that in the fray, "five Indians were killed and four made prisoners, including Le Loup, chief of the Piankeshaw, another Indian from his village, and two domiciled Illinois." Despite the efforts of the mounted pursuit parties, these Indian prisoners would comprise the entirety of the captured conspirators. Le Loup, however, was no mean catch.[8]

Originally a Kickapoo who had become a chief of the Piankeshaw, Le Loup has been described as a French partisan. His record in the 1740s and 1750s reveals him to have been, like many of the Indian leaders of the Illinois Country, caught in the commercial and military rivalry between the French and the English, using the web of kinship and chiefdom allegiances to negotiate for the best outcome in unpredictable circumstances. Although his people lived along the Vermilion River in eastern Illinois—across the Grand Prairie—Le Loup was connected to the Illinois Indians living along the Mississippi. He was one of a group of alliance chiefs circulating around the arch-plotter in the conspiracy of December 7: La Demoiselle, also known as Memeskia or Old Briton.[9]

La Demoiselle's rise to power as a Miami chief (he was likely born a Piankeshaw) reflects the internal splintering and factionalism within the Miami tribe, a complex history involving the consistent mobility and relocation of tribes living in the Detroit area. Decisions to move tribal villages to more advantageous locations did not simply reflect a state of "dependent clientism," as argued by some historians of the 1980s. Reports in 1750, for instance, indicate an epidemic along the Wabash near Ouiatanon, where many Piankeshaw had died. They had set fire to their own village "to drive away the bad air" and blamed the French, saying it was the bad medicine of the French that had killed them. The turnover in French Canadian leadership between 1747 and 1755 was also a factor in Miami disaffection. As the English began to press into the backcountry of Pennsylvania and the Ohio Valley, winning tribal loyalties with rich trade goods and lavish presents, four French governors in succession attempted to implement a sterner policy than the old, familiar gifting-and-negotiating rituals best described by Richard White in *The Middle Ground*. The new policy has been characterized as one of "humilia[tion], subjection . . . and naked force." Perhaps the aspect of humiliation most rankled with the Miami. A visit to Quebec by the Piankeshaw tribe, led by L'Enfant, ended badly. L'Enfant had spread it everywhere that the French wanted to throw him into the sea at Quebec. This story, that "M. the general at Quebec" wished to have the Piankeshaw visitors thrown into the sea, crops up often in L'Enfant's narratives explaining why he rejected the French. Counterbalanced against gossipy personal tales such as these were eye-witness reports flowing in from the upper Ohio Valley describing the winding trains of heavily laden English packhorses—perhaps as many as forty or fifty horse loads of goods—reaching the upper Miami and Maumee rivers in the vicinity where the Ottawa, Potawatomi, Detroit tribes, and the Miami wintered. Although the frontier negotiator Conrad Weiser stated in 1754 that Pennsylvania traders had been "going to the Allegheny" for over thirty years, the flow of British trade goods seems to have increased in the late 1740s. One historian writing about the thirty years following the Treaty of Utrecht in 1713 has called the North American frontiers places of "aggressive instability." It's a succinct summation of a country of rapidly shifting alliances. L'Enfant, for instance, has been characterized with the nebulous phrase, "His loyalty [to the French] was vouched for at times."[10]

La Demoiselle, however, remained vociferously and steadily anti-French. His sending of conspiratorial wampum belts and mats to the Illinois Country to promote warfare against the French settlements drew on a kinship alliance with the Kaskaskia Indians. Their chief Rouensa was brother to La Mouche Noir, a leading pro–Miami alliance chief; the followers of La Mouche Noir lay among both the Wea and the Piankeshaw, Miami tribes. While early in the eighteenth century the Miami had sought the protection and trade advantages of the French at Detroit, by the late 1740s they had changed allegiance. As the territorial competition for the rich North American fur and trade hegemony mounted between France and Britain, leaders such as La Demoiselle, La Mouche Noir, and Le Loup watched. They rapidly learned to exploit factions and allegiances to secure their own power.[11]

During the foiled attack on the French at Kaskaskia and Prairie du Rocher on December 7, 1751, the Miami and Piankeshaw Indians slipped down to the floodplain settlements on foot from the top of the bluffs. The trees would have been stripped of leaves, making night vision clearer and footing surer. These Indians had crossed the upland prairies from the eastern Wabash settlements. In the course of interrogations carried out by Commander Macarty, Indian prisoners stated they had come to the French settlements specifically to acquire pirogues from the Kaskaskia Indians; they were preparing to sail south down the Mississippi against the Chickasaw. This seems to have been a ruse, the means by which a group of Indians arriving from the eastern Wabash valley—the home of the "revolted" Miami tribes—passed into the French towns and apparently succeeded in boarding with some of the inhabitants. Governor Vaudreuil wrote to the Comte de Jouy that the attacking Indians comprised thirty-three men from the village of the Piankeshaw and the Vermilion. In reviewing the plot, Vaudreuil also accused "all the tribes of the Wabash" except the Kickapoo and the Mascouten. He believed La Demoiselle was behind the attack, and more important, linked La Demoiselle to the Illinois Indians, writing that "the Illinois even appeared to be in on the plot."

Some of the Indians who had stayed with French inhabitants that night pilfered small items and clothing from their hosts, as the interpreter Dodie, called out to examine the body of a slain Indian, recognized items from his own home. After securing places to stay, Indians boarding with the French in select homes around the settlements were apparently to have risen up and killed the villagers; yet the fact that individual Indians felt compelled to steal confuses the picture somewhat. Le Loup's eventual explanation for what happened in the villages the night of December 7 was that "it is not you, my father, who slays me; it is my young men." The angry young men of the Piankeshaw and Miami tribes become characterized in the correspondence of Macarty as "the madmen among you." Le Loup himself espoused this heartily, claiming that he did not know who the madmen were. This explanation for the perfidy of some Miami remains a good part of the rationale for the conspiracy: younger, more volatile braves (such as L'Enfant) were recruited and inflamed by La Demoiselle's propaganda and threats, while older, steadier chiefs warned them against hurting the French.[12]

The involvement of some Illinois Indians in this plot has been indicated, but the overall tribal allegiance of the Kaskaskia, Mechigamea, Cahokia, and Peoria does not appear in question. During Macarty's investigation, which lasted over the winter months of 1752, the story came out that La Demoiselle's agents and minions had approached various Illinois tribes at their winter camps on the upland prairies and tried every method imaginable to detach them from the French. Such methods included direct threats. Macarty reports that Chareragoue, a Kaskaskia Indian, recounted to him the arrival of two Miami Indians in the Kaskaskia winter camp at Prairie de l'Orme (French designation for an upland prairie, Meadow of the Elm). These minions of La Demoiselle bore English blankets and a wampum belt, and messengers sketched a conspiracy led by the "great English chief preparing to attack the French." Pro-British Indians numbered a thousand men, they said, and if the Illinois did not join, "we will begin on you." Likely that phrase caused unease at the winter camp. However, representatives of the Kaskaskia and Cahokia swore to Commander Macarty that they had rejected the English blanket, that they had French hearts and French blood. Although admitting they had traded at Pickawillany the previous spring, they thought no more of the English. The Kaskaskia chief Thomas stated that "evil messages" merely passed by the Kaskaskia village. Other groups of the Illinois continued to appear at Fort Chartres, testifying to their loyalty. On January 12, twenty-one Peoria, all chiefs or children of chiefs, marched down from the Illinois River to swear their allegiance to the French, which they called "an ancient alliance."[13]

References to ties by blood and to old alliances were real: the Illinois Indians had been intermarrying with the French along the Mississippi since before 1700. As noted in chapter 2, when the Catholic Seminarian missionaries arrived at the Indian villages along the Illinois River in 1698, their first religious act was the baptism of a son born to a French soldier, La Violette, and an Indian woman, Catherine Ekipakinoua. Parish registers at Kaskaskia and Fort Chartres attest to both French-Indian marriages and baptisms; in the early years especially, 1720–30, Indian women are appearing as godparents. Thus the Illinois Indians were caught between two kinds of blood alliances: their daughters had married French soldiers and traders for over fifty years and had borne their children; but they themselves shared kinship and chieftain ties with the pro-English or "revolted" Miami across the Grand Prairie. In a letter of September 25, 1751, almost three months before the attack on the French settlements, La Jonquiere, governor-general of New France, wrote to Rouille about the activities of La Mouche Noir and La Demoiselle. He noted with unease that La Mouche Noir had two brothers who were Kaskaskia chiefs living near Fort Chartres. French leaders feared English infiltration and influence along the kinship network that bound tribes as diverse as the militant Kickapoo and the farming, pacific Kaskaskia.[14]

Through the early winter months of 1752 Macarty interrogated Le Loup. The fort was visited repeatedly by bands of Peoria and Kaskaskia who asked for the Piankeshaw's release, yet Le Loup remained in chains. Among the French, property continued to change hands. In January there arrived from New Orleans a French surgeon, Michel Gourdeau, who bought property in the town of Chartres from Joseph Buchet, Principal Scrivener of the Commissary Marine. Master Surgeon Gourdeau acquired a mature, choice property: "a house with . . . a yard, well, garden, fence and buildings and conveniences." Perhaps the new surgeon was planning to minister to the French troops. A few months later, in April, one Michel Lejeune sold a tract in St. Philippe. The property and its buildings stood next to the King's Road (Le Chemin du Roi), the ancient road winding across the floodplain from Kaskaskia, rising through Le Grand Passe to the bluffs, and continuing across the ridge prairies to Cahokia. As property continued to change hands, French farmers drove their oxen out to the common fields, hitched them to the two-wheeled plows (charrues) that later American settlers would call "bare-footed carts," and began to plow the black, winter-wet soil, still chilly as it was turned up to the sun. In May, as the rising sap in the great trees of the floodplain turned the prairies a bright yellow-green—especially noticeable in the venerable cottonwoods, green before any other trees—the Mechigamea and Cahokia began to sow their fields. They had agreed to farm communally that spring, having fears of Fox reprisal. Neither a year of anxious alertness nor communal farming saved them.[15]

On June 1, 1752, a party of four or five hundred northern Indians—Fox, Sauk, Sioux, Potawatomi, Winnebago, and Menominee—sailed down the Mississippi to the shores of the Mechigamea villages. As Le Loup spoke once again with Commander Macarty at Fort Chartres, denying any plot to kill the French, northern Indian raiders set fire to at least twelve Mechigamea cabins and then stormed the fields where Mechigamea, Cahokia, and some Peoria were working. They killed or injured seventy people—men, women, and children—and "scattered about the limbs of the dead." They may have taken captive as many as forty Illinois. On the recently sown fields, hilly with carefully planted corn, lay the severed arms, legs, and heads of the Illinois, rolling in the furrows. Perhaps Commander Macarty walked through the ash grove and north along the Mississippi to personally view the carnage, breathing the smoldering air of burning mat lodges and human flesh. The image of hacked-off limbs in Indian fields comes from him. The number of Illinois killed or taken prisoner was much larger than the number of French injured or Indians killed in the fray of the preceding fall, when the Miami had attacked the French villages. Yet no mounted French troops left in hot pursuit of the enemy; no call to arms was sounded. As the Cahokia "bewailed their relatives," the devastated Indians regrouped in a band north of the fort. They would construct a new village about a quarter mile from Fort Chartres, up on a ridge in the middle of an open meadow. The French government did eventually make efforts to arrange for the release of the Indian captives, who were scattered among the different tribes of the attacking alliance. Over the course of two years, nine captives were repatriated to the Illinois Country. However, at the time of the raid itself, French soldiers were outfitting themselves to march on La Demoiselle's trading town of Pickawillany. This effort, as well as the impending war with the British, overshadowed the tragedy of the Illinois Indians. That same June in 1752, French and allied Indians would burn Pickawillany to the ground. Soon after, Le Loup was released from irons.[16]

The only records of French village life during this turbulent year are notarial. From them we learn that in July of 1752, an orphan, Etienne Gouremont, came of age in the small village of St. Philippe. His guardian, Joseph Barron, agreed to let Etienne sell an inherited property, a house that had belonged to Etienne's father. The house, described as a half-timbered, frame structure on sills, sat on a concession stretching back to the Mississippi. It was going to ruin, since Etienne was living not in it but with the Barron family. Etienne received two payments for his property: one hundred francs to be paid in flour and one hundred livres to be paid on All Saints Day, 1753. He left Fort Chartres with his guardian after making the sale verbally, since neither of the two men knew how to write. They returned to St. Philippe along the Chemin du Roi. On its southern boundary, the village of St. Philippe abutted the prairie of the Mechigamea. Somewhere in those meadows in 1753, the Illinois Indians established the new village that would be known to archaeologists as the Waterman Site. Conspicuous from this site, among all excavated Mechigamea village sites, are iron knives, European ceramic and glass vessels—and gun parts and flints. Very few agricultural tools or tool parts have ever surfaced from Waterman, with the exception of a few iron hoes. In addition to suggesting a shift from agriculture to a hunting and trading economy, the Waterman Site may tell a story of increasing focus on protection and defense. When the British arrived in the Illinois Country twelve years later, they found but 650 warriors left in the entire Illinois Confederacy, with the highest number, 150, the Kaskaskia. There were but forty Mechigamea warriors, who, with their families, had crossed the Mississippi to Spanish Missouri, eventually returning to the Illinois. For the splintered Cahokia as well, the years after 1752 were ones of watching their backs.[17]

It had taken less than one hundred years. In 1679 the French explorer Tonti, writing in Paris, described a territory conquered by the Iroquois Indians. The "Irocois," he wrote, had taken possession of virtually all the land in the Great Lakes area, and had elsewhere "conquered the Miamihas and the Illinois, Chavanoues [Shawnee] three great Nations as far as the River Meschacebe." In less than a century, the "great nation" of the Illinois was already endangered. From this point on, their history is a narrative of survival. Equally important in the year of prairie invasions is the shift in action to an upland arena. The Seven Years War is usually described as beginning in 1754 in the Ohio Valley. Some historians, in fact, date the beginning of the violence to the attack on Pickawillany in June 1752. French troops marched south from Detroit and east from the Illinois Country, and the land they crossed would never again be perceived as simply the hunting lands of the Illinois Indians. After the long, bitter war itself, Pontiac's War in 1763 brought even more intrigue and contact among prairie and Great Lakes tribes; and in 1765 a company of the British Black Watch arrived to take possession of the Illinois Country. After those soldiers debarked at the deserted French village of Chartres, having sailed down the Ohio and up the Mississippi, old family oral accounts from French Prairie du Rocher preserve a striking image. British soldiers, wishing to convey that a large number of troops had arrived in the Illinois Country, set huge night bonfires on the edge of the bluffs, those often-burned till plain prairies used for lookout and the grazing of French black cattle. There the soldiers "danced," silhouetted in the smoky orange light, moving in circles to suggest hundreds of men holding aloft their bayonets. If true, it was a fitting symbol of transition, for within only a few years, the British would be building Fort Gage farther south on those bluffs; and the maintenance and defense of British Illinois would involve soldiers appearing on the upland prairies almost daily. If there had been a time of relative insularity and isolation for the Mississippi settlements—Kaskaskia, Prairie du Rocher, Chartres, St. Philippe, and Cahokia—it was over.[18]

PART TWO

Uplands Arena,
1750–78

6

A Ragged Resource War: British in the Illinois

To embed the British experience in the natural history of the Illinois Country, it is important to emphasize emptying processes that occurred across almost fifteen years. The Illinois lands did not emerge as war-ravaged but as war-emptied, and the British soldiers arriving there in 1765 faced a stripped environment. Such processes began early in the war, facilitated by the Mississippi-Ohio river route that enabled a steady stream of Illinois foodstuffs to leave the villages. The French were shipping grain, flour, and animal products up the Ohio River, supplying inland troops. In doing so, they were participating in the long, contested-border history of that river.

Except for the Civil War years, the Mississippi never functioned as a dividing waterway between deeply hostile nations. The Ohio, however, carved out a great north-south political geography much earlier. When the Seven Years War broke out in the Ohio Valley to the east, French began to navigate the Ohio to move troops and supplies, finding that another triad of big-river confluences set up both danger and opportunity. A long-used riverine corridor was created by the "forks of the Mississippi," the confluence of the Ohio near present-day Cairo, the mouth of the Wabash entering from the north, and approximately thirty-six miles east, the Tennessee River pouring in from the south. The long dip of the Tennessee, or Cherakee River as it was known at the time, a curving spoon shape to the south, sheltered clusters of Indian shoreline villages. Chickasaw and Cherokee settlements dotted the banks of the Little and Big Tennessee Rivers. Using water routes that linked into the Savannah and hence to Charles Town, these tribes had established a comfortable deerskin trade with the British. Contact between the earliest English to penetrate this region and southern mountain-river tribes had begun at about the same time as contact between the French and the Illinois Indians. In 1673 a few English explorers reached Cherokee villages on the Tennessee and were amazed to find them already in possession of firearms. Cherokee were using sixty flintlock muskets obtained through trade with Spanish Florida. Ancient ties are sturdy ties. The consistently British-allied tribes south of the Ohio used their intimacy with that watershed to harass the French by water. A romanticized description of this activity occurs in an early Tennessee history, in which the Cherokee are depicted as "sweeping down the Tennessee" in pirogues to "harry the Illinois country." The northern banks of the Ohio were in turn defended by the then French-allied Kickapoo and Mascouten. By the 1770s the Ohio River would enter the dark and bloody ground history of Kentucky, where Americans to the south and Delaware and Shawnee to the north of the river conducted guerrilla raids across the waters. The great, pacific Ohio, termed the Belle, or beautiful river, by the French, was truly a natural boundary between warring peoples long before it separated Union and Confederate states.[1]

Using the Ohio to ascend toward Fort Duquesne, tediously rowing or cordelling, French supply convoys sent out from Illinois had to pass the mouth of the Tennessee River. Cherokee warriors and some Chickasaw easily ambushed the slow-moving, laden bateaux, and French military became convinced that one day, the British themselves would be firing from the timbered banks of the "Cherakaee," using the Tennessee River system to reach the Illinois Country. In 1757, under the command of Captain Charles Philip Aubry, the French accordingly built Fort Massac, originally Fort Ascension, on a spit of land on the Illinois side, "just below the mouth of the Tennessee." The earliest history of this area states that the site was the old French Juchereau buffalo hide tannery, where once had stood a trading post, a "fortlet," and a mission. When the French built Fort Massac, construction was hasty and based on lumber to hand instead of the much more durable oak growing on the uplands. Soldiers split water-loving cottonwoods and willows to construct a typical small, bastioned fort. Predictably, within three years, Fort Massac was rotting.[2]

Despite French fears of a combined Anglo-Indian invasion up the Tennessee, none transpired, and French sacrifice from the Illinois Country involved a different commodity. Indians acting alone did attack the French at this strategic point, however. In autumn of 1757, a large band of Cherokees converged on Fort Massac; the Cherokee are recorded as being put "totally to flight" by the garrison and its artillery. Cherokee attacks on the French near Fort Massac occurred more frequently during the early years of the war and before the official outbreak, as Illinois grain convoys began supplying inland forts in 1753. A total of fifteen men and two officers died near Fort Massac between 1756 and 1758. These men were casualties of the great Seven Years War that engulfed most of North America above the Ohio River and which was fought out as well in Europe. However, the Fort Massac deaths represent the closest the Seven Years War actually came to the Illinois

Bowen and Gibson Map of North America, 1763, showing the Illinois Country and the rivers that dominated it during the Seven Years War: the Mississippi, Ohio, and the Cherokee (Tennessee).

Country. The war drained men and supplies out of the Illinois, whose rich grain crop was termed "a most important asset" for the French. It wasn't just the wheat itself; it was the quality of that wheat. The fertility of land in the Mississippi floodplain was nearly unsurpassed in the *world*. French farmers had built large stone bread ovens in their homestead yards to supply themselves with this formidably nutritious food source. That many French were using horse mills was documented as early as 1732, and although they also constructed water mills and windmills, the local, easily operated horse mill remained the most popular mill throughout the eighteenth century. Notarial records frequently specify a home with such a small, private mill to grind grain; and the daily industry of French villages had developed around wheat and bread. This was especially true of Kaskaskia, Prairie du Rocher, and Chartres. Now the grain that had once been stored for the use of French families, the rich flour that had become a form of legal tender in the buying and selling of property, and the fat skin bags filled with prized bear oil—this surplus began to leave the settlements on military supply boats. One historian who has studied Fort Massac before the fall of Fort Duquesne in 1758 concludes that the support of the Ohio Country during the war came to depend entirely on Illinois flour and other provisions. Other accounts identify French Detroit as a source of grain and foodstuffs supplying the French army in the interior. The military involvement of Fort Chartres occurred at the outset of the war, when a contingent of French Illinois soldiers ascended the Ohio to engage George Washington at Fort Necessity. The shipping of wheat from French Illinois floodplain farms became the principal war effort.[3]

Little is known of the Illinois Indians during the war years. Some "Indian intelligence" enclosed in a letter from William Johnson to Jeffrey Amherst, February 12, 1761, described French efforts to influence the Illinois tribes. The Indians were being pressured to go to war with the (recently disaffected) Cherokee against the British; such efforts were unsuccessful. In 1763 Captain Aubry wrote "An Account of the Illinois Country," a document intended for the incoming British officer Arthur Loftus. Aubry's account mentions the subtribes of the Illinois, especially the Kaskaskia, whom he characterized as "100 Warriors, but they are Idle and very drunken." Aubry felt there might be only 100 French inhabitants left near Fort Chartres, as well as the "Indians which are called Metchis," numbering about forty warriors. Given the amount of foodstuffs shipped out of the Illinois Country during the war, it is likely that at least some of the Illinois were involved in the supply effort. Explicit mention of fats as an item sent east on the convoys suggests bear oil or buffalo tallow; as many as fifteen bateaux carried flour, "biscuit, maize, fats and bacon, tobacco, salt, and lead." Supply shipments stopped after the fall of Fort Duquesne in 1758; and after the surrender of the French at Montreal in 1760, people began trickling out of the Illinois. Both French and Indians were leaving for the Missouri lands across the river. It is possible to infer a collapse of the old provisioning trade, wherein the bounty of French agricultural efforts was exchanged for wild game products. Changes in the environment, exacerbated by the war, played a role in political shifts in the Illinois Country across the next decades. These changes were well under way by the time the land passed to British rule.[4]

"It seems to be a crazy tottering situation at present . . ."

While important histories of the British in Illinois have all stressed this attrition of peoples, there is little analysis of environmental factors affecting the British experience. The floodplain of Fort Chartres, as well as the upland prairies, was in a depleted state in the fall of 1765 when British troops finally arrived. In 1750, well before the start of the war, Father Vivier at Kaskaskia had pointed out that it was "usually necessary to go one or two leagues to find deer, and seven-eight to find oxen [buffalo]." Fifteen years later, the emptying out of the Illinois Country was proceeding apace with both fur-bearing animal and human numbers significantly lower. The gold of the Illinois—its wheat and maize harvests—depended on human labor. In 1763 the French government had expelled the Jesuits from its colonies, a reflection of the European hostility toward that order. The leaving of the Jesuits from the Kaskaskia mission dissolved a mature, productive agricultural base including forges, wind and horse mills, wine presses, orchards, and a considerable contingent of slaves. Prior to this date, the French military had continued to demand the wheat harvest, packing milled flour in barrels for the long spring journey up the Ohio. At the same time, supply convoys from New Orleans had stopped during the war. The result was a string of decaying settlements in which a previously vigorous, integrated foodstuff production system had ground to a halt. This was the riverine world to which British soldiers finally came in 1765 to occupy newly ceded lands. Their ten-year stay in the Illinois was impacted by a matrix of factors: a severe shortage of food, depopulation of both French and Indians, the flooding of the Mississippi and subsequent waves of illness, deforestation and wood scarcity, and the effect of buffalo migration and, later, the intense competition for buffalo meat by French and British hunters. These factors must be accorded a prime role in the experience of the common British foot soldier at Fort Chartres, most of whom arrived with preconceived ideas.

The enthusiastic endorsement in many travel and military accounts of the Illinois Country, some of which at least was hyperbolic, may have created an unrealistic sense of the place in British minds. British preparing to occupy Illinois may have conflated Edenic landscape with opportunity and the pastoral signature of French Illinois with plenitude. The perception of the Illinois as a fertile breadbasket was circulating in New Orleans for years before the British occupation there. Although by the early 1760s the Illinois was so depleted of manpower that it was sustaining only itself, the perception of abundance up in the Illinois Country was deeply ingrained. Only official letters and dispatches remain to detail the British view of country they won, but in the taverns of New Orleans, along the great city levee already notorious for its "bad influences," British soldiers mingled with French inhabitants as well as French soldiers leaving the Illinois. The stories were circulating: rich country, black earth, vast herds of game, and murderous Indians. A study of British expectations running aground on Illinois reality starts with changes in the natural world the British would encounter in 1765.[5]

As tensions increased in the Illinois before the formal outbreak of war in 1756, and as the war itself changed patterns of movement between the Illinois and the Ohio Valley, the earth itself was also changing. Dynamic shifts in the course of the Mississippi River worked oppositionally to the drying out of some parts of the bottomland. Wheat and corn crops, plowing, harvesting, and the grazing of animals had reduced the luxuriant, often rotting vegetative cover of the land. The steaming, rank-smelling floodplain grasses had protected a shimmering, watery surface. Without this heavy green blanket, the earth could be seared by steady sun. In addition, the stripping of intermittent forested areas that had formed the patchy, mosaic quality so consistently described by observers had likely created both drying and erosion. Hints of these processes can be found in notarial land records.

In addition to the shifts in the course of the river and its effect on the village of Chartres, there is some evidence that French fields were beginning to show evidence of soil exhaustion. French farmers did not consistently enrich their land with manure, except through the process called *l'abandon*, the turning out of domestic animals onto harvested fields. Neither did French farmers practice crop rotation, even with well-known soil enhancers like clover. Repeated inundations at midcentury may also have contributed to changes in the soil. At least one British observer wrote in 1766 that the soil of the Illinois settlements was "not so good . . . owing perhaps to the Quantity of Sand mix't with it by the Mississippi." By the time the 1763 Treaty of Paris altered the political face of the Illinois Country, the natural economy had been eroding for at least ten years. In addition to the interruption of trade and consumer goods throughout the Seven Years War, the sixty miles of riverine French settlement had also experienced soil exhaustion, flooding, sickness, deforestation, declining Indian populations (directly affecting the provisioning trade), and changes in hunting, involving new and exploitive patterns. The eighteenth-century environment provides a record of these processes, reflecting to the incoming British a strange world of potential wealth in a depauperate land.[6]

A critical—and measurable—change in the French settlement area can again be traced to the action of water. In 1751 the owner of land in the parish of St. Anne's adjoining Fort Chartres petitioned to auction off one of his arpents. The Canadian heir to this property had discovered that "a piece of ground" was nearly "covered over" with marshes and ditches. He wanted to sell it to avoid the expense of continuously replacing rotting fences. Buried in notarial records, this entry presages the years to come before the British arrived in 1765, debarking from bateaux into a land being redefined by water. The last entry in the Chartres notarial records, June 29, 1765, describes the posting for auction, on the gates of the church after high Mass, of a property in the village. The house was "falling to ruins" down the banks of the river and would soon be washed away. Because of the general moisture level in the soils of the Chartres plains, wooden houses there lasted only twenty years. Close by, to the south, the settlement of Prairie du Rocher was built of lime and stone houses, perhaps a conscious choice of the inhabitants, who had moved their town to the sheltering base of the cliffs after a serious flood. The French had learned to replace their posts and palings, to use limestone from the cliffs, to move dwellings inland, yet they still contended with the Mississippi. One historian who has made comparative studies between original French grants in 1722 and 1734 and the American Public Lands surveys of the early nineteenth century concludes that spring river floods annually eroded the acreage of the original grants. By 1760, in fact, those French who had been granted land in 1722 or as late as 1734 "had lost more than half of it to the new river channel."[7]

Periodically, the Mississippi rampaged over the floodplain. In 1785, known as Annee des Grandes Eaux, or Year of the Great Waters, the entire bottomland stood under so much water that men rowed boats up and down the floating prairies. The Mississippi River reached a watermark twenty feet above any known flood level. There is some suggestion of a similar flood earlier, in the 1740s. Perhaps this flood initiated a change in the river's course; for the west wall of Fort Chartres, the impressive limestone walls built by the French engineer Saucier under the direction of Commander

Macarty in the early 1750s, was threatened and eventually undermined by the river while the British were in Illinois. In 1766 Captain Harry Gordon visited the fort with an assistant British engineer and wrote a considerable description of its incipient collapse. He also furnished specific suggestions on how to prevent the erosion, including "driving a Number of Button Wood short stakes in the Slope." He advocated the French creating makeshift levees from the great floating trees and other debris brought down by the river. Gordon had a low opinion of the French efforts to save the fort. He notes that they had "fascined and piled the banks, but the Torrent soon got Passage behind them." Buttonwood trees are sycamores, rarely mentioned in any of the accounts of trees growing in the French bottomlands. While water-loving and sprouting often in large numbers along streams, sycamores do not seem to have been preferred by the French. The British may have been introducing the idea of using sycamore seedlings in flood control.[8]

In addition to catastrophic flooding, the Mississippi River was channel-changing, moving inland at a rapid pace. In 1765 Captain Philip Pittman, arriving in the Illinois Country with Major Farmar, described the Mississippi as lying "next to the Fort . . . continuing falling in." A sandbank rising from the thickety shore shallows had become an "island of willows." Pittman made a distinction between the two villages of Prairie du Rocher and Chartres. Prairie du Rocher, he wrote, was a small village of twelve houses whose inhabitants were "very industrious," owning almost every kind of

Fort de Chartres on the Mississippi River under American rule. This early-twentieth-century sketch is based on a mural in the Illinois state capitol, 1885. Note the encroachment of the river toward the western wall.

stock. The village of Chartres near the fort, however, once prosperous with forty families, he found nearly abandoned. A few impoverished families were still living in the old village. As early as 1752, Commander Macarty at Chartres had written to Governor Vaudreuil in New Orleans about the need for inhabitants. "This country lacks strength," he observed. He noted that the French children did not take over farms from their fathers and that many farms were deserted. Perhaps the Mississippi was already beginning to erode concessions. Captain Gordon sent his plan to buttress the banks near the fort with "Button Wood stakes" to the British engineers, but he also despaired in his journal of organizing a work detail for the fort: "The Sickly State of the Troops did not allow of getting any Number to work during my stay, nor was the Water low enough or the Heats abated to make much work otherwise advisable."[9]

Fever and sickness along humid river bottoms, intensifying as temperatures and water levels rose farther south, comprise a familiar theme in settlement history on the eastern and southern coasts and in the major river valleys of the North American interior. Both malaria and yellow fever are vector-borne diseases spread through the bite of infected mosquitoes. Three species especially infest watery places in Illinois: *Aedes vexans*, *Anopheles quadrimaculus*, and *Culex pipiens*; the last is a dangerous carrier of St. Louis encephalitis, while Anopheles carries malaria. The life cycle of some species of floodplain mosquitoes reveals an adaptive dependence on intermittent flooding. *Aedes vexans* is a widespread pest mosquito, a floodplain insect laying its eggs on soil often subject to inundation. However, at the time of ovipositing, the soil must not be waterlogged. The eggs will hatch when inundated by flood waters, due to a particular bacterial action in the waters surrounding the raft of eggs. Such action can occur only at times of flood or very high water. On the upper Mississippi, serious flooding was much less common than in the lower river delta. There, both the French and the Spanish civil governments enacted rigorous laws requiring landowners to build and maintain a levee system to protect the riverine fields from annual floods. The first levees appeared near New Orleans in 1731. No such laws were required for the Illinois colony, although the Mississippi flooded severely at least once a decade.[10]

The references to fever and sickness in the American Bottom suggest that newly arrived men and women were contracting malaria and additional "malignant" fevers such as forms of encephalitis. But not everyone who arrived fell ill with fever. The intermittent quality of "sickening" across the American Bottom settlements suggests a possible connection with the life cycle of *Aedes vexans* or *Anopheles deluvialis*. These mosquitoes seek and prefer a specific riverine environment in which sporadic flooding over the previous high-water mark triggers egg hatching. Field entomologists have vividly described the bottomlands of the Mississippi in Illinois, most especially the mercurial quality in which the floating in of debris and upstream flood detritus creates sandy, decaying islands. Such a morass was observed in 1766 by Lieutenant Eddington, who described the woody banks of the Mississippi as "full of Cane, brambles, bulrushes, and underbrush so that it's very difficult to make one's way through them." Almost eighty years later in 1842, Charles Dickens, touring the American Bottom, described a similar environment, calling the atmosphere "deadly." He saw a thick bush on either side of the rough track he traveled on, and "everywhere was stagnant, slimy, rotten, filthy water." It is just such an environment that attracts female floodplain mosquitoes. Despite eye-witness accounts of saturation, the best evidence that the French and Indians along the Mississippi were not contending with *yearly* floods lies in the way they fenced their animals along the riverbanks. In interviews with early American settlers in the old French bottomlands, prior to 1813, for example, witnesses attested that "horses ran in large droves in the canebrakes along the Mississippi River." When Captain Stirling's party arrived at the mouth of the Kaskaskia River on October 10, 1765, Lt. Eddington recorded that they could see "the Horses and Cattle of the Village of Kuskusquias galloping about." Some were lying and rolling, "basking" on the sunny riverbanks. As in the days of the first and second Fort Chartres, the rivers, both the Mississippi and the Kaskaskia, were still providing one-half of a natural fence line, and animals were not considered at risk from constant flooding.[11]

The historical accounts of French Illinois contain a mixed record of elegiac endorsement of "healthful" climate and references to virulent fevers. As late as 1790 the first territorial governor of the old Northwest, Arthur St. Clair, wrote in a report on the Illinois Country to President Washington, "[T]he situation is high, the air pure and healthy, and the soil good." Yet sixteen years earlier, in 1774, the French Canadian trader Charles Gratiot wrote to his father that the Illinois Country was "[a] part of Louisiana, an extremely hot and feverish country." The intermittent nature of upriver flooding and subsequent anopheles hatchings help to explain these contradictions across the eighteenth century. The correlation between the high water advance of the Mississippi and the sickening of British soldiers after 1764 is suggestive. In the year 1766 many persons arriving to the floodplain were stricken with illness. Captain Harry Gordon's journal states that on September 8, he was seized with a fever of "unremitting violence" lasting for eight more days. George Croghan writing from Fort Chartres a few days later admitted, "I have been so ill this fortnight past that I have not been able to write." Along with problems of food supply, nutritional deficiency, and trade shifts caused by French and Indian populations crossing the river to the Spanish side, outbreaks of debilitating fevers were part of the British experience in Illinois.[12]

An irony in the timing of the British arrival concerns the polar forces of riverine destruction and economic development. Despite references in records and correspondence to inundation, erosion, and the washing away of farms, notarial descriptions also reveal a steady maturation of property. French farms that were abandoned, auctioned off in the 1750s and 1760s, or sold to members of the French military garrisoned at Chartres are extensively delineated and inventoried. These properties are replete with many wooden structures, including pigeon coops, windmills, smokehouses, henhouses, barns, and horse mills. Crops and gardens are specified, including fruit trees and orchards. For instance, the Kaskaskia Manuscripts detail the sale of a large farm at St. Philippe in 1759. It contained a stone house, barn, stable, horse mill, water mill, and sawmill, as well as livestock and a slave. At Prairie du Rocher in 1760, there occurred a sale at public auction of a house that had an accompanying tannery. The property included a mill and "160 tanned hides of buckskin, bear and other hides." Property was changing hands across the decade before the French gave up their claim to Illinois. Small numbers of arpents—usually three or four—were being sold, auctioned, or abandoned, and on these arpents stood the structures of an interdependent trade world—horse and water mills, tanneries, and forges. At the same time, the references in notarial and commercial records to the presence of water are difficult to ignore. Watery earth no longer farmed or grazed would invite the return of some presettlement features. By the 1790s, when the French spy Victor Collot toured the bottomlands, he found evidence of a natural recovery process.[13]

That recovery process included many forms of rampant vegetation and woodlands reclaiming the prairies. South of Prairie du Rocher, between the village and Kaskaskia, lay broad, fertile southern meadows, called le Grande Prairie, repeatedly remarked on by the arriving British in the mid 1760s. The surgeon traveling with Captain Stirling's detachment of the Black Watch Regiment described the land on either side of the wagon road running between Kaskaskia and the fort in 1765. He saw "natural meadows without a single Tree in them, and fine long Grass . . . and little runs or brooks here and there intersecting them." Thirty years later those "natural meadows," once maintained for years through autumnal burning and, especially, the grazing of livestock, evinced a virile transformation. Collot noted luxuriant, twenty-one-foot-high grasses along Kaskaskia Road, adding the familiar detail of the man on horseback being obscured. At Fort Chartres, he saw foundational ruins lying half a mile from the long-deserted village of Chartres and the old town site covered over with wild herbs. Between the fort ruin and St. Philippe, seven miles to the north, he described a mosaic of abandoned properties "intersected with woods, with natural meadow, and some marshes." He perceived that St. Philippe itself was "unhealthy." Up at Cahokia, crossing the Meadow of the Bridge, Collot observed large ponds, some three or four miles long, filled with stagnant waters. He felt the deserted lands there bespoke an exodus to avoid fevers.[14]

Historians have usually interpreted the abandonment of the French settlements by 1765 as an exodus west across the river, fueled by fear of British rule. The inhabitants were certainly still leaving when the British arrived; Captain Thomas Stirling, the first commander to successfully reach the Illinois and oversee the changing of international flags at the fort, despaired of his ability to keep the French there. He wrote to Commander Thomas Gage in December 1765 about this problem. Many families had "gone away," he noted, "for fear of the English." They often used stealth in the night, driving off their cattle and crossing the river by moonlight. Most critical for the British, these French families took all their grain with them. An early history of Randolph County states that "most of the Metis population [half-breed]" crossed to Missouri with the Mechigamea in 1765. Yet the consistent sales and auctioning of property in the French settlements during the 1750s suggest that other forces may have been at play besides political fears; many peoples in the 1760s were facing resource exhaustion. The British officer who succeeded Stirling at Fort Chartres, Lieutenant Alexander Fraser, wrote to General Haldimand in May of 1766 that he was having trouble determining the number of French inhabitants at the Illinois, "as they are going & coming Constantly." He described the French as moving between Indian nations as well as up and down the Mississippi, to New Orleans and back. To the British, the Illinois was a world in flux.[15]

In particular, two sets of conflicting information form strong themes during the British occupancy of Illinois. While incoming British accounts are uniformly glowing and admiring of the fertility of the Illinois Country— its beauty, the animal, bird, and fish plenitude—the records, letters, and the behavior of British soldiers suggest that they were hungry, remaining outside the provisioning trade. A second discrepant theme is connected to British perceptions of the Illinois Indians. Fears of Indian unrest, of plots, hostility, of the French stirring up the Indians to attack Fort Chartres are rife in the initial British accounts. But where exactly were the Indians? The

Mechigamea and the Peoria had left the Chartres area in 1765, following many of the French across the river to Spanish Louisiana. The numbers of remaining Illinois, either at Kaskaskia or up at Cahokia, were very small. In 1763 Captain Charles Aubry, reflecting on his sojourn in the Illinois in 1757, wrote that at Kaskaskia, there were one hundred warriors; near Fort Chartres were about fifty Mechigamea; and north, up at Cahokia, were "sixty fighting men." Despite these low numbers, British feared the Illinois kinship and networking systems, especially with tribes to the north and east. Their recent experiences in the Seven Years War and, especially, Pontiac's War in 1763 predisposed them to great wariness, although they also perceived impoverishment and degradation of the Indians. That impoverishment, consistently blamed on alcohol (French rum and brandy), economic dependency, and radical shifts in the number and variety of subsistence activities, is also linked to the decay of the Chartres trade matrix. Philip Pittman perceived that trade was still thriving in the Illinois, despite the cessation of the wheat convoys. Yet the trade he mentions is specifically peltry and fur exchange, "got in traffic from the Indians." He does not mention the provision trade. The importance of foodstuff exchange in a frontier environment cannot be overestimated. The French commander over at Vincennes alluded to the consequences of disappearing Indians in 1752. He wrote that he was "disquieted" over the missing Indians at the post and felt inhabitants were leaving the area, "as they can only live by trade with the Indians." By December of 1765, Lieutenant Fraser was writing to General Gage from Fort Chartres that the Indians living near the fort had also left, crossing to the Spanish side of the Mississippi. The disintegration of the Chartres trade matrix during the 1750s and 1760s may well have contributed to the French exodus.[16]

"I am now in great distress for Want of Provisions"

The first five years of British experience in the Illinois were marked by hunger, illness, privation, and fricative encounters with disparate groups of Indians. In August 1765, the British made the first successful attempt to occupy and command the Illinois Country. Almost two years earlier, in November 1763, General Thomas Gage had succeeded Jeffrey Amherst as commander in chief of the British Army in America. Gage was convinced that occupying the western posts early was critical to British control. He believed such occupations would "interrupt" or "cut off" communications between French and Indians in the wilderness. A close study of Gage's letters over the course of the next few years reveals an exasperated education as he came to realize the extent and depth of those French-Indian communications. Prior to the commissioning of Captain Thomas Stirling and his Black Watch Regiment company, the British had sent Major Arthur Loftus up from New Orleans, the Indian agent George Croghan down the Ohio, and Lieutenant Fraser also out to Fort Chartres. All three attempts failed, specifically due to Indian conflict. Major Loftus's expedition was attacked 240 miles above New Orleans on the Mississippi by "hostile Indians." The first descriptions of those Indians identify them as Quapaw and Tunica, but later, in Loftus's exculpatory letters to Gage, he details the tribes as Ofogoula, Choctaw, Avoyelles, and Tunica, all strongly French-allied. In a deposition, Indian chiefs of these tribes blamed the British for a smallpox epidemic brought into New Orleans: "They have caused nearly all our children to die." In contrast, Indians called the French "our brothers" and felt they had never brought disease. When Major Loftus tried to explain that the British were not going to claim and settle the Illinois land but only to advantage Indian tribes by setting up trading posts, the Indian chiefs were not deceived. One asked, "Do the lands of the Illinois belong to them more than others?"[17]

Arthur Loftus did not attempt to re-ascend the Mississippi. When George Croghan optimistically set out for Fort Chartres, Kickapoo and Mascouten Indians captured him on the Ohio and came near to burning him at the stake; he managed to talk his way free, with the fortuitous (and ironic) intervention of Pontiac. Lieutenant Fraser reached Fort Chartres but stayed only two weeks, finding himself harassed and threatened by Illinois Indians in the area. When Captain Stirling was commissioned to try a fourth time, the British, older and wiser, sent him out on the rivers with a considerable detachment of men. Lieutenant Eddington's journal opens with a dramatic scene of embarkation: "Down the Ohio to the Country of the Illinoise moved the Detachment of the 42 Regt." The detachment included 112 British soldiers and 14 Indians—two interpreters and twelve Iroquois and Delaware warriors. Their charge was to "take possession of the Country of the Illinoese." For this venture, they packed in ten bateaux just three months provisions.[18]

The party arrived at Fort Chartres on October 9. Both the journals kept by Captain Thomas Stirling and Eddington record the number of animals shot at, killed for food and sport, or "dispatched" along the Ohio and the Mississippi. Often multiple numbers of animals are noted, such as Eddington's remark that while descending the Mississippi on the return trip, Chickasaw hunters saw no buffalo but killed as many as six large black bears. Stirling himself had a narrow escape with a black bear. ("He was a monstrous creature. I had him skinned. He measured above 6 feet long.") Other entries mention female bears with cubs, white-tailed deer, buffalo crossing rivers singly or in herds, and multitudes of birds. Some of Stirling's men were apparently encountering pelicans for the first time, for Eddington describes them, writing of "an innumerable quantity of large white fowls. We shot some of them." He precisely observed and recorded features of the birds, saying that upon picking one up, they identified it as a kind of pelican. "The plumage is entirely white, only the Tips of the Wings excepted, which are jett black." In nearly medical terms he describes the pouch as "a skinny, membranous substance." Stirling recounts that on first catching sight of the pelicans in the evening along the Ohio, many of his soldiers identified the massing of white birds in dusk light as a French regiment. "Our sharpsighted soldiers did not know what to make of them."[19]

Mistaking pelicans for French soldiers is an indication of the anticipatory mindset of these British soldiers: fresh from the Seven Years War, dispatched to a far-flung outpost wholly settled and commanded by French, British foot soldiers and artillery alike may have expected to find French troops arrayed in full uniform. The reality of life in French Illinois—the abandonment of farms, the cessation of grain convoys, the draining away of manpower and Indians over the course of the war, and the subsequent reduction in grain production—all played a role in depleting the settlements. As they embarked for the Illinois, the British did not focus on the material state of the colony but on its capacity for loyalty, on the tenor of the Indian temperament, and on the smoothness of the political-military transition. In their introduction to *The New Régime, 1765–1767*, Alvord and Carter note that "the large supply of provisions which the colony had produced in former years seems to have decreased; at any rate it fell short of the expectations of the officers." On the journey down the Ohio and up the Mississippi, the soldiers were prepared for French "resistance" and Indian ambush. Stirling devised meticulous plans for night watches and the formation of attack lines should the convoy be fired on while in midstream. His strategies bespeak a formal, Continental training, in which wading-ashore soldiers would form a file of men. "Then the Enemy to be vigorously pushed with bayonets."[20]

Such precautions were wise, given the failed history of British penetration into the newly ceded French lands and the "difficulties" encountered with various Indian nations all along the rivers. The possibility of violence is the consistent theme in British correspondence. Even though the attempts to reach Fort Chartres all involved conflict with different groups of Indians—as diverse as the lower Mississippi tribes like the Ofogoula and the Tunica or the Peoria up in Illinois—British writers often lumped Indians in broad categories geographically. Indians frequently emerge in correspondence as a single adversarial population to be watched, cajoled, bought off, and fought. General Gage wrote in 1765 that "our Differences with the Western Indians begin to subside very fast." A few weeks earlier, however, he names specific tribes and organizes them along a spectrum of hostility: "the Pouteatamies [Potawatomi] of St. Joseph, and a Tribe of Chippewas of Saguinam, appear the most forward and ready to commit Hostilities."[21]

These incoming British had no credible eyewitness information about land or people in the Illinois Country. In the absence of any real history detailing the near century of interaction between the French and Indians, the British usually interpreted Indian loyalty to the French as a result of either French machinations or of French cultural degradation. They did not often credit the ancient alliances between the French and the Indians, concretely formalized in ritual and artifact. Without focusing on early French sovereignty, General Gage brought himself to acknowledge the superiority of French trade as a product of years of interaction: "of all the Systems of Indian Commerce which have ever come within my Knowledge, I have found none equal to that adopted by the French; which a long Experience proved to be a good one."[22]

In some cases, that "long Experience" was based on specific agreements with western tribes. In 1760–61, as his regiment retreated south to the Illinois Country after the British had taken Fort Detroit, the French commander Captain La Chapelle was shown a skin inscribed with the signature of La Salle. It was a hard, frozen December as La Chapelle's militia unit made its weary way "with shoes and uniforms in a very bad state" past St. Joseph and down the Illinois River. Unexpectedly, they were aided by Indians of the region (likely the Peoria). The Indian chief brought out a skin roll still bearing La Salle's seal of wax, although the imprint had worn off. The words were yet legible in French: "We, Cavalier de Salle, representing his Majesty, the King of France, declare in his name a fair and perpetual alliance with the Nation of the Illinois." La Salle had visited the Peoria on the Illinois about 1689. On the strength of this seventy-year-old skin document, the Indians of the Illinois furnished the French snowshoes, sledges, ten dogs, and fifty Indian guides to see them to Fort Chartres. Yet British letter writers and diarists during the British occupation of Illinois speak almost uniformly of French wiles, of present-day intrigues in which Indians were "influenced." Lieutenant Eddington, for instance, writes as if it were a certainty that the French in New Orleans were "spirit[ing] up the Savages against us" out of fear that when the British took over Fort Chartres, they would "in time beat them out of the Indian Trade." The invisible, seditious, and mysterious ways of the French out in the wilderness, mingling with

Indians in their villages, speaking their languages, calling on a long shared trade history—such ways seemed a ubiquitous and formidable threat. In 1767 William Johnson wrote to General Gage about an incident in West Florida: "The French were doubtless at the bottom of the Affair in West Florida, as they are of all other disturbances on the Continent."[23]

Despite these concerns, in none of the letters exchanged among British officials prior to Stirling's expedition is there a mention of potential problems of supply, of the decay of the provisioning trade, or of food shortages. It is a striking omission in the flurry of letters. The immense distance of the French settlements from the supply warehouses in Philadelphia—the firm of Baynton, Wharton, and Morgan—is mentioned obliquely, almost as a curiosity. In 1770 General Haldimand wrote to General Gage, "What a strange Project is this of settling a new country by passing over such a number of leagues of land, as yet uncultivated, from the present inhabited frontier to the Mississippi!" Exactly how the incoming British soldiers viewed the French settlements in 1763 is an interesting question. At least one scholar believes the soldiers expected to find an empty country with a few "tenuous hamlets clinging precariously to the edge of known civilization." Had this been the case, it is likely Stirling's expedition might have taken more provisions. They carried but a three months' supply of pork, beef, and flour. There is also the general British view of the French in North America, both the French Canadians and the Illinoisans. In many ways, British administering the vast northwest interior came to conflate perceptions of the wilderness with its occupants. British officials learned to "despise and distrust" the many French Canadians at Detroit, Vincennes, Fort Chartres, Michilimackinac, and Green Bay. British correspondence is full of characterizations of the interior French; they are lazy, licentious, "Indianized," and "vagabond." General Gage emerges as one of the most passionate attackers. According to Gage, out in the wilderness the French "lived a lazy kind of Indian life . . . almost as wild as the Savages themselves." He felt the French were "as near as wild as the Country they go in, or the People they deal with, and by far more vicious and wicked." The Indian trader and sometimes agent George Croghan expressed contempt for the French living at Detroit especially, writing in his journal that they were a "lazy idle people, depending chiefly on the savages for subsistence." He believed the Detroit French had completely adopted Indian customs. Given these prejudices, particularly about the level of French industry and agriculture, it is puzzling why the British attempting to occupy French Illinois did not advance upon the rivers realistically prepared to exist in a far-distant country without a strong supply system.[24]

Yet food was certainly on the minds of the men in Stirling's expedition. On the way down the Ohio and up the Mississippi, Stirling and Eddington both discuss the plenitude—or absence—of game. While Eddington uses the phrase "abounds with" consistently to describe a wide variety of game, fish, and birds, conspicuous among both accounts is the focus on buffalo. In early September, twenty-six days from Pittsburgh on the Ohio River, Stirling notes how "shy" the buffalo were on the shores and how Indian hunters' attempts to find them was causing some delay. He speculates that the buffalo had become shy due to the "Shawnese "[Shawnee Indians] "continually hunting them thereabouts." On October 1, having entered the mouth of the Mississippi, he complains again about the elusiveness of buffalo. "We saw a great many Buffaloe Tracks. However, as the French are continually hunting from the Mouth of the Ohio upwards, they are very shy." Attempts to explain buffalo scarcity involved pointing a finger at Indian and French hunters. British observers did not evidently think in terms of buffalo migrations.[25]

Buffalo Tales

Interviews with late-eighteenth-century and early-nineteenth-century pioneers of Illinois, Anglo-Americans who settled the upcountry above the French prior to 1813, reveal a specific buffalo migration pattern. "On account of the green-headed flies," wrote one observer, buffalo would leave the Wabash Country to range west and north of the Illinois River during the hot summer months. The migration of Illinois buffalo, *Bison bison*, seems to have been a result of many factors, including heat, insects, calving, movement to escape snow, movement toward better forage, and proximity to water. As early as 1680, Louis Hennepin was describing the movement of "wild cattle or bulls," saying that they "change country according to the seasons." Hennepin may have been implying that migration functioned as an adaptive insurance against extirpation by humans. The movement of buffalo helps to explain contradictions in historical accounts: some observers claim that for miles, the westward prairie was frequently "blackened." Marquette and Joliet used precise numbers to describe early bison herds in 1673: four hundred to five hundred animals. However, another French missionary, Sebastien Rasle (Rale), wrote of bison along the Illinois River in 1690 as being of "countless numbers." He estimated four thousand to five thousand animals on the prairies, as far as the eye could reach. Estimates are often contradictory. Careful accounts of Illinois bison pinpoint small, enumerated herds. Other descriptions refer to herds darkening the land until the earth looked like "one black robe." Such vivid, blanketing images have much greater resonance in the buffalo biology and culture of the nineteenth-century Great Plains. There, the trans-Mississippi West herds multiplied to extraordinary numbers. One nineteenth-century biologist studying buffalo concluded that while the numbers of Illinois animals may have seemed considerable to people living east of the Mississippi, in reality Illinois prairie buffalo were "mere stragglers from the innumerable mass" out on the western Great Plains.[26]

From the early decades of French settlement, buffalo were more plentiful north of the Mississippi bottomlands. They are described as being commonly seen near the Illinois River while very scarce along the lower Mississippi River. Some historians credit this disparity to French hunting of buffalo. Although Father Vivier in the 1750s wrote that bison "abound everywhere," and although Lieutenant Alexander Fraser in 1766 also observed "vast Numbers of Buffaloe," by the late 1760s, there was a noted scarcity of animals along the Mississippi River in southern Illinois. By the time of the British occupation, the location of the "vast" buffalo herds seems to have shifted. Ecstatic observers were describing, in the area of the Wabash River across the Grand Prairie, "vast numbers of Buffaloe & Deer And every other species of Game common in that country." Lieutenant Fraser wrote of "extraordinary large and frequent herds" near the confluence of the Ohio and the Wabash. Comparative perceptions are important in accounting for observers' beliefs that the herds were indeed "vast." Almost all European accounts, as well as Anglo-Americans' from the Illinois Country, use the language of enormity and inexhaustible abundance to describe wildlife. Their prior experiences should be taken into account. For instance, Father Sebastien Rasle, who described buffalo herds of "four and five thousand" along the Illinois River, was also ministering to the Abenaki Indians in the northern New England area, in what is now Maine. In a 1723 letter to his brother, Rasle describes a northern land stripped of game, without any elk or deer left, and bear and beaver "very scarce." It is in this same letter that he recalls the buffalo herds he saw in 1690 along the Illinois. After the environment of northern New England, beginning to be scoured of game and fur-bearing mammals through at least seventy years of French and Indian hunting, Father Rasle may have felt the Illinois Country to have been almost preternaturally abundant.[27]

Differing accounts of buffalo in Illinois reflect the likelihood that buffalo moved to different locations seasonally. Research on biting flies, Tabanidae, strongly supports this theory. Deerflies and horseflies, including some species of the "green headed flies" mentioned by early pioneers, inflict torment and genuine wounds on buffalo. Grazing herds whose tails move in switching unison often reveal palm-size patches of bloody, hairless flesh, to which Tabanidae are drawn not only for blood meals but to deposit larvae. In this sense Tabanidae may be understood not just as a pest but as a form of seasonal predator. Many species lay eggs right on the edges of trail vegetation, constructing a larval ambush. The flies have evolved particularly to prey on large herbivores; they are drawn to contrasts in color, especially large dark shapes against a lighter background of green, and to exhaled carbon dioxide. In 1816 the surveyor Henry Allyn, working along the Illinois River and east to the Grand Prairie, described an attack by a large greenfly on his horses. He compared these insects to the locusts of Egypt, calling them "voracious . . . their bite was severe." In less than a second after flies lit on an animal, "blood would fly, & run down their sides in streams." Allyn saw that after his party entered upon the prairie, waiting flies "rose from the grass . . . & formed a perfect cloud around our horses, which began to pitch, rear, & snort."[28]

In addition to the famous wallowing, in which buffalo coated themselves with mud to create a dried, protective earthen husk, buffalo in Illinois used migration. Tabanidae also commonly lay their eggs in watery places, often on the edges of streams, bogs, and marshes. The hatching flies tend to stay out of large open areas because of wind. Buffalo migrated to areas that were freer of bogs and marshes, standing water, and sloughs, and to places that were more open and windy. These prairies were often calving grounds. In addition, buffalo, as grazing herbivores, were strongly attracted to recently burned areas because of more tender and nutritious fresh growth. Now, as during the eighteenth century, buffalo most favor grama, buffalo, wheat, blue, bluejoint, June, dropseed, and windmill grasses, most of which are native to the Illinois tallgrass prairies. Much of the evidence for aboriginal burning of prairies in Illinois is taken from central and northern prairies. The clustering of buffalo herds in the northern half of the Illinois Country, especially between the Illinois and the Wabash, can thus be understood as a specific migratory response to avoid Tabanidae and perhaps find a greener, sweeter graze. The early-nineteenth-century observer James Hall wrote of the buffalo "tracts" or traces across the Grand Prairie of Illinois that the animals moved to higher ground to escape "prairie flies" in summer. In winter they sought the margins of large rivers where they could browse on giant cane, *Arundinaria gigantea*, an evergreen. Early accounts of Anglo-Americans settling along the Ohio and Mississippi Rivers stress that in winter, they turned their stock into the tangled stands of cane, often the only forage the animals had over the cold months. Some of this "cane" may actually have been stout scrubbing rush, *Equisetum hyemale*. In 1803

Lewis and Clark noted scrubbing rush while ascending the Mississippi above the Ohio, again using the phrase "abounds with" to describe the plenitude of this plant. Lewis noted that *Equisetum* grew much thicker, and to a much greater height, in the river bottoms. William Clark felt the rush was "agreeable food" for both cattle and horses. Buffalo would also browse on *Equisetum* and would move toward the rivers to find it. Yet migration is such a complex behavior that no single factor can account for it. Andrew Isenberg points out that on the western Great Plains, migration was both complex (a biological-reproductive behavior) and unpredictable; bison aggregation was highly fluid, with coalescing, relocating animals dotting an extensive landscape. Buffalo movement was also connected to migratory and hunting patterns of Indians who became nomadic in pursuit of herds. Judging from contradictory historical accounts in the Illinois Country, the migration of Illinois buffalo was as multifactored and erratic.[29]

The relevance of buffalo migratory patterns to the history of Illinois prairies in the 1760s lies in the British difficulties in procuring food; this in turn stems from the disintegration of the provisioning trade at Fort Chartres. British attempted to understand the scarcity of buffalo by accusing French hunters of profligate slaughter. In 1769 a British officer described the French as "destroy[ing] immense Number of Buffaloes." French hunting parties were ranging south toward the Kentucky lands, pursuing the herds who often sought the salt deposits in those areas. These hunting forays supplied the lucrative New Orleans buffalo market. British officials perceived that the French were hunting "as regularly as the Savages." Another officer at Fort Chartres wrote at the same time that fourteen Chickasaw Indians saved a British expedition by providing buffalo meat to soldiers who were at least five weeks short of provisions. The procuring and selling rhythms of the original trade matrix at the fort had been meshed into Indian summer and winter hunts and, in the case of black bear, into patterns of animal hibernation as well. The French and Indians alike used domestic animals to supplement seasonal hunts. The depletion of human beings from the French settlements, prior to and during the British occupation, reconfigured hunting to some extent. The lapsing of agriculture was also a piece of this reconfiguration. In 1768 Father Meurin, returning voluntarily to the Illinois after the Jesuit Order had been expelled, wrote that he was ministering to only twenty people at Prairie du Rocher and four men at St. Philippe. This was probably not enough of an agricultural workforce to put in a healthy wheat crop.[30]

The effect of uncertain meat supplies caused British officials to hire hunters who would travel long distances on horseback to locate buffalo herds. Eventually, British supply firms employed boatmen to use the river systems, but initially, they sent hunters fanning out over the uplands. The British used Indians and, occasionally, French inhabitants, but they also began to send out commissioned hunters from the fort's supply firm. In addition, French inhabitants found they could sell foodstuffs to the hungry soldiers at "very dear" prices. General Gage thought prices in the Illinois to be excessive. In 1767 he compared Illinois food prices with those in the Fort Pitt area: "It comes much heavier at the Illinois, at the rate you purchase it from the Inhabitants." British soldiers may have been procuring their own food as well. Latrine pit excavations dating from the British occupation of Fort Chartres (renamed Fort Cavendish) reveal large numbers of domestic animal bones, as well as red-eared turtle carapaces ("sliders"). The number of these turtle shells coinciding with the British at Fort Chartres suggests that soldiers were privately setting turtle traps in the river; it wouldn't have been difficult, since the Mississippi was washing up around the western wall. In the fall of 1768 a British letter-writer from Fort Chartres mentioned that these turtles commonly weighed thirty pounds and that soldiers found them nearly as good as sea turtles for making soup. This pattern of private turtle trapping likely developed as a result of a severe food shortage shortly after the British occupation. The second British officer to command at the fort, Major Farmar, wrote to Secretary of War Barrington in March of 1766, "I am now in great distress for Want of Provisions." Farmar felt he was in a critical position, that his command was threatened, as soldiers went often four days without anything but Indian corn and old bread. "The Country cannot afford sufficient Meat for daily Consumption of the Troops," he states.

This country that could not afford sufficient meat had been described only five months before by Lieutenant Eddington as "abound[ing] with incredible quantities of all kinds of Game. Particularly Buffalowes, Elks, Deer of various kinds, Bears, Oppossums, Raccoons, which are very common. . . . Turkies are everywhere." The months between the arrival of Stirling's expedition and the rather frantic letters of Major Farmar in the spring contain a history of British, French, and Indian interaction that suggests the Chartres trade matrix had dissolved. It also suggests that the British soldiers, perhaps those especially of Captain Stirling's Black Watch, were not trained as hunters. However, another factor must be accounted in this history of the British in the Illinois.[31]

The leaving of Illinois Indian tribes from the vicinity of the fort has not been credited historically in the difficulty of British experience at Fort Chartres. These Indians, most especially the Mechigamea, were middlemen in a fluid, evolved food procurement system. While food exchange also drew in French hunters, it depended on the very large meat hauls obtained by Indians on their winter and summer hunts. One factor enabling Indians to return to the Chartres area with heavy packs of smoked tenderloins, haunches, buffalo tongues, rendered fat, and hides was the presence of women on the hunts. Early observers of the Miami tribe, for instance, mention how critical the women were to the seasonal hunts, how they were able to pack exceptionally heavy loads of meat on their backs and to run with these loads for long distances. The Illinois Indian villages decamped en masse to the prairies for the hunts, and all individuals were employed in the production of the salted, smoked buffalo and other game. With the radical reduction in Indian village population—most tragically for the Mechigamea and Cahokia in 1752, when as many as ninety men, women, and children were killed in the Fox raid—the nature of seasonal hunts must have changed. Late in 1765 Major Farmar wrote to Gage suggesting that the "great Numbers" of Indians assembling at Fort Chartres in February, March, April, and May had been used to being supplied by the French "with double what we allow the Soldiers . . . and also Meat." Farmar stresses that the supply of "meat" going to Indians "entirely depends upon the Success the Hunters have in killing Buffalo, which is the Principal Maintenance of this Country." From this letter it seems clear that Indian groups living near the fort and perhaps at some distance from it were obtaining food supplies and were no longer the suppliers themselves.[32]

However, the hunts were still in evidence in 1768 among the Peoria to the north, for the Fort Chartres Commissary for the Philadelphia firm of Baynton, Wharton, and Morgan recorded that Black Dog, a chief of the Peoria, had appeared at the fort twice, in winter and spring. In winter Black Dog revealed that his people had just returned from an upland prairie winter hunt. In the spring he revealed that "a great part of his Nation" were soon leaving for the summer hunt to "provide Meat for their Old Men." There is no mention that the Peoria were routinely supplying Fort Chartres. Of additional interest here is the location of the summer hunt: on the Grand Prairie of north central Illinois, where the habitual migratory movement of buffalo left hard, rutted paths swerving down to ford streams, pushing up again through the rampant grasses on the other side. Here the buffalo had moved into the windier open lands, and here Algonquian tribes had been used to finding them, for at least one hundred years and likely much longer.

Illinois Indians may have continued to trade buffalo meat to the French, despite avoiding that trade with British soldiers. During the tenure of Colonel Reed at Fort Chartres in 1767, he fined a French woman in Kaskaskia

250 livres for trading a pint of rum to an Indian for a "piece of Meat." Some observers found the fine exorbitant, suggesting that the (perhaps clandestine) selling and trading of game to the French was common. Such incidents suggest that the French themselves may have been experiencing food shortages. In letters during these initial years, British observers often mention small groups of Illinois Indians arriving at the fort to trade and to receive presents, but the details of what they brought to trade are missing. Although Baynton, Wharton, and Morgan began to supply Fort Chartres by the end of 1766, the difficulty in procuring meat continued. French hunters were in competition with the hunters sent out by the firm. These French hunters (not all from the Illinois settlements) were sending salted and smoked buffalo tongues and tenderloins down to New Orleans, engaged in a high-profit convoy trade that offered them the same geographical market as their grain shipments earlier in the century. There is little evidence they were selling meat to the British at the fort. The British company hunters preferred to camp near the Ohio and the Wabash, while the French tended to hunt farther west and south into the Kentucky lands. The commissary George Morgan at the fort was responsible for organizing his firm's hunters. Morgan's letters refer to this part of his duties as "Our Buffalo Adventure."[33]

This adventure most seriously impacted buffalo in Illinois. On one highly successful hunt during the late summer and early fall of 1767, the company's hunters along the Ohio River killed nearly seven hundred buffalo. Morgan notes that at the same time, there were "twenty large Perriogues employed in the same Trade on the Ohio from New Orleans." Those pirogues contained French hunters. It is not hard to visualize the scene: British hunters skinning, butchering, and rendering the tallow from a massive buffalo kill spread out on the open prairies of the Ohio River banks, leaving the earth saturated with blood, carcasses, and entrails. Out on the Ohio, at least twenty large boats fully manned with French hunters rowed past like circling vultures. Overhead would have drifted real vultures, and hidden in the underbrush and timber margin additional consumers would have lain in wait: the carnivorous predators—especially the then-populous wolves—and carrion eaters of the natural world. Thickets trembled with patient ravens, while small mammals, many concealed in the earth itself, sniffed an air so redolent with fresh blood the smell would have carried for miles.[34]

While these birds and animals were rich benefactors of southern Illinois buffalo hunts in the late 1760s, one historian has described the British and French attack on southern-ranging bison (migrating south as winter approached) as a "virtual pincers movement." This hunting war hastened the extirpation of buffalo from Illinois. Such political competition, taking the form of animal slaughter, is rarely discussed for its impact on Illinois buffalo; rather, American hunters are credited or, just as often, writers speculate on the "unknown" causes of buffalo extirpation. The British, occupying the Illinois for only ten years, invested significant amounts of money in buffalo hunting. Over time, the firm of Baynton, Wharton, and Morgan invested "30,000 pounds in the enterprise [supplying the Illinois], employing over 300 boatmen." Yet the British still believed that the French were "thinning" the herds. George Morgan, writing to his employers Baynton and Wharton in 1767, complained about the great number of French hunters going after buffalo up the Ohio River; he wanted measures taken to stop them, fearing that "it will in a short Time be difficult to supply even Fort Chartres with Meat." To safeguard their scouting on the Ohio River through pro-British Cherokee territory, French hunters were even using a ruse of "wear[ing] English Colours." Of some significance is the date of this letter—written in winter, when buffalo herds would likely have been ranging to the south. French were following buffalo migration, and they had probably learned this from the Illinois Indians. Only a year later, another British observer journeying down the Ohio toward the Illinois Country described the presence of buffalo herds up to one hundred animals. He bragged that "we killed so many Buffalos that We commonly served out one a day to Each Company, & they Commonly Weigh'd from 4 to 600 lbs."[35]

The relentless competition between British and French hunters in the Ohio Valley and the Illinois Country brought more people out onto the upland prairies. And such hunting wars provided a counterpoint to another kind of interaction: the competition for Indian loyalty. George Croghan's boast in 1765 that "the Indians agree to our taking possession of the Illinois" was based on the agreement of two tribes only, the Kickapoo and the Mascouten, holding him prisoner near the Ohio River. And ironically, at the moment when the Illinois Country passed to the British, no Indian was witness. On the morning of October 10, 1765, the detachment of the Black Watch Regiment under Captain Stirling assembled formally to relieve the French officers at the gate of Fort Chartres. Lieutenant Eddington describes the French Guard as looking like "Invalids without any sort of uniform." He mentions jackets of different colours and "slouch'd Hats," and sneers at the condition of their weapons. There were twenty men under the French commander St. Ange, who insisted that the British should strike the French flag. St. Ange would never himself lower the "Pavilion Francais." In a private letter Lieutenant Eddingstone [Eddington] commented, "The French Troops we relieved here might be called anything but Soldiers, in Short I defy the best drol comick to represent them at Drury Lane." Eddington also had little praise for the fort itself. The buildings and barracks were very dirty, he wrote, and tall weeds grew all over the central square, some reaching the tops of the walls. The official inventory of Fort Chartres, conducted by Captain Stirling, lists many items "of bad quality," "bad," or "damaged." Through these brief impressions can be glimpsed an impoverished country whose material goods had been compromised by seven years of war and not replenished through trade, whose labor force could no longer care for the great limestone fort. The war had also emptied out Indian populations.[36]

In the accounts of the striking of the Fleur-de-Lys and the raising of the St. George, there is no mention of Indians. The ceremony took place in a brief, emotional exchange at the gates of the fort (Lt. Eddington describes the "great Chagrin" of the "Honest Old Veterans" assembled under St. Ange). Well outside the fort sat a structure listed by Captain Stirling in his inventory as a "Pent House for the use of Savages." The French version gives this structure as a "hangard." In this stone building had often slept Indian guests, as well as prisoners, since the completion of the fort in 1754. There seem to have been no Indian witnesses to the French and British flag exchange before the fort gates. Yet the implicit statement of the hangard, its mute witnessing of the shift of empire, and its presence outside the walls of the fort summon Indians nonetheless. Though they were ostensibly absent that October day, their influence on the French and British, as well as their evolving relations with incoming American settlers, strongly determined relations among disparate groups of people in the Illinois Country in the next decade.[37]

7

Predations and Survivals:
French, British, and Indian Illinois

In 1769, when the British and Illinois Indians alike were dismayed by Pontiac's murder, Thomas Hutchins wrote to George Morgan, "We are frequently alarm'd that our Enemies are every day Assembling to strike next and this Alarm is corroborated by the opinion of the Kaskaskia Chief and of our own Indians." Despite food shortages and a flux and flow of peoples, in just four years, Illinois Indians had won some estimation from occupying British. The Indians who had been the French domiciled tribes had become "our own Indians" under the British at Fort Chartres. Across the early 1770s relations among indigenous Indians, visiting and occasionally raiding tribes, old French families, Canadian traders, and British military and merchants can be glimpsed as authentic and human. The record is neither one of constant friction nor harmonious prosperity but a mixture. Especially by the early 1770s there were signs that some British living near Fort Chartres were finding life in the Illinois worth planning a future around. Brief mention in some accounts and letters concerning the Kaskaskia and Mechigamea "who are our friends" indicates that the pejorative dismissals of the Illinois Indians found in all initial British accounts were being tempered by proximity. Yet the ten years of British occupancy also saw increasing pressures on the old French settlements by dissatisfied tribes to the north and south. The impact of Pontiac's War lasted through the early 1770s, as anti-British tribes blamed the Illinois not only for learning to live in peaceful adjacency with the British but also for the murder of Pontiac in 1769. The years of British sojourn were filled with gossip, talk, and rumor about incipient events and upriver and downriver news.[1]

Yet it would be a mistake to analyze the unrest in the Illinois Country from only a political standpoint. Underlying the sporadic violence—the attacks on French and British traders, random raids on settlements—can be found a story of disintegrating livelihoods. While the overall argument of this study has emphasized the ecological shifts engendered through French-Indian interaction across eighty years, not all human privations can be laid at the door of environmental degradation. The erosion of ancient subsistence patterns, patterns that yielded dependable harvests through labor-intensive activity, is also part of the story. During the British years in the Illinois, the disruptive presence of the Potawatomi (and raids by the St. Joseph Potawatomi especially) became much more pronounced. While the focus of this study is on the old French and Illinois Indian tripartite environment, raids into this area by Indian nations from the north can be seen as both political and environmental competition. The increased flow of people throughout the Illinois Country reshaped the boundaries of this ecosystem. The Potawatomi approached most often on horse or foot, over the upland prairies.

These Indians had once lived in a broad loop extending from southern Wisconsin around the tip of Lake Michigan and on up into the Great Lakes Country. By the middle of the eighteenth century, many Potawatomi still lived along and were identified with the rivers of that region. A description of the Potawatomi bands who supported Pontiac mentions "the Potawatomies of the rivers Milwaukee, Chicago, St. Joseph, and Detroit." In that area, they were harvesters of wild rice. A curious lacuna in accounts of early Illinois—French, British, or American—is mention of this protein-rich, sustaining grain. British at Fort Chartres, in fact, ate rice shipped up from New Orleans, white, polished rice from the Carolinas or the bayou lowlands of Louisiana. Yet the wild rice of northern Illinois had once nourished bands who had learned to weave its seasonal harvest into their subsistence patterns. In studying environmental change in one area, it is often necessary to examine shifts in adjacent areas; effects on populations created big-picture changes in human relations.[2]

A Tale of Wild Rice

In his study of the Potawatomi, R. David Edmunds points out that Potawatomi women particularly harvested wild rice as part of their traditional food supply. Early anthropological studies of Great Lakes Indians mention two centers of rice harvesting activity, one along the southern shores of Lake Superior and one in the Fox River Valley. This area is in northern Illinois and today runs north-south across the Wisconsin state line. There,

Menominee, Potawatomi, Sauk and Fox, Mascouten, Miami, and Kickapoo harvested *Zizania aquatica*. The late-nineteenth-century anthropologist who studied the history of these tribes felt the main factor affecting location of Indian villages was the abundant crop of wild rice to be obtained nearby. Parts of the Fox River were so densely choked with wild rice, in fact, that passages for boats had to be cut out of the dense stems. This grain, also called Indian rye, water rye, wild oats, and marsh rye, played multiple roles in Indian subsistence. Wild rice attracted waterfowl in the thousands, perhaps hundreds of thousands, and because of the height of its long, dark, reedy stems, sometimes nine or ten feet, rice also served as a ready-made blind for waterfowl hunters.[3]

Zizania aquatica did not disappear from the northern Illinois Country until the twentieth century. An 1870 survey of Lake and McHenry Counties, for example, found them "widely margined" with wild rice. In 1875 an observer near the Chain of Lakes district of Illinois noted wild rice from four to twelve feet high. Naturalists and botanists have created wild rice maps, finding it in a total of eight of the eleven counties in the Fox valley, and although rice was later seriously impacted by drainage projects, carp foraging, and water pollution, it was still abundant and available to Indian tribes in the Illinois in the eighteenth century.[4]

Since Spanish records of gifts and provisions distributed to Indian tribes appearing in Spanish St. Louis do mention the Potawatomi, questions can be asked about tribes willing to travel fair distances and ford large rivers to obtain food. The abandonment of rice harvesting occurred in the context of an intensely accelerating market economy in skins and peltries. In the Canadian north, among the Ojibway, wild rice had been traded to French fur traders for well over one hundred years. After peltries, *Zizania aquatica* was the most highly desired commodity in the northern fur trade. Although subject to changing value, due to fluctuations in rice harvests, a bushel of *folle avoine*, wild rice, usually equaled a mature beaver pelt in value. The history of Indian tribes living in Illinois reveals that while environmental change did exert both discrete and keen pressures on Indians, and while competition for natural resources may have driven intertribal warfare prehistorically and historically, in some cases, Indian nations had let go of reliable survival mechanisms. Wild rice, however, is dependent on precise environmental factors. If heavy spring flooding occurs, not enough oxygen will reach the seeds to promote germination. Although little evidence is available for eighteenth-century rice growth on the Fox River, a suggestive point concerns the building of mills there. The Fox River was described, in fact, as "the most dammed stream" in all of Illinois. These earliest dams, some perhaps in place by the late 1780s, were constructed of brush, earth, logs and stones; their number may have changed the water levels on the Fox River, impacting rice. When looking for explanations for the marked shifts in Indian lifeways, such as those especially evident in the splintered Potawatomi, both environmental change and external economic stimuli (market economy) have worked together. Richard White has poignantly characterized such shifts with the phrase "the roots of dependency."[5]

On one level, a theme of the last ten years of this study—which saw the most interaction among disparate peoples—is food procurement. The British at Fort Chartres were laying stores by; the French were peddling foodstuffs to the garrison and to Indians, and vice versa; Indians were also traveling to Spanish forts to obtain food; Fox and Potawatomi raiders were attacking French and British hunters anywhere they found them on the Grand Prairie; and the river systems were being used at night to carry on an extensive illicit trade. Captain Forbes detailed this practice back in 1768, when he wrote to General Gage about subjects in British Illinois slipping across the Mississippi at night with furs to obtain French trade goods. He felt the reason for this contraband trade was "the French Goods are 30 p'Cent cheaper." The use of the Illinois rivers by French traders continued to be seen as an outrage by the British. Colonel Wilkins wrote to the British Secretary of War, "The French still carry away all the Trade. . . . They go up our rivers." The final chapter of the Illinois Country in the years before the Americans arrived describes the behavior of peoples in extreme transition. The British had just begun to put down tenuous roots when the American Revolution broke out. Against the backdrop of yet another war, the Illinois Country continued to be exploited by many peoples—and in some cases, animals—looking for any means to survive. Such a reality must be placed next to the tenacious refrain in all early Illinois histories—one that has subtly influenced even later historians: "[In 1796] the [Illinois] country was in a state of almost primeval simplicity."[6]

Three years after the British first wintered in the Illinois, meagerly parceling out their scant provisions, hunting in a desultory way, buying random items of foodstuffs from the remaining French, the memory of "starving" was still fresh. George Morgan, the representative of the Philadelphia merchant firm Baynton, Wharton, and Morgan, made sure he was set for the winter of 1768:

> However there will be no Danger of Starving for I have now two Years Provisions in the House consisting of Salt Petred Gammons, Rounds of Beef, Buffaloe Tongues, Vennison & Bears Hams. . . . So that I am

not in Quite the Same Situation that poor honest Jennings Used to be formerly—When his Letters were fill'd with his Fears of Starving &c.

In addition to his smoked and salt petered meats, Morgan had eleven nesting hens "with 13 Eggs each" and more than two hundred couples of pigeons. He owned six cows and had put in fifteen acres of Indian corn "& expect to have fifty if no Accidents happens to my Horses or Oxen." While working at Fort Cavendish [Chartres], Morgan was still able to build up what he referred to as his plantation. He had constructed a small log house and hired a "New England Man" to build a new barn, stables, and fences. His "negroe Boy" cooked a dish of rice pudding almost daily; Morgan had grown quite fond of this, taking it with a glass of wine. While enjoying such commodities as rice and Madeira shipped up from New Orleans, Morgan was clearly putting in his acres of corn on preworked and plowed French farmland available around the fort (he mentions no ground-breaking activity); he and his helper could easily sow the long ribbon arpents formerly belonging to the French of the village of Chartres. His animals were likely initially housed in the solid French barns, built of sassafras, mulberry, or oak, and pastured in the fenced common grounds. When he was not caring for his stock or hanging up venison and bear haunches in French smokehouses, Morgan walked to the fort. There, every day, he received an uneven flow of peltries from Indians and French traders and dispensed in return a wide variety of goods. He kept track of what passed from hand to hand. In July of 1768 he wrote his partners, "The Red Strouds, Kettles, Wire, and Guns I must have . . . of the following Tin Ware you cannot easily send too much—Nests of Kettles, Milk & Pudding Pans sorted small, Candle Sticks—Brass Iron & Tin . . . Pewter Basons." He was also begging for shipments of shoes, mentioning that the demand for shoes was excessive. Earlier in the spring, the fort commissary Edward Cole had documented a brisk trade in breech clouts. Coats, petticoats, match coats, shirts, "gartering," Indian ribbon, and Leggings were also sold daily.[7]

Patterns of consumption and especially the escalating demand for clothing items suggest that Indian, French, and British peoples were all depending on the storehouse. Although the British occupied Illinois for only ten years, they were there long enough to experience resistance, acceptance, and even a measure of prosperous engagement among the diverse peoples of the Illinois. This tenuously growing social world of trade relationships would be dissolved through invasions of northern Indians whose relationships to the British and to the tribes of the Illinois Confederacy had been permanently changed by Pontiac's War. The gathering momentum of the

American colonial revolt was also a factor in the unrest of the 1770s. Age-old hostilities and newly engendered ones prevented a frontier synthesis of peoples and cultures. For George Morgan in 1768, however, the future looked promising, exemplified in his own storehouse of foodstuffs.

In the great central yard of old Fort Chartres, on any given day that summer, would be found traders' horses strapped with merchandise, Indian horses piled with packs of peltries, and hunters' horses returning weighted with huge, darkly stained leather bags. Following spotty trails of blood, dogs skulked along the chalk-white walls, darting out among groups of French formed into militia and drilling under British command, black slaves sent on errands to the fort, and Indians on foot or arriving on glistening, dripping horses, as when the Osage crossed the Mississippi in "a large party of warriors." In the high heat and humidity of the August floodplain, British soldiers' wives originally from Yorkshire or Providence toiled in from their houses in the former French village of Chartres. They would likely have met French women from Prairie du Rocher, comfortably peddling garden produce and bread, long used to the heavy, saturated air and immune to the "miasmic" diseases that were plaguing British arrivals. The empty country to which Captain Stirling had come three years ago, occupying a fort overgrown with weeds and filthy from neglect, was reestablishing itself. The letters sent out from Fort Cavendish/Chartres by British men writing their wives, as well as commissary and military correspondence, sketch a busy world. Despite General Gage's dim view of the potential of the Illinois Country, in the year 1768 the human traffic there was considerable.[8]

The British in the Illinois Country most aware of trade and hunting patterns were merchants. Although British military commanded at the fort, it was the merchant firm representative and the commissary, the keeper of storehouse goods, that Indians most often sought. On a day-to-day basis, these men became skilled assessors of the number and quality of furs passing through the gates of the fort. They recognized and knew personally a great number of Indians, members of diverse tribes who converged from all four directions. It is in the letters of merchants and their representatives that Indians are most often named as individuals. For instance, in his diary, Matthew Clarkson wrote on December 23, 1766, "Another party of Osages came to the fort, about fifteen in number. Tawanaheh the chief. Shakewah, an old man who interpreted into the Illinois language. Saheshinga, another Indian." British military correspondence rarely names individual Indians unless they were chiefs, but the commercial men in British Illinois traded with individual people. After only a year or two of living in the Illinois Country, some British writers often identified Indians. Because so many

French of the riverine settlements were illiterate, they left scant accounts and letters of their daily lives. Yet over the course of the sixty-six-year French and Indian history there, how many Mechigamea, Cahokia, and Peoria could have entered the historical record as named people? The fleeting proper names in British letters provide some of the only recognition of Indians as named persons—tribal members who may not have had status as chiefs. There is virtually no evidence for what Illinois Indians thought about British, Spanish, or even their long-time neighbors, the riverine French. Indian perceptions and adaptations must be inferred from a close analysis of their actions.[9]

Among these Indians visiting Fort Chartres it is likely there was an increasing number of mixed-blood men and women. The British acknowledged this to some extent. General Haldimand wrote to General Gage in 1770, "If any French do come to us, it will be from the Illinois where they are half-Indians." Yet it was commercial men who had the most intimate dealings with Indians; they admitted the realities of Indian-French trade loyalties and the deep, decades-old ties Illinois Indians especially had to French families. In 1767 Baynton and Wharton were writing to Lauchlin Maclean, Lord Shelburne's private secretary, about the state of affairs in the Illinois Country. "The Influence of the French is so great, with the Numerous Tribes of Indians, in the Country, That They have engrossed the greatest Part of the Trade." This was seen as France "interfering with" the British nation. In the same letter, the writers inform Maclean, "with the utmost Concern . . . That the greatest Discontent and Jealousy, Now prevail Among the Western Nations." The merchants had had "certain Intelligence" concerning twelve tribes meeting at Shawnee Town. There, the merchants believed, the gathering nations would "determine On Measures," a perhaps violent response to injuries received from the British.[10]

Tracing the origins of such reports, of the "intelligence" making its way to Fort Chartres, is often impossible. British writers only sometimes identify the source of their information. By its frequency, however, and given that the Illinois Indians were the tribes most consistently at the fort, an inference can be made about sources. In 1768 the commissary at the fort, Edward Cole, wrote a lengthy "Account of Philadelphia Merchants." Some of this manuscript has unfortunately been burned, but partial entries indicate that Cole and Captain Gordon Forbes were attempting to track down sources of rumor. In listing the merchandise dispersed as gifts to various Indian tribes, Cole writes of two parties of Vermilion and Kaskaskia Indians who had come to discuss a chief, Black Fly. Cole indicates that he and Forbes had sent a message to these Indians to determine the truth of a "report spread abroad." This report suggested that Indians were planning "to strike their fathers the English." The merchant report in its entirety is an invaluable reflection of the numbers and nations of Indians who came to the fort to impart information and receive gifts. "Piorias," "Missouris," "Kaskaskias and other Indians living at and around [MS. Burned]" "Piorias at Pain Court [St. Louis]," "the Chief of the Osage," "Seven Chiefs of the Putawatomies," "a Chief of the Arcanzas," "Pondiac and His Attendants," as well as "Sundry Chiefs and Partys of Ottaways and Chippaways"—all passed under the limestone arch of the fort, and Edward Cole dispersed appreciative gifts to the amount of 601 pounds, 10 shillings.

From the Osage west across the Mississippi, the Arkansas nations to the south, the Potawatomi and Chippewa to the north, and Pontiac from the northeast, Indians converged on a fort slipping slowly into a bend of a giant river. All peoples arriving at the fort would have seen and heard the Mississippi, and a good many would have been on it or in it. In addition to the horse traffic, there would have been many river craft gently bobbing along the shoreline: hollowed-out pirogues of cottonwood, lighter bark canoes, cane rafts, and rough log ferries. The Illinois tribes living closest to the fort, the Mechigamea (and sometimes the Cahokia and Peoria) would have taken footpaths to the gates. Trails led down from "the heights" of the uplands and crossed the floodplain prairies. Edward Cole and the military commander, Captain Forbes, extracted promises of trade fidelity from all these arriving Indian nations. Especially vocal about wanting to support the English in the burgeoning competition were the Osage, who were already pushing south to the Arkansas River to reach unlicensed French and Spanish traders. Also in 1768, General Gage wrote a frustrated account about settlers and traders from the Spanish side of the Mississippi. He described men "who go up the Rivers Ilinois, Ohio, and Oubache," trading with Indians living in British territories of the Illinois and hunting on their lands. Gage believed these "Spanish side" traders—who were just as likely to have been French as Spanish—encouraged "Mischief" as well as illicit trade, desiring the Indians to "keep their Hatchets ready to strike."[11]

The belief that contraband traders were also warmongers is clear in British correspondence. French and Spanish traders were thought to act with the design of an international conspiracy, agents in a vast trade war brewing in all directions. Yet the British themselves were key participants in such intrigues. Colonel Wilkins, for instance, on his arrival in the Illinois in 1768, likely sent "a Gentleman to be depended on" over to scout out the Spanish fort being built at the confluence of the Mississippi and Missouri. "This Gentleman was so curious as to measure the Fort several times." Those specific measurements are included in the letter sent to General Gage, as well as exact counts of the numbers of Spanish soldiers stationed at the fort. Probably Illinois Indians crossing into Missouri lands, such as the Peoria who occasionally hunted there, also provided the British in the Illinois with information about the Spanish trade. Yet it was the French who continued to interact most often with the Illinois Indians. The English language was heard consistently for the first time in the Illinois Country during the Seven Years War. French had been spoken there since 1699 and had become the language of trade, a Creole patois containing a vibrant blend of native vocabulary, old French Canadian, and place names arising from joint usage of the land. Many Illinois Indians understood it, and in return, quite a few French could speak some Algonquian. In May of 1768, Peoria Indians reported to a Frenchman in "Caho" (Cahokia) that Potawatomi Indians were plotting against the British. "They immediately gave intelligence to . . . Monsieur Longvall, who could speak their language."[12]

In maintaining trade with and affective loyalties to the French under British rule, the Illinois Indians were able to influence the course of occupation even before some expeditions arrived in the Mississippi bottomlands. One of the early signs was the downriver flow of ominous tidings about how Indians would receive the first British to arrive in their country. In 1765, while Major Farmar was organizing his expedition to relieve Captain Stirling up at Fort Chartres, he was plagued with desertions of his troops. Down the long, populated stretch of the Mississippi to New Orleans ran accounts, canoe to village, village to pirogue, pirogue to sandbar camp, of the angry native inhabitants of the Illinois Country, resentful of the incoming British and ready to ambush the soldiers of His Britannic Majesty. In 1764 the last French governor, D'Abbadie, wrote of the Illinois Country, "The news which M. de Villiers sends me is very disquieting to him: the savages are visiting him in companies of twenty and thirty, and it is necessary that he give them something or run the risk of their threats." Yet a year before, in 1763, the British at Fort Detroit complained that Indians were abandoning the country. References in the correspondence of the French and the British, prior to their final occupation of the Illinois, reflect this peculiar theme: the absence of Indians, both as fur providers and as suppliers of provisions, but also, paradoxically, their continued threat. By February of 1765 the French minister at New Orleans was receiving frantic letters from his commanders. St. Ange wrote that his "feeble garrison and the inhabitants of the Illinois" would be exposed to the "furor of the savages," ostensibly so desperate at being abandoned by the French that they might have recourse to attack, to "proceeding to the most terrible extremities."[13]

The (potential) "furor of the savages" was likely perceived by the common British foot soldiers stationed in New Orleans as equal to the ferocity of Indians in the Ohio Valley during the Seven Years War. British held captive by Indians, those who lived to tell of Indian treatment of prisoners, spread gruesome accounts. For instance, although captured early, in 1755, Colonel James Smith watched as a dozen injured prisoners were burned at the stake beside the Allegheny River. In the same year, Mary Jemison, captured at thirteen, saw "heads, arms, legs, and other fragments of the bodies of some white people who had just been burned." She recounted that it "was like pork . . . hanging on a pole." By the time the British arrived in New Orleans and sat waiting for the provisioning of their transport, these stories would have been circulating for at least ten years. In 1769 the French priest Father Gibault wrote to his superior in Quebec, justifying his being armed with a gun and two pistols. Father Gibault is credited with a romantic imagination by his biographers, but he was drawing on history when he wrote of fending off an attack by an Indian, "a miserable barbarian who seeks only to gratify his barbarism, who only wants my scalp, who would as soon take my hair as that of my horse, or who would slowly burn me alive just for the pleasure of seeing me suffer, who would make me eat my own flesh after having roasted some part of my body." Gibault feared ambush by fierce Indians of the Grand Prairie, such as the Kickapoo or the Miami.[14]

The truth of the Illinois Country, however, was that except for the foiled plot of 1751, in which Miami Indians and a few kinship-allied Kaskaskias fired on some French villagers, no Illinois Indian tribe had ever directly attacked the French villages, the fort, or Frenchmen in their fields (ambush by the Fox was common earlier in the century). While ambush of lone traders on the Grand Prairie was all too common, the "furor of the savages" was a haunting invocation of other times and places, other Indian-European frontiers. Conflation of Indian practices—merging the Ohio and Mississippi Valley Indians as similar populations—seems to have been likely. Desertions in the British ranks were common. Major Farmar and his officers wrote of finding ways to prevent such desertions. Farmar blamed the proximity of New Orleans for desertions, calling it an "asylum . . . where [deserters] find encouragement from ill-disposed people." Even after the occupation of the Illinois, British soldiers still deserted. In 1768 General Gage noted that forty-one deserters from "Louisiana" had been sent to "the Grenadoes." Earlier, in 1765, Major Fraser wrote to General Gage about the reception of his men up in the Illinois Country, saying the men were ill-treated by Indians who were drunk and destitute. Likely fearing worse than simply ill treatment, Fraser sent his men "away" while the Indians were attending a council at Fort Chartres.[15]

That ambiguous adverb *away* obscures the destination of Fraser's men, the destination of most people leaving the Illinois country in a hurry: New Orleans, easily and quickly reached on the steady, south-running river currents. River news traveled fast, and it was borne on the river systems by all peoples. Communication spread from east to west as well as north to south. In the summer of 1765, for instance, General Gage wrote to William Penn about his concerns over a "large convoy of goods [that went] from New Orleans to Illinois in February." Gage felt it was necessary to open trade back at Fort Pitt as soon as possible, and to "give notice of it," to the Indians of the Ohio. If the Ohio Valley tribes were to learn of the goods convoy in the Illinois, especially if trade were postponed at Fort Pitt, Indians would soon discover the source of supplies and might defect to the French. The location of Fort Pitt at the confluence of three rivers, and especially its connections to the Ohio, assured that Indian tribes would discover trade commodity surpluses and deficits quickly.[16]

A riverine relay system connected the eastern and western tribes; the ease of river travel also allowed for networks of Indian alliances. At an Indian Council in New Orleans in February of 1765, a Shawnee chief named Charlot Kaske (Cornstalk or Corn Cob) showed French authorities a belt depicting forty-seven separate Indian villages who were all willing "to die attached to the French," who would defend the French in battle. While the French governor D'Abbadie tried to dissuade the Shawnee from attacking the English, an Illinois Indian chief, Levacher, also spoke. He displayed "a little round piece of skin to which were attached 60 porcelain beads." According to the eyewitness who wrote of the moment, the beads represented the number of nations to which Levacher and the Illinois Indians were allied. This visual symbol of alliance—a skin world rimmed with sixty porcelain nations—helps to explain the importance of the Illinois Indians both to other tribes and to the Europeans. With some of the smallest numbers of people by 1765, the four Illinois subtribes were nonetheless wooed by Pontiac, sought out by the Osage from across the Missouri, and identified by the British in their correspondence as key players in the contraband French fur trade.[17]

The Shawnee and Illinois chiefs had traveled to New Orleans, to the "warm town," to see if it were true that the country had been ceded to the English. These Indian chiefs returned to their lands bearing news, and that news spread to the villages and nations with whom they were allied. The back-and-forth exchange of both accurate information and rumor created a different kind of matrix for the British at old Fort Chartres. Levacher, for instance, interpreted the British injunction against the sale of gunpowder as "they wish that we starve." He declared passionately that "we [the Illinois tribes] shall not be embarrassed, having bows and arrows, and if there is no wood, we should find rushes." Despite nearly seventy years of access to French firearms, the Illinois chief still affirmed the use of bow and arrow among his people. Such sentiments certainly were reiterated back in the villages of the Illinois. Their kinship connections, especially to the eastern Illinois prairie bands of Miami, Wea, Piankeshaw, and Mascouten ensured the spread of such suspicions.

Into this land of rumor arrived the British. The eastern shore Indians, finding that the fur trade was shifting into the rich Missouri lands across the river, experiencing the dissolution of their old provisioning trade relations with Europeans, at risk through the 1760s and 1770s from attacks by northern allied bands of Sauk, Fox, Potawatomi, and some Sioux, used the resource of information to survive in the English-controlled lands of the Illinois. Survival was centered directly on the British storehouse and artillery at old Fort Chartres. It was maintained indirectly through relationships with the remaining French in the Illinois Country. Yet even this explanation is too simple. The loyalty of the Mechigamea to the French still located near the fort and at Prairie du Rocher—peoples who had lived near each other on adjacent lands since 1720—was concomitant with an imposed political loyalty to the British. The two allegiances were very different emotionally and arose out of two opposite historical tracks. An aborted attack of Potawatomi on the French and British living outside the fort in May of 1768 illustrates this complex relationship.[18]

"The alarm word King George was made known to all the inhabitants"

The old French and Indian landscape had been considerably changed by 1768. Kaskaskia was the most populous village left in French Illinois, with mere scatterings of French at Prairie du Rocher, St. Philippe, and Cahokia. Back in 1752 Kaskaskia had fifty-eight French males, while Prairie du Rocher had ten men and Cahokia eighteen. In addition, thirty-one Indian men and forty-four Indian women lived at Kaskaskia; Prairie du Rocher had only five Indian inhabitants. By 1769 Father Meurin described Prairie du Rocher as "a little village of twenty-four souls," including two inhabitants living at old Fort Chartres about a league away. The French village of Chartres, sometimes called the "L'Establishment" in French records, whose construction and property sales furnished so many detailed notarial records, was abandoned in 1765; some British soldiers and their families moved into empty homes between the fort and Prairie du Rocher. From the bluffs stretched bottomland prairie, partially cleared by French farmers, dotted with copses of hazel and some considerable stands of fruit trees planted by the people of Chartres. Many of the farms remained deserted, however. St. Philippe, which in 1765 had ten or twelve French houses and a church, was almost completely emptied; all inhabitants "but one" crossed to the Spanish side. Up at Cahokia, the land was as vacant. Father Gibault left a description of French Cahokia, written in 1768 to Bishop Briand in Quebec. Gibault was arguing to be posted at Kaskaskia rather than at Cahokia. He characterizes Cahokia as a place "small and distant from all others, that mission formerly so flourishing is nothing any more, not a slave." Gibault saw that "mills are in ruins, the milldams have been carried away by the waters, barns have fallen, the orchard for lack of a fence has been destroyed by animals, which have eaten the bark off the trees clear to the sap." He makes no mention of the Cahokia Indians, nor the Peoria who sometimes lived with them. Yet to the south, the Mechigamea continued to occupy a village three quarters of a mile from Fort Chartres, north along the river. Back toward the bluffs perhaps two miles, nestled under the protective rise of sheer limestone and granite, lay the tiny village of Prairie du Rocher. As such, it was the closest French village to the Mechigamea. Fleeting references in British letters describe the land around the fort as "wide and open," or coated with immensely tall grasses, cordgrass and big bluestem. In May, however, those grasses would just have begun to grow again, making the approach of attacking Indians quite visible.[19]

Between May 5 and May 10, according to the terse entries in the journal of John Jennings, Potawatomi Indians launched an attack on a place identified by Jennings as "the village." It is not entirely clear whether this refers to the British occupying the old Chartres site or to Prairie du Rocher. Mention of "the church" makes it more likely to have been Prairie du Rocher, since St. Anne's chapel near the fort was long abandoned and St. Joseph's church in Prairie du Rocher, with its adjacent cemetery, was the place of worship. Jennings's account begins with Peoria Indians meeting sixty Potawatomi while hunting; the Potawatomi told the Peoria of plans to attack the English. The location of this information exchange was likely somewhere along the Illinois River, between its confluence with the Mississippi and the northeast turn into the Kankakee. Potawatomi had settled in the Kankakee valley and ranged south to hunt and meet (illegal) Spanish traders. The Peoria immediately relayed the news of the impending attack to the British, using the intermediary of an Algonquian-speaking Frenchman at Cahokia. Jennings recounts that sentinels were stationed in the streets and night patrols organized. The French and British inhabitants were "muster'd together and armed." Despite these precautions, a British soldier and his wife were kidnapped by Potawatomi right out of the village. Immediately twenty soldiers and "a party of the Mitchigamie, who are our friends," went in pursuit. Across the next few days, Jennings records even more elaborate precautions. Double sentinels were placed at the village avenues, and the alarm cry of "King George!" given as the warning. Hearing this, all inhabitants were to gather armed at a rendezvous site. Through the night several times the alarm was given, as sentinels saw strange Indians "creeping close" or "advancing." Eventually, some Kaskaskia Indians also set out in pursuit of the Potawatomi war party, while village guards and sentinels continued to watch both night and day. At noon on May 9 again "the drums beat to Arms," as a relay system sent news of an approaching party of Indians on the Mississippi. The Kaskaskia chief Tomera and his warriors, acting in support of the British, went to determine who was coming. Near the Mechigamea village they met some Chippewa men and women crossing from St. Louis. These Indians were immediately suspected of being spies, and the guard was maintained around the village. After May 10, however, there seems to have been no further alarm.[20]

While both the Mechigamea and the Kaskaskia are described as defending the village, this five-day tale illustrates more than political loyalty. The Illinois Indians had been habitually attacked by the Potawatomi, often allied with the Fox and Sauk (see chapter 5 for the combined Potawatomi-Fox raid on the Mechigamea and Cahokia villages, 1752). However, the Potawatomi were a splintered tribe by the 1760s, with two major factions divided geographically and politically. The Potawatomi living around Fort Detroit had made peace with the British after Pontiac's War, while the St. Joseph Potawatomi maintained a bitter hostility to them. By the late 1760s, "St. Joseph Potawatomi" had become a cluster term describing bands of Indians living everywhere but Detroit and led mostly by younger men. While the Potawatomi at the French St. Joseph mission had a long history of occupying the area, most of the original dissenting Potawatomi had dispersed south into the Illinois Kankakee River Valley. There they were able to participate in illegal trade with Spanish and French using the waterways of Illinois to penetrate deep into the north-central area. Early accounts of the land south of Detroit identify it as exceptionally wet and marshy, also a riverine world traced with many waterways and the timbered shorelines of great lakes. Southern Michigan, in fact, was a land of salt springs and abundant "salt brine." Studies have estimated Michigan's reserves of salt as immense.

Despite these deposits, which Indians knew about and used, curiously, salt was so expensive up at Detroit that very little meat was salted for sale. Salt was also available to the south along the Illinois River, on the east bank above the mouth of the Vermilion. These saline deposits were described in 1773 as "two salt ponds 100 yards in circumference . . . water is stagnant and of a yellowish colour; but the French and natives make good salt from it." Salt deposits were thus strategically placed between the northwestern Potawatomi and the Mississippi, providing a means of preserving meat and game and perhaps allowing the independence of the tribal factions from the main Potawatomi around Detroit. One account of the activities of a French priest along the Illinois River near Peoria makes note of his participation in a buffalo hunt with "the Indians north of Peoria." It is not known who these Indians were, but the Grand Prairie of Illinois was clearly a theater for the meeting of many peoples, including the French, not all of whom had crossed the river. The relocation of Great Lakes Algonquian tribes at mid-eighteenth century changed patterns of resource use in all of the Illinois Country.[21]

The French around Detroit and south near St. Joseph maintained cultural traditions similar to those of the French along the Mississippi. They built houses of oak and cedar and marked off their property with "pickets of red cedar" ten to twelve feet high. Incoming American settlers often mentioned the orchards of apples and cherries. An account from 1837 describes some of the red cedar posts still standing in Detroit; and red cedar was used extensively by the French as far west as Ste. Genevieve in Missouri. Thus the natural and cultural landscape of French Illinois would have felt very familiar to Potawatomi raiders in 1768: marshy earth interspersed with some stands of thick timber, a landscape mosaic including improved agricultural lands, and dwellings displaying the familiar closely set, high pickets running along property lines. Potawatomi approaching on horses would have been at home wending their way through the wet prairies and inundated floodplain of the Mississippi in May. These western Potawatomi had relocated to the Kankakee area, another river system, one in which they were more available to both Spanish and French and northern tribes like the Fox and Sauk. Along the Kankakee they were reinforced in their belief that the British should be driven from the Illinois. One historian has described the clashes between St. Joseph Potawatomi and the British in the late 1760s as "the western-Potawatomi-British feud."[22]

The feud took the predominant form of guerrilla attacks on British traders. The raid on the Chartres area was but one incident in a long chain of attacks. The ubiquitous George Croghan in his role of Indian agent met with the Potawatomi at Detroit in 1767 but achieved little. The Potawatomi living around the St. Joseph River area of Michigan and south into Illinois "bragged" that they "would not Suffer an English Man to come near their Place." These Illinois Potawatomi remained loyal to Pontiac's vision of western lands emptied of British and restored to the Indians who had lived there, despite the ancient intertribal warfare that characterized relationships among the tribes of the upper Mississippi River Valley.[23]

While Pontiac was working to unite the western tribes, the Illinois Indians, assisted by the French, had been supplying him with ammunition and supplies. Their anti-British sentiments and loyalty to Onontio, the French father, mirrored the feelings of the St. Joseph Potawatomi. At least one historian believes this activity—especially the supplying of ammunition to Pontiac—prompted the British to occupy the Illinois lands earlier than they had planned. When the Illinois Indians appeared to have capitulated under British rule and to have traitorously abandoned the good fight, the Potawatomi were fiercely retaliatory. Somewhat astonishing in this tale of political anger and betrayal is the great disparity in numbers among the Potawatomi, the Sauk, the Fox—and the Illinois. The Fox Indians, in fact, had experienced a resurgence of population during the post-1763 fur trade years. Between 1700 and 1763, however, the number of Illinois Indians fell from six thousand to two thousand. Some historians believe this number is too conservative, with one estimate placing the loss of Illinois peoples at more than 90 percent of their precontact numbers. The Potawatomi numbers remained higher; the Detroit Potawatomi, who supported Henry Hamilton's western warfare plan during the American Revolution, were able to contribute at least one hundred warriors to the one thousand mixed-nation force Hamilton sent south to raid Kentucky in 1777. In 1778 George Morgan estimated the Potawatomi at Detroit as having four hundred men. Despite population differences, tribes in northern Illinois and Michigan saw the greatly reduced Illinois Indians as traditional enemies to be "cut off." However, the two groups of Potawatomi continued to be perceived differently by most Europeans. Back in 1769 the St. Joseph Potawatomi were listed on a "Report of the Various Indian Tribes Receiving Presents in the District of Ylinoa or Illinois, 1769." In addition to the four Illinois tribes—the "Kaskaskia, Kaokias, Peorias, and Metchigamia"—the roster, prepared by the outgoing French commander St. Ange for the incoming Spanish, identifies "Puotuatami" "of the river of San Joseph and that of Ylinnese." St. Ange wrote at the end of this report, "I certify the tribes here above expressed are the same ones who are accustomed to come here to get presents." It is important to keep careful track of the timing of these reports and activities. The Potawatomi raid on the Chartres area occurred in May of 1768; a year later in May of 1769 both the Illinois and the Potawatomi are identified as habitually receiving presents from the French; in a similar document prepared in 1777, both the Potawatomi and the "Peorias and Kaskaskias" are listed as receiving presents from the Spanish. In this last report, the St. Joseph Potawatomi are counted as having 150 warriors, while the two tribes of the Illinois combined have 100 (the Mechigamea and the Cahokia are not mentioned).[24]

Despite the fact that both nations—the Illinois and the Potawatomi of St. Joseph—were using the resources of the French and the Spanish, great heated feeling seethed under these international pseudoalliances. In addition to cultural patterns of retaliation, tribes experiencing dislocation and the breakdown of internal leadership structures often projected their feelings of vulnerability onto lesser tribes, blaming them for changing allegiances. One study of the Potawatomi in this period points out that each tribal faction or society had specific, different adaptations arising from distinctive histories of interaction with Europeans and with other Indian nations. Within one hundred years, in fact, the Potawatomi had reversed their patterns of trade and cultural allegiance with the Illinois Indians. They had initially adopted the calumet ceremony from Illinois tribes after 1667, as they traded to the south. They incorporated this important pipe stem and bowl ritual into their own practices as an act of closure to an intertribal compact or agreement. Also like the Illinois, the Potawatomi in the first half of the eighteenth century were dominated by the Fox Wars and Fox raids. The Fox considered the Potawatomi "their most desperate enemies," and Potawatomi joined the massive French and Indian force that nearly exterminated the Fox on the Grand Prairie in the early 1730s. Fighting beside them were Illinois Indians. Less than twenty-five years later, the Illinois had taken the place of the Fox as those most desperate enemies, and the Fox and Potawatomi were allied. In this shifting, unstable world of recombining allegiances, the kind of anger fueled by acts of perceived betrayal could be completely disproportionate to the incident. In 1751, for example, the Potawatomi became incensed over the death of a fractious chief named La Grue (The Crane). He was killed in a northern Peoria village along the Illinois River as Potawatomi passed through the area. Documents establish that La Grue was in fact "a notorious trouble-maker" who had started the quarrel, yet the Potawatomi could not forget the incident. The tradition of retaliation among the Potawatomi was documented as early as 1677 when Father Allouez, the successor to Father Marquette, stayed with "Poueteouatamis" near Green Bay. He described a "bear war," in which the Potawatomi killed more than five hundred bears in retaliation for the death of a single Potawatomi brave who was mauled.[25]

The Potawatomi were no different from other Great Lakes and prairie Indian tribes in preserving deep patterns of retaliatory warfare. In addition to the many historical and anthropological studies establishing tribal warfare as a constant, archaeological evidence has revealed striking evidence of murderous assault in the Oneota culture, the prehistoric Indian group occupying the Illinois land in the centuries before the French descent of the rivers. Studies of fractures in interred skeletons found in one Oneota burial site in west-central Illinois, circa 1300, suggest not only surprise attack but repeated attacks. Of 264 burials, forty-three partial or complete skeletons indicated violent death. Archaeologists conclude that "lethal trauma . . . is unambiguous" at this grave site: numerous skull fractures were caused by the wielding of stone-ground celts, and mutilation was present as well, including scalping and decapitation. Many remains show evidence of old injuries. Although the connection between the Oneota culture and the historic Indian tribes is uncertain, the tradition of small-scale attacks among localized tribes did persist. The earliest recorder of Illinois Indian culture, the Frenchman Deliette who stayed with the Peoria around 1700, describes flamboyant rituals of warring and attack on other nations, especially the northern Fox and Sauk. One historian characterizes the Fox-Illinois "vendetta" as "bitter and of long duration." The lodges of the Fox proudly displayed many "Cahokia and Kaskaskia scalps." In one 1730 Illinois Indian ambush of Fox prisoners, three women were killed and fifteen Fox taken prisoner. Even after the defeat of the Fox on the Grand Prairie in 1730, the Illinois conducted retaliatory raids north along the Mississippi and Illinois Rivers, especially on isolated Fox hunters.

Yet by the time of the British occupation, the Illinois had departed from these patterns; they were more consistently focused on survival, on food and clothing procurement, than on resource-driven warfare. Perhaps their nearly seventy-year interaction with Europeans in intimate quarters, as the domiciled Indians of the French villages, had changed them. Yet despite shifts that may have occurred within their own culture, the Peoria certainly understood the Potawatomi retaliatory tradition. After the death of La Grue, they sent gifts to his family, but La Grue's relatives and kinsmen remained focused on revenge. The Peoria even sent a message to the Potawatomi:

> Why do you disturb the earth for a fool who has been killed? What is your reason for coming to such extremes? Some of our people who were married in your villages have been killed there and we have never

taken up arms to revenge ourselves. Moreover, if you attack us we will avenge ourselves; the earth will be disturbed and the roads will be closed through your fault.

Such pleas were to no avail. Revenge for La Grue's death took the form of the catastrophic raid on the Mechigamea village in 1752. The memory of that raid—the scattered, hacked-off limbs of men, women, and children macerating in riverine cornfields—was yet searingly vivid. In the late 1760s the Illinois Indians aligned themselves with the ruling power who could best protect them from northern enemies. They used a skillful, swift relay system of reporting information to keep themselves safe. That today at least two of the Illinois tribes survive in Oklahoma is testament to the way these Indians read and used the political system of the late eighteenth century, at a time when their own livelihood was highly compromised through environmental degradation and the influx of many peoples. One way of reading the historical record has invited interpretations of dependency and weakness. This is most strongly expressed in analyses of how the Illinois behaved at the time of Pontiac's murder in 1769.[26]

"There came to Fort Chartres . . . a party of the Peoria with the greatest Apprehensions"

On April 20, 1769, a Peoria Indian stabbed Pontiac to death in Cahokia, possibly in the nearby Indian village, "au Millieu du Village des Kahoquias." At least one historian interprets this attack as an act of vengeance: months earlier, Pontiac himself had stabbed Black Dog, the great Peoria chief. Pontiac's murderer was a grandson of Black Dog. The death of La Grue in the Peoria village back in 1751 was much less significant than the death of Pontiac at the hands of a Peoria warrior in 1769. A bitter international war had been fought in the interim. Land had changed hands and had been changed itself through British occupancy: the influx of soldiers, traders, merchandise convoys, and new Indian tribes inscribed the abandoned French lands with new trails, paths, landing places, and roads. Pontiac's vision had temporarily united western Indian nations; yet that war was driven by a fiery purpose and passionate dream that burned intensely and briefly, succeeding only at first through the Indian traditional warfare tactic of swift, surprise attack. Siege warfare requiring steady flows of ammunition, powder, and foodstuffs to attacking nations asked too much of the Indian supply systems of the old Northwest. After Pontiac negotiated a peace with the British, he was instrumental in stopping further violence at the time the British arrived in the Illinois. On at least two occasions, he prevented the murder of British envoys: once in the case of Lieutenant Fraser at Fort Chartres and once in the case of George Croghan, held captive along the Ohio River. However, most British, including those out in the Illinois Country, held a bitter view of Pontiac. After learning of Pontiac's murder, Thomas Hutchins wrote in 1769, "God grant that every ill-disposed Rascal of his Colour may step out of this world in the same manner that he has done."[27]

Historians have commented on the waste and ignominy of Pontiac's death outside a trading post on the muddy streets of Cahokia. To the Illinois Indians, waste and ignominy were the least concerns; they were extremely alarmed. The impact of Pontiac's murder on a single Indian has been movingly documented in a letter from Thomas Hutchins to George Morgan in 1769. "When I informed your Ottaway Indian of the Death of Pondiac his countenance changed and was so confused as not to be able to speak for some time," Hutchins wrote. "At last he gave us to understand that the Pondiac was dead his Death would be avenged. For God's sake take care of yourself when you come this way."[28]

The log of Colonel Wilkins in command at old Fort Chartres documents that the Peoria arrived in May, barely a month after Pontiac's murder, traveling downstream in thirty canoes, as well as overland in a large party. Wilkins tried to reassure them, asking them to return, but they refused. Four chiefs negotiated with Wilkins to obtain British protection. They eventually settled with the Mechigamea in their village, yet five Illinois Indians were scalped between the fort and the Indian village. In July, in the middle of a storm of rumors that angry northern tribes were massing against the Illinois, the Cahokia arrived, "to Settle here with the Peories & Mitches." The tribes worked together to fortify a village with a stockade on an elevated area ("a rising ground") within full sight of the fort and British canon mounted on the great stone walls. Rumors of attacks, retaliation for the death of Pontiac, continued from 1769 through the early 1770s. As the months passed, a messaging fervor created a swirl of "rumors and misinformation" drifting down the Mississippi to New Orleans. Sporadic raiding by Potawatomi against the Illinois British and Indian settlements also continued, although there was no definitive attack on the Illinois Indians in their new, combined encampment. This reality underscores the way the Illinois were focusing on survival and had managed to insure it. In 1773–74, when the British Indian commissioner Sir William Johnson attempted to negotiate an intertribal peace among the western nations, the Illinois did not attend the conference but sent a reply through a Shawnee chief. He brought "a Message from the three Illinois Indian Nations called the Kaskaskeys," who described themselves as being "continuingly at war" and "always be[ing] in dread of being struck . . . and therefore cou'd not leave their Families exposed."[29] It is clear the Illinois continued to feel vulnerable. During these early years of the 1770s, the Illinois Country was perceived by all who lived in it as unstable and dangerous. In command at Fort Chartres, Colonel Wilkins, who has entered history as "the notorious Colonel Wilkins" for his financial intrigues and high-handedness with commercial traders and French alike, perceived the vulnerability of the Illinois Indians. One historian grudgingly admits that Wilkins "had a way with the Indians that they liked." In addition to sometimes dispensing gifts more liberally than the British policies at the time permitted, Wilkins took seriously the information given to him by the Illinois. In 1769 three Kaskaskia chiefs came to the fort—Baptiste, Tomeroy, and Laudeviet. They told Wilkins, "express[ing] strong fear," that the Chickasaw Indians intended to cut them off. Wilkins successfully calmed the Kaskaskia, inviting them to settle under English protection. In 1771 Wilkins's log between April 19 and 27 details the arrival of twenty young Chickasaw braves, who made their way surreptitiously to the fort. Wilkins's efforts to keep animosities from breaking out between these Chickasaw and the Illinois Indians were really quite extraordinary. He housed the Chickasaw in a room inside the fort instead of in the hangard (savage house) that stood outside the gates; he also listened patiently to their concerns. The Indians privately expressed to the Colonel their hatred of Illinois Indians. In the tradition of many skilled negotiators, Wilkins approached the problem from both sides. He knew of a Chickasaw married to a Peoria woman and invited this man to the fort to negotiate a peace agreement. Colonel Wilkins spent four days "in Counsil with parties of the nations of the Illinois, Chickasaws, and Shawanes." In a complicated negotiation, he offered presents to the Chickasaw—brass bells and Jews harps, powder, lead, clothing, and knives—and sent them south to their villages. Despite being recalled by the British in 1772 for financial mismanagement, Colonel Wilkins protected the Illinois Indians from both their northern and southern enemies. Part of his success may simply have been the magnitude of the immense, French-constructed fort, its imposing size and range of cannon atop the limestone walls. Those walls were being undermined by the Mississippi, however, and in 1772 the British abandoned the fort. They moved south to Kaskaskia, occupying the old Jesuit mission grounds and house, also built of stone. This new location they named Fort Gage. It was from Fort Gage in April of 1773 that Captain Hugh Lord wrote to General Gage about his namesake fort, describing large numbers of Indians gathering there, "great Numbers of Indians of different Nations being almost continually here." General Haldimand also reported to General

Gage in 1773 that disorder in the Illinois Country was "increasing every day." It is not known whether the Peoria, Cahokia, and Mechigamea were among those Indians massing near Fort Gage or whether they continued to live near the abandoned and crumbling old Fort Chartres. It is clear, however, that they used two other means to insure their survival: they sold off more land, and they migrated south into Arkansas (the Kaskaskia) and west to the St. Louis area (the Peoria). For a time, they were much farther away from Potawatomi and Fox raiders.[30]

Shifts in population of the Illinois Country were accompanied by changes in land ownership. In the early 1770s members of newly formed land companies that had grown out of merchant involvement in British Illinois acquired land from the Illinois Indians. In his introduction to *The Illinois-Wabash Land Company Manuscript*, Clarence Alvord begins with a ringing exhortation to land speculation. Alvord's analysis underscores the zeal and determination of eastern land speculators, as well as his admiration for their efforts. The original deed of sale is preserved, carefully drawn up as a legal document and notarized in Kaskaskia in 1773; on it appears the list of goods the Illinois obtained for selling two large tracts of land to William Murray, representative of the Illinois-Wabash Land Company (these sales were subsequently declared illegal by General Gage and also never acknowledged by any American court, despite repeated efforts of the investors to that end). The merchandise, the price of their land, tells a revealing story of the Illinois nations on the eve of the American Revolution. In exchange for two rich tracts, "one on the Illinois River and one on the Ohio," the Illinois asked for the following:

> Two hundred and Sixty Strouds, Two hundred and fifty Blankets, Three hundred and fifty Shirts, One hundred and fifty pairs of Stroud and half thicke Stockings, One hundred and fifty Stroud Breech Cloaths, Five hundred pounds of Gun Powder, Four thousand pounds of Lead—Thirty pounds of Vermilion, Two thousand gun flints, Two hundred pounds of brass kettles, One Groce [gross] of knives, Two hundred pounds of Tobacco, Three Dozen gilt looking glasses, One groce of gun worms [?], Two groce of awls, One Groce of fire Steels, Sixteen dozen of gartering, Ten thousand pounds of flour, Five hundred bushels Indian corn, Twelve horses, Twelve horned Cattle, Twenty Bushels Salt, and Twenty Guns.

Conspicuous for its absence on this list is brandy or "eaudevie," as the French traders referred to it. The British were certainly dispensing alcohol to Indians, for George Morgan even wrote a proposal to build a distillery in Illinois to accommodate the brisk trade in it. In 1768 Lieutenant Fraser had observed of the Illinois Indians that "nothing can equal their passion for drunkenness, but that of the French Inhabitants." While the effect of alcohol on the Illinois is clearly documented, in the early 1770s the goods they asked as the price of their land did not include it. Just as significant is the appearance of 12 horses as part of the price. In fact, there are suggestions that at this time, despite the diffusion of horses all across the century to Indians of the Missouri and Illinois tribes, the domiciled Illinois nations were horse-poor.

Horse Tales

The account left by Commander Macarty of the arrival of Mechigamea, Cahokia, and Peoria Indians at Fort Chartres in 1752 contains one of the few descriptions in which the mode of travel of Illinois Indians is documented. A week after a decimating attack by the northern Indians (see chapter 5), the Indians received a false report of a second attack. They abandoned their villages and converged on the fort for safety. "All the men, women, and children of the three Illinois villages reached here early in the morning, having walked all night in a continual rain," Macarty noted. The three villages mentioned here are the two villages of the Mechigamea and the Cahokia village, all north of Fort Chartres. Only the settlement of the Kaskaskia Indians lay to the south. Some of the Cahokia, in fact, lived at least thirty miles to the north. Why weren't these Indians, traveling at night through the rain, desperate for the protection of the fort, using horses? While all their animals may have been stolen in the Fox and Sioux raid, those attacking Indians had converged on the Illinois Indian villages by canoe. Stealing an entire horse herd would have been difficult. So few accounts of the Illinois Indians mention them on horseback that there is a general historical sense of the Cahokia and Mechigamea especially: people conducting their lives and daily activities on foot. Paths leading to their villages inscribe a landscape of pedestrian traffic; and except in deepest winter, when the river bottoms lay silent under scarves of heavy mist and ice plates shimmered from bank to bank, the rivers provided a constant transport. Summer and winter hunts would have required horses, and Commander Macarty states specifically that the Mechigamea "traded horses" with the Missouri tribes. But accounts of horses in the Illinois settlements after 1750 usually link the animals to the French, the "sturdy French ponies," the "point ponies."

Earlier in the century, Illinois tribes appear to have had horses. The De Gannes memoir of the early eighteenth century, describing the Peoria Indians, states they obtained horses from the Pawnee and Wichita Indians

Facsimile page of the Illinois-Wabash Land Company deed of sale, circa 1796, appearing in Clarence W. Alvord, *The Illinois-Wabash Land Company Manuscript* (1915). Illinois Indian and allied chiefs have drawn their personal symbols on this deed. The original was notarized in 1773.

to use for buffalo hunts. The horses came branded on their hindquarters and were called *canatis*. French accounts of the Mechigamea village north of Fort Chartres, along the river, mention Indian livestock "running" there. One of the early memorials of Bienville, describing his plans to build a fort out in the Spanish borderlands, describes obtaining "a quantity of horses . . . from the Indians of the upper part of this river [the Mississippi]." It is not clear which Indian tribes he had in mind, but at that time, the 1720s and 1730s, the upper Mississippi Valley Indians were obviously seen as sources for horses. The decimation of the Illinois in the Chickasaw Campaign and the Fox Wars likely changed this and perhaps affected their horse populations as well. By 1752 Commander Macarty was identifying the Osage as the source of Illinois Indian horses.

Although horses would provide natural increase if well cared for, the grazing lands of the domiciled Illinois Indians were circumscribed by ancient French grants. The edges of the "Mechigamea Prairie," for instance, north of Fort Chartres, abutted the French village of St. Philippe. Indian horses may have been overworked in hunting and packing meat; and as also occurred with Osage horses across the Mississippi, exhausted mares did not foal. Caring for horses was directly connected to the yield of the land. Both the French ponies and aboriginal horses had a relatively small body size; live weights ranged from six hundred to nine hundred pounds. Even so, these horses needed to consume a great deal of forage. Providing that forage in winter was extremely labor-intensive for tribes living in areas of cold winters. In the eighteenth century, the upper Mississippi Valley had such cold and icy winters. Plains Indians living along the Missouri River are described as having to cut down cottonwood trees, haul them to village or camp, thaw them by fires, and then cut or peel off the bark for horses. A meager diet for horses affected reproductive capacity as well, leading to limited natural increase. Such tribes, known as "horse-poor," resorted to horse raiding and stealing as the means of keeping up their horse herds. However, replenishing horses through raiding did not seem to have been a pattern in the Illinois Country. Over sixty years, the Illinois Indians had gradually relinquished their role as tribal raiders. By the time of the British occupation, the horse reserves of the Illinois Indians could never have equaled those of other, competing Indian tribes, especially the Osage.[31]

Most Indian tribes were trading with each other, or raiding, to obtain horses. While the Kaskaskia Indians had been the most successful agriculturally, and are documented in the French regime as having livestock and horses, the other Illinois tribes seem to have "crossed the river" to obtain their horses. Buying or trading for horses via the old Spanish trade networks that crisscrossed the Plains Indians' territory would involve swimming or transporting the animals across inland Missouri territory rivers and across the Mississippi, that chimerical, unpredictable waterway. Efforts of the French to float horses and cattle downriver to supply such military efforts as the Chickasaw Campaign in the 1730s had sometimes been disastrous. Mention of capsizement and drowned animals occurs in letters. In 1719 a trader obtained at least fourteen horses from the Osage but lost six horses and a colt while crossing a stream. Preparing for his Chickasaw Campaign of 1739, Bienville bought seventy-seven yoke of oxen and eighty horses from the Illinois colonies but documents that thirty horses perished on the way to Arkansas Post. Water levels in the eighteenth century were significantly higher; in heavy rain, streams and rivers rose dangerously. In the inland Ozark highlands especially were streams and springs dissecting the slopes, creating an erosional landscape through which waterways ran with "devious courses." Hydrographic studies of stream rise and flash flooding in the Ozarks have found valleys "without the semblance of a stream in the evening [holding] torrents the next morning which a man on horseback could not ford." As also occurring in the Illinois Country, natural springs in the Missouri lands were profuse: in one Ozark county alone were counted twenty-four hundred vital springs! Rampant, often dangerous streams made a constant horse trade through the area and then across the Mississippi difficult to sustain. And across the Mississippi, in the country of the Illinois, lay prairies and plains, punctuated with oak-hickory savannas. There were no highlands to speak of, no steep gradients (excepting the river bluffs) and no mountainous terrain. This meant no miles of sheltering woods in which to guard horse reserves. And at the time the deerskin trade was becoming important in the Missouri lands, the Illinois lived on the British side of the river. The Mississippi was an international boundary that eventually became policed and patrolled by the Spanish. The Osage, even in their traditional village sites along the Missouri, faced few transportation or boundary issues. They could trade with (and also raid) tribes to the southwest without crossing a clear international border. They claimed and roamed the land on both sides of the internal Osage and Gasconnade Rivers and would have known ideal fording spots.[32]

The Osage became consummate horse raiders, often of European herds. In the late 1790s, at the height of the trouble among the Osage, the Spanish, and the French, Nicolas de Finiels left a vivid account of their horse-stealing methods. He observed that Osage "disdained to flee upon the animals' backs" but rather ran behind the startled horses, "spurring them on with their own speed," until all were beyond pursuit. The predation of Osage on the hunting, trapping, and living of both Europeans and Indians has been well documented. A significant aspect of their horse acquisition was the connection to deer hunting. The horse made possible a consummate mastery of the deerskin trade. During the "prairie hegemony" of the Osage, the horse and the deer combined in a twenty-year period of staggering deerskin extraction. In 1757 the Osage marketed eight thousand pounds of bear- and deerskins; by 1773 they were producing twenty-two thousand pounds. The ascendancy of the Missouri Osage, both Little and Great bands, is an important factor in understanding the experience of the British and the Illinois Indians. And that ascendancy had much to do with the reality of the Osage population: they remained "numerically strong" in their forested Ozark highlands and western prairies, rarely experiencing the decimation of disease that periodically swept across the open prairies of the Illinois Country. Their domination of the deerskin trade has led historians to use the phrase "robber economy" to characterize the fur and peltry trade of the Mississippi and Missouri lands.[33]

Across the river among the Illinois Indians, a robber economy in deerskin trade had been possible only during the years when the woodlands of the floodplain and upland bluffs could support herds of deer. Such herds had been described much earlier in the century as "vast" and "roving." While archaeological site studies of both the French and Indian villages have consistently revealed the presence of deer bones, domesticated animal remains also appear, in increasing numbers among the French and especially among the earliest Anglo-American settlers in the 1790s. Some limited evidence of the Illinois Indian trapping and hunting harvests pinpoints the concentration more on furbearing mammals such as bobcat, bear, wolf, and fox, as well as otter, muskrat, mink, marten, and fisher. The enormous deerskin hauls taking place across the Mississippi were not replicated in the Illinois Country after 1763. In 1769 Colonel Wilkins at Fort Chartres wrote [somewhat ambiguously] that "Peltries here are abundant, but inferior to those of the Mississippi, the Major Part being Deer Skins." He also noted that the "Missouri is better peopled than the Mississippi." Due to the remaining French in the Illinois colonies ranging to the south and trading with the Indians there for deerskins, Colonel Wilkins also felt Illinois Indians were "jealous" of the Cherokees and Chickasaws. General Gage himself saw that the trade potential of the Illinois was uncertain: "Some Trade has been carried on there, not very great," he wrote, "and it is a doubt, whether the Adventurers in the Trade will not fail."[34]

Across the three decades prior to the arrival of the Americans under George Rogers Clark but especially after the British moved into the Illinois, relations among all groups of peoples were unstable. One historian has perceptively summarized pre-Revolutionary Illinois as "thirty-odd years of temporary ends and makeshift means." He describes forces "beyond the control of any government." Such forces included aggressive hunting competition by horse-rich tribes such as the Osage and raids into old French Illinois by northern tribes, increasing as word spread of the impending conflict between Britain and her colonies. A letter sent to Commander Rocheblave from Cahokia in 1777 tersely outlines the level of unrest: "There have been . . . two Frenchmen killed while coming from St. Joseph, and by the Potawatomies. Also Mr. Chartranc had a finger cut off by the Renards. Four traders have abandoned their house, and all their effects in the country along the river of the Illinois." The same writer adds later, "Both the Potawatomies and the Renards say that they wish St. Joseph ravaged and destroyed. There is nothing but war on every side."[35]

The Illinois Country was also reorganizing itself along new lines of trade and livelihood. Some French families who had crossed the river to live in Spanish Missouri had returned to British Illinois. In 1777 a Frenchman from Vincennes, Paul Des Ruisseaux, traveled through the old French settlements. He found that tiny St. Philippe, once almost completely abandoned, had eight or ten houses reoccupied by *Canadiens*. However, the young Frenchmen of the region were more drawn to hunting and trading than to agriculture, as Philip Pittman observed in the late 1760s. While the oldest French families at Prairie du Rocher continued to raise stock and to farm, Cahokia had become almost entirely a trade center, fortuitously located almost directly across the Mississippi from burgeoning Spanish St. Louis. Cahokia was a long, straggling, ragged village with a "great deal of poultry" but had infrequent and poorly tended crops. The Cahokia "fort," wrote Pittman, was only a small house standing in the middle of the village. "It was formerly enclosed with high palisades, but these were torn down and burnt." (It is likely the palisades were used as fuel). Independent French traders, including those traveling up the Mississippi from New Orleans and the young hunters of the French settlements, became interested in trading south toward the Ohio River, serving the needs of the Shawnee who had moved farther west, living south of Ste. Genevieve. Convoys of wheat, corn, and trade goods left the Kaskaskia area for the confluence of the Ohio and Mississippi; business was often conducted on river islands. Fur trade on the eastern shores of the Mississippi began to list toward a localized market economy in which Indians and French alike exchanged one or two furs to secure goods as needed. The old pattern of tribes converging at the end of summer and winter hunts with large packs of furs and skins was disintegrating into patterns of individual Indians trading single furs for rum or gunpowder. The *Kaskaskia Records* contain an account of an Indian visiting the wife of the British commander at Kaskaskia, M. de Rocheblave, and throwing two beaver skins at her feet. He then demanded *eaudevie*, which she refused him.[36]

This incident is documented in a lengthy court of inquiry conducted by the British only one year before George Rogers Clark surprised the sleeping village of Kaskaskia and the Illinois Country changed hands again. A close reading of this inquiry reveals persistent patterns of old loyalties in a maelstrom year. M. de Rocheblave, a Frenchman commanding for the British, was accused of treason by an Anglo-American merchant with whom he had a long-standing feud. A central charge involved a large party of Fox and Sauk Indians—perhaps as many as six hundred—who were approaching Kaskaskia, apparently with the goal of eradicating thirty Illinois Indians who had taken refuge in the town. Rocheblave asked some French inhabitants to take a British flag out to meet the Indians, a visual symbol of British military presence. Somehow, en route to the prairies where the Fox were massed, the British flag became a French flag. Rocheblave denied he had sent a French flag. During the inquiry, the French inhabitants confessed they were "burdened by the weight of the said flag," so they had substituted a "white towel" attached to a pole. The lighter flag would allow them "to pass more easily through the woods."[37]

Although Rocheblave was exonerated, the important point about the Fox not attacking Kaskaskia seems to have been missed in the inquiry. However they perceived the white towel on the pole, at that moment, the Fox were deterred. We don't know what passed between the Fox-Sauk Indians and a few French residents of Kaskaskia who staggered out of the woods at the edge of the prairie, hoisting what was clearly a French flag. The French dissatisfaction with British rule would lead to French support during the invasion of George Rogers Clark in 1778, seen by all historians who write of the bloodless takeover as a critical factor. In turn, the French may have been instrumental in persuading Indians to accept American rule. Before the American invasion, Commander Rocheblave confessed himself to be "a little crazed," as he was forced to imprison young men in Kaskaskia every day. These young Frenchmen demanded first that he follow English law and then demanded a return to French laws. In July of 1778, one month before being taken prisoner by George Rogers Clark, Rocheblave was writing letters of alarm from Fort Gage, begging the British to send troops at once. He mentions as well the difficulty in controlling Indians, although they were "in general well enough disposed." By the Indians, Rocheblave may have been specifically referring to the Kaskaskia and the Mechigamea, although many Indian nations continued to visit Fort Gage.[38]

The British had withdrawn their garrison from the Illinois in 1774–75 after rebelling eastern colonists invaded Quebec. Captain Hugh Lord was recalled; the British who had marched in under Captain Stirling in 1765 marched out in 1775. The evacuation of Fort Gage left Commander Roche-blave, in his own words, "in charge without troops, without money, without resources." From that point until August of 1778, when the Illinois Country became part of the state of Virginia, the land lay in an uneasy limbo. Land speculators and dreamers planned colonies and settlements with names like Charlotina, Vandalia, and New Wales—ephemeral, paper settlements in which happy, orderly subjects would live an elegiac life. Indian nations would be "controlled," relegated to a buffer zone where animal, fish, and bird resources would replenish themselves forever. Flowing out of the lim-itless reservoir would be a steady stream of peltries enriching the British crown. Of all the unrealistic conceptions that fueled British dreams for the management of western lands, lack of ecological understanding was perhaps the most trenchant; it has also been the least explored by scholars. In the eighteenth-century view of the frontier, it was possible to carve out tracts of land, even millions of acres in extent, surround those tracts with enforced barriers such as a string of military posts and forts, and isolate animal and plant populations into perpetuity. The intimate and intricate relationships of adjacent ecosystems, the myriad processes in which reciprocal exchanges contribute to sustainability—these relationships were unacknowledged in the thinking of even the most advanced geographers of the time. As a wolf lopes out of its territory, crossing from one habitat to another, its coat may be filled with seeds. Those seeds are shaken off, take root and grow, and a fringe of nutrient-rich northern dropseed appears to feed both deer and mice many leagues away. Similarly, wood ducks and upland game birds redistribute the seeds of rough-leaved dogwood, browsed heavily by deer. Territories and ranges are imbricated and fluid and depend on animal—and human—movement. The encapsulated Indian buffer zone, part of the vision the British were fighting to preserve in the American Revolution, was a chimera. In the real world, on the banks of the Mississippi, the old French and Indian villages of Kaskaskia, Prairie du Rocher, St. Philippe, and Cahokia hung tenuously on.[39]

Epilogue: Losses

Despite the persistent narrative of the Illinois Country as untouched virgin land, on the eve of the American takeover, both the Illinois Indians and the French were already living in an environment depleted of fur-bearing animals and the kinds of trees many of those animals depended on. In addition, introduced vegetation was thriving. On the cleared lands in the floodplain, the French had put in significant numbers of fruit trees. Early American accounts mention numerous apple and pear. While Indian agriculture was limited to the acreage granted tribes around their villages, changes in Indian subsistence overall affected the land in other ways. Indians had long burned sections of prairie to create a mosaic environment attractive to specific types of game: wild turkey, upland ruffed grouse and quail—and deer. Nut groves may have been tended on bluff tops, and the burning of prairie vegetation insured the survival of stands of fire-resistant, sun-loving oaks as well and eliminated fire-sensitive trees like red cedar and sugar maple. By the 1790s Indians living in the tripartite ecosystem of what would become the American Bottom were no longer routinely involved with maintaining through burning. Seasonal patterns of planting had been disturbed. Indians living in villages near old Fort Chartres and new Fort Gage were not clearing more land, and there is little evidence of Indian agriculture in these years. With the phasing out of autumnal burning, the invasion of woody species from the prairie-woodland edge proceeded apace. Incoming American accounts of the prairies mention that the native bluejoint (likely big bluestem) grew to the height of a man's head on horseback. Accounts also describe "reeds, cane, foxtail, millet, and broom or beard grass," the somewhat puzzling "thirty kinds of elm," and giant cottonwoods. The land held sloughs "hundreds of miles in extent," as well as prairies that were rapidly named by white settlers: Prairie Tamaroa, Twelve

Mile Prairie, Looking Glass Prairie, and Horse Prairie, lying between the Kaskaskia River and Horse Creek. In this fertile expanse of grassland, herds of wild horses grazed and multiplied, breeding from original stock that had escaped from French settlements. (See discussion of Horse Prairie in chapter 1, "Illinois Country Ecology.") These horses became prized hunting animals, for they were capable of bursts of speed and had an "additional vigor and toughness." One early history states that a French pony was "a proverb for endurance." Up at Cahokia a horse trade developed in which the French were selling large numbers of horses to Indians, an ironic inversion of the old trade patterns of the early eighteenth century. And in all areas of old French Illinois, even extending to the prairie savanna of the uplands, nearly a century of wood use had resulted in widespread deforestation.[1]

Neighborhoods of Trees

Since 1699 French-occupied lands had mandated a steady use of wood for heating and cooking; as with the Illinois Indians, the preferred tree was hickory. While most accounts maintain that Illinois Indians constructed traditional homes of bent saplings and woven cattail mats, one history does specify that in 1732, a tribe of Mechigamea built a village of log cabins near Fort Chartres. French settlers preferred what has become known as French Creole architecture. Seventy years of house and barn construction in which all property was surrounded by upright pickets and posts had resulted in premium prices being paid for rot-resistant woods like red cedar. In Ste. Genevieve by 1790, for instance, eastern red cedar, *Juniperus virginiana*, a prime post wood, was selling for three times the amount of oak. Red cedar is the common native pioneer tree of old fields and previously cleared or burned lands; it also furnishes food for deer who browse it heavily in the winter months. Some ecologists and botanists classify red cedar as a native invasive species, so quickly does it seed and spread; however, in French Missouri and Illinois, it wasn't spreading quickly enough to keep up with the demand for cedar posts. French builders also exploited another tree routinely. The shingle oak, *Quercus imbricaria*, provided thousands—perhaps hundreds of thousands—of shingles for French houses. In addition to using prairie cordgrass as thatch, French carpenters employed the froe to split the shingle oak into thin, overlapping sheets. A typical entry in the Chartres notarial records, 1763, reads, "One old house, built of pickets, covered with shingles, situate in New Chartres near the Mississippi River." A record from 1764 is even more precise in detailing the number of wooden structures on the property: "one horse mill built of posts . . . one barn covered with straw [thatch] . . . one stable built of pickets, and the lot belonging to said

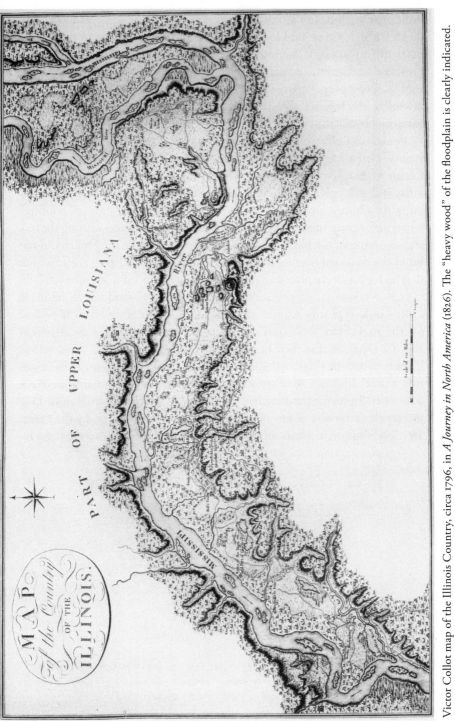

Victor Collot map of the Illinois Country, circa 1796, in *A Journey in North America* (1826). The "heavy wood" of the floodplain is clearly indicated.

buildings, enclosed all around with posts . . . and the shingles, posts, and pickets which are on said lot." One of the earliest mentions of these posts occurs in a Kaskaskia manuscript from 1723, and the repeated mention of pickets references the French manner of running sharp, closely spaced palings all along property lines. Posts and pickets were milled at early French sawmills; the lumber was hauled from the uplands when the floodplain forests were exhausted.[2]

French use of wood to demarcate property and create defined spaces, such as gardens, horse mill enclosures, orchards, and barnyards, is a marked feature of their settlement. Twentieth-century sketches of old French Illinois villages depict this high wood use. Neighborhoods fairly bristle with picketing. In addition, repeated references in the notarial records to "hauling" wood in for construction suggest that French workers were mining the oak stands on top of the bluffs, especially white oak. While the French did not build the standard frontier log cabin, preferring vertical-post construction in which posts were placed in the ground or embedded in a horizontal sill, log cabin construction provides a good measure of wood use. A standard cabin could typically require nearly eighty logs, in addition to the wood for the roof. French notarial records of contracts for home construction are often specific that their homes be built of walnut or oak. Observers of French homes in the Prairie du Chien area of Wisconsin area also mention that the houses were wrapped in bark sheets—cedar, elm, or black ash—although this practice has not been documented for Illinois. Due to French extraction of key tree species from upland groves, by the 1780s, arriving Anglo-American settlers on the ridge prairies may have been re-

Typical Illinois French village of the eighteenth century, drawn by Gordon Peckham. French settlers used wood extensively. Reprinted with permission from Margaret Kimball Brown and Lawrie Cena Dean, *The French Colony in the Mid-Mississippi Valley* (1995).

sorting to using woodlots (stream-margin timber) at a distance from their farms. Finally, soil analysis from the northern American Bottom, including an alluvial fan between the Cahokia Mounds and the bluffs, has revealed a zone in which specialized sediments show a "renewed instability" that bespeaks forest clearance activities, accelerating in the late eighteenth and early nineteenth centuries. The high moisture content of the alluvial bottomlands, where wooden structures would rot within twenty years, required consistent rebuilding.[3]

At the same time, right across the Mississippi, adjacent Missouri lands revealed a completely different tree neighborhood by the 1770s. Miles of forest, a blend of deciduous and conifer, coated the unglaciated southern Missouri hills south of St. Louis. The lush trees of the Missouri Ozark highlands, dominated by an oak-hickory overstory raining down delectable acorns for deer, had no parallel by the 1770s in the Illinois Country. And in some areas, those miles of forest contained superlative stands of pure oak. Studies conducted early in the twentieth century still showed upland forests composed almost exclusively of oaks, in fact, one of the largest pure oak forests in the United States. The same study showed an extraordinary number of species of oak. The adjacency of this oak phenomenon to the oak-poor lands of the Illinois Country must be acknowledged in the history of both areas. The presence of unusually concentrated oak varieties in the Missouri lands may well have contributed to its bountiful deer population. Surveys of white-tailed deer diet in timbered regions of America have shown that as much as one-third of deer diet in the fall is acorns. The high fat and carbohydrate content of acorns rapidly builds up deer reserves for the winter. In times of "acorn abundance," deer may eat so many acorns that the mast comprises nearly 80 percent of their diet!

Scientists who have used Government Land Office records (the GLO survey) to reconstruct the presettlement floodplain landscape along the Illinois and Mississippi rivers have found that perhaps 56 percent of the floodplain was forested; however, those records, drawn in part from the selection of witness trees by surveyors, were set down in the decades following 1800. At that time, the abandonment of French Illinois had begun to be reversed by the influx of American settlers. Forty years of untended tree growth on the floodplain and uplands would have seen the beginnings of successional resurgence of woodland. Back in the 1780s, however, the prairie margins and cutover timber were only beginning a recovery process. In addition, this succession would not involve a resurgence of slow-growing, fire-resistant oaks. A study of forest regeneration in southern Illinois, using the same interval—approximately forty-three years of abandoned lands—

established that the first pioneers into old, burned, but unfarmed fields were sweet gum and sugar maple.[4]

In the Illinois Country, the complex, linked factors of predominant, fire-managed prairies, oak depletion, and thinning deer populations created a strong, environmental pressure on remaining Illinois Indians. The southern tip forests of Illinois, the swampy cypress country just north of the Ohio River, as well as the wide swath of hardwood known today as Shawnee National Forest, were far enough away from Illinois Indian villages to make aggressive deer hunting impractical. Researchers attempting to pinpoint the hunting grounds of the Illinois during the British period, for instance, have located the Kaskaskia Indians "out upon a Prairie hunting about one hundred Miles from the village of Kaskaskia." The historian compiling these records comments that during the winter of 1770–71, at least, the Illinois were hunting at such a distance from old Fort Chartres that they could not make trading visits. There is also evidence that the Kaskaskia occasionally hunted across the Mississippi. An entry in the logs of Baynton, Wharton, and Morgan records the Kaskaskia as receiving presents at Fort Cavendish (Chartres). Early in Colonel Wilkins's tenure at the fort, in 1769, his journal of transactions with Indians shows interactions "almost exclusively" with the four Illinois Indian tribes, who came regularly to trade and receive the small gifts by which the old Indian traditions of gifting and honoring were meagerly maintained. The Wilkins log and other scattered references in British correspondence compile a picture of Illinois Indians continuing to use the central magnet of the fort as their base. The out-and-back movement of their hunts and their regular appearance at the great limestone arch suggest that the British storehouse and Indian trade policies were gradually replacing the familiar French liaisons, despite the Indians' initial resistance. Colonel Wilkins wrote grandiose estimates to General Gage of what might be possible in trade revenues from the Illinois. He felt that the upper Illinois River country was too sparsely inhabited by Indians to bring in much trade, but that if motivated, the Peoria, Kaskaskia, and Cahokia "might furnish 3 or 400 packs P[er] Annum." It is not clear what peltries or skins would comprise these packs. To place the number of three or four hundred packs in perspective, one observer of the deerskin trade far south, in Augusta, Georgia, between 1783 and 1799, felt that the export "has never been less than 240,000 skins." In the first decade of the nineteenth century, Choctaw and Chickasaw nations alone sent 105,039 pounds of deerskins to New Orleans. Deerskins probably averaged about one and a half pounds each, and typical packhorse loads were 150 to 200 pounds. Colonel Wilkins's estimate for a potential Illinois Indian haul was therefore an improbable forty thousand pounds of skins! Across the river in Missouri, using large numbers of horses on highland trails, the Osage were increasing their deerskin packloads to a high of twenty-two thousand pounds per year.

It seems clear that the Illinois Indians were not competing in the deer-skin trade. The oak-hickory woodlands were likely compromised; and there were no dense miles of sheltering woods for horse thieves to fade into with contraband animals. A few tribes had stolen horses from the garrison of the fort in the first year of British occupation, but they returned the animals during a negotiation with George Croghan in 1766. The traditional loca-tion of floodplain Illinois Indian villages placed these Indians between two populations. Across the Mississippi were burgeoning European settlements, satellite villages of the French surrounding the new fur-trading entrepôt of St. Louis; and to the east of the Illinois villages, Ohio Valley and Wabash River tribes were crisscrossing the prairies. In the late eighteenth century, the Illinois Indians were caught in the peculiar nature of their land: not undisturbed prairie enough to promote the rapid replenishing of buffalo herds; not canopied forest enough to maintain the forest-meadow mosaic preferred by deer; and finally, ribboned by so many waterways that humans were almost ubiquitous by 1770.[5]

Other tribes emulated the patterns of trade modeled by the Osage, of engaging in legal activities close to the monitoring eye of the Spanish authorities in the settlements and trading on the instant with any willing individual in the interior. During the decades of the 1760s and 1770s, for instance, the Missouria Indian tribe "became familiar," to the point of spending summers with French inhabitants. The (greatly reduced) Mis-souria camped outside St. Louis, where Missouria women found work in the building and construction trades of the new settlement. This custom, of Indian tribes migrating to the St. Louis area to camp and trade, began to pull in the more aggressive, northwestern tribes as well. Eventually even the Sauk and the Fox used the market center of St. Louis to trade hard-wood products like maple sugar and pecans. This riverine activity was developing directly across the Mississippi River from the British and then the American Illinois Country, reflecting a commercial, population, and resource shift to a dynamic new center. The effect on the Indian populations of the true Illinois Country was to increase their dissatisfaction, heighten their anxiety about their livelihood and future, and create a different kind of trafficking to authorities at Fort Cavendish, Fort Gage, and then the Americans governing out of Old Kaskaskia. Purveyors of furs also became purveyors of information. Tribal "unrest" and potential intertribal war are the dominant themes not only of the British occupation of the Illinois but also of the first decades of American occupation. One early historian of the St. Louis area asserts that the Illinois Indians "never crossed the river." While this is a generalization and clearly erroneous, as some Peoria, especially, did cross the Mississippi to establish a permanent camp south of St. Louis, the perception that the trade life of the Illinois Country was vitalized through the Missouri Indian tribes and not the Illinois is likely accurate. By January of 1769, French merchants living in Spanish St. Louis petitioned to be allowed to trade up the Missouri River. The merchants state that they also presented the same request to St. Ange, commanding in the Illinois Country, "in regard to what concerns the district of the Misisipi, where it is absolutely necessary to send traders for the tranquillity of the tribes." Merchants perceived Indians as competitors for European trade. With St. Louis merchants beginning to send traders both east and west, the sixty-mile stretch of Mississippi River to which the French had come marveling in 1699 was never again empty of craft, flowing wide and open, glinting with undisturbed light.[6]

Changes in human occupancy of the area had greatly accelerated at midcentury. The "distant Illinois" of Captain Thomas Stirling's expedition may have been distant, but it was not trackless wilderness punctuated with isolated smoke plumes. Indian tribes had engaged in periodic riverine migrations and relocations for most of the eighteenth century. French trappers and voyageurs descended the Mississippi from the Falls of St. Anthony, converging on the trade matrix at Fort Chartres. Tediously rowing and cordelling upriver from New Orleans, French Creoles and recently emigrated traders and merchants stopped at early settlements like Natchez, Baton Rouge, Arkansas Post, and the bluff outpost of latter-day Memphis. From the Great Lakes streamed trappers, traders, and Indians using the portage at St. Joseph near the Kankakee to reach the Illinois River and descend to the heart of the Illinois Country.[7]

Historical records can only hint at the amount of traffic on the rivers in the decades preceding the American Revolution. Figures available at midcentury from Montreal, listing the number of *conges* (trade licenses) granted to voyageurs as well as the number of men and canoes engaged in the trade down the Mississippi, give some indication of the numbers of legally-sanctioned traders.

1740	32 *conges*	57 canoes	336 men engaged
1743	54 *conges*	68 canoes	417 men engaged
1750		74 canoes	419 men engaged

The number of unlicensed French traders and trappers was almost certainly greater. One study of the French trading posts above the American Bottom, those "farflung" bluff and high hill country outposts of French Wisconsin, summarizes the human traffic on the rivers: "They came and went without record." While no thorough historical investigation exists into the flow of men in an illegal riverine trade on the upper Mississippi and Missouri, there is evidence, especially from the increasingly hostile interactions of the Missouria and Osage Indians and the French, that unlicensed and unscrupulous traders were cheating their suppliers. The pattern escalated as a result of war. At the end of King George's War (1744–48), tantalizingly higher prices for beaver lured French Canadian voyageurs across the Mississippi. Although estimates in the 1740s and 1750s of Missouria and Osage Indian tribe populations were quite low—at five hundred "men" and fewer—there was yet "much trouble" between Indians and, especially, unlicensed French traders. These traders were often found murdered on the banks of rivers. A "Memoir upon the State of the Colony of Louisiana in 1746" noted efforts of French voyageurs to induce Indians to overwinter in beaver country of the interior. This practice, of French traders following Indians into rich fur country, distinguished the French fur harvesting from that of the British.[8]

The British initially planned to set up scattered posts and trading sites throughout their new holdings in the western lands. There are repeated references in British correspondence to the necessity of building forts at the mouths of the Illinois, the Wabash, and the Ohio. Yet even these proposed forts (which never materialized) would have required Indians to travel fair distances to trade. One historian has commented that the proposed British system of setting up a handful of forts was "running contrary to customs a hundred years old." Ironically, however, it was the presence of French Canadian traders and trappers in the Indian camps and villages that created animosity. Abuses of trade by coureurs de bois resulted in the murder of French traders during and after the Seven Years War.[9]

After the British arrived in the Illinois, British traders poured into the Great Lakes region and fanned out into the Upper Mississippi. Their numbers eventually caused General Gage to change his mind about the efficacy of building forts at the mouths of the Illinois and Ohio Rivers. The British policy of controlling all trade through forts and outposts would be futile, since the Indian tribes were so numerous. Skilled traders and Indians long used to the river systems and their character could silently skiff by the forts at night. Gage believed that regulation of traders was necessary, via a system of strict licenses and trading rules. Yet just as French and British hunters competed for buffalo on the Grand Prairies, subjects from both countries—as well as Spanish emigrating north—were thronging on the rivers and crossing into the Missouri lands in a drive to reach the fur basin of the trans-Mississippi West. As French and Indians migrated across the Mississippi to Spanish Louisiana in the 1760s, new French settlements on the western banks of the Mississippi began to appear. St. Louis and Carondelet (Vide-Poche) grew upriver from the earlier, southernmost French village of Ste. Genevieve. With the exception of Ste. Genevieve, an early lead-mining, saltworks, and agricultural village, these new settlements were wholly thriving on the fur trade. French and Spanish trappers were pushing west and then north, up the Missouri River, meeting descending Indian nations who had transferred their trade activities from Fort Chartres to St. Louis.

With the relocating of numerous prairie tribes, eventually the burning of the thick prairie grasses was taken over by white hunters. William Faux left a vivid account of these grasses and their burning in Illinois in 1819: "*the Indian summer* . . . is caused by millions of acres, for thousands of miles around[,] being in a wide-spreading, flaming, blazing, smoking fire, rising up through the wood and prairie, hill and dale." Faux observed that both shrubs and trees could be kindled by flames running through long, coarse prairie grasses, and that such fires, once set by native tribes, were now "perpetuated by the White Hunters." American hunters and settlers began to appear in the early 1780s, even before the Northwest Territories were officially opened for land purchase. The earliest American arrivals, a colony of settlers to the Kaskaskia area, came in 1780, lured by promising reports of the Illinois Country spread by the soldiers in George Rogers Clark's expedition. The fledgling American government tried to control squatters, but official rulings did not deter settlement. In 1779 the county-lieutenant of the newly created Virginia Territory, Colonel John Todd, had issued a proclamation forbidding "new settlements upon the flat lands of said rivers, or within one league of said lands" (Mississippi, Ohio, Illinois, and Wabash Rivers). Directive had come from the government that French land claims must be legally decided and the original French farms surveyed. In issuing the injunction against settling the flatlands of the rivers, Colonel Todd was acknowledging the tremendous alluvial potential of riverine earth and perhaps, as well, noting the lure of those friable lands already cleared by both prehistoric and historic Indians and the French. When they settled along the Kaskaskia River, these earliest American squatters were clearly ignoring Todd's proclamation. They rapidly imprinted the land with a different set of cultural traditions, one focused on surveying, fencing, and using even small tributary streams to send produce to market. Around

La Belle Fontaine spring on the uplands, settlement initially began along the old Cahokia-Kaskaskia Road, the Chemin du Roi of the French. This settlement was called New Design, and in 1787, the first recorded white child of English parentage was born in a log home there. These upland settlers shared in common with the remaining French a dependence on the white *capot* or blanket coat; they were also typically barefoot or wore moccasins. In the absence of leather, they made horse collars plaited from maize husks sewn together. Their cabins had ceilings covered with pelts— raccoon, opossum, and wolf.[10]

Wolf Tales

The mention of wolf pelts being used as cabin insulation is one of the last references to the wolf as a useful animal, outside its role in the fur trade. Modern studies of the intricate ecological relationships among deer, moose, wolves, and forests have indisputably established the importance of wolf predation on large herbivores. In the absence of deer herds, wolf packs will prey on livestock and possibly on people. This pattern surfaced in the Illinois Country in the eighteenth century and accelerated into the nineteenth. In 1769 Father Gibault, making his first visit across the prairies to Vincennes, wrote to Bishop Briand, "I have been told the story of some deaths which certainly cannot be heard without drawing tears; this portion of your flock is terribly a prey to the wolves." Before the depletion of deer herds and their own numbers through the fur trade, gray wolves, *Canis lupus*, sought the edge habitats where deer ranges overlapped. Ironically, such habitats, the stream margins and emergent prairie-savanna, became the prized settlement corridors for incoming American settlers. Research on settlement patterns in northeastern Missouri, for instance, establishes that over and over, settlers chose the ecotonal prairie, or edge habitat, an area highly preferred by early frontier farmers in Illinois as well. Such lands were transition zones that provided access to a variety of trees for cabin and barn construction, water, pasture for stock, small game for food, and soil that was "sparsely timbered." Geographers call these early settled strips of ecotonal habitat staging areas. From there, settlers made forays out into woodlands and sent their stock to graze. While most hogs were permitted to range freely on the uplands in Illinois, farmers tried to protect their other animals with fences. Yet the graceful worm fence, the sloping rail border so easily constructed by American settlers and brought with them as part of the southern hearth culture, never kept out a hunting wolf.[11]

The hunting and eating patterns of wolves in the wild are tied to a capacity to live a feast-or-famine existence. Consummate stalkers and long-distance travelers, wolves are naturalized to find and digest enormous amounts of meat at one time. They need to eat an average of five to ten pounds of meat a day but may consume up to eighteen pounds. Nor are wolves usually wasteful predators. They eat the heart, lungs, liver, and some other internal organs; they crush bones to extract marrow and sometimes eat hair and hooves. Their attacks on livestock would have been not opportunistic assaults but strategies for survival. Wolf hunting territories are marked by scent and droppings, and such territories overlap and shift seasonally, what Barry Lopez, in comparing hunting territories of Pawnee and Omaha Indians to wolf territories, has called an ebb and flow of boundaries. While such historians as Carl Ekberg have written movingly of the eradication of French communal agriculture under American property laws, those same laws imposed a territorial rigidity on deer and wolf ranges equally as destructive. The ebb and flow of natural boundaries stopped. Fencing, ditching, and timber removal overrode sensitive animal responses to a variety of earth and climate factors, including seasonal fluctuation in water. The loose, changing, adaptive habitat of the Illinois watery world, characterized by natural movement of rivers, streams, animals, and people, entered another phase of alteration under American rule. New species of plants, insects, fish, birds, and some mammals would appear even as others disappeared. Yet the means by which these species arrived was no longer so often tied to the fluctuation of water, nor was it gradual. The dynamic influx was tied much more directly to human real estate: who bought and sold, which persons and how many entered the habitat.[12]

Under American governance, many of the new arrivals were aggressive eradicators of animals. By the early 1800s Randolph County commissioner records describe payment for wolf bounties. On one day in session, June 5, 1804, the court accepted five wolf scalps, two grown wolf carcasses, and seven wolf scalps again. Prairie du Rocher and Kaskaskia are in Randolph County; the wolves taken there in 1804 were preying on American livestock. The attractiveness of the cash wolf bounty, coupled with ridding the area of predators, took precedence over the value of a wolf fur in trade. The bounty system was a direct cause of extirpation and extinction of wolf subspecies and fueled the two-hundred-year-old conflict that Barry Lopez has termed "the wolf war in North America." Today seven wolf subspecies are completely gone—including the Great Plains wolf and the Texas gray wolf; both the northern and southern Rocky Mountain subspecies of wolves are extinct. In the areas of old French Illinois and Missouri, the wolf war had its roots in the deerskin and fur trade. The emptying out of the "vast" deer herds of early accounts left wolves, as predators of large mammals,

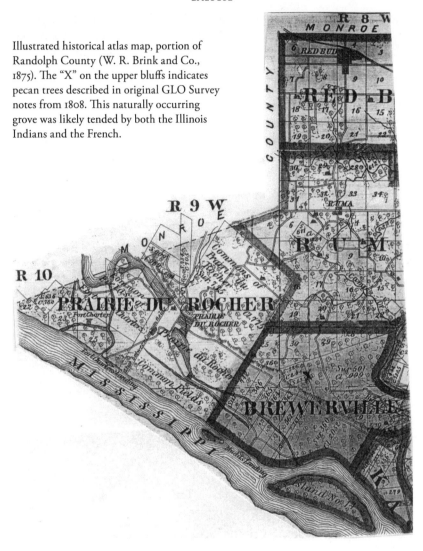

Illustrated historical atlas map, portion of Randolph County (W. R. Brink and Co., 1875). The "X" on the upper bluffs indicates pecan trees described in original GLO Survey notes from 1808. This naturally occurring grove was likely tended by both the Illinois Indians and the French.

without much recourse. Elk were also disappearing by the time of the American occupation. The delectable, amniotic smell of newborn calves, colts, and lambs drew hungry wolves to early American homesteads. By 1818 Gershom Flagg, a settler in Madison County just above the French settlements, noted, "Sheep will do very well here if they can be kept from the Wolves but this cannot well be done in the newsettled parts the wolves are so very numerous." Flagg also mentioned that wolves were killing sows and their newborn shoats. While letters and accounts from the 1780s and

1790s continue to note the availability of deer and buffalo in Illinois, these references must be carefully weighed against the total picture of imbalanced animal populations. The 1804 Wood River journals of Lewis and Clark, for instance, describe the killing of deer not as members of vast herds but as one or two animals. An entry for January 29, 1804, reads, "Shields Killed a Deer Today." Other entries describe two deer killed, or one deer and one turkey. Ten hunters took five deer on January 30, the largest number recorded. Such entries are in contrast to the references to "roving deer herds" and the "vast" or "immeasurable" numbers of animals, both deer and buffalo, consistently mentioned by observers before 1750. A suggestive account written by a traveler to the Illinois Country in 1790 mentions the number of times Indians appeared with sturgeon to trade. So often did this occur that the diarist, Hugh Heward, wrote, "An Indian came with sturgeon but we would not buy having had enough to that time." Accounts of Indians offering sturgeon or other fish are rare before this period. They usually traded buffalo or venison.[13]

In the growth of wolf predation on livestock, two forces were in operation: long-disturbed mammal populations, especially deer, and the substitution of domestic animals for those deer. Also disturbed—long before the first American settler applied for a land title—was the Illinois Indian sense of the cosmological world as knit together in a series of processes. Barry Lopez has described this circle of processes in his seminal work on wolves and Native Americans, *Of Wolves and Men* (1978):

> When, for example, the Indian left his buffalo kill, he called out to the magpies and others to come and eat. The dead buffalo nourished the grasses, the grasses in turn fed the elk and provided the mouse with straw for a nest; the mouse, for his part, instructed the Indian in magic; and the Indian called on his magic to kill buffalo.

Anthropologists interviewing members of surviving Kickapoo in Oklahoma have also documented a cosmology of reciprocal processes. Yet overlapping the Kickapoo cosmology since the middle of the eighteenth century was a vigorous association with Europeans and their trade world. One historian has commented that Kickapoo old ways included a "strong connection with European culture." The Illinois Indian connection with the European trade world—not to mention the influence of domesticating French Catholicism—goes back to the mid-1600s and especially 1699, when the Seminarians floated down the Illinois River to establish the Holy Family Mission at Cahokia. Nor was this a maiden voyage. For twenty years before that, Europeans had been traveling the interlaced rivers, streams, and lakes of northern Illinois. In 1687 Pierre Deliette had glided in a canoe from Lake Michigan through the Chicago Portage, then down the Des Plaines River to the merging in of the Kankakee. Soon he was moving south on the waters of the Illinois River, mentioning a tributary he called the Mazon flowing in from the south. *Mazon* is derived from an Algonquian word for "nettles." Already the riverine cartography of the Illinois Country, the maps on paper and in the mind, reflected the meetings of two cultures.[14]

When George Rogers Clark entered Kaskaskia in 1778, the Illinois Indians had experienced over one hundred years of close contact with Europeans and trade culture. They had adapted their subsistence in response to rising and falling levels of game, as well as climate extremes of drought and flood. One year might bring more agriculture, then perhaps a year of longer and farther winter and summer hunts; one year, in response to rising prices in the French fur exchange, they might exploit the northern Mississippi watershed for small fur-bearing mammals; another year they might hunt more buffalo. By the 1770s the French in the Illinois were doing the same thing, refocusing trade to the south among the newly opened markets with Ohio River Indians. Trade also flourished to the north, out of Cahokia. In 1774 Charles Gratiot established a "grand depot for Indian trade at Cahokia." Between 1780 and 1800, Cahokia became known as the residence of a large number of northwestern Indian traders. It was also the most wholly French of all the east-bank settlements. One early account claims that before 1788, there were only two non-French residents in the town. In 1778 while exchanging furs at Michilimackinac, Gratiot was able to trade for five canoe loads of store merchandise valued at four thousand pounds. An inventory from his store suggests a new, ornamental style in clothing. Gratiot carried flowered flannels, Irish linens, printed calico, black knitted breeches, hats with piping, gold and silver lace, "silver, rose, red, black, yellow, green, and flowered ribbands," artificial flowers, and satin shoes. French traders, Illinois Indians, other Indian nations from the north and east, Anglo-Americans, and occasional Spanish, as well as the French families living in Cahokia, would have traded for these clothing items. Other goods for sale included combs "for curling hair," razors, and eyeglasses. This emphasis on gentility and decoration is markedly different from the lists of British trade goods shipped out to Fort Cavendish/Chartres ten years before. The year of the Gratiot inventory is also the year that the Illinois Country changed hands, passing to American rule. Clearly cultural and social shifts engendered by sheer population growth were already under way.[15]

The story has been told of a sudden, invasive, and catalytic change through American settlement. In the rapid influx of American settlers and in the confiscation of Indian lands through the aggressive treaty policies of Thomas Jefferson, political and social changes were certainly intensified. The oldest extant assessment of lands in Randolph County, 1808, indicates that 435,800 acres were "in the possession of individuals." These enormous grants numbered as many as 12,600, 15,200, 24,800, or 34,000 acres. The largest grant was for 130,400 acres. As early as 1774, an American speculator named George Castles, one of twenty-two owners, obtained a deed for a tract of land so immense, it encompassed more than a third of the present-day state of Illinois, a jagged rectangular puzzle piece taking up most of the Grand Prairie. Castles then sold his 1/22 of this tract to another person, likely sight unseen. In comparison, the typical French grant, a two-by-fifty-arpent farm, would measure out to around 130 acres. Only small portions of these widespread American grants were "in fields," and the productive land was recorded nearest Kaskaskia and Prairie du Rocher. Clearly some of those fields included old French arpents: black, prodigiously rich earth that itself had supported human beings since at least 1000 A.D. The emptying out of the Illinois Country after 1763, as well as heightened internal conflicts among tribes and between Europeans and Indians, allowed the land to begin a recovery process. Portions of prairie especially were rebounding, with tallgrass vegetation becoming rampant; however, the gradual cessation of burning by Indians was encouraging the growth of fire-sensitive trees and creating a weedy understory. The Mississippi River, too, was changing course again. After washing away the western wall of old Fort Chartres, it inexplicably began a retreat. By the early nineteenth century, a gazetteer was recording the presence of a "ravine" to the immediate west of the fort site. That ravine was in fact the abandoned river channel; and the deposition of alluvium there invited sand-loving willows, which eventually gave way to bottomland hardwoods like cottonwood, hackberry, and elm. A new fringe of floodplain forest developed. Observers in the 1790s wrote of "Bottoms low & levell & very full of heavy wood." Slowly, the look of the land of big rivers was changing.[16]

When the unwieldy and imprecise surveying system of metes and bounds passed into the Jeffersonian rectilinear survey, edges of grants and property lines tightened up. Instinct in this survey system was an expectation of control and eradication of some animal and plant populations, an expectation that at least had the merit of realism. Surveying and settlement are intrusive processes; in the first nineteenth-century histories of the area, animal and bird populations were inventoried and evaluated ruthlessly. One section of a geographical assessment was even specifically titled "These Birds Should Be Exterminated." The environmental controls being exerted on the Illinois

Country—now a territory—mirrored the eager determination of a newly formed nation to define itself, to lay with surveying chains the imprint of both public and private domain. The distinctive nature of the Illinois Country across almost one hundred years had been its indefinite borders, its malleable riverine edges, a land that merged into prairie both subtly and suddenly. When had a traveler left the French lands and embarked into "the open"? What and where were Indian hunting grounds "out on the prairie"? Were the strange, hooded, one-thousand-year-old cypress along the Cache River near the Ohio River part of the Ohio Valley or the Illinois Country? Within the Mississippi channel of islands, sandbars, and changing riverbanks, was a boatman in Britain or in Spain?

The ambiguous character of the Illinois Country symbolized its presettlement ecology as well. Watery exchanges, life-cycle relationships, adaptations so complex it would be three centuries before science caught up to name them—this land was never static, virgin, or predictable. Perhaps the dynamic presence of water contributed to the "boundaryless" character of this early Illinois. Here was an ecosystem of great continental rivers and confluences, marshy floodplains, bluffs streaming with waterfalls, and mesic prairies dotted with lush, noisy upland springs; parts of the rolling till plain held year-round wetlands. Green slashes, corridors of luxuriant grasses, signaled the unusually high water table. A nineteenth-century historian wrote that when in 1778 Virginia extended her jurisdiction west to the Mississippi, [she] "included in a country called 'Illinois,' the only one ever formed without a boundary." The alteration in, especially, the Mississippi floodplain of this unbounded land had been ongoing for millennia, but the historic peoples who lived the longest there—the Illinois Indians and the French—had endured strong processes of disintegration and deracination. Neither the British nor the Americans ever experienced the loss of a powerfully fecund riverine environment in which succeeding generations of their own people had been born.[17]

Notes

Bibliography

Index

Notes

Introduction

1. Carl J. Ekberg, *Colonial Ste. Genevieve: An Adventure on the Mississippi Frontier* (Gerald, Mo.: Patrice, 1985); *French Roots in the Illinois Country: The Mississippi Frontier in Colonial Times* (Urbana: University of Illinois Press, 2000); and *François Valle and His World: Upper Louisiana before Louis and Clark* (Columbia: University of Missouri Press, 2002). Margaret Kimball Brown's important 1979 dissertation, *Cultural Transformations among the Illinois: An Application of a Systems Model*, has been published by Michigan State University, and she has subsequently, with Lawrie Cena Dean, collated, translated, and published a critical collection of French notarial records from the first half of the eighteenth century. See *The Village of Chartres in Colonial Illinois 1720–1765* (New Orleans: Polyanthos, 1977); see also Brown and Dean as coauthors of *The French Colony in the Mid-Mississippi Valley* (Carbondale, Ill.: American Kestrel, 1995). In addition to Brown's study of change and acculturation among the Illinois Indians, two other collections of archaeological work are particularly important: *Calumet & Fleur-de-Lys: Archaeology of Indian and French Contact in the Midcontinent*, ed. John A. Walthall and Thomas E. Emerson (Washington, D.C.: Smithsonian Institution Press, 1992), and *French Colonial Archaeology: The Illinois Country and the Western Great Lakes*, ed. John A. Walthall (Urbana: University of Illinois Press, 1991). See also Charles J. Bareis and James W. Porter, *American Bottom Archaeology: A Summary of the FAI-270 Project Contribution to the Culture History of the Mississippi River Valley* (Urbana: University of Illinois Press, 1984); see Emily J. Blasingham, "The Depopulation of the Illinois Indians," part 1, *Ethnohistory* 3, no. 3 (summer 1956), and part 2, *Ethnohistory* 3, no. 4 (autumn 1956).

2. Robert M. Owens, "Jean-Baptiste Ducoigne, the Kaskaskias, and the Limits of Thomas Jefferson's Friendship," *Journal of Illinois History* 5, no. 2 (summer 2002).

3. See Carl J. Ekberg, *Stealing Indian Women: Native Slavery in the Illinois Country* (2007); Timothy Silver, *A New Face on the Countryside: Indians, Colonists, and Slaves in the South Atlantic Forests, 1500–1800* (Cambridge: Cambridge University Press, 1990), 6.

4. Peter C. Mancall, ed., *Land of Rivers: America in Word and Image* (Ithaca, N.Y.: Cornell University Press, 1996), 1.

1. Illinois Country Ecology

1. Gilbert Imlay, *A Topographical Description of the Western Territory of North America*, 3rd ed. (London: J. Debrett, 1797), 504; see also letter from Major Butricke

at Fort Chartres, 1768, describing catfish of one hundred pounds or more he encountered in the lower Ohio River, in Theodore Calvin Pease, ed., *Illinois on the Eve of the Seven Years War*, Collections of the Illinois State Historical Library 29 (Springfield: Trustees of the State Historical Library, 1940), 409; Imlay, *Topographical Description*, 504; although the terms "Illinois Country" and "the Illinois" are used interchangeably by French, British, and American writers across the eighteenth century, the clearest definition of the geographic area is provided by the British Lieutenant Eddington in 1765: "The Country of the Illinoise is very extensive, comprehending all the Country on the East Side of the Mississippi from about thirty leagues above the mouth of the Ohio to a considerable distance above the mouth of the Illinoise River junction with the Mississippi. The name of Illinoise applies to all the Country on both sides of the Illinoise River and E. of the Mississippi almost to the bottom of Lake Michigan, the latter formerly the Illinoise Lake." "Journal of Lt. Eddington or the Surgeon," in Robert G. Carroon, ed., *Broadswords and Bayonets: The Journals of the Expedition under the Command of Captain Thomas Stirling of the 42nd Regiment of Foot, Royal Highland Regiment (The Black Watch) to Occupy Fort Chartres in the Illinois Country, August 1765 to January 1766* (Society of Colonial Wars in the State of Illinois, 1984), 89.

2. James R. Gammon, *The Wabash River Ecosystem* (Bloomington: Indiana University Press, 1998), 10–11.

3. W. H. Perrin, H. H. Mill, and A. A. Graham, *The History of Edgar County, Illinois* (Chicago: Le Baron, 1879).

4. Brink, McDonough, and Co., *A History of St. Clair County* (Philadelphia, 1881), 30; J. L. McDonough & Co., *The Combined History of Randolph, Monroe, and Perry Counties, Illinois* (Philadelphia, 1883), 82; Brink, McDonough, and Co., *An Illustrated Historical Atlas Map of Monroe County* (Philadelphia, 1875), 11; *American State Papers: Public Lands. Documents, Legislative and Executive, of the Congress of the United States from the Second Session of the Eleventh to the Third Session of the Thirteenth Congress* (Washington, D.C.: Walter Lowrie and Walter S. Franklin, 1832–61), 5:168.

5. McDonough, *Combined History*, 11; Imlay, *Topographical Description*, 55; Brink, *History of St. Clair County*, 31; Kaskaskia Manuscripts, Randolph County Courthouse, Chester, Ill., 82:8:5:1 and 82:7:9:1; Pierre Deliette, "Memoir of De Gannes concerning the Illinois Country," in T. C. Pease, *The French Foundations, 1680–1693* (Springfield: Illinois State Historical Library, 1934), 340; Census of 1800, St. Clair County, Illinois Territory, in John W. Allen, *It Happened in Southern Illinois* (Carbondale: Southern Illinois University, 1968), 349; McDonough, *Combined History*, 11.

6. For the concept of an enclosing quadrilateral, see Edward Countryman, "Indians, the Colonial Order, and the Social Significance of the American Revolution," *William and Mary Quarterly*, 3rd ser., 53, no. 2 (April 1996): 342–62; Brink, *History of St. Clair County*, 30; J. White, "How the Terms *Savanna, Barrens,* and *Oak Openings* Were Used in Early Illinois," in J. S. Fralish et al., *Living in the Edge:*

Proceedings of the North American Conference on Savannas and Barrens, Illinois State University, Normal, Ill., October 15–16, 1994 (Great Lakes National Program Office: U.S. Environmental Protection Agency, 1994), 25–63; Major Butricke letter, Sept. 15, 1768, in Clarence W. Alvord and Clarence Carter, eds., *Trade and Politics, 1767–1769*, Collections of the Illinois State Historical Library 16 (Springfield: Trustees of the Illinois State Historical Library, 1921), 411; Carl J. Ekberg, *French Roots in the Illinois Country: The Mississippi Frontier in Colonial Times* (Urbana: University of Illinois Press, 2000), 82.

7. McDonough, *Combined History*, 75; E. W. Gould, *Gould's History of River Navigation* (St. Louis: Nixon-Jones, 1889), 246; Kaskaskia Manuscripts, 65:6:29:1.

8. Brink, *History of St. Clair County*, in Robert Mazrim, *Now Quite Out of Society: Archaeology and Frontier Illinois* (Illinois Department of Transportation, 2002), 55; Father Meurin to Bishop Briand, June 14, 1769, in Joseph P. Donnelly, *Pierre Gibault, Missionary 1737–1802* (Chicago: Loyola University Press, 1971), 42; Macarty and Buchet to Vaudreuil, Jan. 15, 1752, in Pease, *Illinois on the Eve*, 424; Major Butricke to Barnley, Sept. 15, 1768, in Alvord and Carter, *Trade and Politics*, 411; Macarty to Vaudreuil, Jan. 20, 1752, in Pease, *Illinois on the Eve*, 432–33; Father Louis Hennepin, *A New Discovery of a Vast Country in America*, vol. 1, ed. Reuben Gold Thwaites (Chicago: McClurg, 1903), 186.

9. Edward B. Jelks, Carl J. Ekberg, and Terrance C. Martin, *Excavations at the Laurens Site: Probable Location of Fort de Chartres I* (Springfield: Illinois Historic Preservation Agency, 1989), 15; Charles J. Bareis and James W. Porter, *American Bottom Archaeology: A Summary of the FAI-270 Project Contribution to the Culture History of the Mississippi River Valley* (Urbana: University of Illinois Press, 1984), 3; Almon Ernest Parkins, *The Historical Geography of Detroit* (Lansing: Michigan Historical Commission, 1918), 9.

10. Alvin G. Lugn, *Sedimentation in the Mississippi River between Davenport, Iowa, and Cairo, Illinois* (Rock Island, Ill.: Augustana, 1927), 83; J. W. Foster, *The Mississippi Valley: Its Physical Geography* (Chicago: Griggs, 1869), 9; see also discussion of river "dynamism" in Jelks, Ekberg, and Martin, *Excavations at the Laurens Site*, 19; Foster, *Mississippi Valley*, 9; Lugn, *Sedimentation*, 83; Imlay, *Topographical Description*, 405; Foster, *Mississippi Valley*, 8.

11. Glenn J. Speed, *Ghost Towns of Southern Illinois* (Royalton, Ill., 1977), 131; see also Victor Collot's observations on the Illinois side of the Ohio River and the Black Bottoms, in 1796. Collot wrote that his party "perceived nothing but a vast extent of low and swampy ground." In Collot, *A Journey in North America, Containing a Survey of the Countries Watered by the Mississippi, Ohio, Missouri, and Other Affluving Rivers; with Exact Observations on the Course, and Soundings of these Rivers; and on the Towns, Villages, Hamlets, and Farms of That Part of the New-World; Followed by Philosophical, Political, Military, and Commercial Remarks and by a Protected Line of Frontiers and General Limits* (Florence, Italy: O. Lange, 1924), 1:190; Captain Thomas Stirling, in Carroon, *Broadswords and Bayonets*, 43; General Harmar to the Secretary of War, Jan. 10, 1788, in William Henry Smith,

ed., *St. Clair Papers: The Life and Public Services of Arthur St. Clair, Soldier of the Revolutionary War, President of the Continental Congress, and Governor of the North-Western Territory, with His Correspondence and Other Papers* (1881; repr., New York: De Lupo Press, 1971), 38; Imlay, *Topographical Description*, 499; *Thomas' Travels in the West*, in William Hayden English, *Conquest of the Country Northwest of the River Ohio, 1778–1783; and Life of General George Rogers Clark* (Indianapolis: Bowen-Merrill, 1896, 1985), 302; Hugh Heward, "The Journal of a Voyage Made by Hugh Heward to the Illinois Country" (1970), unpublished manuscript, Hugh Heward Collection, Chicago Historical Society, 23.

12. See "A Fire-Dominated Landscape," in J. White, *A Survey of Native Vegetation in the Big Rivers Blufflands of Calhoun, Greene, and Jersey Counties with Recommendations for Protection, Restoration, and Management* (Urbana: Illinois Department of Natural Resources, 2001), 19.

13. Ekberg, *French Roots*, 79–80; see map labeled "Carte de la Pays des Illinois ca. 1752," in Winstanley Briggs, "The Forgotten Colony: Le Pays des Illinois" (PhD dissertation, University of Chicago, 1985), 88. Briggs's map is a composite based on the U.S. Geological Survey of 1956 and the Nicolas de Finiels 1797 map "La Louisiane Superieure".

14. Terrance J. Martin and Mary Carol Masulis, "Preliminary Report on Animal Remains from Fort de Chartres (11R127)," appendix D, in "Archaeological Excavations at Fort de Chartres: 1985–87," ed. David Keene (unpublished technical report on file at the Illinois Historic Preservation Agency, Springfield).

15. Jelks, Ekberg, and Martin, *Excavations at the Laurens Site*, 19.

16. Omer C. Stewart, *Forgotten Fires: Native Americans and the Transient Wilderness* (Norman: University of Oklahoma Press, 2002), 126; Stewart, *Forgotten Fires*, 118–19; Collot, *Journey in North America*, 1:244; John Francis McDermott, ed., *The Western Journals of Dr. George Hunter, 1796–1805*, Transactions of the American Philosophical Society, n.s., 53, pt. 4 (Philadelphia, 1963), 30. I am indebted to John White, Ecological Services, Urbana, Ill., for bringing these observations to my attention.

17. Kenneth R. Robertson et al., "Fifty Years of Change in Illinois Hill Prairies," *Erigenia* 14 (Nov. 1995), 48. John White, *A Survey of Native Vegetation in the Big Rivers Blufflands of Calhoun, Greene, and Jersey Counties with Recommendations for Protection, Restoration, and Management* (Urbana: Illinois Department of Natural Resources, 2001), 22.

18. Reuben Gold Thwaites, ed., *The Jesuit Relations and Allied Documents, 1610–1791*, vol. 66 (Cleveland: Burrows, 1900), 287; Engelmann quoted in Stewart, *Forgotten Fires*, 119.

19. Three such prairies were mentioned by incoming Americans, one in Pike County, one in southwestern Madison County, and one farther east, in Perry County. See J. M. Peck, *A Gazetteer of Illinois, in Three Parts*, 2nd ed. (Philadelphia: Grigg and Elliot, 1837), 293.

20. See for instance, William Oliver writing in 1841 about Looking Glass Prairie in early St. Clair County, or Charles Dickens on the same prairie in 1842, in *History*

NOTES TO PAGES 26–29

of St. Clair County, Illinois (St. Clair Genealogical Society, Curtis Media Corporation, 1992), 2:13; Solomon Koepfli, *The Story of the Settling of Highland*, trans. Jennie Latzer Kaeser (Highland Bote, 1859; privately printed, 1970), 25 (copy available at Madison County Historical Museum and Archives, Edwardsville, Ill.); see listing for Worthen et al., 1868, in White, "How the Terms," 25–63 (available online; see bibliographic entry); use of "point" terminology is documented especially for Missouri settlers by Walter A Schroeder in *Pre-settlement Prairie of Missouri*, 2nd ed. (Missouri Dept. of Natural Resources, 1982); H. M. Hill, "What and Where Is Round Prairie?" in an unpublished memoir, "Sketches," likely written in the 1920s (copy available at Morrison-Talbott Library, Waterloo, Ill.).

21. See Steven R. Ahler, "Stratigraphy and Radiocarbon Chronology of Modoc Rock Shelter, Illinois," *American Antiquity* 58, no. 3 (1993); see also T. E. Emerson, D. L. McElrath, and J. A. Williams, "Patterns of Hunter-Gatherer Mobility and Sedentism during the Archaic Period in the American Bottom," in *Foraging, Collecting, and Harvesting: Archaic Period Subsistence and Settlement in the Eastern Woodlands*, ed. S. Neusius, Occasional Paper no. 6, Center for Archaeological Investigations (Carbondale: Southern Illinois University, 1986); Reuben Gold Thwaites, ed., *Atlas Accompanying the Original Journals of the Lewis and Clark Expedition, 1804–1806*, vol. 8 (New York: Arno Press, 1969), xi, "Map of Upper Mississippi, Lower Ohio, and Lower Missouri," contemporary French manuscript map.

22. See the list of named and known prairies in Illinois, available as an attached appendix on http://dnr.state.il.us/conservation/naturalheritage/prairie/appen1.htm.

23. Phillip J. Swank, James P. Geaghan, and Donna A. Dewhurst, "Foraging Differences between Native and Released Mississippi Sandhill Cranes: Implications for Conservation," *Conservation Biology* 2, no. 4 (Dec. 1988), 389; for a comprehensive overview of crane diet, see also "[Sandhill Crane] Occurrence in Illinois," at http://www.inhs.uiuc.edu/chf/pub/ifwis/birds/sandhill-crane.html; Patrick J. Munson, Paul W. Parmalee, and Richard A. Yarnell, "Subsistence Ecology of Scovill, a Terminal Middle Woodland Village," *American Antiquity* 36, no. 4 (1971), 430.

24. Daniel H. Usner Jr., "A Cycle of Lowland Forest Efficiency: The Late Archaic-Woodland Economy of the Lower Mississippi Valley," *Journal of Anthropological Research* 39, no. 4 (1983), Table 2, 436.

25. Lauren Brown, *Grasses: An Identification Guide* (New York: Houghton Mifflin, 1979), 124; Brink, McDonough, and Co., *A History of Madison County, Illinois* (Edwardsville, Ill., 1882), 54; Terry A. Messmer et al., "A Landowner's Guide to Common North American Predators of Upland-Nesting Birds," Berryman Institute publication no. 13 (Logan: Utah State University, 1997), 5; Kathy Love, "Save the Last Dance," *Missouri Conservationist*, Feb. 2004, 25.

26. Paul W. Parmalee, "The Faunal Complex of the Fisher Site, Illinois," *American Midland-Naturalist* 68, no. 2 (1962), see table, 409; Ronald W. Loos, "A Walk through Marine, from the Past to the Present: A History of Marine and Marine Township, Madison County, State of Illinois, 1813–1988," 12 (copy available at Madison County Historical Society, Edwardsville, Ill.); Messmer, "Landowner's Guide,"

10. See also T. Edwards, "Buffalo and Prairie Ecology," in D. C. Glenn-Lewin and R. Q. Landers, Jr., eds., *Proceedings of the Fifth Midwest Prairie Conference* (Ames: Iowa State University, 1978), 110–12; William B. Collins et al., "Canadian Bluejoint Response to Heavy Grazing," *Journal of Range Management* 54, no. 3 (May 2001).

27. See this finding in "Transportation History," a history of the Bridgeport Canal System, 1998, http://www.uic.edu/orgs/LockZero/II.html; Janet Roney, "Kaskaskia Reflections: Where the Buffalo Roamed," *Community Record*, Dec. 14, 2005; Brink, *History of Madison County, Illinois*, 65.

28. N. M. Miller Surrey, *The Commerce of Louisiana during the French Regime: 1699–1763* (New York: Columbia University Press, 1916), 83; Jefferson Chapman, Robert B. Stewart, and Richard A. Yarnell, "Archaeological Evidence for Pre-Columbian Introduction of *Portulaca oleracea* and *Mollugo verticillata* into Eastern North America," *Economic Botany* 28 (Oct.–Dec. 1974), 411. See also Lawrence Kaplan, "Ethnobotany of the Apple Creek Archaeological Site, Southern Illinois," *American Journal of Botany*, 60, no. 4 (supplement; Apr. 1973); Euell Gibbons, *Stalking the Healthful Herbs* (New York: McKay, 1966), 278; Thomas D. Morgan, "Purslane," *Prairie Falcon* 33, no. 1 (Sept. 2004); Bradford Angier, *Free for the Eating* (Harrisburg, Pa.: Stackpole, 1966), 80.

29. See, for instance, extracts from the 1820s account of Daniel Harmon Brush, *Growing Up with Southern Illinois*, appearing in John White, *Early Accounts of the Ecology of the Big Rivers Area*, Big Rivers Area Assessment 5 (Springfield: Illinois Department of Natural Resources, 2000), 115; see "Farms and Residence of Alfred Gant, Sec. 14, Town 6, Range 7, Randolph County, Illinois," in McDonough, *Combined History*, 95; William Oliver, *Eight Months in Illinois; with Information to Emigrants* (Newcastle on Tyne: William Andrew Mitchell, 1843), 97, copy available at Edwardsville, Ill., Historical Society and Archives.

30. Kenneth R. Robertson, et al., "Fifty Years of Change in Illinois Hill Prairies," *Erigenia* 14 (Nov. 1995), 45; Robertson et al., "Fifty Years of Change," 46; Ibid; McDonough, *Combined History*, 59; Robertson et al., "Fifty Years of Change," 41; Mark W. Schwartz et al., "The Biogeography of and Habitat Loss in Hill Prairies," in *Conservation in Highly Fragmented Landscapes* (New York: Chapman , 1997), 279; *Kaskaskia River Area Assessment*, Living Resources 3 (Illinois Department of Natural Resources, 2000), 53; remnant or relict studies can function as fairly legitimate predictors of eighteenth-century environments. Personal communication, John White, Ecological Services, Urbana, Ill., December 5, 2003.

31. See the records of these newspapers in Lola Frazier Crowder, *Early Kaskaskia, Illinois, Newspaper Abstracts, 1814–1852* (1992), copy at Morris-Talbott Library, Waterloo, Ill.; Llewellyn L. Manske et al., "Spring-seeded Winter Cereals Can Extend the Northern Plains Grazing Season," in www.grazinghandbook.com/, North Dakota State University, Dickinson Research Extension Center; "Cool Season Grasses," in *Range of Grasses of Kansas*, Kansas Cooperative Extension Service (Manhattan: Kansas State University, July 1983), 3.; Dennis C. Nelson and Roger C. Anderson, "Factors Related to the Distribution of Prairie Plants

along a Moisture Gradient," *American Midland Naturalist* 109, no. 2 (Apr. 1983), 367–75; William Oliver records this usage in the late 1830s during his travels from Kaskaskia to Looking Glass Prairie in eastern Madison County. See Oliver, *Eight Months in Illinois*, 23; H. M. Hill, "Horse Prairie," in "Sketches."

32. Marian Smith et al., "Effect of the Flood of 1993 on *Boltonia decurrens*, a Rare Floodplain Plant," *Regulated Rivers Research & Management*, no. 14 (1998), 191–302; M. A. Stoecker, "Survival and Aerenchyma Development under Flooded Conditions of *Boltonia decurrens*, a Threatened Floodplain Species, and *Conyza canadensis*, a Widely Distributed Competitor," *American Midland Naturalist* 134, no. 1 (July 1995), 117–26; Richard E. Sparks, "Need for Ecosystem Management of Large Rivers and Their Floodplains," *BioScience* 45, no. 3 (Mar. 1995); B. S. Middleton, ed., *Flood Pulsing and Wetland Restoration in North America* (New York: Wiley, 2001).

33. Jelks, Ekberg, and Martin, *Excavations at the Laurens Site*, 19; Dan Hechenberger, Nipundikan Organization, personal communication, January 27, 2004; Surrey, *Commerce*, 59; Ekberg, *French Roots*, 276; Nicolas de Finiels, *An Account of Upper Louisiana*, ed. Carl J. Ekberg and William E. Foley, trans. Carl J. Ekberg (Columbia: University of Missouri Press, 1989), 100, and n., 193; Macarty to Vaudreuil, Jan. 1752, in Pease, *Illinois on the Eve*, 452.

34. April Allison Zawacki, *Early Vegetation of Lower Illinois Valley; a Study of the Distribution of Floral Resources with Reference to Prehistoric Cultural-Ecological Adaptations*, Report of Investigations/Illinois State Museum, no. 17 (Springfield, Ill., 1969), 60; B. Styles, S. R. Ahler, and M. L. Fowler, "Modoc Rock Shelter Revisited," in J. L. Phillips and J. A. Brown, eds., *Archaic Hunters and Gatherers in the American Midwest* (New York: Academic Press, 1983); See Table 32, "Estimated Minimum Annual Nut Yields (in bushels) Per Square Mile," in Zawacki, *Early Vegetation*, 63.

35. François Xavier Charlevoix, *Journal d'un voyage fait par ordre du roi dans L'Amerique septentriole*, 20 vols. (Paris, 1744), 2:238; and Deliette, "Memoir," 340; Donald Culross Peattie, *A Natural History of Trees of Eastern and Central North America* (New York: Bonanza, 1968), 122–23.

36. Jelks, Ekberg, and Martin, *Excavations at the Laurens* Site, 20; Ekberg, *French Roots*, 60; George Morgan to Baynton and Wharton, Dec. 10, 1767, George Morgan Letters Book, in Alvord and Carter, *Trade and Politics*, 132.

37. Macarty to Vaudreuil, Jan. 20, 1752, in Pease, *Illinois on the Eve*, 443; Daniel H. Usner Jr., *Indians, Settlers, and Slaves in a Frontier Exchange Economy: The Lower Mississippi Valley before 1783* (Chapel Hill: University of North Carolina Press, 1992); for a discussion of the nature of game and Indian trails as appropriated by the French, see Surrey, *Commerce*, 82–87. Surrey has established the principal horse and footpath routes used by the French. The prairie trails, despite being laid over buffalo traces at times wide enough for two wagons side by side, were cut so deeply into the sod, and were so often inundated, that "not during the French period, nor for many years afterward, was it possible to traverse this route with a cart." *Commerce*, 86–87; Kaskaskia Manuscripts, 37:10:9:1.

NOTES TO PAGES 39–46

38. Mcdonough, *Combined History,* 59.

39. Usner, *Indians, Settlers, and Slaves,* 219; George Morgan Letter Book, Dec. 6, 1767, in Alvord and Carter, *Trade and Politics,* 130.

2. Cahokia: French and Indian Struggles

1. Thomas E. Emerson and James A. Brown, "The Late Prehistory and Proto-history of Illinois," in *Calumet & Fleur-de-Lys: Archaeology of Indian and French Contact in the Midcontinent,* ed. John A. Walthall and Thomas E. Emerson (Washington, D.C.: Smithsonian Institution Press, 1992), 104; see also Robert L. Hall's discussion of Cahokia earthworks, "The Cahokia Site and Its People," in *Hero, Hawk, and Open Hand: American Indian Art of the Ancient Midwest and South,* ed. Robert F. Townshend (New Haven: Yale University Press, 2004). The origin and decline of Cahokia mound-builder civilization continue to be of high interest to scholars. Hall has argued elsewhere that "the post-Mississippian decline in the north Mississippi valley was not so much a cultural death as a transition to a mode of adaptation allowing settlements in new areas of the prairies." Hall, *Archaeology of the Soul: North American Indian Belief and Ritual* (Urbana: University of Illinois Press, 1997), 153. Thomas E. Emerson, *Cahokia and the Archaeology of Power* (Tuscaloosa: University of Alabama Press, 1997), especially chapter 3, "The Cultural-Historical Contexts." For the importance of the Mississippi River to the prehistoric inhabitants of Cahokia, see chapter 2, "A Huge Silver Serpent," in George R. Milner, *The Cahokia Chiefdom: The Archaeology of a Mississippian Society,* (Washington, D.C.: Smithsonian Institution Press, 1981).

2. See "The Hunter Returns," in *Illinois: Man and Resources, Past and Present: A Guide to the Exhibits in the Museummobile* (Springfield: Illinois State Museum, n.d.); John Bartram, in Chuck Williams, "Lessons from Pigeon," *Natural Areas Journal* 22, no. 3 (2002), 179; Williams, "Lessons from Pigeon," 179.

3. Patrick J. Munson, Paul W. Parmalee, and Richard A. Yarnell, "Subsistence Ecology of Scovill, a Terminal Middle Woodland Village," *American Antiquity* 36, no. 4 (1971), 430.

4. Zenobius Membre, collected in J. G. Shea, *Discovery and Exploration of the Mississippi Valley* (New York: J. S. Redfield, 1852); Charles J. Bareis and James W. Porter, *American Bottom Archaeology: A Summary of the FAI-270 Project Contribution to the Culture History of the Mississippi River Valley* (Urbana: University of Illinois Press, 1984), 185; Richard E. Sparks, "Need for Ecosystem Management of Large Rivers and Their Floodplains," *BioScience* 45, no. 3 (Mar. 1995), 171.

5. John White, *Early Accounts of the Ecology of the Big Rivers Area,* Big Rivers Area Assessment 5 (Springfield: Illinois Department of Natural Resources, 2000), 1; White, *Big Rivers,* ix; Louis Hennepin, *A New Discovery of a Vast Country in America,* vol. 1, ed. R. G. Thwaites (Chicago: McClurg, 1903); Jean Francoise Busson de St. Cosme, in M. M. Quaife, ed., *The Development of Chicago, 1674–1914* (Chicago: Caxton Club, 1916).

6. H. David Bolen, *The Birds of Illinois* (Bloomington: Indiana University Press, 1989), 20; Paul A. Johnsgard, *Waterfowl of North America* (Bloomington: Indiana University Press, 1975), 12; Munson et al., "Subsistence Ecology," 415; on woodland and subarctic Indian identification with fur-bearing mammals, see Calvin Martin, *Keepers of the Game: Indian-Animal Relations and the Fur Trade* (Berkeley: University of California Press, 1978).

7. For a good sketch of Deliette, see Judith A. Franke, *French Peoria and the Illinois Country, 1673–1846* (Springfield: Illinois State Museum Society, 1995), 28–31; Charles Callender, "Illinois Indians," in William C. Sturtevant, *Handbook of North American Indians* (Washington, D.C.: Smithsonian Institution, 1978), 674; Callender, "Illinois Indians," 674; see discussion of a fire-managed environment in chapter 1.

8. Letters of M. De la Source and St. Cosme both are discussed in J. H. Schlarman, *From Quebec to New Orleans: the Story of the French in America, Fort de Chartres* (Belleville, Ill.: Beuchler, 1929), 141; Joseph Zitomersky, *French Americans–Native Americans in Eighteenth-Century French Colonial Louisiana: The Population Geography of the Illinois Indians, 1670s–1760s* (Lund, Sweden: Lund University Press, 1994), 203; for formulas on estimating populations, see 219; Thorne Deuel, *American Indian Ways of Life: An Interpretation of the Archaeology of Illinois and Adjoining Areas* (Springfield: Illinois State Museum, 1958), 46; Pierre Deliette, "Memoir of De Gannes concerning the Illinois Country," in *The French Foundations, 1680–1693*, ed. T. C. Pease (Springfield: Illinois State Historical Library, 1934), 308; Charles Callender, "Illinois Indians," 678; Fathers Mercier and Courier, April 12, 1735, letters in Schlarman, *From Quebec*, 282; see letter from Father Mercier, April 12, 1735.

9. Deliette, "Memoir of De Gannes," 345; see also Marquette's references (1673–77) to melons "which are excellent, especially those which have red seeds," in the memorial "Of the Character of the Illinois, of their Habits and Customs," in Reuben Gold Thwaites, *The Jesuit Relations and Allied Documents, 1610–1791* (Cleveland: Burrows, 1900), 59:129; John A. Walthall, F. Terry Norris, and Barbara D. Stafford, "Woman Chief's Village: An Illini Winter Hunting Camp," in *Calumet & Fleur-de-Lys: Archaeology of Indian and French Contact in the Midcontinent*, ed. John A. Walthall and Thomas E. Emerson (Washington, D.C.: Smithsonian Institution Press, 1992), 137; Deliette, "Memoir of De Gannes," 312; LaHontan, *New Voyages to North America*, 2:4, and 2:77. See LaHontan's impressions in J. Nick Perrin, *Perrin's History of Illinois* (1906), 45; Deliette, "Memoir of De Gannes," 319.

10. Callender, "Illinois Indians," 676; for a description of the making of these dyed reed mats, see Deliette, "Memoir of De Gannes," 375–76; Callender, "Illinois Indians," 676–77.

11. John A. Walthall, "Aboriginal Pottery and the Eighteenth-Century Illini," in Walthall and Emerson, eds., *Calumet & Fleur-de-Lys*, 170; letter from Father Vivier, 1750, in Thwaites, *Jesuit Relations*, vol. 69; Andre Penicaut discusses the Kaskaskian use of plows as early as 1711, in Pierre Margry, *Memoires et Documents,*

Decouvertes et Establishments des Francais dans L'Ouest et dans la Sud de L'Amerique Septentrionale (1661–1754) (Paris, 1879–1888), English translation, 5:448–93.

12. See Carl J. Ekberg's discussion of wheat in the Illinois Country, *French Roots in the Illinois Country: The Mississippi Frontier in Colonial Times* (Urbana: University of Illinois Press, 2000), 173; Mary Borgias Palm, "The First Illinois Wheat," *Mid-America* 13 (July 1930), 72–73.

13. Dan Hechenberger, "The Metchigamea Tribe," *M'Skutewe Awandiangwi* I, no. 2 (1998), 1; Wayne Temple, *Indian Villages of the Illinois Country: Historic Tribes* (Springfield, Ill.: Department of Registration and Education, 1958), 41, 45–46.

14. Schlarman, *From Quebec*, 47. For a discussion of English, Spanish, and French claiming ceremonies and how they differed in practice and meaning, see Patricia Seed, "Taking Possession and Reading Texts: Establishing the Authority of Overseas Empires," *William and Mary Quarterly*, 3rd ser., 49 (1992), 183–209; LaSalle's entire speech is reproduced in Henry Brown, *The History of Illinois from Its First Discovery and Settlement to the Present Time* (New York: J. Winchester, New World Press, 1844), 132–33; Schlarman, *From Quebec*, 131; Mary Borgias Palm, *The Jesuit Missions of the Illinois Country, 1673–1763* (Cleveland: Saint Louis University, 1931), 24 and 80–81.

15. Dan Hechenberger, "Towards Understanding the Illinewek View of the French at Cahokia," *Journal of the St. Clair County Historical Society* 5, no. 9 (1999), 15, 39.

16. Raymond Douville and Jacques Casanova, *Daily Life in Early Canada*, trans. Carola Congreve (New York: MacMillan, 1968), 108–9; letter from Father Sebastien Rasle, in Edna Kenton, ed., *The Indians of North America* (New York: Harcourt, 1927), 370; Douville and Casanova, *Early Life*, 111.

17. Bruce G. Trigger, *Natives and Newcomers: Canada's "Heroic Age" Reconsidered* (Kingston: McGill-Queen's University Press, 1985), 293; see also discussion in Palm, *Jesuit Missions*, 96.

18. Nicolas de Finiels, *An Account of Upper Louisiana*, ed. Carl J. Ekberg and William E. Foley, trans. Carl J. Ekberg (Columbia: University of Missouri Press, 1989), 99.

19. See Marest letter, 1712, in Thwaits, *Jesuit Relations*, 65:253, 257; Schlarman, *From Quebec*, 141.

20. Dan Hechenberger, "The Cahokia Tribe," *M'Skutewe Awandiangi Nipundikun* I, no. 3 (1998), 1; Dean L Anderson, "Variability in Trade at Eighteenth-Century French Outposts," in John A. Walthall, *French Colonial Archaeology: The Illinois Country and the Western Great Lakes* (Urbana: University of Illinois Press, 1991); Robert Mazrim, *Now Quite Out of Society: Archaeology and Frontier Illinois—Essays and Excavation Reports*, Transportation Archaeological Bulletins I (Urbana: University of Illinois, 2002); Henry M. Majors, "Fort Ouiatanon and the Wabash River, 1700–1824" (unpublished manuscript, Lilly Library, Indiana University, Bloomington, 1970).

21. N. M. Miller Surrey, "The Fur Trade of Louisiana," in Miller, *The Commerce of Louisiana during the French Regime: 1699–1763* (New York: Columbia University

Press, 1916), 345; Carl J. Ekberg believes that the presence of seven French inhabitants on a 1723 census of Cahokia reveals that "Cahokia was in the process of becoming an agricultural community." Ekberg, *French Roots*, 58.

22. Schlarman, *From Quebec*, 142; footnote references the Taschereau MS, *Mission du Seminaire de Quebec chez les Tamarois,* in the Quebec Seminary Archives; Ekberg, *French Roots*, 55; Ekberg, *French Roots*, 58; Schlarman, *From Quebec*, 207; this practice of extending longlots from geographical features has its origins in medieval France, described by Marc Bloch in *Les Caracteres Origineux de l'histoire Rurale de France* and further discussed in Carl J. Ekberg, *French Roots*, 9.

23. Ekberg, *French Roots*, 60; George Washington Smith, *A History of Southern Illinois: A Narrative Account of Its Historical Progress, Its People, and Its Principal Interests* (Chicago: Lewis, 1912), 535; *Michigan Pioneer and Historical Collections* (Lansing: W. S. George, 1877), 1:352; Rinita A. Dalan et al., *Envisioning Cahokia: A Landscape Perspective* (DeKalb: Northern Illinois University Press, 2003), especially 81–84. The authors note that even the "General Land Office notes of 1810 describe the land in the vicinity of the mound groups . . . (prairie and Mississippi Bottom) as "wet"; Ekberg, *French Roots*, 172; see also Ekberg on visitors' comments about the fine quality of wheat grown at Kaskaskia in the first two decades of the eighteenth century, 191; Margaret Kimball Brown and Lawrie Cena Dean, *The Village of Chartres in Colonial Illinois 1720–1765* (New Orleans: Polyanthos, 1977), Document K-118 (H768), 463; Ekberg, *French Roots*, 217–18; Thomas Stirling, "Stirling's Personal Journal of the Expedition: General Accounts of British Attempts to Occupy the Illinois Country," in Robert G. Carroon, ed., *Broadswords & Bayonets* (Society of Colonial Wars in the State of Illinois, 1984), 91.

24. See discussion of maize growing on the uplands after 1000 A.D. in chapter 1; Schlarman, *From Quebec*, 148; Schlarman, *From Quebec*, 206. See Ekberg's discussion of this census in *French Roots*, 58; John A. Walthall and Elizabeth D. Benchley, *The River L'Abbe Mission: A French Colonial Church for the Cahokia Illini at Monk's Mound* (Springfield: Illinois Historic Preservation Agency, 1987), 1; Father Mercier letter, Apr. 12, 1735, to the Quebec Seminary, printed in its entirety in Schlarman, *From Quebec*, 280–84. This letter is important in that it specifically describes land and climate constraints at the Cahokia mission, including annual flux and flow of water (creating problems in the building of mills), drainage of water, location of arable land, and location of bluff forests of white walnut whose wood "is very clear." This walnut was used for the construction of the new mission house. Father Mercier letter of May 25, 1732, in Schlarman, *From Quebec*, 288. The fact that it was timber hauled down from the bluffs suggests depletion of the wood reserves on the floodplain of the Cahokia grant, despite a low French settler population. It may reflect the need for fuel of the Cahokia-Tamaroa Indians, whose village was nearby on the grant; Mercier letter, August 3, 1732, in Schlarman, *From Quebec*, 290; Mercier letter, April 20, 1743, in Schlarman, *From Quebec*, 284; Bonnie L. Gums, *Archaeology at French Colonial Cahokia* (Springfield: Illinois Historic Preservation Agency, 1988), 18; Ekberg, *French Roots*, 58.

25. Schlarman, *From Quebec,* 280; Fathers Mercier and Courier, letter of Apr. 12, 1735, in Schlarman, *From Quebec,* 280; See "The Trade of the Illinois Country" in Surrey, *Commerce,* 288; Carl J. Ekberg, *French Roots,* 266; Palm, *Jesuit Missions,* 49; Natalia Maree Belting, *Kaskaskia under the French Regime* (New Orleans: Polyanthos, 1975), 58; Dan Hechenberger, "The Peoria Tribe," in *M'Skutewe Awandiangwi* 1, no. 3 (1998), 1; see also the August 3, 1732, letter from Father Mercier, printed in Schlarman, *From Quebec,* 290.

26. Personal communication, John White, Ecological Services, Urbana, Illinois, February 2004; see Table 4, "Illinois Indian Locales: 1699–1700" in Zitomersky, *French Americans–Native Americans,* 203; 1699 letter from Father Binneteau, in Edna Kenton, *The Jesuit Relations,* 326–27; Brown and Dean, *Village of Chartres,* Doc. K-25 (H173), 359.

27. Terrance J. Martin, "Animal Remains from the Cahokia Wedge Site," in Gums, *Archaeology,* 230; Martin, "Animal Remains," 233.

28. Bolen, *Birds of Illinois,* 20; Daniel W. McKinley, "The Carolina Parakeet in Pioneer Missouri," *Wilson Bulletin* 72, no. 3 (Sept. 1980), 275; Deliette, "Memoir of De Gannes," 391; Thwaites, *Jesuit Relations,* 59:131; see photograph and caption in Callender, "Illinois Indians," 675; see a reproduction of this painting in Callender, 677; several of George Catlin's paintings of the Peoria appear in Callender, 679.

29. Archaeologists posit that the abandonment in the fourteenth and fifteenth centuries of the American Bottom by the Middle-Mississippian agrarian culture was likely due to soil exhaustion on constantly worked plots, expressed as "localized environmental degradation caused by an overexploitation of the resources." Thomas E. Emerson and James A. Brown, "The Late Prehistory and Protohistory of Illinois," in Walthall and Emerson, *Calumet & Fleur-de-Lys,* 97; Bossu, in Schlarman, *From Quebec,* 293; Thomas Stirling, in Carroon, *Broadswords & Bayonets,* 94; Stirling writes only five short sentences about Cahokia, mentioning, "It contains betwixt sixty and seventy houses and has a Church." He furnishes no description of the land or habitat. Stirling in Carroon, *Broadswords & Bayonets,* 90.

30. Father Marest letter of 1712, in Thwaites, *Jesuit Relations,* vol. 66; letter from Father Vivier, November 17, 1750, in Thwaites, *Jesuit Relations,* 69:209 (for lower Mississippi); see 69:219 for French settlements in the Illinois Country. Also see William Cronon on perceptions left by Europeans and on ways to estimate or reconstruct animal and bird populations, in *Changes in the Land: Indians, Colonists, and the Ecology of New England* (New York: Hill and Wang, 1983), 6–8. Cronon discusses "those awkward situations in which an ecological change which undoubtedly must have been occurring in the colonial period has left little or no historical evidence at all."

31. Letter of Father Mercier to M. Lyon of Quebec Seminary, Aug. 3, 1732, in Schlarman, *From Quebec,* 290. Mercier exclaims, "If only the Peoria were away from here!—they will leave this fall—we could have some hopes of doing something with several Kahos [Cahokia Indians]"; Zitomersky, *French Americans–Native Americans,* 17; see Table 29, "Illinois Indian Estimated Village Populations," in Zitomersky, *French Americans–Native Americans,* 321; Palm, *Jesuit Missions,* 71.

32. Walthall and Benchley, *River L'Abbe Mission*, 8; Daniel H. Usner Jr., *Indians, Settlers, and Slaves in a Frontier Exchange Economy: The Lower Mississippi before 1783* (Chapel Hill: University of North Carolina Press, 1992), 72; see the account of the massacre in the letter from Father le Petit, missionary, to Father d'Avaugour, procurator of the missions in North America, July, 1730, in Edna Kenton, ed., *The Indians of North America* (New York: Harcourt, 1927), 439–40; Usner, *Indians, Settlers, and Slaves*, 66; letter from Father Le Petit, in Kenton, *Indians*, 430; *Mississippi Provincial Archives*, French Documents: "Narrative of the Hostilities Committed by the Natchez against the Concession of St. Catherine, October 21, November 4, 1722" (Baton Rouge: Louisiana State University Press, 1927); St. Ange letter in Walthall and Benchley, *River L'Abbe Mission*, 8–10; Table 29, "Illinois Indian Estimated Village Populations," in Zitomersky, *French Americans–Native Americans*, 321.

33. Emily J. Blasingham, "The Depopulation of the Illinois Indians, Part II," *Ethnohistory* 3, no. 4 (1956), 386–96; Schlarman, *From Quebec*, 215; R. David Edmunds and Joseph L. Peyser, *The Fox Wars: The Mesquakie Challenge to New France* (Norman: University of Oklahoma Press, 1993), especially 138–57, for careful reconstruction of the Fox-French battle on Sept. 8–9, 1730; for the Chickasaw Wars, see the account of the orders to D'Artaguiette to "raise as many men as he could—soldiers, Canadians, French, and Illinois Indians," in Schlarman, *From Quebec*, 273; see 277 for an account of the second campaign in 1739 in which Illinois Indians also fought; Blasingham, "Depopulation," 378–79. For raids against English settlements, see Blasingham, "Depopulation," 379; for continuing French use of Illinois ("Mississippi") Indians in raids against western Pennsylvania through the 1740s, see *Minutes of the Provincial Council of Pennsylvania* (Harrisburg: Theo. Penn, 1855), 5:1–5; Zitomersky, *French Americans–Native Americans*, 351–53.

34. Macarty to Vaudreuil, Jan. 1752, in Pease, *Illinois on the Eve*, 451.

3. Chartres: French and Indian Successes

1. Betty I. Madden, *Art, Crafts, and Architecture in Early Illinois* (Urbana: University of Illinois Press, 1974), 16. In at least two other periods of the eighteenth century, French administrators argued for the location of Fort Chartres at Kaskaskia and at Cahokia. Both areas were seen as more advantageous due to river confluences. The Fort Chartres location lay on a level prairie between the Kaskaskia River, seventeen miles to the south, and the Big Rivers area to the north.

2. Mary Borgias Palm, *The Jesuit Missions of the Illinois Country, 1673–1763* (Cleveland: Saint Louis University, 1931), 50.

3. Carl J. Ekberg points this out in *French Roots in the Illinois Country: The Mississippi Frontier in Colonial Times* (Urbana: University of Illinois Press, 2000), 33; George Washington Smith, *History of Illinois and Her People* (Chicago: American Historical Society, 1927), 1:118–19; Palm, *Jesuit Missions*, 50–51. De Boisbriant (or Boisbriand) was commandant in the Illinois Country between 1719 and 1724. A French Canadian from Montreal, he is described as "very popular with the Indians

because he knew Indian languages and had an interest in their welfare." *Dictionary of Canadian Biography*, vol. 2 (Toronto: University of Toronto Press, 1969); Smith, *History of Illinois*, 119; Wayne C. Temple, *Indian Villages of the Illinois Country: Historic Tribes* (Springfield: Illinois State Museum, 1958), 41. Temple bases this point on documents in the *Mississippi Provincial Archives*: French Dominion, French Documents (Baton Rouge: Louisiana State University Press, 1927), 3:514; Palm, *Jesuit Missions*, 49.

4. Charlevoix, in Palm, *Jesuit Missions*, 49; Carl J. Ekberg argues that De Boisbriant was concerned about the effect of brandy on the Kaskaskia Indians and wanted to remove them from the "ready supply of spiritous liquors" in French Kaskaskia. Ekberg, *Francois Valle and His World: Upper Louisiana before Louis and Clark* (Columbia: University of Missouri Press, 2000) 9. See a good discussion by Cornelius J. Jaener on French policies in Quebec, segregating Huron Indians from French villagers, and Indian reaction to this practice. Jaener, "Amerindian Views of French Culture in the Seventeenth Century," in *American Encounters: Natives and Newcomers from European Contact to Indian Removal, 1500–1850*, ed. Peter C. Mancall and James H. Merrell (New York: Routledge, 2000) 86; Margaret Kimball Brown and Lawrie Cena Dean, *The Village of Chartres in Colonial Illinois 1720–1765* (New Orleans: Polyanthos, 1977) Record D-2, 5; Brown and Dean, *Village of Chartres*, Record D-9, 11.

5. The evidence for the ash grove is taken from notarial records (property descriptions) in Brown and Dean, *Village of Chartres*, for the years 1724–65. This ash grove, noted at times as "the hill of the ash grove" or "the ash grove by the coulee" appears in property descriptions for the entire period of the French Regime, with the first mention occurring in 1726 (record K-23, H169, 357); as late as 1761 property is inventoried as running from "the ash grove" (see record E-295, H424, 734). The ash grove functioned as a western property marker, along with the Mississippi River and "the prairie of the Mechigamea Indians." The significance of this ash grove being left untouched as a fuel source will be discussed in the next chapter; enumeration of trees in the American Bottom in the area around the first Fort Chartres is given in Edward B. Jelks, Carl J. Ekberg, and Terrance J. Martin, *Excavations at the Laurens Site: Probable Location of Fort de Chartres I*, Studies in Illinois Archaeology 5 (Springfield: Illinois Historic Preservation Agency, 1989), 19; see also discussion of cordgrass (*Spartina pectinata/Michauxiana*) on early Illinois river floodplains in Homer C. Sampson, "An Ecological Survey of the Prairie Vegetation of Illinois," *Bulletin of the Illinois Laboratory of Natural History* 13, no. 16 (1921), 523–77; Lewis M. Turner, "Grassland in the Floodplain of Illinois Rivers," *American Midland Naturalist* 15 (1934), 770–80, especially 778.

6. Gordon G. Whitney, *From Coastal Wilderness to Fruited Plain: A History of Environmental Change in Temperate North America from 1500 to the Present* (Cambridge: Cambridge University Press, 1994), 255. Whitney also points out that under the pressure of livestock grazing, prairie leadplant (*Amorpha canascens*) was one of the significant "decreasers" (see 258). French livestock would thus have

assisted in the conversion of the tallgrass prairies; Lewis, Meriwether, and William Clark, *The Journals of the Lewis and Clark Expedition August 30, 1803–August 24, 1804* (Lincoln: University of Nebraska Press, 1986), 117.

7. Brown and Dean, *Village of Chartres,* preface, ix; map of Laurens site and its relation to the third stone Fort Chartres, yet standing (rebuilt) on its original location, in Jelks et al., *Excavations at the Laurens Site,* 17.

8. Smith, *History of Illinois,* 120: "Tradition insists that there was a sort of warehouse or blockhouse at this place." For the most detailed account of the Crozat venture and the subsequent involvement of the Scottish speculator John Law, see Marcel Giraud, *A History of French Louisiana,* vol. 2: *Years of Transition, 1715–1717,* trans. Brian Pearce (1958; repr., Baton Rouge: Louisiana State University Press, 1993), 38–49. Giraud presents Crozat in a more favorable light, stressing his realism and business acumen about the necessity of support and fortification in the Louisiana colonies.

9. Louis Hennepin, *A New Discovery of a Vast Country in America,* vol. 1, ed. Reuben Gold Twaites (Chicago: McClurg, 1903); Louis Hennepin, *A Description of Louisiana,* trans. John Gilmeary Shea (Ann Arbor: University Microfilms, 1966), 150: "We are convinced that the soil is capable of producing all kinds of fruits, herbs, and grain, and in greater abundance than the best lands of Europe"; Le Page du Pratz, *The History of Louisiana, or of the Western Parts of Virginia and Carolina: Containing a Description of the Countries That Lye on Both Sides of the River Mississippi: With An Account of the Settlements, Inhabitants, Soil, Climate, and Products* (London: T. Becket and P. A. De Hondt, 1763), 2:302; Robert Kirk, *Through So Many Dangers: The Memoirs and Adventures of Robert Kirk, Late of the Royal Highland Regiment,* ed. Ian McCulloch and Timothy Todish (New York: Purple Mountain, 2004), 104; Timothy Flint, *A Condensed Geography and History of the Western States, or the Mississippi Valley* (Cincinnati: E. H. Flint, 1828; Gainesville, Fla.: Scholars' Facsimiles and Reprints, 1970), 118; Louis Hennepin, *New Discovery;* Giraud, *History of French Louisiana,* 2:459.

10. D'Artaguiette, "Journal of Diron D'Artaguiette," in *Travels in the American Colonies,* ed. Newton D. Mereness (New York: Antiquarian, 1961), 74 and 69; this perception comes from Carl J. Ekberg's analysis of land grants in *French Roots,* 79; Brown and Dean, *Village of Chartres,* Record K-6 (H145), 341–42; see records K-7 (H146), K-10 (H161) and K-11 (H163), 345–47; Record K-341, in Brown and Dean, *Village of Chartres,* 806; Memorial of De Boisbriant, in Ekberg, *French Roots,* 177.

11. Monsieur Lallement, observations in Ekberg, *French Roots,* 177; Ekberg, *French Roots,* 79; J. H. Schlarman, *From Quebec to New Orleans: The Story of the French in America, Fort de Chartres* (Belleville, Ill.: Buechler, 1929), 209–10; the mosaic pattern of maize fields interspersed with "many abandoned fields" in alluvial canebrakes has been specifically documented in historical description for the southeastern Indians: Creek, Choctaw, Chickasaw, and Shawnee. William I. Woods, "Maize Agriculture and the Late Prehistoric: A Characterization of Settlement Location Strategies," in *Emergent Horticultural Economies of the Eastern*

Woodlands, ed. William F. Keegan, Center for Archaeological Investigations, Occasional Paper no. 7 (Southern Illinois University, 1987), 277.

12. Schlarman, *From Quebec to New Orleans*, 155; record K-341 in Brown and Dean, *Village of Chartres*, 807; Natalia Maree Belting, *Kaskaskia under the French Regime* (New Orleans: Polyanthos, 1975), 53; illustrations of French farming tools in Belting, 55, drawn from Louis Liger, *La nouvelle maison rustique, ou, Économie generale de tous les biens de campagne: la maniere de les entretenir & de les multiplier* (Paris: Chez la veuve Prudhomme . . . , 1736); Dale Miquelon, *New France: 1701–1744* (Toronto: McClelland and Stewart, 1987), 200.

13. Neal H. Lopinot, "Spatial and Temporal Variability in Mississippian Subsistence: The Archaeobotanical Record," in *Late Prehistoric Agriculture: Observations from the Midwest*, ed. William I. Woods, Studies in Illinois Archaeology 8 (Springfield: Illinois Historic Preservation Agency, 1992), 46; Woods, "Maize Agriculture," 283.

14. Woods, "Maize Agriculture," 280–81.

15. Sara Jones Tucker, *Indian Villages of the Illinois Country*, Scientific Papers 2 (Springfield: Illinois State Museum, 1942 and 1975), pt. 1, atlas, plate 14; William I. Woods, "Soil Chemical Investigations in Illinois Archaeology: Two Example Studies," *American Chemical Society* (1984), 70. John W. Weymouth and William I. Woods, "Combined Magnetic and Chemical Surveys of Forts Kaskaskia and de Chartres Number 1, Illinois," *Historical Archaeology* 18, no. 2 (1984), 20–37.

16. Merle C. Rummel, *The Four Mile* (Boston, Ind., 1998); Adolph B. Suess, *Glimpses of Prairie du Rocher, Its Past and Present, 1722–1942* (Belleville, Ill.: Buechler, 1942), 4; Belting, *Kaskaskia*, 54; see also French oxen and charrues in Ekberg, *French Roots*, 178–80. Ekberg contrasts the English and American views of French agriculture as "defective" or "non-progressive" with the actual French tillage habits using oxen teams, charrues, and common lands. Evidence exists from estate inventories of the French settlers that "virtually every substantial habitant in the Illinois Country owned a team of oxen and a charrue." (179); Record K-380 in Brown and Dean, *Village of Chartres*, 851–52; Record K-404 in Brown and Dean, *Village of Chartres*, 884; Robert H. Mohlenbrock, *Forest Trees of Illinois* (Springfield: Illinois Department of Conservation, Division of Forestry, 1975), 101; Thomas D. Morgan, "Tree of the Month: Hop Hornbeam," *Prairie Falcon* 31, no. 4 (Dec. 2002); D'Artaguiette, "Journal," 74.

17. Lopinot, "Spatial and Temporal Variability," 53; William I. Woods and George R. Holley, "Upland Mississippian Settlement in the American Bottom Region," in *Cahokia and the Hinterlands: Middle Mississippian Cultures of the Midwest*, ed. Thomas E. Emerson and R. Barry Lewis (Urbana: University of Illinois Press, 1991), 60.

18. Morgan, "Tree of the Month"; such themes are especially prevalent in William Cronon, *Changes in the Land: Indians, Colonists, and the Ecology of New England* (New York: Hill and Wang, 1983), and Carolyn Merchant, *Ecological Revolutions: Nature, Gender, and Science in New England* (Chapel Hill: Univer-

sity of North Carolina Press, 1989). A comparison of the population of French
Louisbourg and the entire Illinois Country in 1752 shows a striking disparity:
Louisbourg "was occupied by 1,500 military personnel, 674 fishermen, 437 engagés
and other servants, and 1,349 residents." The Illinois Country claimed "151 soldiers,
670 habitants or farmers, 401 black slaves, and 133 native Indian slaves." In David
Keene, "Fort de Chartres: Archaeology in the Illinois Country," in *French Colonial
Archaeology: The Illinois Country and the Western Great Lakes*, ed. John Walthall
(Urbana: University of Illinois Press, 1991), 38. There is a strong literature on the
introduction of European swine to New World locales. Important works include
two studies by Alfred W. Crosby, *Ecological Imperialism: The Biological Expansion
of Europe, 900–1900* (Cambridge: Cambridge University Press, 1986), and *Germs,
Seeds, & Animals: Studies in Ecological History* (New York: M. E. Sharpe, 1994).
Crosby points out the high adaptability of omnivorous hogs and states, "The impact
of the animals the Europeans brought with them to the Americas transformed
whole ecosystems." See *Germs, Seeds, & Animals*, 55. See also Cronon, *Changes
in the Land*, 135–37. Both Crosby and Cronon term hogs the "weed animals" for
their reproductive and disseminating behaviors.

19. See Marest letter in Reuben Gold Thwaits, *The Jesuit Relations and Allied
Documents* (Cleveland: Burrows, 1900), 66:257; John A. Walthall, F. Terry Nor-
ris, and Barbara D. Stafford, "Woman Chief's Village: An Illini Winter Hunting
Camp," in *Calumet & Fleur-de-Lys: Archaeology of Indian and French Contact in the
Midcontinent*, ed. John A. Walthall and Thomas E. Emerson (Washington, D.C.:
Smithsonian Institution Press, 1992), 145; record K-376 in Brown and Dean, *Village
of Chartres*, 846; record K-388, Brown and Dean, *Village of Chartres*, 868; numbers
of swine provided in Ekberg, *French Roots*, 206–7; Raymond E. Hauser, "The
Ethnohistory of the Illinois Indian Tribe, 1673–1832," PhD dissertation, Northern
Illinois University, 1973 (Ann Arbor, Mich.: University Microfilms, 1973), 99.

20. Ekberg, *French Roots*, 80–81 and 206–8; Lewis R. Binford, "An Ethnohistory of the Nottoway, Meherrin, and Weacock Indians of Southeastern Virginia,"
Ethnohistory 14, no. 3/4 (summer 1967), 146, 163, and 178; Joshua Micah Marshall,
"A Melancholy People": Anglo-Indian Relations in Early Warwick, Rhode Island,
1642–1675," *New England Quarterly* 68, no. 3 (Sept. 1995), 407–9.

21. See chapter 2 for an overview of the Cahokia revolt; for a careful study
of escalating friction between eastern colonists and Indians over livestock, see
Virginia DeJohn Anderson, "King Philip's Herds: Indians, Colonists, and the
Problem of Livestock in Early New England," *William and Mary Quarterly*, 3rd
ser., 51, no. 4 (Oct. 1994), 601–24; Jean-Baptiste Le Moyne, Sieur de Bienville,
"Louisiana, May 15, 1733," *Mississippi Provincial Archives* (Jackson: Press of the Mississippi Department of Archives and History, 1927), 1:201; Hauser, "Ethnohistory,"
263–64; Macarty to Vaudreuil, Jan. 1952, in Theodore Calvin Pease, ed., *Illinois on
the Eve of the Seven Years War*, Collections of the Illinois State Historical Library
29 (Springfield: Trustees of the State Historical Library, 1940), 451; Jean-Bernard
Bossu, *Jean-Bernard Bossu's Travels in the Interior of North America, 1751–1762*, ed.

and transl. Seymour Feiler (Norman: University of Oklahoma Press, 1962), 81 and 81, n. 9; Bossu, *Travels*, 108, in Hauser, "Ethnohistory," 116; Virginia DeJohn Anderson, *Creatures of Empire: How Domestic Animals Transformed Early America* (New York: Oxford University Press, 2004), 160; E. W. Hilgard, "Botanical Features of the Prairies of Illinois in Ante-Railroad Days" (manuscript on file at the Illinois Historical Survey; n.p, n.d), 19–20; Marc D. Abrams, "Where Has All the White Oak Gone?" *Bioscience* 53, no. 10 (Oct. 2003).

22. Frances B. King, *Plants, People, and Paleoecology: Biotic Communities and Aboriginal Plant Usage in Illinois*, Scientific Papers 20 (Springfield: Illinois State Museum, 1994), 29; John White, personal communication, May 17, 2004.

23. Winston P. Smith et al., "A Comparison of Breeding Bird Communities and Habitat Features between Old-Growth and Second-Growth Bottomland Hardwood Forests," in *Bottomland Hardwoods of the Mississippi Alluvial Valley: Characteristics and Management of Natural Function, Structure, and Composition,* General Technical Report SRS-42 (Fayetteville, Ark.: U.S. Department of Agriculture, 2001), 78; Winston P. Smith and Patrick A. Zollner, "Seasonal Habitat Distribution of Swamp Rabbits, White-Tailed Deer, and Small Mammals in Old Growth and Managed Bottomland Hardwood Forests," in *Bottomland Hardwoods,* 94.

24. Nancy M. Miller Surrey, *The Commerce of Louisiana during the French Regime: 1699–1763* (New York: Columbia University Press, 1916), 289; D. W. Moodie, "Agriculture and the Fur Trade," in *Old Trails and New Directions: Papers of the Third North American Fur Trade Conference,* ed. Carol M. Judd and Arthur J. Ray (Toronto: University of Toronto Press, 1980); E. J. Montague, "The History of Randolph County, Illinois, Including Old Kaskaskia Island," 1859, copied by Elisabeth Pinkerton Leighty (Sparta, Ill., 1948), 10; Inventory of Andre Chaverneau, Kaskaskia Mss., 47:9:30:1. Margaret Kimball Brown, *The Voyageur in the Illinois Country: The Fur Trade's Professional Boatman in Mid America*, Extended Publication Series, no. 3 (Naperville, Ill.: Center for French Colonial Studies, 2002), 26.

25. Morris S. Arnold, *Unequal Laws unto a Savage Race: European Legal Traditions in Arkansas, 1686–1836* (Fayetteville: University of Arkansas Press, 1985), 5; Paul B. Hamel et al., "Chainsaws, Canebrakes, and Cotton Fields: Sober Thoughts on Silviculture for Songbirds in Bottomland Forests," in *Bottomland Hardwoods of the Mississippi Alluvial Valley,* Table 1, 99; Tom Foti, Chief Ecologist, Arkansas Heritage Association, personal communication, May 4, 2004.

26. Journal of Pierre Marquette, in John Upton Terrell, *American Indian Almanac* (New York: World Publishing, 1961), 234; W. David Baird, *The Quapaws* (New York: Chelsea House, 1989), 14; for the best account of initial Quapaw-French encounters before 1700, see Morris S. Arnold, *The Rumble of a Distant Drum: The Quapaws and the Old World Newcomers, 1673–1804* (Fayetteville: University of Arkansas Press, 2000); Samuel D. Dickinson, "Shamans, Priests, Preachers, and Pilgrims at Arkansas Post," in *Arkansas before the Americans,* ed. Hester A. Davis (Arkansas Archaeology Survey Research Series no. 40, 1991), 98.

27. Arnold, *Unequal Laws,* 8–9; Father François-Xavier Charlevoix, *Journal*

d'un voyage fait par ordre du roi dans l'Amerique septentriole (Paris, 1744), cited in Arnold, *Unequal Laws*, 8–9.

28. Arnold, *Unequal Laws*, 34; Daniel H. Usner Jr. *Indians, Settlers, & Slaves in a Frontier Exchange Economy: The Lower Mississippi Valley before 1783* (Chapel Hill: University of North Carolina Press, 1992), 81; Arnold in his study of colonial Arkansas states, "It is safe to conclude that there were never more than eight or ten real farmers at any one time at the Post in the colonial period. . . . Although the state of the agricultural art, and the number of people engaged in it, certainly increased during the last decade of the eighteenth century, John Treat, writing from the Post in 1805, notes even at that late date that 'agriculture here is yet in its infancy.'" See Morris S. Arnold, *Colonial Arkansas, 1686–1804: A Social and Cultural History* (Fayetteville: University of Arkansas Press, 1991), 61.

4. Trade Matrix at Fort Chartres: Farmers, Traders, and Provisioners

1. Father Marquette in Reuben Gold Thwaites, *The Jesuit Relations and Allied Documents, 1610–1791* (Cleveland: Burrows, 1900), 59:91; account of this exchange by Nancy M. Miller Surrey, *The Commerce of Louisiana during the French Regime: 1699–1763* (New York: Columbia University Press, 1916), 98; see a map of Michigan portages and informed discussion in Susan Sleeper-Smith, *Indian Women and French Men: Rethinking Cultural Encounter in the Western Great Lakes* (Amherst: University of Massachusetts Press, 2001), 20.

2. Richard White, *The Middle Ground: Indians, Empires, and Republics in the Great Lakes Region, 1650–1815* (Cambridge: Cambridge University Press, 1991); James Axtell documents changes in Indian village archaeology of the eastern woodlands, reflecting what he calls a "consumer revolution" in the seventeenth century. See *Natives and Newcomers: The Cultural Origins of North America* (New York: Oxford University Press, 2001), 115–18. For Miami horticulture, see Stewart Rafert, *The Miami Indians of Indiana: A Persistent People, 1654–1994* (Indianapolis: Indiana Historical Society, 1996), 12, 65.

3. Natalia Belting, "The Native American as Myth and Fact," *Journal of the Illinois State Historical Society* 69, no. 2 (May 1976), 119–26. Belting states that "Indian alliances were . . . essential to its [New France's] economy." Indians were "the hunters and trappers, the harvesters, and the tanners of the pelts." See Belting, "Native American," 122. This view can be contrasted with Raymond Hauser's, who believes the French "did deliberately destroy Illinois self-sufficiency . . . in order to secure the cooperation of the tribe in French colonial ventures." He cites La Salle as writing, "So long as it can be contrived to keep them dependent on us, they may be readily held to their duty. . . ." Hauser, "The Illinois Indian Tribe: From Autonomy and Self-Sufficiency to Dependency and Depopulation," *Journal of the Illinois State Historical Society* 69, no. 2 (May 1976), 135. La Salle did not establish the entire colonial policy for New France, and his initial perceptions should not be taken as a template for the following century. The reciprocity of French-Indian trade, advantaging both sides, is a more realistic assessment.

4. "Journal of Diron D'Artaguiette," in *Travels in the American Colonies*, ed. Newton D. Mereness (New York: Antiquarian, 1961), 70–71.

5. D'Artaguiette, "Journal," 82; Winstanley Briggs, "The Forgotten Colony: Le Pays d'Illinois," PhD dissertation, University of Chicago, 1985, 249–51.

6. Wayne C. Temple, *Indian Villages of the Illinois Country: Historic Tribes* (Springfield, Ill.: Department of Registration and Education, 1958), 42. For defeat of the Fox on Grand Prairie, see chapter 2, n. 122; Eric Hinderaker, *Elusive Empires: Constructing Colonialism in the Ohio Valley, 1673–1800* (Cambridge: Cambridge University Press, 1999), 12–13. See also Margaret Kimball Brown, *Cultural Transformations among the Illinois: An Application of a Systems Model* (East Lansing: Museum, Michigan State University, 1979), 244–45. The initial discussion of the "mourning war" appears in Daniel K. Richter's analysis of Iroquois war patterns, "War and Culture: The Iroquois Experience," *William and Mary Quarterly*, 3rd ser., 40 (1983), 528–59. See Richter's discussion of the term *mourning-war* in footnote 4, comparing the usage to that in a 1951 report by Marian W. Smith for the New York Academy of Sciences; see chapter 6 for a discussion of Illinois buffalo; R. David Edmunds and Joseph L. Peyser, *The Fox Wars: The Mesquakie Challenge to New France* (Norman: University of Oklahoma Press, 1993), 33–35; Edmunds and Peyser, *Fox Wars*, 93; *Wisconsin Historical Collections* 16, 456–61, in Joseph Jablow, *Indians of Illinois and Indiana: Illinois, Kickapoo, and Potawatomi Indians* (New York: Garland Press, 1974), 164.

7. John A. Walthall and Elizabeth D. Benchley, *The River L'Abbe Mission: A French Colonial Church for the Cahokia Illini on Monks Mound* (Springfield: Illinois Historic Preservation Agency, 1987), 11–12. See also Raymond E. Hauser, "The Fox Raid of 1752: Defensive Warfare and the Decline of the Illinois Indian Tribe," *Illinois State Historical Journal* 86 (1993), 210–24; Temple, *Indian Villages*, 95–96; D'Artaguiette, "Journal," 78; for Fox depredations and ambushes of Indians and French, see Jablow, *Indians*, 164–66.

8. Minutes of the Council of Commerce Assembled at Dauphine Island on the Thirteenth of September, 1719, in *Mississippi Provincial Archives* (Baton Rouge: Louisiana State University Press, 1927), 3:260–61.

9. Wilbur R. Jacobs, *Diplomacy and Indian Gifts: Anglo-French Rivalry along the Ohio and Northwest Frontiers, 1748–1763* (Stanford: Stanford University Press, 1950), 55–57; Inventory of Louis Bienvenu *dit* Delisle in Margaret Kimball Brown, *The Voyageur in the Illinois Country: The Fur Trade's Professional Boatman in Mid America,* Extended Publication Series (Center for French Colonial Studies), no. 3 (Naperville, Ill.: Center for French Colonial Studies, 2002), 21; Vaudreuil to Maurepas, March 15, 1747, in Theodore Calvin Pease, *Illinois on the Eve of the Seven Years War,* Collections of the Illinois State Historical Library 29 (Springfield: Trustees of the State Historical Library, 1940), 9–10.

10. Edward B. Jelks, Carl J. Ekberg, and Terrance C. Martin, *Excavations at the Laurens Site: Probable Location of Fort de Chartres I,* Studies in Illinois Archaeology 5 (Springfield: Illinois Historic Preservation Agency, 1989), 112; David Keene, "Fort

NOTES TO PAGES 97–99

de Chartres: Archaeology in the Illinois Country," in *French Colonial Archaeology: The Illinois Country and the Western Great Lakes*, ed. John Walthall (Urbana: University of Illinois Press, 1991), 31; "Table of Selected Vertebrate Remains" in Jelks, Ekberg, and Martin, *Excavations*, 106. The excavations of faunal remains at the Laurens site contrast with those discovered at the more remote Ouiatanon post on the Wabash. The French diet at Ouiatanon reflected a higher incidence of wild game; see Record K-206 (H223) for a 1755 description of a property on Royal Street in the village of Chartres, bounded "on the other [side] by the run used as a discharge of the marsh." In Margaret Kimball Brown and Lawrie Cena Dean, *The Village of Chartres in Colonial Illinois, 1720–1765* (New Orleans: Polyanthos, 1977), 594.

11. "Journal of Diron D'Artaguiette," cited in Jablow, *Indians*, 161; Pierre Margry, *Memoires et Documents, Decouvertes et Etablissments des Francais dans l'Ouest et dans la Sud de L'Amerique Septentrionale (1616–1754)*, English trans. (Paris: 1879–1888), 6:548.

12. Surrey, *Commerce*, 347, citing Margry, *Memoires et Documents*, 6:427; Surrey, *Commerce*, 354; see discussion in Surrey, *Commerce*, 360. The Archives Nationale, Colonies, records do not clearly differentiate the source of the peltries—from the upper Missouri Country across from French Illinois, from the Arkansas tribes, or from the lower Mississippi Valley. Earlier records do make this distinction, as noted by Surrey in drawing from the Archives, Bibliotheque du Department des Affaires Etrangeres, Paris. See the list of furs obtained from lower Mississippi tribes, 348. The Abikas tribe alone furnished eight thousand skins.

13. Notarial record K-411 in Brown and Dean, *Village*, 891–95; declaration of Jean Jacques Desmanets, in notarial record K-411, Brown and Dean, *Village*, 893.

14. See the detailed account of the expedition of Veniard de Bourgmont in 1723–24 into the Missouri Country for the purposes of establishing the short-lived Fort d'Orleans, in Marcel Giraud, *A History of French Louisiana*, trans. Brian Pearce (Baton Rouge: Louisiana State University Press, 1987), 5:445–55; census is in the *Documents Relative to the Colonial History of the State of New York*, ed. E. B. O'Callaghan and Berthold Fernow (Albany: 1856–87), 9:1055–57; Jablow, *Indians*, 188; Theresa J. Piazza, "The Kaskaskia Manuscripts: French Traders in the Missouri Valley before Lewis and Clark," *Missouri Archaeologist* 53 (Dec. 1992), 20–21.

15. Note 1 in a document titled "Proposed Colony in the Illinois," in Theodore C. Pease, ed., *Illinois on the Eve of the Seven Years War*, Collections of the Illinois State Historical Library 29 (Springfield: Illinois State Historical Library, 1940), 135. This 1749 plan detailed a French colony on the Wabash (the Ohio), an idea resurfacing across the 1750s and 1760s as a strategic benefit but never acted upon. The plan contains river designations such as "the Green, Bon Secours, and Michecaco Rivers." As explained by Pease on a 1755 map, the "Michecaco" was noted as a tributary of the Illinois River; Pease identified it as possibly "Crooked Creek, Spoon River, Copperas Creek, or Kickapoo Creek"; Louise Phelps Kellogg, *French Regime in Wisconsin and the Northwest* (Madison: State Historical Society

NOTES TO PAGES 100-103

of Wisconsin, 1925), especially her chapter "Changes in Fur Trade Methods." As Kellogg points out, "the licensed traders also were but a few of those who trafficked in the wilderness" (366). Margaret Kimball Brown also discusses the leasing of Missouri posts and the use of the *conge* (trading permit) in *The Voyageur in the Illinois Country*; Louise Kellogg provides a concise overview of the claims of various French governors in both Louisiana and Canada, especially the Memorial of Vaudreuil in 1748. In Kellogg, *French Regime*, 371–73.

16. Ekberg, *French Roots*, appendix, 273–79; for analysis of contracts for the building of river craft, see Margaret Kimball Brown, *Voyageur*, 8–11; Record K-416 in Brown and Dean, *Village*, 901; Kaskaskia Manuscripts, 1743, in Brown, *Voyageur*, 8; Brown, *Voyageur*, 24; Brown, *Voyageur*, 28; see lists of furs obtained in 1747 and 1745, respectively, in Brown, *Voyageur*, 21; these exchange rates are for the year 1765, listed on a "Schedule of equivalents for barter of goods and skins," and appear in Brown, *Cultural Transformations*, 250.

17. E. W. Gould, *Fifty Years on the Mississippi, or Gould's History of River Navigation* (St. Louis: Nixon-Jones, 1889), 28; "Instructions for Exploration of Louisiana," in Pease, *Illinois on the Eve*, 5.

18. Arthur J. Ray, "Indians as Consumers in the Eighteenth Century," in *Old Trails and New Directions: Papers of the Third North American Fur Trade Conference* (Toronto: University of Toronto Press, 1980), 267. Northern Canadian Indians rejected any substandard kettle or cooking pot and would assess the iron or copper quality of kettles minutely; an equal scrutiny was given to knives. There is no reason to think that Illinois Indians could not shape the nature of their trade with the French in similar ways; Carl J. Ekberg, *Francois Valle and His World: Upper Louisiana before Louis and Clark* (Columbia: University of Missouri Press, 2002), 9; Memorial of Bienville, in *Mississippi Provincial Archives* 3:533–34; Jablow, *Indians*, 165.

19. Hugh Prince, *Wetlands of the American Midwest: A Historical Geography of Changing Attitudes* (Chicago: University of Chicago Press, 1997), 99; Donald L. Hey and Nancy S. Phillipi, "Reinventing a Flood Control Strategy," *Wetlands Initiative*, Sept. 1994, 7.

20. Hey and Phillipi, "Reinventing," 4–8.

21. Robert J. Naiman, Carol A. Johnston, and James C. Kelley, "Alteration of North American Streams by Beaver," *BioScience* 38 (Dec. 1988), 753–62; Charles D. Dieter and Thomas R. McCabe, "Factors Influencing Beaver Lodge-Site Selection on a Prairie River," *American Midland Naturalist* 122, no. 2 (Oct. 1989), 408–11; Jeanne M. Kay, Table 3.2, "Value of Habitats for Game Animals in Wisconsin," in Prince, *Wetlands*, 99; Brandi M. Sangunett, "Reference Conditions for Streams in the Grand Prairie Natural Division of Illinois," (masters thesis, Southern Illinois University Carbondale, 2000), 6; See William Oliver's observations in Hey and Philippi, "Reinventing," 4; Alice Outwater, *Water: A Natural History* (New York: Harper, 1996), 31–32. See especially Outwater's chapter on beaver as "nature's hydrologists."

22. Letter in *Collections of the State Historical Society of Wisconsin* (Madison: The Society, 1888–1931), 17:336, quoted in Jablow, *Indians*, 191; Perier letter of August 15, 1729, in Chicago Historical Society; Temple, *Indian Villages*, 41; Glenn J. Speed, *Ghost Towns of Southern Illinois* (Royalton, Ill., 1970), 184.

23. For a protohistoric Quapaw connection with the Mechigamea, see W. David Baird, *The Quapaw Indians: A History of the Downstream People* (Norman: University of Oklahoma Press, 1980), 6. Baird has a single piece of evidence implying the Quapaw had "forcibly displaced the Tonnika [Tunica] and the Illinois Indians." More consistent accounts in the historic period indicate that the Mechigamea and the Quapaw were allies; Morris S. Arnold, *The Rumble of a Distant Drum: The Quapaws and Old World Newcomers, 1673–1804* (Fayetteville: University of Arkansas Press, 2000), 70; Dan Hechenberger, "The Metchigamea Tribe," *M'Skutewe Awandiangwi Nipundikan* 1, no. 2 (1998), 1; this livestock "peninsula" was noted by Nicolas de Finiels in the 1790s. Here the French bred and contained their sturdy ponies, an intermixed breed of some Arabian and French stock, possibly some mustang. One early history of the Prairie du Rocher area calls these horses "point ponies," perhaps referring to the peninsular point where they were grazed. The peninsula made stealing these horses very difficult; their naturally increasing numbers lessened the need for Indian horses procured from the trans-Mississippi tribes, thereby affecting a trade network that had existed since before 1700. For "point ponies," see E. J. Montague, "The History of Randolph County, Illinois, Including Old Kaskaskia Island" (1859; copied by Elisabeth Pinkerton Leighty, Sparta, Ill., 1948), 10; John A. Walthall, "Aboriginal Pottery and the Eighteenth-Century Illini," in *Calumet & Fleur-de-Ly*s: *Archaeology of Indian and French Contact in the Midcontinent*, ed. John A. Walthall and Thomas Emerson (Washington, D.C.: Smithsonian Institution Press, 1992), 169.

24. Sarah Jones Tucker, *Indian Villages of the Illinois*, Scientific Papers 2, part 1, atlas, (1942; repr., Springfield: Illinois State Museum, 1975), plates 4 and 5; for discussion of Grigsby site artifacts and the profile of the Mechigamea in the 1670s, see Dan F. Morse, "The Seventeenth-Century Michigamea Village Location in Arkansas," in Walthall and Emerson, *Calumet & Fleur-de-Lys*, 55–74; Morse, "Seventeenth-Century Michigamea," 62; John A. Walthall, F. Terry Norris, and Barbara D. Stafford, "Woman Chief's Village: An Illini Winter Hunting Camp," in Walthall and Emerson, *Calumet & Fleur-de-Lys*, emphasizes the importance of knives: "Knives were among the earliest and most demanded trade goods brought into the Illinois Country." Walthall inventories trade goods from 1688 as containing twenty-three dozen case knives of standard size, three dozen case knives of large size, and six dozen clasp knives (citing Theodore C. Pease and Raymond Werner, *The French Foundations: 1680–1693*, Collections of the Illinois State Historical Library 23 [French Series 1; Springfield: Illinois State Historical Library, 1934]).

25. Surrey, *Commerce*, 262; Le Page du Pratz, *The History of Louisiana, or of the Western Parts of Virginia and Carolina: Containing a Description of the Countries That Lye on Both Sides of the River Mississippi; with an Account of the Settlements,*

Inhabitants, Soil, Climate, and Products (London: T. Becket and P. A. De Hondt, 1763), 2:62. See also Arnold, *Rumble,* for a "fawn of oil" and subsequent description of Quapaw Indians' production of bear oil, 39–41; this illustration resides in the Peabody Museum, Harvard University. See a good photograph of this drawing, with accompanying explanation, in Arnold, *Rumble,* 43; Herbert B. Battle, "The Domestic Use of Oil among the Southern Aborigines," *American Anthropologist* 24, no. 2 (Apr.–May 1922), 173; Ian W. Brown, "Certain Aspects of French-Indian Interaction in Lower Louisiana," in Walthall and Emerson, *Calumet & Fleur-de-Lys,* 21, and Daniel H. Usner, Jr., *Indians, Settlers, and Slaves in a Frontier Exchange Economy: The Lower Mississippi Valley before 1783* (Chapel Hill: University of North Carolina Press, 1992), 206; Surrey, *Commerce,* 262. Brown, *Voyageur,* 5, n. 5, and 21, has an overview of the meaning of the term *pot* in conjunction with the shipping of both bear oil and brandy. A Canadian half gallon "was a pot or quarte, equal to 63.4 ounces." Brown indicates that a barrel would hold twenty pots (about ten gallons).

26. See page 1 of two, http://www.ku.edu/-mammals/ursus-amer.html.

27. Kaskaskia Manuscripts, 1740, in Brown, *Voyageur,* 7; statistic of 120 pots from one bear appears in Brown, *Voyageur,* 8. Arnold, *Rumble,* 40, discusses a "more realistic" estimate—eighty pots of oil from a single animal, as estimated by C. C. Robin in 1807; Brown, *Voyageur,* 12.

28. Manifest is in Briggs, "Forgotten Colony," 373–74; Macarty to Rouille, Feb. 1, 1752, in Pease, *Illinois on the Eve,* 481; Macarty and Buchet to Vaudreuil, Jan. 15, 1752, in Pease, *Illinois on the Eve,* 426; "Inventory of the Goods at Fort De Chartres," in Clarence W. Alvord and Clarence Carter, *The New Régime, 1765–1767* (Springfield: Illinois State Historical Library, 1916), 102–4.

29. Manifest in Briggs, *Forgotten Colony,* 374–77; for instance, see Bruce G. Trigger's discussion of seventeenth-century Huron trade good preferences, 209–10, and Indians' reuse of broken iron implements and artifacts through metal and iron reworking, 216, in Trigger, *Natives and Newcomers: Canada's "Heroic Age" Reconsidered* (Kingston, Ont.: McGill-Queen's University Press, 1985); for discussion of the archaeology of trade goods in the Middle Historic Period, 1670–1760, see George Irving Quimby, *Indian Culture and European Trade Goods* (Madison: University of Wisconsin Press, 1966), 71–72. Quimby posits that pieces of iron kettles may have been detached and used as hoes; John Walthall, "Aboriginal Pottery," in Walthall and Emerson, *Calumet & Fleur-de-Lys,* 168; Piazza, "Kaskaskia Manuscripts," 26; these trade lists are furnished by Margaret Kimball Brown in her study *Cultural Transformations among the Illinois,* 149–50. Father Marest's list appears in Thwaites, *Jesuit Relations,* vol. 66; Robert G. Carroon, ed., *Broadswords and Bayonets: The Journals of the Expedition under the Command of Captain Thomas Stirling of the 42nd Regiment of Foot, Royal Highland Regiment (the Black Watch) to Occupy Fort Chartres in the Illinois Country, August 1765 to January 1766* (Society of Colonial Wars in the State of Illinois, 1984), 26; See inventory comparison of Zimmerman, Waterman, and Guebert sites in Brown, "Cultural Transformation," 251.

30. Mary Borgias Palm, *The Jesuit Missions of the Illinois Country, 1673–1763* (Cleveland: Saint Louis University, 1931), 54. According to the etymology listed in the *American Heritage Dictionary of the English Language*, 2004, *pesle mesle* is probably a reduplication of *mesle*, the imperative of *mesler*, "to mix"; *American State Papers, Public Lands. Documents, Legislative and Executive, of the Congress of the United States from the Second Session of the Eleventh to the Third Session of the Thirteenth Congress.* (Washington, D.C.: Walter Lowrie and Walter S. Franklin, 1832–61), 2, 186, in Palm, *Jesuit Missions*, 55.

31. Record K-87 (H698) in Brown and Dean, *Village of Chartres*, 425; Record K-136 (H760) in Brown and Dean, *Village of Chartres*, 485.

32. Record K-171 (H74) in Brown and Dean, *Village of Chartres*, 532; Record K-181 (H1018) in Brown and Dean, *Village of Chartres*, 547.

33. Joseph Zitomersky, *French Americans–Native Americans in Eighteenth-Century French Colonial Louisiana: The Population Geography of the Illinois Indians, 1670s–1760s* (Lund, Sweden: Lund University Press, 1994), 321; see chapter 2, 35, n. 21, on Emily Blasingham's analysis of population decline among the Illinois Indians; Brown, "Cultural Transformation," 248; Martin Pring (1625), in Gordon G. Whitney, *From Coastal Wilderness to Fruited Plain: A History of Environmental Change in Temperate North America from 1500 to the Present* (Cambridge: Cambridge University Press, 1994), 102. See Whitney's excellent discussion of Indian agricultural practices, 100–107.

34. See record K-203 (H246) in Brown and Dean, *Village of Chartres*, 587; map appears in Briggs, *Forgotten Colony*, 91.

35. J. Nick Perrin, *The Jewel of Cahokia* (Belleville, Ill.: Belleville Advocate, 1936), 5. The *Grand Dictionnaire Francais-Anglais*, 1864, defines a "rigole" as "a trench, a little ditch or furrow, drain, gutter (for water to pass in)." This definition seems to suggest a manmade waterway; both naturally occurring feeder streams and constructed "rigolets" crisscrossed French lands; see Macarty to Vaudreuil, Mar. 27, 1752, in Pease, *Illinois on the Eve*, 557; notarial records K-128 (H568) and K-314 (H483) in Brown and Dean, *Village of Chartres*, 475 and 762. Wood use for the posts surrounding all French buildings, even henhouses, was very high. For example, in 1725 in a house sale contract, the seller agreed to furnish the buyer with "six hundred posts to fence said lot." Record K-14 (H154), 349. These posts were initially red mulberry; by the 1750s, a stated preference for cedar posts begins to appear in the records. One inference is the exhaustion of red mulberry in the bottomlands; Robert H. Mohlenbrock, *Forest Trees of Illinois* (Springfield: Illinois Department of Conservation, Division of Forestry, 1986), 73 and 76; Whitney, *From Coastal Wilderness*, 212; Frances B. King, *Plants, People, and Paleoecology: Biotic Communities and Aboriginal Plant Usage in Illinois*, Scientific Papers 20 (Springfield: Illinois State Museum, 1984), 135. For green ash and erosion control, see H. A. Fowells, *Silvics of Forest Trees of the United States*, Agriculture Handbook no. 271 (Washington, D.C.: U.S. Department of Agriculture, 1965), 188; A. F. Yeager, "Root systems of certain trees and shrubs grown on prairie soils," *Journal of Agricultural Research* 51 (1935), 1085–92.

36. Giraud, *History of French Louisiana*, 5:465; chapter 3, 82–83, for discussion of livestock foraging; Hechenberger, "Metchigamea Tribe," 1; Macarty to Vaudreuil, Sept. 1752, in Pease, *Illinois on the Eve*, 680.

37. Palm, *Jesuit Missions*, 56; record D-168, Brown and Dean, *Village of Chartres*, 118; records D-248, 175, and D-74, 53, respectively, in Brown and Dean, *Village of Chartres*. For a thorough study of French-Indian liaisons along the Mississippi and the resultant kinship network, see Tanis C. Thorne, *The Many Hands of My Relations: French and Indians on the Lower Missouri* (Columbia: University of Missouri Press, 1996).

38. Order of Command for Macarty, 1751, in Pease, *Illinois on the Eve*, 315.

5. Prairie Invasions, 1751–52

1. These details appear in the letters of Macarty Mactigue, referred to hereafter as Macarty, French commander at Fort Chartres across 1751–52; letters in Theodore Calvin Pease, "Macarty's Command of the Illinois, January-February, 1752," in *Illinois on the Eve of the Seven Years War, 1747–1755*, Collections of the Illinois State Historical Library 29 (Springfield: Illinois State Historical Library, 1940).

2. I am indebted to Dr. Geoffrey Plank of the University of Cincinnati for this point. For most important works: Mary Borgias Palm on the Jesuits; Carl J. Ekberg on the French merchants and farmers; Wayne C. Temple on Indians and their villages; Margaret Kimball Brown on the Illinois Indians in particular and Brown and Lawrie Cena Dean on French culture and the role of the voyageur; Reginald Horsman, Clarence Carter, and Clarence Alvord on the British occupation; Theodore Calvin Pease on the French regime; Abraham Nasatir on the Spanish in the Illinois; and Clarence Alvord on the "Virginia Anarchy" of the earliest American influx; Brink, McDonough and Co., eds., *A History of St. Clair County* (Philadelphia, 1881), 59.

3. Carl J. Ekberg, *French Roots in the Illinois Country: The Mississippi Frontier in Colonial Times* (Urbana: University of Illinois Press, 2000), 180–81; D'Abbadie, the last governor of French Louisiana, writes in 1764, "The savages of the different posts of the Illinois are reduced today to a very small number; war and tafia have almost destroyed them." In Joseph Jablow, *Indians of Illinois and Indiana: Illinois, Kickapoo, and Potawatomi Indians* (New York: Garland Press, 1974), 237; Bienville to Maurepas, May 18, 1733, in *Mississippi Provincial Archives*, 3:614. Raymond Hauser, "An Ethnohistory of the Illinois Indian Tribe, 1673–1832" (PhD diss., Northern Illinois University, 1973; Ann Arbor, Mich.: University Microfilms, 1973), 108; a good discussion of the French population that examines these contrasts and provides texture is Walter J. Saucier and Katherine Wagner Spineke, "Francois Saucier, Engineer of Fort de Chartres, Illinois," in *Frenchmen and French Ways in the Mississippi Valley*, ed. John Francis McDermott (Urbana: University of Illinois Press, 1969). Winstanley Briggs, "The Forgotten Colony: Le Pays des Illinois" (PhD diss., University of Chicago, 1985).

4. Carl J. Ekberg, *Colonial Ste. Genevieve: An Adventure on the Mississippi Frontier* (Gerald, Mo.: Patrice Press, 1985), 20; Clarence W. Alvord, *The Centennial History of Illinois* (Springfield: Illinois Centennial Commission, 1920), 1:238; Ekberg, *Colonial Ste. Genevieve*, 21.

5. See Richard White's analysis of Indian discontent with the amount and quality of French trade goods at the end of King George's War (1744–48). White states, "By 1745, there were serious shortages of trade goods in the West." *The Middle Ground: Indians, Empires, and Republics in the Great Lakes Region, 1650—1815* (Cambridge: Cambridge University Press, 1991), 199; Hamilton to Clinton, Sept. 20, 1750, in "An Anthropological Report on the Piankeshaw Indians, Dockett 99 (part of Consolidated Docket no. 315, Dr. Dorothy Libby)," in *The Ohio Valley–Great Lakes Ethnohistory Archives: The Miami Collection* (Bloomington: Glenn A. Black Laboratory of Archaeology, Indiana University; R. Louis Gentilcore, "Vincennes and French Settlement in the Old Northwest," *Annals of the Association of American Geographers* 47, no. 3 (Sept. 1957), 265; Henry M. Majors, "Fort Ouiatanon and the Wabash River, 1700–1824" (Seattle: independently published, 1970), 103–4, 108; A. M. Gibson, *The Kickapoos: Lords of the Middle Border* (Norman: University of Oklahoma Press, 1963), 22–23.

6. White, *Middle Ground*, 200. Note also Governor Vaudreuil reporting in 1748 that "some Shawnees" were "settled at the forks of the Wabash" in part "because of quarrels with other Indian groups." See Vaudreuil, cited in "An Anthropological Report on the Piankeshaw Indians, Dockett 99"; John Mack Faragher, *Sugar Creek: Life on the Illinois Prairie* (New Haven: Yale University Press, 1986), 24; N. M. Miller Surrey, *The Commerce of Louisiana during the French Regime 1699–1763* (New York: Columbia University Press, 1916), 84–86.

7. Margaret Kimball Brown and Lawrie Cena Dean, *The Village of Chartres in Colonial Illinois, 1720–1765* (New Orleans: Polyanthos, 1977), Record K191 (H878), 565–66; Brown and Dean, *Village of Chartres*, Record K-193 (H861), 569; letters of Commander Macarty Mactigue, in Joseph Jablow, *Indians of Illinois and Indiana*, 216–17. For the most comprehensive treatment of the vendetta between the Illinois and the northern tribes at this time, see Raymond E. Hauser, "The Fox Raid of 1752: Defensive Warfare and the Decline of the Illinois Indian Tribe," *Illinois State Historical Journal* 86 (1993), 210–24.

8. Jean Jacques Macarty Mactigue was born in France "to a family of Irish military refugees." He entered the French Marines and rose through the ranks to become senior captain of the New Orleans colony by 1749. He was appointed to succeed the Chevalier de Bertet as Commander of the Illinois in 1749 and served France during the Seven Years War in Illinois. See William P. McCarthy, "The Chevalier Macarty Mactigue," *Journal of the Illinois State Historical Society* 61, no 1 (spring 1968), 41–57; Macarty to Vaudreuil, Jan. 1752, in Pease, *Illinois on the Eve*; for description of the difficulty ascending the rivers, see 432–33; for events of Dec. 7, see 435. Pierre Rigaud de Vaudreuil became governor of Louisiana in

1742 and then of Canada in 1755. He was the son of the more famous Vaudreuil, Philippe de Rigaud de Vaudreuil, "chevalier and marquis, musketeer, commander of the troops, naval captain, Governor of Montreal, and Governor-general of New France" between 1703 and 1725. Vaudreuil's twenty-three-year sojourn as an early-eighteenth-century governor saw the French Louisiana proprietary colony founded and struggling. The proper placement of the Illinois Country was debated hotly under his regime, and the territory finally was awarded to Louisiana. See *Dictionary of Canadian Biography*, vol. 2 (Toronto: University of Toronto Press, 1969); Macarty to Vaudreuil, in Pease, *Illinois on the Eve*, 435.

9. White, *Middle Ground*, 229; Ian K. Steele, *Warpaths: Invasions of North America* (New York: Oxford University Press, 1994), 182. At least one historian, Fred Anderson, discusses the activities of La Demoiselle solely as Memeskia. See Fred Anderson, *Crucible of War: The Seven Years' War and the Fate of Empire in British North America, 1754–1766* (New York: Knopf, 2000), 25–29.

10. Francis Jennings, *Empire of Fortune: Crowns, Colonies, and Tribes in the Seven Years War in America* (New York: Norton, 1988), 50; reports to Raymond, Mar.–April 1750, in Pease, *Illinois on the Eve*, 174–75; Steele, *Warpaths*, 182; reports to Raymond, in Pease, *Illinois on the Eve*, 176; see additional account in Pease, *Illinois on the Eve*, 173; Steel, *Warpaths*, 165; reports to Raymond in Pease, *Illinois on the Eve*, 173, n. 1; See Conrad Weiser's report in Peter Wraxall, *An Abridgment of Indian Affairs Contained in Four Folio Volumes, Transacted by the Colony of New York, from the Year 1678 to the Year 1751*, ed. Charles H. McIlwain (Cambridge: Harvard University Press, 1915), xvi; W. Neil Franklin, "Pennsylvania-Virginia Rivalry for the Indian Trade of the Ohio Valley," *Mississippi Valley Historical Review* 20, no. 4 (March 1934).

11. See Richard White's discussion of kinship loyalties and political alliances among the lower Great Lakes tribes, a pattern he calls "intermarried leadership," in *The Middle Ground*, 212–13; See La Motte Cadillac, Sept. 25, 1702, in which eighteen Miami came to the fort at Detroit "on behalf of their tribe, to ask me for lands and to beg the savages who are there to approve of their coming to settle there and joining them." In *Cadillac Papers*, portfolio 127, document 45, *Michigan Pioneer and Historical Collections*, vol. 33 (Lansing: Robert Smith, 1904), 138. For a clarifying discussion of the split in Miami allegiance and relocation, see Stewart Rafert, *The Miami Indians of Indiana: A Persistent People, 1654–1994* (Indianapolis: Indiana Historical Society, 1996), 33–36.

12. See Le Loup's statement to Macarty in Macarty to Vaudreuil, Jan. 1752, in Pease, *Illinois on the Eve*, 455; Vaudreuil to Rouille, Apr. 8, 1752, in Pease, 572; Macarty to Vaudreuil, January, 1752, in Pease, 434; Le Loup's statement appears in Macarty to Vaudreuil, Jan. 1752, in Pease, 438; Macarty to Vaudreuil, Jan. 1752, in Pease, 447; Le Loup, reported in Macarty to Vaudreuil, Jan. 1752, in Pease, 455.

13. Words of Chareragoue, reported by Macarty, Macarty to Vaudreuil, Jan. 1752, in Pease, *Illinois on the Eve*, 436; reported in Macarty to Vaudreuil, Jan. 1752, in Pease, 449; Macarty to Vaudreuil, Jan. 1752, in Pease, 453.

14. Mary Borgias Palm, *The Jesuit Missions of the Illinois Country, 1673–1763* (Cleveland: Saint Louis University, 1931), 24; see the parish records of St. Anne's in Brown and Dean, *Village of Chartres*, 3–20; La Jonquiere to Rouille, Sept. 25, 1751, in Pease, *Illinois on the Eve*, 366–67.

15. Brown and Dean, *Village of Chartres*, Record K-195 (H851), 572–73; Brown and Dean, *Village of Chartres*, Record K-196 (H236), 574; Brink et al., *History of St. Clair County*, 31; Macarty Mactigue, in Jablow, *Indians of Illinois and Indiana*, 216.

16. *M'Skutewe Awandiangwi, Nipundikan* puts the date of the attack as June 6 and the number of attackers at one thousand. See Dan Hechenberger, "The Metchigamea Tribe," vol. 1, no. 2, 1998; Macarty Mactigue, in Jablow, *Indians of Illinois and Indiana*, 216; description of the site is taken from Jean-Bernard Bossu, *Jean-Bernard Bossu's Travels in the Interior of North America, 1751–1762*, ed. and trans. Seymour Feiler (Norman: University of Oklahoma Press, 1962), and Margaret Kimball Brown, "The Search for the Michigamea Indian Village," *Outdoor Illinois* (Mar. 1972); Hauser, "Fox Raid," 218. Hauser presents an argument for the complicity of Commander Macarty in the attack on the Illinois villages. His evidence is extremely circumstantial and ignores the yearlong efforts of Macarty to keep peace in the Illinois Country by interrogating rather than executing Le Loup; see correspondence of Commander Macarty in Jablow, *Indians of Illinois and Indiana*, 217; White, *Middle Ground*, 230–31. See also Macarty to Vaudreuil, Sept. 2, 1752, in Pease, *Illinois on the Eve*, 680–81.

17. Brown and Dean, *Village of Chartres*, Record K-197 (H237), 574–75; "Comparative Table 6: Native Materials and Technology," in Margaret Kimball Brown, *Cultural Transformations among the Illinois: An Application of a Systems Model* (East Lansing: Museum, Michigan State University, 1979), 251; See "Table 2: Population Figures for the Illinois," in Brown, *Cultural Transformations*, 232.

18. "Coxe's Account of the Activities of the English in the Mississippi Valley in the Seventeenth Century, A Memorial by Dr. Daniel Cox," in Clarence W. Alvord and Lee Bidgood, *The First Explorations of the Trans-Allegheny Region by the Virginians, 1650–1674* (Cleveland: Clark, 1912), 233; R. David Edmunds, "Pickawillany: French Military Power versus British Economics," *Western Pennsylvania Historical Magazine*, 58, no. 2 (Apr. 1975); see this account in Margaret Kimball Brown, *History as They Lived It: A Social History of Prairie du Rocher, Illinois* (New Orleans: Patrice Press, 2005).

6. A Ragged Resource War: British in the Illinois

1. Donald E. Worcester and Thomas F. Schilz, "The Spread of Firearms among the Indians on the Anglo-French Frontier," *American Indian Quarterly* 8, no. 2 (spring 1984), 105; Donald Davidson, *The Tennessee: The Old River—Frontier to Secession, a Facsimile Edition of Volume 1* (Knoxville: University of Tennessee Press, 1946), 96.

2. O. J. Page, *History of Massac County, Illinois, with Life Sketches and Portraits, Part One—Historical* (Massac County, 1900), 26; Norman W. Caldwell, "Fort

Massac during the French and Indian War," *Journal of the Illinois State Historical Society* 43, no. 2 (summer 1950), 105 and 112, n. 58. John B. Fortier, "New Light on Fort Massac," in *Frenchmen and French Ways in the Mississippi Valley*, ed. John Francis McDermott (Urbana: University of Illinois Press, 1969).

3. John A. Walthall, "French Colonial Fort Massac: Architecture and Ceramic Patterning," in *French Colonial Archaeology: The Illinois Country and the Western Great Lakes*, ed. John A. Walthall (Urbana: University of Illinois Press, 1991), 45; Caldwell, "Fort Massac," 107, n. 30, citing Kelerec memorandum, Dec. 12, 1758; Caldwell, "Fort Massac," 104. See the thorough account of French Illinois expeditions and the few battles in which French Illinois soldiers fought in Clarence Alvord, *The Illinois Country, 1673–1818* (Springfield: Illinois Centennial Commission, 1920), 238–45; Almon Ernest Parkins, *The Historical Geography of Detroit* (Lansing: Michigan Historical Commission, 1918), 79. Parkins describes a population boom in Detroit between 1749 and 1755, despite the war; Margaret Kimball Brown and Lawrie Cena Dean, "French and Indian War," in *The French Colony in the Mid-Mississippi Valley* (Carbondale, Ill.: American Kestrel Books, 1995), 21–22; Alvord, *Illinois Country*, 238–39; Carl J. Ekberg, *French Roots in the Illinois Country: The Mississippi Frontier in Colonial Times* (Urbana: University of Illinois Press, 2000), 266.

4. Caldwell, "Fort Massac," 113, n. 61; "Aubry's Account of the Illinois Country, 1763," in Clarence W. Alvord and Clarence Carter, eds., *The Critical Period, 1763–1765*, Collections of the Illinois State Historical Library 10 (Springfield: Illinois State Historical Library, 1915), 4; Caldwell, "Fort Massac," 104.

5. Ekberg, *French Roots*, 223–25. Ekberg documents the reality of war-stressed New Orleans, a city desperate for foodstuffs from the Illinois, which were scant or unavailable.

6. For *l'abandon*, see Ekberg, *French Roots*, 115–18; see discussion of possible soil exhaustion on the eastern shores of the Mississippi in Carl J. Ekberg, *Colonial Ste. Genevieve: An Adventure on the Mississippi Frontier* (Gerald, Mo.: Patrice Press, 1985), 20. Ekberg also points out the subdivision of large French farms through filial inheritance. French Canadians were beginning to emigrate to the Illinois, often sons and daughters from previous marriages. One petitioner to the French commander Macarty in 1752 mentions "the large number of children [near Kaskaskia]." See Ekberg, *Colonial Ste. Genevieve*, 21. Macarty also uses the French word *fatiguee* (exhausted) to describe the French farmlands. However, such observations must be kept in the context of the year 1752, when a major drought stressed the area; Fraser to Haldimand, May 4, 1766, in Clarence W. Alvord and Clarence Carter, eds., *The New Régime, 1765–1767* Collections of the Illinois State Historical Library 11 (Springfield: Illinois State Historical Library, 1916), 227.

7. Margaret Kimball Brown and Lawrie Cena Dean, *The Village of Chartres in Colonial Illinois, 1720–1765* (New Orleans: Polyanthos, 1977), Record K-193 (H861), 569; Brown and Dean, *Village of Chartres*, record K-340 (H523), 804; Brown and Dean, *French Colony*, 9; T. P. Fadler, *Memoirs of a French Village: A Chronicle of*

Old Prairie du Rocher, 1722–1972 (self-published, 1972), 17; Natalia Maree Belting, Kaskaskia under the French Régime (New Orleans: Polyanthos, 1975), 53.

8. See account by August Chouteau before Theodore Hunt, recorder of land titles, Apr. 18, 1825, in John McDermott, The Early Histories of St. Louis (St. Louis: St. Louis Historical Documents Foundation, 1952), 92; "Captain Gordon's Journal," Aug. 20, 1766, in Alvord and Carter, New Régime, 298.

9. Philip Pittman, The Present State of European Settlements on the Mississippi (Cleveland: Clark, 1906), 88; Pittman, Present State, 87; Pittman, Present State, 90; Macarty to Vaudreuil, Jan. 1752, in Theodore C. Pease, Illinois on the Eve of the Seven Years War (Springfield: Illinois State Historical Library, 1940), 468–69; "Captain Gordon's Journal," 298–99.

10. Craig Vetter, "Bloodsucker Zen," in Chicago Wilderness 7, no. 3 (spring 2004), 17; Truls Jensen, Paul E. Kaiser, and Donald R. Barnard, "Adaptation to Intermittently Flooded Swamps by Anopheles quadrimaculus Species C1 (Diptera Culicidae), Environmental Entomology 23, no. 5 (1994), 1150. This study describes the ovipositing and hatching behavior of a species of mosquito in Florida; however, many species of floodplain mosquitoes inhabit river valleys in North America, including the upper Mississippi; William R. Horsfall, Robert J. Novak, and Forrest L. Johnson, "Aedes vexans as a Flood-plain Mosquito," Environmental Entomology 4, no. 5 (Oct. 1975), 675; Helmut Blume, The German Coast during the Colonial Era, 1722–1803 (Geographisches Institut der Universitat Kiel, Germany, 1956), trans. and ed. Ellen C. Merrill (Destrehan, La.: German-Acadian Coast Historical and Genealogical Society, 1990), 79; Rivers of North America, ed. Michael P. Dineen et al. (Waukesha, Wis.: Outdoor World, 1973), 43–44.

11. Claudia M. O'Malley, "Aedes vexans (Meigen): An Old Foe," Proceedings of the New Jersey Mosquito Control Association, 1990, 90–95; see Horsfall et al., "Aedes vexans," 675; "The Official Journal Kept by Lt. Eddington or the Surgeon," in Carroon, Broadswords and Bayonets, 77; Charles Dickens, in William I. Woods, "Changes in the Landscape of the American Bottom—A.D. 1000 to Now," paper presented in a roundtable symposium: Changes in the Landscape: The Lower Valley and Elsewhere—A.D. 1000 to Now at the Joint Meetings of the Southern Archaeological Conference and the Midwest Archaeological Conference, Lexington, Ky., Nov. 11, 1984; Nehemiah Matson, Pioneers of Illinois, Containing a Series of Sketches That Occurred Previous to 1813 (Chicago: Knight and Leonard, 1882), 114; "Official Journal Kept by Lt. Eddington," in Carroon, Broadswords and Bayonets, 79.

12. The Arthur St. Clair Papers, vol. 2, in John White, Early Accounts of the Ecology of the Big Rivers Area (Springfield: Illinois Department of Natural Resources, 2000), 43; "A Business Venture at Cahokia: The Letters of Charles Gratiot, 1778–1779," in Old Cahokia: A Narrative and Documents Illustrating the First Century of Its History, ed. John McDermott (St. Louis: St. Louis Historical Documents Foundation, 1949); "Journal of Captain Gordon," in Alvord and Carter, New Régime, 301; Croghan, in "Journal of Captain Harry Gordon," in Newton D. Mereness, ed., Travels in the American Colonies (New York: Macmillan, 1916), 478, n. 1.

13. In 1763 a traveler, "Mr. Hamburgh," observed that the French settlements in the Illinois "Produces Some fruit: Apples, Pears, Quinses, and Peaches. The land is low And the Missippi [*sic*] Gennerally over flows in June; the Excessive Heat that followeth afterwards occasioneth the fevers to Be Very frequent." "Minutes of Mr. Hamburgh's Journal," 1763, in Mereness, *Travels in the American Colonies*, 364. French orchards at Detroit were described by the British as containing "several hundred of fruit trees." Their apple varieties included Detroit Red and Pomme de Neige. Information gathered anecdotally from "old people" suggests these fruit trees were originally obtained from Montreal and, before that, from Normandy and Provence. *Michigan Pioneer and Historical Collections* (Lansing: W. S. George & Co., 1877), 1:355; Kaskaskia Manuscripts 59:12:17:1; Kaskaskia Manuscripts, 60:1:13:1.

14. "The Official Journal Kept by Lt. Eddington," in *Broadswords and Bayonets*, 90; Victor Collot, *A Journey in North America, Containing a Survey of the Countries Watered by the Mississippi, Ohio, Missouri, and Other Affluving Rivers; with Exact Observations on the Course and Soundings of These Rivers; and on the Towns, Villages, Hamlets, and Farms of That Part of the New World; Followed by Philosophical, Political, Military, and Commercial Remarks and by a Projected Line of Frontiers and General Limits* (Florence, Italy: O. Lange, 1924), 1:239–40; Collot, *Journey*, 241, 242.

15. Stirling to Gage, Dec. 15, 1765, in Alvord and Carter, *New Régime*, 125; Glenn J. Speed, *Ghost Towns of Southern Illinois* (Royalton, Ill.: Glenn J. Speed, 1977), 172–73; Fraser to Haldimand, May 4, 1766, in Alvord and Carter, *New Régime*, 231.

16. Numbers from Aubry are given in Joseph Jablow, *Indians of Illinois and Indiana: Illinois, Kickapoo, and Potawatomi Indians* (New York: Garland Press, 1974), 236; for the best recent treatment of British-Indian relations before and during Pontiac's War, see Gregory Evans Dowd, *War under Heaven: Pontiac, the Indian Nation, & the British Empire* (Baltimore: Johns Hopkins University Press, 2002); see especially 168–73, "The Struggle for Illinois"; Philip Pittman, *Present State*, 97; St. Ange to Vaudreuil, Feb. 1752, in Pease, *Illinois on the Eve*, 485; Fraser to Gage, Dec. 16, 1765, in Alvord and Carter, *New Régime*, 131.

17. Major Farmar, of the 34th Regiment of Foot, to British Secretary of War Barrington, Mar. 19, 1766, in Alvord and Carter, *New Régime*, 191; Clarence Carter, *Great Britain and the Illinois Country, 1763–1774* (Washington, D.C.: American Historical Association, 1910), 31; Loftus to Gage, Apr. 9, 1764, in Alvord and Carter, *Critical Period*, 230; deposition of Indians in Alvord and Carter, *Critical Period*, 235–36.

18. Bradley Gericke, "To the Distant Illinois Country: The Stirling Expedition to Fort de Chartres, 1765," *Journal of Illinois History* 2, no. 2 (1999), 89; Alvord and Carter, *Critical Period*, xvii–lvii; see Croghan's own account of this capture and release in "Croghan's Journal," June 8, 1765, in Alvord and Carter, *New Régime*, 30–31. Croghan identifies the Indian attackers as "Kickapers and Musquatimes." Alvord and Carter's footnote may erroneously identify the "Musquatimes" as Foxes

(Mesquatchie); it is more likely, that far south to the Ohio River, that they were Mascoutens; Fraser's "treatment" by the Illinois Indians is variously described. George Croghan mentions "an Account of the bad reception & ill treatment M. Frazier & M. Sinnott met with on their Arrival there." Croghan, June 15, 1765, in Alvord and Carter, *New Régime*, 40. Captain Harry Gordon writing to William Johnson on August 10 of the same year is more specific: "we had the accounts of Lieut. Fraser being taken out of the Commandants House at Fort Chartres by the Indians and delivered to Pontiac. His party was sent down the Mississippi." See Gordon to Johnson, Aug. 10, 1765, in Alvord and Carter, *New Régime*, 67; "Journal Kept by Lt. Eddington," in Carroon, *Broadswords and Bayonets*, 48–49.

19. "Official Journal Kept by Lt. Eddington," in Carroon, *Broadswords and Bayonets*, 97; "Journal of Captain Thomas Stirling," in Carroon, *Broadswords and Bayonets*, 37; "Journal Kept by Lt. Eddington," 67; "Journal of Captain Thomas Stirling," 37.

20. See the excellent overview of the military operations of the Black Watch Regiment in Gericke, "To the Distant Illinois." The Black Watch "participated in the assault on Fort Ticonderoga in 1758 and was present at the capture of Montreal in 1760." The Black Watch also fought in Pontiac's War in 1764. See Gericke, "To the Distant," 91; Alvord and Carter, *New Régime*, xii; "The Journal of Captain Stirling," in Carroon, *Broadswords and Bayonets*, 28; Peter E. Russell, "Redcoats in the Wilderness: The British Officer and Irregular Warfare in Europe and America, 1740–1760," *William & Mary Quarterly*, 3rd. ser., 35, no. 4 (Oct. 1978), 629–52.

21. Gage to Conway, Sept. 23, 1765, in Alvord and Carter, *New Régime*, 85; Gage to Halifax, Aug. 10, 1765, in Alvord and Carter, *New Régime*, 69.

22. Bradley Gericke, "To the Distant Illinois," 81; General Gage to Lord Shelburne, Feb. 22, 1767, in Mereness, *Travels*, 484.

23. Louise Kellogg, "La Chapelle's Remarkable Retreat through the Mississippi Valley, 1760–61," *Mississippi Valley Historical Review* 22, no. 1 (June 1935), 63–81; "Official Journal Kept by Lt. Eddington," in Carroon, *Broadswords and Bayonets*, 102; Johnson to Gage, Jan. 15, 1767, in Alvord and Carter, *New Régime*, 483.

24. See, for instance, the letters between Lieutenant Fraser and George Croghan, or those between General Thomas Gage and Sir William Johnson, 1765–67, in Alvord and Carter, *New Régime*. It isn't until the actual possession of Fort Chartres by Captain Stirling that letters explicitly about provisions, stores, and supplies begin to appear. The urgent tone of many of these letters suggests the occupying British were surprised and dismayed to find a depleted country; Haldimand to Gage, May 16, 1770, in Thomas Gage Papers, British Museum Additional Mss., 21664:148 and 21665:289, photostats in the Illinois Historical Survey; Bradley T. Gericke, "To the Distant Illinois," 82; "Journal of Captain Thomas Stirling," in Carroon, *Broadswords and Bayonets*, 26; see also the discussion of provisions in Gericke, "To the Distant Illinois," 91–92; Jack M. Sosin, *Whitehall and the Wilderness: The Middle West in British Colonial Policy, 1760–1775* (Lincoln: University of Nebraska Press, 1961); Kerry A Trask, "To Cast Out the Devils: British Ideology and the French Canadians of

the Northwest Interior, 1760–1774," *American Review of Canadian Studies* 15, no. 3 (1985), 249. Trask demonstrates the power of an entrenched ideology in shaping a national policy; Thomas Gage to Jeffrey Amherst, Mar. 26, 1762, in Trask, "To Cast Out the Devils," 254; Thomas Gage to Lord Shelburne, Feb. 22, 1767, in Mereness, *Travels in the American Colonies*, 462; "Journal of George Croghan," in *Michigan Pioneer and Historical Collections* 3, 14.

25. "Journal of Captain Thomas Stirling," in Carroon, *Broadswords and Bayonets*, 60.

26. Matson, *Pioneers of Illinois*, 145; J. Dewey Soper, "History, Range, and Home Life of the Northern Bison," *Ecological Monographs* 11 (1941), 384; John White, *A Review of the American Bison in Illinois, with an Emphasis on Historical Accounts* (Urbana, Ill.: Nature Conservancy, 1996), 14; Matson, *Pioneers of Illinois*, 145; counts by Marquette and Joliet given in White, *Review*, 8; See Sebastien Rasle (Rale) in White, *Review*, 9; this famous phrase appears in many articles and accounts of buffalo on both sides of the Mississippi. See the *1997–1998 Marysville, Kansas, Tourism Guide*, 34; Frank Gilbert Roe, *The North American Buffalo: A Critical Study of the Species in Its Wild State*, 2nd ed. (Toronto: University of Toronto Press, 1970). Roe cites William Hornaday on buffalo numbers, 256. For the most recent and convincing ecological analysis of the disappearance of the Great Plains buffalo, see Andrew C. Isenberg, *The Destruction of the Bison: An Environmental History* (New York: Cambridge University Press, 2000). I am indebted to Dr. David Stradling for emphasizing to me the importance of Isenberg's work.

27. White, *Review*, 10; Vivier and Fraser reported in White, *Review*, 11; Alexander Fraser, in White, *Review*, 11; for the best initial discussion of perceptions of inexhaustible abundance in the New World, see William Cronon, *Changes in the Land: Indians, Colonists, and the Ecology of New England* (New York: Hill and Wang, 1983), especially chapter 3, "Seasons of Want and Plenty," 34–53; Father Sebastien Rasle [Rale] to his brother, October 12, 1723; letter appears in Edna Kenton, ed., *The Indians of North America* (New York: Harcourt, 1927), 384.

28. L. L. Pechuman, Donald W. Webb, and H. J. Taskey, *The Diptera or True Flies of Illinois: I. Tabanidae*, Illinois Natural History Bulletin 33, no. 1 (Champaign: Illinois Department of Energy and Natural Resources, 1983), 11; H. Allyn and J. A. Smeltzer, *Henry Allyn, Autobiography* (Portland, Ore.: Jean Allyn Smeltzer, 1974).

29. John Burger, "Yellowstone's Insect Vampires," *Yellowstone Science* 4, no. 4 (1996), 14. This article corroborates the movement of buffalo to escape biting flies in Yellowstone National Park. See also P. D. Taylor and S. M. Smith, "Activities and physiological states of male and female *Tabanus sackeni*," *Medical Veterinary Entomology* 3 (1989), 203–12; Pechuman et al., *Diptera*, 11; Forrest Rose, "Ring in the Old: Study of Tree Rings Brings Perspective to Human Life," *Focus* 21 (spring 1999), 15, for discussion about the setting of fires by Native Americans and pioneers to foster growth for forage. Said A. Damhoureyeh and David C. Hartnett, "Effects of Bison and Cattle on Growth, Reproduction, and Abundance of Five Tall-Grass Prairie Forbs," *American Journal of Botany* 84, no. 12 (1997), 1719–28;

Tom McHugh, *The Time of the Buffalo* (New York: Knopf, 1972), 150; James Hall, *Notes on the Western States, Containing Descriptive Sketches of Their Soil, Climate, Resources, and Scenery* (Philadelphia: Harrison Hall, 1838), 110–11; Meriwether Lewis and William Clark, *The Journals of the Lewis and Clark Expedition, August 30, 1803–August 24, 1804* (Lincoln: University of Nebraska Press, 1986), 102; Isenberg, *Destruction of the Bison*, 66–68.

30. White, *Review*, 12; see John A. Jakle, "The American Bison and the Human Occupance of the Ohio Valley," *Proceedings of the American Philosophical Society* 112, no. 4 (August 1968), especially fig. 1, 300. Jakle identifies salt licks on either side of the Ohio River and probable buffalo traces connecting these sites; Stirling to Gage, Dec. 15, 1765, in Alvord and Carter, *New Régime*, 125; Farmar to Stuart, Dec. 16, 1765, in Alvord and Carter, *New Régime*, 128; John Rothensteiner, *History of the Archdiocese of St. Louis in the Various Stages of Development from A.D. 1673 to A.D. 1928* (St. Louis: Catholic Historical Society, 1923), 1:126.

31. Gage to Reed, July 15, 1767, in Alvord and Carter, *New Régime*, 584–85; Terrance J. Martin and Mary Carol Masulis, "Preliminary Report on Animal Remains from Fort de Chartres (11R127)," appendix D in "Archaeological Excavations at Fort de Chartres: 1985–87," ed. David Keene (unpublished technical report on file at the Illinois Historic Preservation Agency, Springfield); Butricke to Barnsley, Sept. 15, 1768, in Clarence W. Alvord and Clarence Carter, *Trade and Politics, 1767–1769*, Collections of the Illinois State Historical Library 16 (Springfield: Illinois State Historical Library, 1921), 409; Farmar to Barrington, Mar. 19, 1766, in Alvord and Carter, *New Régime*, 191; "Official Journal Kept by Lt. Eddington," in Carroon, *Broadswords and Bayonets*, 93–94.

32. James Scott, "A History of the Illinois Nation of Indians from Their Discovery to the Present Day" (notes from meetings, Streator Historical Society, 1973), 10–11, manuscript in the Ayer Collection, Newberry Library, Chicago; Farmar to Gage, Dec. 16–19, 1765, in Alvord and Carter, *New Régime*, 133.

33. "Account of Commissary Edward Cole and Captain Gordon Forbes," in Jablow, *Indians of Illinois and Indiana*, 263; George Morgan to Baynton and Wharton, Dec. 10, 1767, "George Morgan Letter Book," in Alvord and Carter, *New Régime*, 130. The fine imposed was in reference to the trading or selling of alcohol to an Indian. In 1765 the British issued a set of "Orders for the Regulation of Trade" from their headquarters in New York. These general regulations were to apply to all trade. Traders bringing "spiritous liquors" to a fort or post were to store them, labeled, in the forts until the transactions were completed. No liquors were to be sold to Indians in or near posts or forts, but after the completion of trade, traders could carry the liquor "two leagues away" and deliver it to Indians. It is not clear from George Morgan's letter where the trading of the pint of rum for the meat took place. "Orders for the Regulation of Trade," Jan. 16, 1765, in Alvord and Carter, *Critical Period*, 400.

34. Morgan's correspondence appears in Jablow, *Indians of Illinois and Indiana*, 260–61; for a contrasting view of the economy and skill of the Great Plains Indians

in butchering buffalo, especially the complete use made of the animal, see "Indians as Consumers," in McHugh, *Time of the Buffalo*, 83–109. White hunters typically left much more of the animal. Eventually, the attraction of wolves to the halfway-butchered carcasses ("the stench of rotting buffalo") began to be a problem for Anglo-American settlers; the wolves then also attacked domestic stock. See Stephen Aron, "Pigs and Hunters: 'Rights in the Woods' on the Trans-Appalachian Frontier," in *Contact Points: American Frontiers from the Mohawk Valley to the Mississippi, 1750–1830*, ed. Andrew R. L. Cayton and Fredrika J. Teute (Chapel Hill: University of North Carolina Press, 1998), 197.

35. Jablow, *Indians of Illinois and Indiana*, 261; Clarence W. Alvord, *The Mississippi Valley in British Politics: A Study of the Trade, Land Speculation, and Experiments in Imperialism Culminating in the American Revolution* (Cleveland: Clark, 1917), 1:301; Morgan to Baynton and Wharton, Dec. 10, 1767 (George Morgan Letter Book), in Alvord and Carter, *Trade and Politics*, 132; Butricke to Barnsley, Sept. 15, 1768, in Alvord and Carter, *Trade and Politics*, 409.

36. See Croghan's 1765 dispatches in Larry C. Nelson, *A Man of Distinction among Them: Alexander McKee and British-Indian Affairs along the Ohio Country Frontier, 1754–1799* (Kent, Ohio: Kent State University Press, 1999), 55.

37. "Official Journal Kept by Lt. Eddington," in Carroon, *Broadswords and Bayonets*, 83; Captain Louis St. Ange de Bellerive was at the time of the French surrender sixty years old. He had served in the French armies in Canada and the Illinois for about forty years. After surrendering Fort Chartres, he and his men crossed the Mississippi to St. Louis. See James F. Keefe, "The Inventory of Fort Des Chartres, "in *Muzzleloader* 18, no. 6 (Jan.-Feb. 1992), 45–46; "Journal of Captain Thomas Stirling," in Carroon, *Broadswords and Bayonets*, 45; letter from Lt. Eddingstone, Oct. 16, 1765, in Alvord and Carter, *New Régime*, 106; "Official Journal Kept by Lt. Eddington," 84; see "Inventory of the Goods at Fort De Chartres," in Alvord and Carter, *New Régime*, 102–4; "Official Journal Kept by Lt. Eddington," 83; See "Cession of Fort de Chartres, Oct. 10, 1765," in Alvord and Carter, *New Régime*, 100.

7. Predations and Survivals: French, British, and Indian Illinois

1. Thomas Hutchins Collection, Chicago Historical Society. Thomas Hutchins to George Morgan, Apr. 6, 1769.

2. Wilshire Butterfield, "Chicago," *Magazine of Western History* 3, no. 5 (March 1886), 446.

3. Edmunds, *The Potawatomis: Keepers of the Fire* (Norman: University of Oklahoma Press, 1978). H. Clyde Wilson, "A New Interpretation of the Wild Rice District of Wisconsin," disagrees that Potawatomi were rice harvesters, but his evidence is taken almost wholly from the early *Jesuit Relations*. Wilson, *American Anthropologist*, n.s., 58, no. 6 (Dec. 1956), 1059–64; Gardener P. Stickney, "Indian Use of Wild Rice," *American Anthropologist* 9, no. 4 (Apr. 1986), 155–22. See page 121 for quotes above; Stickney, "Indian Use," 115–20.

4. These descriptive accounts are in John White, *Early Accounts of the Ecology of the Fox River Area*, Fox River Area Assessment 5 (Springfield: Illinois Department of Natural Resources, 2000), 27.

5. Gilbert Quaal, *Wild Plant Uses (Both Past and Present)* (Deer River, Minn.: White Oak Society, 1995), 26 and 5; Thomas Vennum Jr., *Wild Rice and the Ojibway People* (St. Paul: Minnesota Historical Society Press, 1988); *Wild Rice* (U.S. Fish and Wildlife Service, Department of the Interior, Sept. 1987); John White, *Early Accounts*, 23; Richard White, *The Roots of Dependency: Subsistence, Environment, and Social Change among the Choctaws, Pawnees, and Navajos* (Lincoln: University of Nebraska Press, 1983).

6. "Information on the State of Commerce in the Illinois Country Given by Captain Forbes 34th Regiment," enclosed in a Jan. 6, 1769, letter to General Gage, in Clarence W. Alvord and Clarence Carter, eds., *Trade and Politics, 1767–1769*, Collections of the Illinois State Historical Library 16 (Springfield: Illinois State Historical Library, 1921), 382; Wilkins to Barrington, Secretary of War, Dec. 5, 1769, in Alvord and Carter, *Trade and Politics*, 632; Arthur Clinton Boggess, *The Settlement of Illinois, 1778–1830*, Collection no. 5 (Chicago: Chicago Historical Society, 1908), 13.

7. George Morgan to his wife, after Sept. 5, 1768, in Alvord and Carter, *Trade and Politics,* 480–81; George Morgan to Baynton and Wharton, July 20, 1768, in *Trade and Politics*, 359–61; see "Account of Philadelphia Merchants" in *Trade and Politics,* 391–408.

8. "Account of Philadelphia Merchants" in Alvord and Carter, *Trade and Politics*, 406; George Morgan mentions, for instance, that his "New England man" hoped to send for his wife back in Providence. *Trade and Politics*, 480–81.

9. "Clarkson's Diary, August 6, 1766–April 16, 1767," in Clarence W. Alvord and Clarence Carter, eds., *The New Régime, 1765–1767*, Collections of the Illinois State Historical Library 11 (Springfield: Illinois State Historical Library, 1916), 359; more Kaskaskia Indians are identified across the French regime than any other group. The Rouensa family had early been important in helping Kaskaskia Indians to accept Catholicism. Later, members of the French Canadian Ducoigne and Rouensa families married and produced an important metis chief named Jean Baptiste Ducoigne. Robert M. Owens, "Jean Baptiste Ducoigne, the Kaskaskias, and the Limits of Thomas Jefferson's Friendship," *Journal of Illinois History* 5, no. 2 (summer 2002), 112; Cornelius J. Jaenen, "Amerindian Views of French Culture in the Seventeenth Century," in Peter C. Mancall and James H. Merrell, eds., *American Encounters: Natives and Newcomers from European Contact to Indian Removal, 1500–1850* (New York: Routledge, 2000).

10. Haldimand to Gage, May 16, 1770, Thomas Gage Papers, British Museum Additional Manuscripts 21664:148 and 21665:289 (photostats at the Illinois Historical Survey); for a good study of the way the fur trade post or fort functioned as a social institution in a mixed-blood community, see Gary Clayton Anderson, *Kinsmen of Another Kind: Dakota-White Relations in the Upper Missouri Valley, 1650–1862* (Lincoln: University of Nebraska Press, 1984). For the earliest sound appraisal along

these lines, see Frederick Jackson Turner, *The Character and Influence of the Indian Trade in Wisconsin: A Study of the Trading Post as an Institution,* ed. David Harry Miller and William W. Savage Jr. (Norman: University of Oklahoma Press, 1977; originally published, 1891). Turner concludes, "The history of commerce is the history of the intercommunication of peoples"; Baynton and Wharton to Macleane, Oct. 9, 1767, in Alvord and Carter, *Trade and Politics,* 84–85.

11. "Account of Philadelphia Merchants" in Alvord and Carter, *Trade and Politics,* 405; "Account of Philadelphia Merchants," 408. Clarence Carter provides the figure of "more than six thousand pounds sterling" for the "Indian expense alone" at Fort Chartres between September 1766 and September 1767. See Carter, *Great Britain and the Illinois Country, 1763–1774* (Washington, D.C.: American Historical Association, 1910; repr., Freeport, N.Y.: Books for Libraries Press, 1971), 95; Gage to Shelburne, Apr. 24, 1768, in Alvord and Carter, *Trade and Politics,* 267.

12. Wilkins to Gage, Sept. 13, 1768, in Alvord and Carter, *Trade and Politics,* 388–89; Jennings Journal, May 5–10, 1768, in *Trade and Politics,* 275.

13. Journal of D'Abbadie, Feb. 1764, in Clarence W. Alvord and Clarence Carter, eds., *The Critical Period, 1763–1765,* Collections of the Illinois State Historical Library 10 (Springfield: Illinois State Historical Library, 1915), 170–71; Montressor to Bassett, Nov. 2, 1763, Detroit, in Alvord and Carter, *Critical Period,* 535; Aubry to the minister of New Orleans, Feb. 4, 1765, in Alvord and Carter, *Critical Period,* 434.

14. These examples appear in John A. Jakle, *Images of the Ohio Valley: A Historical Geography of Travel, 1740–1860* (New York: Oxford University Press, 1977), 74; Gibault to Briand, Oct. 1769, in Alvord and Carter, *Trade and Politics,* 622.

15. "Memorial of Major Farmar and the Officers of the Thirty-Fourth Regiment of Infantry of His Britannic Majesty, Who Had Been Commanded to Take Possession of the Illinois via the Mississippi River," in Alvord and Carter, *Critical Period,* 498–99; Gage to Hillsborough, Aug. 17, 1768, in Alvord and Carter, *Trade and Politics,* 377. The French also had difficulty with desertions. The Kaskaskia Records detail "criminal proceedings" against ten French soldiers in 1753. See Kaskaskia Manuscripts, 53:11:28:2; Fraser to Gage, May 26, 1765, in Alvord and Carter, *Critical Period,* 515.

16. Gage to Penn, June 16, 1765, in Alvord and Carter, *Critical Period,* 518–19.

17. Indian Council of Feb. 24, 1765, in Alvord and Carter, *Critical Period,* 450.

18. Indian Council of Feb. 24, 1765, in Alvord and Carter, *Critical Period,* 451.

19. Journal of John Jennings, May 8, 1768, in Alvord and Carter, *Trade and Politics,* 276; "Recencement General Du Pais Des Illinois 1752," in Margaret Cross Norton, ed., *Illinois Census Returns, 1810, 1818* (Springfield: Illinois State Historical Library, 1935), xxvi–xxvii; Meurin to Briand, June 14, 1769, in Alvord and Carter, *Trade and Politics,* 550; Paul L. Stevens, "One of the Most Beautiful Regions of the World": Paul Des Ruisseaux's *Memoire* of the Wabash-Illinois Country in 1777," *Indiana Magazine of History* 83, no. 4 (1987), 378, n. 30; Gibault to Briand, Oct. 1769, in Alvord and Carter, *Trade and Politics,* 615.

20. See the account of this intrigue in Jennings' journal, May 5–10, 1768, in Alvord and Carter, *Trade and Politics*, 275–78.

21. George Pare, "The St. Joseph Mission," *Mississippi Valley Historical Review* 17, no. 1 (June 1930), 24–54. See Joseph L. Peyser's introduction to *On the Eve of the Conquest: The Chevalier de Raymond's Critique of New France in 1754* (East Lansing: Michigan State University Press, 1997), 41, n. 38; information on salt taken from Willis F. Dunbar, *Michigan: A History of the Wolverine State* (Grand Rapids: Eerdmans, 1970), 413; *Michigan Pioneer & Historical Collections* (Lansing: W. S. George and Co., 1877), 1:102; Patrick Kennedy describes these deposits in Raymond Hauser, "An Ethnohistory of the Illinois Indian Tribe, 1673–1832," (PhD diss., Northern Illinois University, 1973; Ann Arbor, Mich.: University Microfilms, 1973), 97; Nehemiah Matson, *Pioneers of Illinois, Containing a Series of Sketches That Occurred Previous to 1813* (Chicago: Knight and Leonard, 1882), 178–79.

22. *Michigan Pioneer and Historical Collections*, 1:358; Edmunds, *Potawatomis*, 97, but especially the chapter titled "Serving Two Fathers," which discusses the factions in the Potawatomi. Elders of the Potawatomi offered the same explanations for violence and intrigue as did the Illinois Indians in accounting for the 1751 conspiracy (see chapter 5). Older chiefs claimed they could not control younger, intemperate men.

23. Edmunds, *Potawatomis*, 98; Gregory Evans Dowd, "The French King Wakes Up in Detroit: 'Pontiac's War' in Rumor and History," *Ethnohistory* 37, no. 3 (summer 1990), 254–78.

24. Carter, *Great Britain and the Illinois Country*, 35; Jeanne Kay, "The Fur Trade and Native American Population Growth," *Ethnohistory* 31, no. 4 (autumn 1984), 265–87. Note especially the population growth charts on 273; the Fox show a steady resurgence following a low in numbers during the Fox Wars of the 1730s. By 1800 they may have numbered between fifteen hundred and two thousand; Helen Hornbeck Tanner, *Atlas of Great Lakes Indian History*, chap. 8, nn. 4, 42, in Charles J. Balesi, *The Time of the French in the Heart of North America, 1673–1818* (Chicago: Alliance Française Chicago, 1992), 243. John K. White believes the drop was even more significant: "By the mid 1700s a century of continual warfare had reduced the Illinois by 90%." See White's article, "Illinois," in the *Encyclopedia of North American Indians*, ed. Fred E. Howe (New York: Houghton-Mifflin, 1996); Edmunds, *Potawatomi*, 100; Joseph Jablow, *Indians of Illinois and Indiana: Illinois, Kickapoo, and Potawatomi Indians* (New York: Garland Press, 1974), 283; this phrase, "cut off," seems to have been used by Black Dog, a Peoria chief, to Commander Wilkins. The Kaskaskias also may have used it in referring to a rumor of nations coming in "150 Canoes who have long since threaten'd to Cutt off the nations of the Illinois." Both instances appear in Jablow, *Indians of Illinois and Indiana*, 269; "Report of the Various Indian Tribes Receiving Presents in the District of Ylinoa or Illinois, 1769," in Louis Houck, *The Spanish Regime in Missouri* (Chicago: Donnelly, 1909), 1:44; "Report of the Indian Tribes Who Receive Presents at St. Louis, Dated November 15, 1777" in Houck, *Spanish Regime*, 141–48.

25. James A Clifton, *The Prairie People: Continuity and Change in Potawatomi Indian Culture, 1665–1965* (Lawrence: Regents Press of Kansas, 1977), 132; Clifton, *Prairie People*, 124; Reuben Gold Thwaites, ed., *The Jesuit Relations and Allied Documents* (Cleveland: Burrows, 1900), 60:153.

26. George R. Milner, Eve Anderson, and Virginia G. Smith, "Warfare in Late Prehistoric West-Central Illinois," *American Antiquity* 56, no. 4 (Oct. 1991), 582–83; R. David Edmunds and Joseph L. Peyser, *The Fox Wars: The Mesquakie Challenge to New France* (Norman: University of Oklahoma Press, 1993), 163–64; reported by La Jonquiere to the French minister, Sept. 25, 1751, *Wisconsin Historical Collections*, 18:89.

27. Quote appears in Jablow, *Indians of Illinois and Indiana*, 274; Gregory Evans Dowd, *War under Heaven: Pontiac, the Indian-Nations, and the British Empire* (Baltimore: Johns Hopkins University Press, 2002), 249; Thomas Hutchins to George Morgan, Apr. 16, 1769, Hutchins, *Letters to George Morgan* (Thomas Hutchins Collection, Chicago Historical Society).

28. Francis Parkman, "Thus basely perished this champion of a ruined race," in *The Conspiracy of Pontiac and the Indian War after the Conquest of Canada* (Boston: Little, Brown, 1917), 2:329; Howard Peckham, in *Pontiac and the Indian Uprising* (New York: Russell and Russell, 1947), describes the Peoria as having "a reputation for ambush and assassination as a policy of foreign relations, with the bully's surprise and outraged cry when they were drubbed for their cowardly attacks." See Peckham, *Pontiac*, 310; Thomas Hutchins to George Morgan, Apr. 6, 1769, in Hutchins, *Letters to George Morgan*.

29. Gregory Evans Dowd believes that Wilkins refused the Peoria admittance to Fort Chartres. See Dowd, *War under Heaven*, 261; Wilkins's accounts in Jablow, *Indians of Illinois and Indiana*, 268; Wilkins, in Jablow, 269; Dowd, *War under Heaven*, 172; this message appears in its entirety in Jablow, *Indians of Illinois and Indiana*, 279.

30. Colton Storm, "The Notorious Colonel Wilkins," *Journal of the Illinois State Historical Society* 40 (Mar. 1947), 17; log of Colonel Wilkins, in Storm, "Notorious," 20; the original "Journal of Transactions and Presents Given to the Indians from 23rd December, 1768, to March 12, 1772," is preserved among the General Gage Papers in the William Clements Library, Ann Arbor, Mich.; Carter, *Great Britain and the Illinois Country*, 156; Captain Lord to General Gage, Apr. 9, 1773, in British Museum Additional Manuscripts 21664:148 and 21665:289 (photostats at the Illinois Historical Survey); Haldimand to Gage, Oct. 5, 1773, in British Museum Additional Manuscripts (see above); see Stanley Faye, "Illinois Indians on the Lower Mississippi, 1771–1781," *Illinois State Historical Society* 35 (1942), 56–72. The Kaskaskia sought refuge among the Quapaw and tried to establish a fur trading niche in the Spanish empire. One group of Kaskaskia even took furs all the way to the British settlements in South Carolina. See Faye, "Illinois Indians," 60.

31. Commander Macarty writing in Theodore Calvin Pease, ed., *Illinois on the Eve of the Seven Years War, 1747–1755*, Collections of the Illinois State Historical

Library 29 (Springfield: Illinois State Historical Library, 1940), 657. Jablow, *Indians of Indiana and Illinois*, 217; Pierre Deliette, "Memoir of De Gannes Concerning the Illinois Country," in *The French Foundations 1680–1693*, ed. T. C. Pease (Springfield: Illinois State Historical Library, 1934), 389; Memorial of Bienville, *Mississippi Provincial Archives*, 3:315; Commander Macarty, in Hauser, "Ethnohistory," 149.

32. Nancy M. Miller Surrey, *The Commerce of Louisiana during the French Regime: 1699–1763* (New York: Columbia University Press, 1916), 302; see Bienville's "Deliberations of the Council of War" in *Mississippi Provincial Archives*, 1:428; Carl O. Sauer, *The Geography of the Ozark Highland of Missouri* (New York: Greenwood, 1920), 49–52; Brink, McDonough, and Co., *A History of St. Clair County* (Philadelphia, 1881), 30–31; Abraham P. Nasatir, *Spanish War Vessels on the Mississippi, 1792–1796* (New Haven: Yale University Press, 1968).

33. James Taylor Carson, "Horses and the Economy and Culture of the Choctaw Indians, 1690–1840," *Ethnohistory* 41, no. 3 (summer 1995), 497; Carson, "Horses," 497–98; Willard Hughes Rollings, "Prairie Hegemony: An Ethnohistorical Study of the Osage, from Early Times to 1840" (PhD diss., Texas Tech University, 1983), 177; also Carl H. Chapman and Eleanor F. Chapman, *Indians and Archaeology of Missouri*, Missouri Handbook no. 6 (Columbia: University of Missouri Press, 1964), 107–9. Paul S. Gardener, "The Ecological Structure and Behavioral Implications of Mast Exploitation Strategies," in *People, Plants, and Landscapes: Studies in Paleoethnobotany*, ed. Kristen J. Gremillion (Tuscaloosa: University of Alabama Press, 1997), especially 165; Andrea A. Hunter and Deborah M Pearsall, "Paleoethnobotany of the Osage and Missouri Indians: Analysis of Plant Remains from Historic Village Sites," *Missouri Archaeologist* 47 (Dec. 1986), 173–196, especially 184 and 194; Carson, "Horses," 499; Glenn T. Trewartha, "A Second Epoch of Destructive Occupance in the Driftless Hill Land (1760–1783: Period of British, Spanish, and Early American Control)," *Annals of the Association of American Geographers* 30, no. 2 (June 1940), 109.

34. Robert Mazrim, ed., *"Now Quite Out of Society": Archaeology and Frontier Illinois—Essays and Excavation Reports*, Transportation Archaeological Bulletins 1 (Urbana: University of Illinois, 2002), 151; see the itemized list of fur equivalents in Matthew Clarkson's diary, Aug. 6, 1766–Aug. 16, 1767, in Alvord and Carter, *New Régime*, 361; Wilkins to Barrington, Dec. 5, 1769, in Alvord and Carter, *Trade and Politics*, 633; Wilkins to Gage, Jan. 2, 1769, in Alvord and Carter, *Trade and Politics*, 483; Gage to Hillsborough, June 16, 1768, in Alvord and Carter, *Trade and Politics*, 317.

35. Clifton, *Prairie People*, 131; Richard McCarty to Rocheblave, Feb. 6, 1777, in Edward G. Mason, ed., *Early Chicago and Illinois* (Chicago: Fergus, 1890), 384.

36. Paul Des Ruisseaux, "Memoire of the Wabash-Illinois Country in 1777," in Paul L. Stevens, "'One of the Most Beautiful Regions of the World': Paul Des Ruisseaux's *Memoire* of the Wabash-Illinois Country in 1777," *Indiana Magazine of History* 83, no. 4 (1987), 378; "Most of the young men rather chuse to hunt and trade amongst the Indians, than apply [themselves] to agriculture or become handicrafts

[men]." Captain Philip Pittman, letter in McDermott, "French Settlers," in *Old Cahokia: A Narrative and Documents Illustrating the First Century of Its History*, ed. John Francis McDermott (St. Louis: St. Louis Historical Documents Foundation, 1949), 11; McDermott, "French Settlers," 10; this Ohio River trade is mentioned as "common" in a document titled "Defense of Thomas Bentley, August 1, 1777," in Clarence W. Alvord, *Kaskaskia Records, 1778-1790*, Collections of the Illinois State Historical Library 5 (Springfield: Illinois State Historical Library, 1909), 13; Alvord, *Kaskaskia Records*, 30.

37. See the detailed account of this incident in *Kaskaskia Records*, 18-40.

38. Jack M. Sosin, *The Revolutionary Frontier, 1763-1783* (New York: Holt, 1967), 118. Sosin mentions a wealthy French merchant in Cahokia, Godfrey de Linctot, who was "invaluable in winning over the neighboring Indians"; Rocheblave to Lieut.-Gov. Hamilton, May 5, 1777, in Mason, *Early Chicago*, 391; Rocheblave to Carleton, July 4, 1778, in Mason, *Early Chicago*, 416-17.

39. Rocheblave to Lord George Germaine, Feb. 28, 1778, in Mason, *Early Chicago*, 407. Sosin describes the Illinois Country after the withdrawal of British troops as a "military vacuum." *Revolutionary Frontier*, 117.

Epilogue: Losses

1. J. L. McDonough & Co., *The Combined History of Randolph, Monroe, and Perry Counties, Illinois* (Philadelphia: J. L. McDonough & Co., 1883), 89; stands of mature pecan were identified on early American surveys and maps. These nut trees flourished on top of the river bluffs above Prairie du Rocher. Brink, McDonough, and Co., *A History of St. Clair County* (Philadelphia, 1881), 42; *History of St. Clair County*, 30-31; J. L. McDonough and Co., *Combined History*, 67 and 64; Harmar to Knox, Nov. 24, 1787, in Gayle Thornbrough, *Outpost on the Wabash, 1787-1791* (Indianapolis: Indiana Historical Society, 1957), 50.

2. Glenn J. Speed, *Ghost Towns of Southern Illinois* (Royalton, Ill.: Glenn J. Speed, 1977), 172; Carl J. Ekberg, *Colonial Ste. Genevieve: An Adventure on the Mississippi Frontier* (Gerald, Mo.: Patrice Press, 1985), 286; *Native Tree Guide* (Shaw Arboretum of the Missouri Botanical Garden, 1987), 5; Margaret Kimball Brown and Lawrie Cena Dean, *The Village of Chartres in Colonial Illinois, 1720-1765* (New Orleans: Polyanthos, 1977), Record K-330 (H496), 785; Brown and Dean, *Village of Chartres*, Record K-338 (H504), 800; Jay D. Edwards, "The Origins of the Louisiana Creole Cottage," in *French and Germans in the Mississippi Valley: Landscape and Cultural Traditions*, ed. Michael Roark (Cape Girardeau, Mo.: Center for Regional History and Cultural Heritage, 1988), 28.

3. Gordon G. Whitney, *From Coastal Wilderness to Fruited Plain: A History of Environmental Change in Temperate North America from 1500 to the Present* (Cambridge: Cambridge University Press, 1994), 146; Mary Antoine de Julio, "Prairie du Chien and the Rediscovery of Its French Log Houses," in *French and Germans in the Mississippi Valley: Landscape and Cultural Traditions*, ed. Michael Roark (Cape Girardeau, Mo.: Center for Regional History and Cultural Heritage, 1988), 101.

Descriptions of the earliest American cabins on the upland, however, mention the use of basswood bark (linden tree) as indoor insulation. See Brink, *History of St. Clair County*, 56–57; William I. Woods, "Population nucleation, intensive agriculture, and environmental degradation: The Cahokia example," *Agriculture and Human Values* 21 (2004), 155. For deforestation of the Mississippi Valley, see F. Terry Norris, "Where Did the Villages Go? Steamboats, Deforestation, and Archaeological Loss in the Mississippi Valley," in *Common Fields: An Environmental History of St. Louis*, ed. Andrew Hurley (St. Louis: Missouri Historical Society Press, 1997).

4. Carl O. Sauer, *The Geography of the Ozark Highland of Missouri* (New York: Greenwood Press, 1920), 58–59; See "White-Tailed Deer: Seasonal Use of Forage Classes" in *Studies of the Cross Timbers Region of Oklahoma and Texas*, The Samuel Roberts Noble Foundation, 1997–2009, http://www.noble.org/Ag/wildlife/DeerFoods/habitatReq4.html; John C. Nelson, Anjela Redmond, and Richard E. Sparks, "Impacts of Settlement on Floodplain Vegetation at the Confluence of the Illinois and Mississippi Rivers," *Transactions of the Illinois State Academy of Science* 87, nos. 3 and 4 (1994); William Ashby and George T. Weaver, "Forest Regeneration on Two Fields in Southwestern Illinois," *American Midland Naturalist* 84, no. 1 (July 1970), 90–104; Walter Schroeder, "The Environmental Setting of the St. Louis Region," in Hurley, *Common Fields*.

5. Joseph Jablow, *Indians of Illinois and Indiana: Illinois, Kickapoo, and Potawatomi Indians* (New York: Garland, 1974), 273; commercial log entries in Jablow, *Indians of Illinois and Indiana*, 264; Jablow, 267; Report by Colonel Wilkins, Dec. 1769, in Jablow, 267; Charles E. Hanson Jr., "The Southern Trade: A Slightly Different Story," *Museum of the Fur Trade Quarterly* 22, no. 1 (1986), 3. For a good general overview of the southern deerskin trade, see Daniel H. Usner Jr., "The Deerskin Trade in French Louisiana," *Proceedings of the Meeting of the French Colonial Historical Society* 10 (1984), 75–93. See also James Axtell's discussion of the deerskin trade as "big business" in "Making Do: Trade in the Eighteenth-Century Southeast," in *Natives and Newcomers: The Cultural Origins of North America* (New York: Oxford University Press, 2001). Axtell also provides good figures to document acceleration in the deerskin trade among the Creeks—80,000 skins in 1720 but 140,000 skins by 1760. This southeastern market exerted a strong centripetal force on the outlier hunting of deer in Missouri. Axtell, "The First Consumer Revolution: The Seventeenth Century," in *Natives and Newcomers*, 107; Hanson, "Southern Trade," 2–3; Croghan to Johnson, Sept. 10, 1766, in Clarence W. Alvord and Clarence Carter, *The New Régime, 1765–1767*, Collections of the Illinois State Historical Library 11 (Springfield: Illinois State Historical Library, 1916), 374.

6. Joseph N. Nicollet, "Sketch of the Early History of St. Louis," in John Francis McDermott, ed., *The Early Histories of St. Louis* (St. Louis: St. Louis Historical Documents Foundation, 1952), 146; Louis Houck, *The Spanish Regime in Missouri* (Chicago: Donnelly, 1909), 1:37; "Petition of the Merchants," in Houck, *Spanish Regime*, 38.

7. John Francis Bannon, *The Spanish Borderlands Frontier, 1513–1821* (Albuquerque: University of New Mexico Press, 1963), 194. Bannon has used the term
"Quasi-Borderland" to describe the Spanish province of "Luisiana"; A. P. Nasatir,
"The Anglo-Spanish Frontier in the Illinois Country during the American Revolution, 1779–1783," *Journal of the Illinois State Historical Society* 21, no. 3 (Oct. 1928),
292; Nicollet, "Sketch of the Early History of St. Louis," 136; Brink, *History of St.
Clair County*, 59.

8. *Conge* is defined in the *Mississippi Provincial Archives* as "a technical term
referring to permits to trade directly with the Indians for fur, which were granted
by the governor of Canada." See *Mississippi Provincial Archives* (Baton Rouge: Louisiana State University Press, 1927), 4:248; this data selected from a table in Norman
W. Caldwell, *The French in the Mississippi Valley, 1740–1750* (Urbana: University
of Illinois Press, 1941; PhD diss. in the Newberry Library, Chicago). See table on
p. 60; Glenn T. Trewartha, "A Second Epoch of Destructive Occupance in the
Driftless Hill Land (1760–1832: Period of British, Spanish, and Early American
Control)," *Annals of the Association of American Geographers* 30, no. 2 (June 1940),
109; for the best study of the illegal fur trade in Canada and New York, see Jean
Lunn, "The Illegal Fur Trade out of New France, 1713–1760," *Canadian Historical Association Annual Report* (1939), 61–76. Lunn states that "in the early years
of the period, . . . some estimates placed the annual export at roughly a half or
two-thirds of the total quantity of beaver produced in Canada each year," (65).
Her interesting conclusion, unexplored in subsequent scholarship, is that the illegal fur trade between Montreal and Albany dictated the course of empire. "Had
the trade with Montreal been cut off, Albany must have tried much earlier and
much more vigorously than it did to establish direct relations with the Indians
in the west." See Lunn, "Illegal Fur Trade," 76; See Caldwell, *French*, 60–61, 74.

9. See for instance, General Gage's discussion of the ideas put forth by Captain
Harry Gordon "to erect Posts on the Rivers Ohio and Illinois near their Junction
with the Mississippi, in order to prevent all Furrs and Skins from coming into the
River from the Eastern Branches," in Gage to Shelburne, Feb. 22, 1767, in Newton
D. Mereness, ed., *Travels in the American Colonies* (New York: Macmillan, 1916;
repr., New York: Antiquarian, 1961), 459; Clarence W. Alvord, *The Mississippi Val-
ley in British Politics: A Study of the Trade, Land Speculation, and Experiments in
Imperialism Culminating in the American Revolution* (Cleveland: Arthur H. Clark
Co., 1917), 1:296; see detailed analysis of French-Indian trade relations in Theresa
J. Piazza, "The Kaskaskia Manuscripts: French Traders in the Missouri Valley
before Lewis and Clark," *Missouri Archaeologist* 53 (Dec. 1992), 1–42. Animosity
persisted into the French settlement phase as well (and under the Spanish regime).
Kathleen Brotherton, "Osage Occasionally Killed Early French Settlers," *River
Hills Traveler* (January-February 2004).

10. William Faux, in John White, ed., *Early Accounts of the Ecology of the Big
Rivers Area*, Big Rivers Area Assessment 5 (Springfield: Illinois Department of
Natural Resources, 2000), 53; J. L. McDonough and Co., *The Combined History*

of Randolph, Monroe, and Perry Counties, Illinois (Philadelphia, 1883), 64; "Proclamation of John Todd, June 14, 1779," in McDonough, *History of Randolph, Perry, and Monroe Counties*, 93; Brink, *History of St. Clair County*, 32; John W. Allen, *It Happened in Southern Illinois* (Carbondale: Southern Illinois University, 1968), 348–49; Brink, *History of St. Clair County*, 56–59.

11. L. David Mech, *The Wolf: The Ecology and Behavior of an Endangered Species* (Minneapolis: University of Minnesota Press, 1981); K. Kunkel and D. H. Pletscher, "Species-Specific Population Dynamics of Cervids in a Multipredator System," *Journal of Wildlife Management* 63, no. 4 (1999), 1082–93; E. Post et al., "Ecosystem Consequences of Wolf Behavioral Response to Climate," *Nature* 401, no. 6756 (1999), 905–7; Gibault to Briand, Feb. 15, 1769, in Clarence W. Alvord and Clarence Carter, eds., *Trade and Politics, 1767–1769* Collections of the Illinois State Historical Library 16 (Springfield: Illinois State Historical Library, 1921), 504; Robert E. Warren and Michael J. O'Brien, "A Model of Frontier Settlement," in *Grassland, Forest, and Historical Settlement: An Analysis of Dynamics in Northeast Missouri*, ed. Michael J. O'Brien (Lincoln: University of Nebraska Press, 1984), 48.

12. Barry Holstun Lopez, *Of Wolves and Men* (New York: Scribner, 1978), 54; Lopez, *Of Wolves*, 65; Alan Burdick, "The Truth about Invasive Species," *Discover* 26, no. 5 (May 2005), 39.

13. *Randolph County, Illinois, Commissioners' Court Records, 1802–1807* (published by Wanda Warkins Allers and Eileen Lynch Gochanour, April 1996), 57–59. Lopez, *Of Wolves*, 194; Lopez, *Of Wolves*, 13; for wolf diet and habits, see J. Knox Jones Jr. et al., *A Field Guide to Mammals of the Plains States* (Lincoln: University of Nebraska Press, 1985), 258; one of the rare references to "packs of elk skins" occurs in a letter from Thomas Hutchins at Fort Chartres to George Morgan in July 1770. In the Thomas Hutchins Collection, Chicago Historical Society; Gershom Flagg in John White, *Early Accounts*, 78; *The Field Notes of Captain William Clark, 1803–1805*, in White, *Early Accounts*, 51; Hugh Heward, "Journal of a Voyage Made by Hugh Heward to the Illinois Country" (1790; unpublished manuscript in Hugh Heward Collection, Chicago Historical Society), 26.

14. Lopez, *Of Wolves*, 104; Dillingham, "The Oklahoma Kickapoo," in John Mack Faragher, *Sugar Creek: Life on the Illinois Prairie* (New Haven: Yale University Press, 1986), 21; Faragher, *Sugar Creek*, 23; see this description by Deliette and accompanying notes in John White, *Early Accounts of the Fox River Area*, Fox River Area Assessment 5 (Springfield: Illinois Department of Natural Resources, 2000), 32–33.

15. See Jeanne Kay's discussion of the adaptations of Wisconsin Indians to changes in the fur trade, "Wisconsin Indian Hunting Patterns," *Annals of the Association of American Geographers* 69, no. 3 (Sept. 1979), 402–18. Kay finds that "Indian use of wildlife reflected the price of pelts, species' fertility, and the varying distribution of wildlife habitats"; Brink, *History of St. Clair County*, 45; letters of Charles Gratiot, in John Francis McDermott, ed., *Old Cahokia: A Narrative and Documents Illustrating the First Century of Its History* (St. Louis: St. Louis Historical Documents Foundation, 1949), 193.

16. George Castles, George Castles Collection, Oversize Collections, Chicago Historical Society. Deed of Sale for George Castles' 1/22 of a vast tract of land in the Illinois Country to Thomas Johnson of Annapolis, Md., May 31, 1774; U.S. GLO Survey notes, 1804–10, in Winstanley Briggs, "Le Pays des Illinois," *William and Mary Quarterly*, 3rd ser., 47, no. 1 (Jan. 1990), 38; "Extract from the Assessment of 1808," in McDonough, *Combined History of Randolph, Monroe, and Perry Counties*, 98; Heward, "Journal of a Voyage," 22; "Plan du Fort de Chartres," in Lewis C. Beck, *A Gazetteer of the States of Illinois and Missouri* (1823; New York: Arno Press, 1975).

17. Wilshire Butterfield, "Chicago," *Magazine of Western History* 3, no. 5 (Mar. 1886), 456.

Bibliography

Primary Sources

Allyn, H., and J. A. Meltzer. *Henry Allyn, Autobiography.* Portland, Oregon: Jean Allyn Meltzer, 1974.

Alvord, Clarence W., ed. *Cahokia Records, 1778–1790.* Collections of the Illinois State Historical Library 2 (Virginia Series 1). Springfield: Illinois State Historical Library, 1907.

———. *The Illinois-Wabash Land Company Manuscript.* Chicago: Cyrus H. McCormick, 1915.

———. *Kaskaskia Records, 1778–1790.* Collections of the Illinois State Historical Library 5. Springfield: Illinois State Historical Library, 1909.

Alvord, Clarence W., and Clarence Carter, eds. *The Critical Period, 1763–1765.* Collections of the Illinois State Historical Library 10. Springfield: Illinois State Historical Library, 1915.

———. *The New Régime, 1765–1767.* Collections of the Illinois State Historical Library 11. Springfield: Illinois State Historical Library, 1916.

———. *Trade and Politics, 1767–1769.* Collections of the Illinois State Historical Library 16. Springfield: Illinois State Historical Library, 1921.

American State Papers: Public Lands. Documents, Legislative and Executive, of the Congress of the United States from the Second Session of the Eleventh to the Third Session of the Thirteenth Congress. Washington, D.C.: Walter Lowrie and Walter S. Franklin, 1832–61.

Bossu, Jean-Bernard. *Jean-Bernard Bossu's Travels in the Interior of North America, 1751–1762,* edited and translated by Seymour Feiler. Norman: University of Oklahoma Press, 1962.

Brown, Margaret Kimball, and Lawrie Cena Dean. *The Village of Chartres in Colonial Illinois, 1720–1765.* New Orleans: Polyanthos, 1977.

Carroon, Robert G., ed. *Broadswords and Bayonets: The Journals of the Expedition under the Command of Captain Thomas Stirling of the 42nd Regiment of Foot, Royal Highland Regiment (the Black Watch) to Occupy Fort Chartres in the Illinois Country, August 1765 to January 1766.* Society of Colonial Wars in the State of Illinois, 1984.

Castles, George. George Castles Collections, Chicago Historical Society.

Charlevoix, François-Xavier. *Journal d'un voyage fait par ordre du roi dans L'Amérique septentriole.* 6 vols. Paris, 1744.

Collections of the State Historical Society of Wisconsin. 20 vols. Madison: The Society, 1888–1931.

Collot, Victor. *A Journey in North America, Containing a Survey of the Countries Watered by the Mississippi, Ohio, Missouri, and Other Affluving Rivers; with Exact Observations on the Course, and Soundings of These Rivers; and on the Towns, Villages, Hamlets, and Farms of That Part of the New World; Followed by Philosophical, Political, Military, and Commercial Remarks and by a Protected Line of Frontiers and General Limits.* Vol. 1. Paris: Arthus Bertrand, 1826. Reprint, Florence, Italy: O. Lange, 1924.

Crowder, Lola Frazier. *Early Kaskaskia, Illinois, Newspaper Abstracts, 1814–1852.* 1992. Copy at Morris-Talbott Library, Waterloo, Illinois.

D'Artaguiette, Diron. "Journal of Diron D'Artaguiette." In Mereness, *Travels in the American Colonies.*

Deliette, Pierre. "Memoir of De Gannes concerning the Illinois Country." In *The French Foundations, 1680–1693,* edited by T. C. Pease. Springfield: Illinois State Historical Library, 1934.

Dictionary of Canadian Biography. Toronto: University of Toronto Press, 1969.

Documents Relative to the Colonial History of the State of New York, edited by E. B. O'Callaghan and Berthold Fernow. 15 vols. Albany, 1856–87.

Eddington, Lt. "The Official Journal Kept by Lt. Eddington or the Surgeon." In Carroon, *Broadswords and Bayonets.*

Finiels, Nicolas de. *An Account of Upper Louisiana,* edited by Carl J. Ekberg and William E. Foley, translated by Carl J. Ekberg. Columbia: University of Missouri Press, 1989.

Flint, Timothy. *A Condensed Geography and History of the Western States, or the Mississippi Valley.* Cincinnati: E. H. Flint, 1828.

Gage, Thomas. Thomas Gage Papers, British Museum Additional Manuscripts. Photostats in the Illinois Historical Survey, Urbana-Champaign.

Hall, James. *Notes on the Western States, Containing Descriptive Sketches of Their Soil, Climate, Resources, and Scenery.* Philadelphia: Harrison Hall, 1838.

Hennepin, Louis. *A New Discovery of a Vast Country in America.* Vol. 1, edited by Reuben Gold Thwaites. Chicago: A. C. McClurg and Company, 1903.

Heward, Hugh. "Journal of a Voyage Made by Hugh Heward to the Illinois Country" (1790). Hugh Heward Collection, Chicago Historical Society.

Hill, H. M. "Horse Prairie." In unpublished memoir, "Sketches," likely written in the 1920s. Copy available at Morrison-Talbott Library, Waterloo, Illinois.

———. "What and Where Is Round Prairie?" In unpublished memoir, "Sketches," likely written in the 1920s. Copy available at Morrison-Talbott Library, Waterloo, Illinois.

Houck, Louis. *The Spanish Regime in Missouri.* Vol. 1. Chicago: R. R. Donnelly and Sons, 1909.

Hutchins, Thomas. "Letters to George Morgan." Thomas Hutchins Collection, Chicago Historical Society.

Hutchins, Thomas, and F. C. Hicks, eds. *A Topographical Description of Virginia, Pennsylvania, Maryland, and North Carolina.* Cleveland: Burrows Brothers Company, 1904.

Imlay, Gilbert. *A Topographical Description of the Western Territory of North America.* 3rd ed. London: J. Debrett, 1797.

Jennings, John. "Journey from Fort Pitt to Fort Chartres in the Illinois Country, March–April, 1766." *Pennsylvania Magazine of History and Biography* 31, no. 122 (April 1907).

Kaskaskia Manuscripts. Randolph County Courthouse, Chester, Illinois.

Kirk, Robert. *Through So Many Dangers: The Memoirs and Adventures of Robert Kirk, Late of the Royal Highland Regiment.* Edited by Ian McCulloch and Timothy Todish. New York: Purple Mountain Press, 2004.

Koepfli, Solomon. *The Story of the Settling of Highland,* translated by Jennie Latzer Kaeser. Highland Bote, 1859. Reprint, 1970. Copy available at Madison County Historical Museum and Archives, Edwardsville, Illinois.

Lewis, Meriwether, and William Clark. *The Journals of the Lewis and Clark Expedition, August 30, 1803–August 24, 1804.* Lincoln: University of Nebraska Press, 1986.

Loos, Ronald W. *A Walk through Marine, from the Past to the Present: A History of Marine and Marine Township, Madison County, State of Illinois, 1813–1988.* Copy available at Madison County Historical Society, Edwardsville, Illinois.

Margry, Pierre. *Mémoires et Documents, Découvertes et Establishments des Français dans L'Ouest et dans la Sud de L'Amérique Septentrionale (1661–1754).* English translation, vols. 5, 6. Paris: 1879–1888.

Mason, Edward G., ed. *Early Chicago and Illinois.* Chicago: Fergus Printing Company, 1890.

McDermott, John Francis, ed. *The Early Histories of St. Louis.* St. Louis: St. Louis Historical Documents Foundation, 1952.

———, ed. *Old Cahokia: A Narrative and Documents Illustrating the First Century of Its History.* St. Louis: St. Louis Historical Documents Foundation, 1949.

———, ed. *The Western Journals of Dr. George Hunter, 1796–1805.* Transactions of the American Philosophical Society, n.s., 53, pt. 4. Philadelphia, 1963.

Mereness, Newton D., ed. *Travels in the American Colonies.* New York: Macmillan, 1916. Reprint, New York: Antiquarian, 1961.

Michigan Pioneer and Historical Collections. Lansing: Robert Smith, 1904.

Minutes of the Provincial Council of Pennsylvania. Vol. 5. Harrisburg: Theo Penn and Company, 1855.

Mississippi Provincial Archives. Vols. 1–5, French Documents. Baton Rouge: Louisiana State University Press, 1927.

Nasatir, Abraham P., ed. *Before Lewis and Clark: Documents Illustrating the History of the Missouri, 1785–1804.* Lincoln: University of Nebraska Press, 1990.

Norton, Margaret Cross, ed. *Illinois Census Returns, 1810, 1818.* Springfield: Illinois State Historical Library, 1935.

Oliver, William. *Eight Months in Illinois; with Information to Emigrants*. Newcastle upon Tyne, Eng.: William Andrew Mitchell, 1843. Copy available at Edwardsville, Illinois, Historical Society and Archives.

Pease, Theodore Calvin, ed. *Illinois on the Eve of the Seven Years War, 1747–1755*. Collections of the Illinois State Historical Library 29. Springfield: Illinois State Historical Library, 1940.

Pease, Theodore C., and Raymond Werner. *The French Foundations: 1680–1693*. Collections of the Illinois Historical Library 23 (French series 1). Springfield: Illinois State Historical Library, 1934.

Peyser, Joseph L., ed. *On the Eve of the Conquest: The Chevalier de Raymond's Critique of New France in 1754*. East Lansing: Michigan State University Press, 1997.

Pittman, Philip. *The Present State of European Settlements on the Mississippi*. Cleveland: Arthur H. Clark Co., 1906.

Pratz, Le Page du. *The History of Louisiana, or of the Western Parts of Virginia and Carolina: Containing a Description of the Countries That Lye on Both Sides of the River Mississippi; with an Account of the Settlements, Inhabitants, Soil, Climate, and Products*. Vol. 2. London: T. Becket and P. A. De Hondt, 1763.

Randolph County, Illinois, Commissioners' Court Records, 1802–1807. Published by Wanda Warkins Allers and Eileen Lynch Gochanour, April, 1996. Copy at the Illinois Historical Survey, Urbana-Champaign.

Smith, William Henry, ed. *The St. Clair Papers: The Life and Public Services of Arthur St. Clair, Soldier of the Revolutionary War, President of the Continental Congress, and Governor of the North-Western Territory, with His Correspondence and Other Papers*. 1881. Reprint, New York: De Lupo Press, 1971.

Stirling, Thomas. "Stirling's Personal Journal of the Expedition: General Accounts of British Attempts to Occupy the Illinois Country." In Carroon, *Broadswords and Bayonets*.

Thwaites, Reuben Gold, ed. *Atlas Accompanying the Original Journals of the Lewis and Clark Expedition, 1804–1806*. Vol. 8. New York: Arno Press, 1969.

———, ed. *The Jesuit Relations and Allied Documents. 1610–1791*. 71 vols. Cleveland: Burrows Brothers Company, 1900.

White, John, ed. *Early Accounts of the Ecology of the Big Rivers Area*. Big Rivers Area Assessment 5. Springfield: Illinois Department of Natural Resources, 2000.

———. *Early Accounts of the Ecology of the Fox River Area*. Fox River Area Assessment 5. Springfield: Illinois Department of Natural Resources, 2000.

Wilkins, John. "Journal of Transactions and Presents Given to the Indians from 23rd December, 1768, to March 12, 1772." General Gage Papers, William Clements Library, Ann Arbor, Michigan.

Secondary Sources (Books and Monographs)

Allen, John W. *It Happened in Southern Illinois*. Carbondale: Southern Illinois University, 1968.

Alvord, Clarence W. *The Centennial History of Illinois*. Vols. 1 and 2. Springfield: Illinois Centennial Commission, 1920.

———. *The Mississippi Valley in British Politics: A Study of the Trade, Land Speculation, and Experiments in Imperialism Culminating in the American Revolution*. 2 vols. Cleveland: Arthur H. Clark Company, 1917.

Alvord, Clarence W., and Lee Bidgood. *The First Explorations of the Trans-Allegheny Region by the Virginians, 1650–1674*. Cleveland: Arthur H. Clark Company, 1912.

Anderson, Fred. *Crucible of War: The Seven Years' War and the Fate of Empire in British North America, 1754–1766*. New York: Knopf, 2000.

Anderson, Gary Clayton. *Kinsmen of Another Kind: Dakota-White Relations in the Upper Missouri Valley, 1650–1862*. Lincoln: University of Nebraska Press, 1984.

Anderson, Virginia DeJohn. *Creatures of Empire: How Domestic Animals Transformed Early America*. New York: Oxford University Press, 2004.

Angier, Bradford. *Free for the Eating*. Harrisburg, Pennsylvania: Stackpole Books, 1966.

Arnold, Morris S. *Colonial Arkansas, 1686–1804: A Social and Cultural History*. Fayetteville: University of Arkansas Press, 1991.

———. *The Rumble of a Distant Drum: The Quapaws and Old World Newcomers, 1673–1804*. Fayetteville: University of Arkansas Press, 2000.

———. *Unequal Laws unto a Savage Race: European Legal Traditions in Arkansas, 1686–1836*. Fayetteville: University of Arkansas Press, 1985.

Axtell, James. *Natives and Newcomers: The Cultural Origins of North America*. New York: Oxford University Press, 2001.

Baird, W. David. *The Quapaw Indians: A History of the Downstream People*. Norman: University of Oklahoma Press, 1980.

———. *The Quapaws*. New York: Chelsea House Publishers, 1989.

Balesi, Charles J. *The Time of the French in the Heart of North America, 1673–1818*. Chicago: Alliance Française Chicago, 1992.

Bannon, John Francis. *The Spanish Borderlands Frontier, 1513–1821*. Albuquerque: University of New Mexico Press, 1963.

Bareis, Charles J., and James W. Porter. *American Bottom Archaeology: A Summary of the FAI-270 Project Contribution to the Culture History of the Mississippi River Valley*. Urbana: University of Illinois Press, 1984.

Beck, Lewis C. *A Gazetteer of the States of Illinois and Missouri, 1823*. New York: Arno Press, 1975.

Belting, Natalia Maree. *Kaskaskia under the French Regime*. New Orleans: Polyanthos, 1975.

Blume, Helmut. *The German Coast during the Colonial Era, 1722–1803*. Geographisches Institut der Universitat Kiel, Germany, 1956. Translated and edited by Ellen C. Merrill. Destrehan, Louisiana: German-Acadian Coast Historical and Genealogical Society, 1990.

Boggess, Arthur Clinton. *The Settlement of Illinois, 1778–1830*. Collection no. 5. Chicago: Chicago Historical Society, 1908.

Bolen, H. David. *The Birds of Illinois*. Bloomington: Indiana University Press, 1989.

Brink, McDonough, and Co. *A History of Madison County, Illinois*. Edwardsville, Illinois, 1882.

——. *A History of St. Clair County*. Philadelphia, 1881.

——. *An Illustrated Historical Atlas Map of Monroe County*. Philadelphia, 1875.

Brooks, James F. *Captives and Cousins: Slavery, Kinship, and Community in the Southwest Borderlands*. Chapel Hill: University of North Carolina, 2002.

Brown, Henry. *The History of Illinois from Its First Discovery and Settlement to the Present Time*. New York: J. Winchester, New World Press, 1844.

Brown, Lauren. *Grasses: An Identification Guide*. New York: Houghton-Mifflin, 1979.

Brown, Margaret Kimball. *Cultural Transformations among the Illinois: An Application of a Systems Model*. East Lansing: Museum, Michigan State University, 1979.

——. *History as They Lived It: A Social History of Prairie du Rocher, Illinois*. New Orleans: Patrice Press, 2005.

——. *The Voyageur in the Illinois Country: The Fur Trade's Professional Boatman in Mid America*. Extended Publication Series (Center for French Colonial Studies), no. 3. Naperville, Illinois: Center for French Colonial Studies, 2002.

Brown, Margaret Kimball, and Lawrie Cena Dean. *The French Colony in the Mid-Mississippi Valley*. Carbondale, Illinois: American Kestrel Books, 1995.

Carter, Clarence. *Great Britain and the Illinois Country, 1763–1774*. Washington, D.C.: American Historical Association, 1910. Reprint, Freeport, New York: Books for Libraries Press, 1971.

Chapman, Basil Berlin. *Oto and Missouri Indians*. New York: Garland Publishing Company, 1974.

Chapman, Carl H., and Eleanor F. Chapman. *Indians and Archaeology of Missouri*. Missouri Handbook no. 6. Columbia: University of Missouri Press, 1964.

Clifton, James A. *The Prairie People: Continuity and Change in Potawatomi Indian Culture, 1665–1965*. Lawrence: Regents Press of Kansas, 1977.

Cronon, William. *Changes in the Land: Indians, Colonists, and the Ecology of New England*. New York: Hill and Wang, 1983.

Crosby, Alfred W. *Ecological Imperialism: The Biological Expansion of Europe, 900–1900*. Cambridge: Cambridge University Press, 1986.

——. *Germs, Seeds, & Animals: Studies in Ecological History*. New York: M. E. Sharpe, 1994.

Dalan, Rinita A., et al. *Envisioning Cahokia: A Landscape Perspective*. DeKalb: Northern Illinois University Press, 2003.

Davidson, Donald. *The Tennessee: The Old River—Frontier to Secession, a Facsimile Edition of Vol. I*. Knoxville: University of Tennessee Press, 1946.

Deuel, Thorne. *American Indian Ways of Life: An Interpretation of the Archaeology of Illinois and Adjoining Areas*. Springfield: Illinois State Museum, 1958.

Din, Gilbert C., and Abraham Nasatir. *The Imperial Osages: Spanish-Indian Diplomacy in the Mississippi Valley*. Norman: University of Oklahoma Press, 1983.

Dineen, Michael P., et al., eds. *Rivers of North America*. Waukesha, Wisconsin: Outdoor World, 1973.

Donnelly, Joseph P. *Pierre Gibault, Missionary, 1737–1802*. Chicago: Loyola University Press, 1971.

Douville, Raymond, and Jacques Casanova. *Daily Life in Early Canada*, translated by Carola Congreve. New York: Macmillan, 1968.

Dowd, Gregory Evans. *War under Heaven: Pontiac, the Indian Nations, & the British Empire*. Baltimore: Johns Hopkins University Press, 2002.

Dunbar, Willis F. *Michigan: A History of the Wolverine State*. Grand Rapids, Michigan: Eerdmans, 1970.

Eccles, W. J. *The Canadian Frontier, 1524–1760*. New York: Holt, 1969.

———. *France in America*. New York: Harper, 1972.

Edmunds, R. David. *The Potawatomis: Keepers of the Fire*. Norman: University of Oklahoma Press, 1978.

Edmunds, R. David, and Joseph L. Peyser. *The Fox Wars: The Mesquakie Challenge to New France*. Norman: University of Oklahoma Press, 1993.

Ekberg, Carl J. *Colonial Ste. Genevieve: An Adventure on the Mississippi Frontier*. Gerald, Missouri: Patrice Press, 1985.

———. *François Valle and His World: Upper Louisiana before Louis and Clark*. Columbia: University of Missouri Press, 2002.

———. *French Roots in the Illinois Country: The Mississippi Frontier in Colonial Times*. Urbana: University of Illinois Press, 2000.

Emerson, Thomas E. *Cahokia and the Archaeology of Power*. Tuscaloosa: University of Alabama Press, 1997.

Emerson, Thomas E., and R. Barry Lewis, eds. *Cahokia and the Hinterlands: Middle Mississippian Cultures of the Midwest*. Urbana: University of Illinois Press, 1991.

English, William Hayden. *Conquest of the Country Northwest of the River Ohio, 1778–1783; and Life of General George Rogers Clark*. Indianapolis: Bowen-Merrill, 1896.

Faragher, John Mack. *Sugar Creek: Life on the Illinois Prairie*. New Haven: Yale University Press, 1986.

Foster, J. W. *The Mississippi Valley: Its Physical Geography*. Chicago: S. C. Griggs and Company, 1869.

Fowells, H. A. *Silvics of Forest Trees of the United States*. Agriculture Handbook no. 271. Washington, D.C.: U.S. Department of Agriculture, 1965.

Franke, Judith A. *French Peoria and the Illinois Country, 1673–1846*. Springfield: Illinois State Museum Society, 1995.

Fuller, George D., ed. *Forest Trees of Illinois and How to Know Them*. Springfield, Illinois: Department of Conservation, Division of Forestry, 1955.

Gammon, James R. *The Wabash River Ecosystem*. Bloomington: Indiana University Press, 1998.

Gibbons, Euell. *Stalking the Healthful Herbs*. New York: McKay, 1966.

Gibson, A. M. *The Kickapoos: Lords of the Middle Border*. Norman: University of Oklahoma Press, 1963.

Giraud, Marcel. *A History of French Louisiana*. Vol. 2, *Years of Transition, 1715–1717*, translated by Brian Pearce. 1958. Reprint, Baton Rouge: Louisiana State University Press, 1993.

———. *A History of French Louisiana*. Vol. 5, *The Company of the Indes*, translated by Brian Pearce. Baton Rouge: Louisiana State University Press, 1987.

Gould, E. W. *Fifty Years on the Mississippi, or Gould's History of River Navigation*. St. Louis: Nixon-Jones, 1889.

Gums, Bonnie L., ed. *Archaeology at French Colonial Cahokia*. Springfield: Illinois Historic Preservation Agency, 1988.

Hall, Robert L. *Archaeology of the Soul: North American Indian Belief and Ritual*. Urbana: University of Illinois Press, 1997.

Hilgard, E. W. "Botanical Features of the Prairies of Illinois in Ante-Railroad Days." Manuscript on file at the Illinois Historical Survey, Urbana-Champaign. N.p., n.d.

Hinderaker, Eric. *Elusive Empires: Constructing Colonialism in the Ohio Valley, 1673–1800*. Cambridge: Cambridge University Press, 1999.

Hodge, Frederick Webb. *Handbook of American Indians North of Mexico, Parts I and II*. Washington, D.C.: Government Printing Office, 1907.

Hurley, Andrew, ed. *Common Fields: An Environmental History of St. Louis*. St. Louis: Missouri Historical Society Press, 1997.

Isenberg, Andrew C. *The Destruction of the Bison: An Environmental History, 1750–1920*. New York: Cambridge University Press, 2000.

Jablow, Joseph. *Indians of Illinois and Indiana: Illinois, Kickapoo, and Potawatomi Indians*. New York: Garland Press, 1974.

Jacobs, Wilbur R. *Diplomacy and Indian Gifts: Anglo-French Rivalry along the Ohio and Northwest Frontiers, 1748–1763*. Stanford: Stanford University Press, 1950.

Jakle, John A. *Images of the Ohio Valley: A Historical Geography of Travel, 1740–1860*. New York: Oxford University Press, 1977.

Jelks, Edward B., Carl J. Ekberg, and Terrance C. Martin. *Excavations at the Laurens Site: Probable Location of Fort de Chartres I*. Studies in Illinois Archaeology 5. Springfield: Illinois Historic Preservation Agency, 1989.

Jennings, Francis. *Empire of Fortune: Crowns, Colonies, and Tribes in the Seven Years War in America*. New York: Norton, 1988.

Jensen, Richard. *Illinois: A History*. Urbana-Champaign: University of Illinois Press, 2001.

Johnsgard, Paul A. *Waterfowl of North America*. Bloomington: Indiana University Press, 1975.

Jones, J. Knox, Jr., David M. Armstrong, and Jerry R. Choate. *Guide to Mammals of the Plains States*. Lincoln: University of Nebraska Press, 1985.

Kaskaskia River Area Assessment. Living Resources 3. Illinois Department of Natural Resources, 2000.

Kellogg, Louise Phelps. *French Regime in Wisconsin and the Northwest*. Madison: State Historical Society of Wisconsin, 1925.

Kenton, Edna, ed. *The Indians of North America*. New York: Harcourt, 1927.

———. *The Jesuit Relations*. New York: Vantage Press, 1954.

King, Francis B. *Plants, People, and Paleoecology: Biotic Communities and Aboriginal Plant Usage in Illinois*. Scientific Papers 20. Springfield: Illinois State Museum, 1984.

Lopez, Barry Holstun. *Of Wolves and Men*. New York: Charles Scribner's Sons, 1978.

Lugn, Alvin G. *Sedimentation in the Mississippi River between Davenport, Iowa, and Cairo, Illinois*. Rock Island, Illinois: Augustana Library Publications, 1927.

Madden, Betty I. *Art, Crafts, and Architecture in Early Illinois*. Urbana: University of Illinois Press, 1974.

Mancall, Peter C., ed. *Land of Rivers: America in Word and Image*. Ithaca, New York: Cornell University Press, 1996.

Mancall, Peter C., and James H. Merrell, eds. *American Encounters: Natives and Newcomers from European Contact to Indian Removal, 1500–1850*. New York: Routledge, 2000.

Martin, Calvin. *Keepers of the Game: Indian-Animal Relations and the Fur Trade*. Berkeley: University of California Press, 1978.

Matson, Nehemiah. *Pioneers of Illinois, Containing a Series of Sketches That Occurred Previous to 1813*. Chicago: Knight and Leonard, 1882.

Matthews, John Joseph. *The Osage: Children of the Middle Waters*. Norman: University of Oklahoma Press, 1961.

Mazrim, Robert. *Now Quite Out of Society: Archaeology and Frontier Illinois—Essays and Excavation Reports*. Transportation Archaeological Bulletins 1. Urbana: University of Illinois, 2002.

McDermott, John Francis, ed. *Frenchmen and French Ways in the Mississippi Valley*. Urbana: University of Illinois Press, 1969.

McDonough, J. L., and Company. *The Combined History of Randolph, Monroe, and Perry Counties, Illinois*. Philadelphia, 1883.

McHugh, Tom. *The Time of the Buffalo*. New York: Knopf, 1972.

McPherson, John, and Geri McPherson. *Primitive Wilderness and Survival Skills*. Randolph, Kansas: Prairie Wolf, 1993.

Mech, L. David. *The Wolf: The Ecology and Behavior of an Endangered Species*. Minneapolis: University of Minnesota Press, 1981.

Meinig, D. W. *The Shaping of America: A Geographical Perspective of 500 Years of History*. Vol. 1: *Atlantic America, 1492–1800*. New Haven: Yale University Press, 1986.

Merchant, Carolyn. *Ecological Revolutions: Nature, Gender, and Science in New England*. Chapel Hill: University of North Carolina Press, 1989.

Middleton, B. S., ed. *Flood Pulsing and Wetland Restoration in North America*. New York: Wiley, 2001.

Milner, George R. *The Cahokia Chiefdom: The Archaeology of a Mississippian Society*. Washington, D.C.: Smithsonian Institution Press, 1981.

Miquelon, Dale. *New France: 1701–1744*. Toronto: McClelland and Stewart, 1987.

Mohlenbrock, Robert H. *Forest Trees of Illinois*. Springfield: Illinois Department of Conservation, Division of Forestry, 1986.

Nasatir, Abraham P. *Spanish War Vessels on the Mississippi, 1792–1796*. New Haven: Yale University Press, 1968.

Native Tree Guide. Shaw Arboretum of the Missouri Botanical Garden, 1987.

Neill, R. F. *The End of National Policy: Very Long Run Economic Factors in Canadian Economic Development*. Prince Edward Island: University of Prince Edward Island, 2004.

Nelson, Larry C. *A Man of Distinction among Them: Alexander McKee and British-Indian Affairs along the Ohio Country Frontier, 1754–1799*. Kent, Ohio: Kent State University Press, 1999.

O'Brien, Michael J., ed. *Grassland, Forest, and Historical Settlement: An Analysis of Dynamics in Northeast Missouri*. Lincoln: University of Nebraska Press, 1984.

Outwater, Alice. *Water: A Natural History*. New York: Harper Collins, 1996.

Page, O. J. *History of Massac County, Illinois, with Life Sketches and Portraits, Part One—Historical*. Massac County, 1900.

Palm, Mary Borgias. *The Jesuit Missions of the Illinois Country, 1673–1763*. Cleveland: Saint Louis University, 1931.

Parkins, Almon Ernest. *The Historical Geography of Detroit*. Lansing: Michigan Historical Commission, 1918.

Parkman, Francis. *The Conspiracy of Pontiac and the Indian War after the Conquest of Canada*. Boston: Little, Brown, 1917.

Peattie, Donald Culross. *A Natural History of Trees of Eastern and Central North America*. New York: Bonanza, 1968.

Peckham, Howard. *Pontiac and the Indian Uprising*. New York: Russell and Russell, 1947.

Perrin, J. Nick. *The Jewel of Cahokia*. Belleville, Illinois: Belleville Advocate Printing Company, 1936.

———. *Perrin's History of Illinois*. 1906.

Perrin, W. H., H. H. Mill, and A. A. Graham. *The History of Edgar County, Illinois*. Chicago: William Le Baron Jr. and Company, 1879.

Prince, Hugh. *Wetlands of the American Midwest: A Historical Geography of Changing Attitudes*. Chicago: University of Chicago Press, 1997.

Quaal, Gilbert. *Wild Plant Uses (Both Past and Present)*. Deer River, Minnesota: White Oak Society, 1995.

Quaife, M. M., ed. *The Development of Chicago, 1674–1914*. Chicago: Caxton Club, 1916.

Quimby, George Irving. *Indian Culture and European Trade Goods*. Madison: University of Wisconsin Press, 1966.

Rafert, Stewart. *The Miami Indians of Indiana: A Persistent People, 1654–1994*. Indianapolis: Indiana Historical Society, 1996.

Roe, Frank Gilbert. *The North American Buffalo: A Critical Study of the Species in Its Wild State*. 2nd ed. Toronto: University of Toronto Press, 1970.

Rothensteiner, John. *History of the Archdiocese of St. Louis in the Various Stages of Development from A.D. 1673 to A.D. 1928.* St. Louis: Catholic Historical Society, 1923.

Rummel, Merle C. *The Four Mile.* Boston, Indiana, 1998.

Sauer, Carl O. *The Geography of the Ozark Highland of Missouri.* New York: Greenwood Press, 1920.

Schlarman, J. H. *From Quebec to New Orleans: The Story of the French in America, Fort de Chartres.* Belleville, Illinois: Buechler Publishing Company, 1929.

Schroeder, Walter A. *Pre-settlement Prairie of Missouri.* 2nd ed. Missouri Department of Conservation, 1982.

Scott, James. "A History of the Illinois Nation of Indians from Their Discovery to the Present Day." Notes from meetings, Streator Historical Society, 1973. Manuscript in the Ayer Collection, Newberry Library, Chicago.

Shea, J. G. *Discovery and Exploration of the Mississippi Valley.* New York: J. S. Redfield, 1852.

Silver, Timothy. *A New Face on the Countryside: Indians, Colonists, and Slaves in the South Atlantic Forests, 1500–1800.* Cambridge: Cambridge University Press, 1990.

Smith, George Washington. *History of Illinois and Her People.* Vol. 1. Chicago: American Historical Society, Inc., 1927.

———. *A History of Southern Illinois: A Narrative Account of Its Historical Progress, Its People, and Its Principal Interests.* Chicago: Lewis Publishing Company, 1912.

Sosin, Jack M. *The Revolutionary Frontier, 1763–1783.* New York: Holt, Rinehart, and Winston, 1967.

———. *Whitehall and the Wilderness: The Middle West in British Colonial Policy, 1760–1775.* Lincoln: University of Nebraska Press, 1961.

Speed, Glenn J. *Ghost Towns of Southern Illinois.* Royalton, Illinois, 1977.

Steele, Ian K. *Warpaths: Invasions of North America.* New York: Oxford University Press, 1994.

Stewart, Omer C. *Forgotten Fires: Native Americans and the Transient Wilderness.* Norman: University of Oklahoma Press, 2002.

Suess, Adolph B. *Glimpses of Prairie du Rocher, Its Past and Present, 1722–1942.* Belleville, Illinois: Buechler Printing Company, 1942.

Surrey, Nancy M. Miller. *The Commerce of Louisiana during the French Regime: 1699–1763.* New York: Columbia University Press, 1916.

Temple, Wayne C. *Indian Villages of the Illinois Country: Historic Tribes.* Springfield: Illinois State Museum, 1958.

Terrell, John Upton. *American Indian Almanac.* New York: World Publishing Company, 1961.

Thornbrough, Gayle. *Outpost on the Wabash, 1787–1791.* Indianapolis: Indiana Historical Society, 1957.

Thorne, Tanis C. *The Many Hands of My Relations: French and Indians on the Lower Missouri.* Columbia: University of Missouri Press, 1996.

Townshend, Robert F., ed. *Hero, Hawk, and Open Hand: American Indian Art of the Ancient Midwest and South.* New Haven: Yale University Press, 2004.

Trigger, Bruce G. *Natives and Newcomers: Canada's "Heroic Age" Reconsidered.* Kingston, Ontario: McGill-Queen's University Press, 1985.

Tucker, Sarah Jones. *Indian Villages of the Illinois Country.* Scientific Papers 2, part 1, atlas. 1942. Reprinted, Springfield: Illinois State Museum, 1975.

Turner, Frederick Jackson. *The Character and Influence of the Indian Trade in Wisconsin: A Study of the Trading Post as an Institution,* edited by David Harry Miller and William W. Savage Jr. Norman: University of Oklahoma Press, 1977; originally published, 1891.

Usner, Daniel H., Jr. *Indians, Settlers, and Slaves in a Frontier Exchange Economy: The Lower Mississippi Valley before 1783.* Chapel Hill: University of North Carolina Press, 1992.

Vennum, Thomas, Jr.. *Wild Rice and the Ojibway People.* St. Paul: Minnesota Historical Society Press, 1988.

Walthall, John A., and Elizabeth D. Benchley. *The River L'Abbe Mission: A French Colonial Church for the Cahokia Illini on Monk's Mound.* Springfield: Illinois Historic Preservation Agency, 1987.

Walthall, John A., and Thomas E. Emerson, eds. *Calumet & Fleur-de-Lys: Archaeology of Indian and French Contact in the Midcontinent.* Washington, D.C.: Smithsonian Institution Press, 1992.

White, Richard. *The Middle Ground: Indians, Empires, and Republics in the Great Lakes Region, 1650–1815.* Cambridge: Cambridge University Press, 1991.

———. *The Roots of Dependency: Subsistence, Environment, and Social Change among the Choctaws, Pawnees, and Navajos.* Lincoln: University of Nebraska Press, 1983.

Whitney, Gordon G. *From Coastal Wilderness to Fruited Plain: A History of Environmental Change in Temperate North America from 1500 to the Present.* Cambridge: Cambridge University Press, 1994.

Wild Rice. U.S. Fish and Wildlife Service. Department of the Interior, September 1987.

Zawacki, April Allison. *Early Vegetation of Lower Illinois Valley: A Study of the Distribution of Floral Resources with Reference to Prehistoric Cultural-Ecological Adaptations.* Report of Investigations/Illinois State Museum, no. 17. Springfield, Illinois, 1969.

Zitomersky, Joseph. *French Americans–Native Americans in Eighteenth-Century French Colonial Louisiana: The Population Geography of the Illinois Indians, 1670s–1760s.* Lund, Sweden: Lund University Press, 1994.

Secondary Sources (Articles, Chapters, and Reports)

Abrams, Marc D. "Where Has All the White Oak Gone?" *BioScience* 53, no. 10 (October 2003).

Ahler, Steven R. "Stratigraphy and Radiocarbon Chronology of Modoc Rock Shelter, Illinois." *American Antiquity* 58, no. 3 (1993).

Anderson, Dean L. "Variability in Trade at Eighteenth-Century French Outposts." In Walthall, *French Colonial Archaeology.*

Angle, Paul M., and Richard L. Beyer. "A Handbook of Illinois History." In *Papers in Illinois History and Transactions for the Year 1941.* Springfield: Illinois State Historical Society, 1943.

"An Anthropological Report on the Piankeshaw Indians, Dockett 99 (part of Consolidated Docket no. 315, Dr. Dorothy Libby)." *The Ohio Valley–Great Lakes Ethnohistory Archives: The Miami Collection.* Bloomington: Glenn A. Black Laboratory of Archaeology, Indiana University.

Aron, Stephen. "Pigs and Hunters: 'Rights in the Woods' on the Trans-Appalachian Frontier." In *Contact Points: American Frontiers from the Mohawk Valley to the Mississippi, 1750–1830,* edited by Andrew R. L. Clayton and Fredrika J. Teute. Chapel Hill: University of North Carolina Press, 1998.

Ashby, William, and George T. Weaver. "Forest Regeneration on Two Fields in Southwestern Illinois." *American Midland Naturalist* 84, no. 1 (July 1970).

Auger, J., et al. "Selection of Ants by the American Black Bear (*Ursus americanus*)." *Western North American Naturalist* 64, no. 2 (2004).

Bannon, John Francis. "The Spaniards and the Illinois Country, 1762–1800." *Journal of the Illinois State Historical Society* 69, no. 2 (May 1976).

Battle, Herbert B. "The Domestic Use of Oil among the Southern Aborigines." *American Anthropologist* 24, no. 2 (April–May 1922).

Belting, Natalia. "The Native American as Myth and Fact." *Journal of the Illinois State Historical Society* 69, no. 2 (May 1976).

"Black Bear: *Ursus americanus* Pallas." In Robert M. Timm et al., *Mammals of Kansas.* University of Kansas Field Station. http://www.ku.edu/~mammals/ursus-amer.html (accessed 2009).

Blasingham, Emily J. "The Depopulation of the Illinois Indians," part 2. *Ethnohistory* 3, no. 4 (1956): 386–96.

Bottomland Hardwoods of the Mississippi Alluvial Valley: Characteristics and Management of Natural Function, Structure, and Composition. General Technical Report SRS-42. Fayetteville, Arkansas: U.S. Department of Agriculture, 2001.

Briggs, Winstanley. "Slavery in French Colonial Illinois." *Chicago History* 18 (winter 1989–90).

Brotherton, Kathleen. "Osage Occasionally Killed Early French Settlers." *River Hills Traveler,* January-February 2004.

Brown, Ian W. "Certain Aspects of French-Indian Interaction in Lower Louisiana." In Walthall and Emerson, *Calumet & Fleur-de-Lys.*

Brown, Margaret Kimball. "The Search for the Michigamea Indian Village." *Outdoor Illinois,* March 1972.

Burdick, Alan. "The Truth about Invasive Species." *Discover* 26, no. 5 (May 2005).

Burger, John. "Yellowstone's Insect Vampires." *Yellowstone Science* 4, no. 4 (1996).

Butterfield, Wilshire. "Chicago." *Magazine of Western History* 3, no. 4 (March 1886).

Caldwell, Norman W. "Fort Massac during the French and Indian War." *Journal of the Illinois State Historical Society* 43, no. 2 (summer 1950).

Callender, Charles. "Illinois Indians." In William C. Sturtevant, *Handbook of North American Indians*. Washington, D.C.: Smithsonian Institution, 1978.

Carson, James Taylor. "Horses and the Economy and Culture of the Choctaw Indians, 1690–1840." *Ethnohistory* 41, no. 3 (summer 1995).

"Cartographic and Pictorial Introduction to Cahokia Mounds and the American Bottom." Department of Geography and Office of Contract Archaeology. Southern Illinois University Edwardsville, 2002.

Chapman, Jefferson, Robert B. Stewart, and Richard A. Yarnell. "Archaeological Evidence for Pre-Columbian Introduction of *Portulaca oleracea* and *Mollugo verticllata* into Eastern North America." *Economic Botany* 28 (October–December 1974).

Collins, William B., et al. "Canadian Bluejoint Response to Heavy Grazing." *Journal of Range Management* 54, no. 3 (May 2001).

"Cool Season Grasses." In *Range of Grasses of Kansas*. Kansas Cooperative Extension Service. Manhattan: Kansas State University, July 1983.

Damhoureyeh, Said A., and David C. Hartnett. "Effects of Bison and Cattle on Growth, Reproduction, and Abundance of Five Tall-Grass Prairie Forbs." *American Journal of Botany* 84, no. 12 (1997).

Dickinson, Samuel D. "Shamans, Priests, Preachers, and Pilgrims at Arkansas Post." In *Arkansas before the Americans*, edited by Hester A. Davis. Arkansas Archaeology Survey Research Series no. 40, 1991.

Dieter, Charles D., and Thomas R. McCabe. "Factors Influencing Beaver Lodge-Site Selection on a Prairie River." *American Midland Naturalist* 122, no. 2 (October 1989).

Dowd, Gregory Evans. "The French King Wakes Up in Detroit: 'Pontiac's War' in Rumor and History." *Ethnohistory* 37, no. 3 (summer 1990).

Edwards, Jay D. "The Origins of the Louisiana Creole Cottage." In *French and Germans in the Mississippi Valley: Landscape and Cultural Traditions*, edited by Michael Roark. Cape Girardeau, Missouri: Center for Regional History and Cultural Heritage, 1988.

Edwards, T. "Buffalo and Prairie Ecology." In *Proceedings of the Fifth Midwest Prairie Conference*, edited by D. C. Glenn-Lewin and R. Q. Landers Jr. Ames: Iowa State University, 1978.

Effects of Fire on Water: A State-of-the-Knowledge Review. U.S. Department of Agriculture Forest Service General Technical Report WO-10. Denver, Colorado: National Fire Effects Workshop, April 10–14, 1978.

Emerson, T. E., D. L. McElrath, and J. A. Williams. "Patterns of Hunter-Gatherer Mobility and Sedentism during the Archaic Period in the American Bottom." In *Foraging, Collecting, and Harvesting: Archaic Period Subsistence and Settlement in the Eastern Woodlands*, edited by S. Neusium. Occasional Paper no. 6, Center for Archaeological Investigations. Carbondale: Southern Illinois University, 1986.

Emerson, Thomas E., and James A. Brown. "The Late Prehistory and Protohistory of Illinois." In Walthall and Emerson, *Calumet & Fleur-de-Lys*.

Etling, Kathy. "The Bear Truth." *Missouri Conservationist*, April 2000.

Ewers, John C. "The Horse in Blackfoot Indian Culture: With Comparative Material from Other Western Tribes." *Bureau of American Ethnology Bulletin*, no. 159 (1955).

———. "Were the Blackfeet Rich in Horses?" *American Anthropologist*, n.s., 45, no. 4, part 1 (October–December 1943).

Fadler, T. P. *Memoirs of a French Village: A Chronicle of Old Prairie du Rocher, 1722–1972.* Self-published, 1972. Copy in Illinois Historical Survey, Urbana-Champaign.

Faye, Stanley. "Illinois Indians on the Lower Mississippi, 1771–1781." *Illinois State Historical Society* 35 (1942).

Fortier, John B. "New Light on Fort Massac." In McDermott, *Frenchmen and French Ways* (under Secondary Sources [Books and Monographs]).

Gardener, Paul S. "The Ecological Structure and Behavioral Implications of Mast Exploitation Strategies." In *People, Plants, and Landscapes: Studies in Paleoethnobotany*, edited by Kristin J. Gremillion. Tuscaloosa: University of Alabama Press, 1997.

Gericke, Bradley. "To the Distant Illinois Country: The Stirling Expedition to Fort de Chartres, 1765." *Journal of Illinois History* 2, no. 2 (1999).

Haines, Francis. "The Northward Spread of Horses among the Plains Indians." *American Anthropologist*, n.s., 40, no. 3 (July–September 1938).

———. "Where Did the Plains Indians Get Their Horses?" *American Anthropologist*, n.s., 40, no. 1 (January–March 1938).

Hamel, Paul B., et al. "Chainsaws, Canebrakes, and Cotton Fields: Sober Thoughts on Silviculture for Songbirds in Bottomland Forests." In *Bottomland Hardwoods*.

Hanson, Charles E., Jr. "The Southern Trade: A Slightly Different Story." *Museum of the Fur Trade Quarterly* 22, no. 1 (1986).

Hauser, Raymond E. "The Fox Raid of 1752: Defensive Warfare and the Decline of the Illinois Indian Tribe." *Illinois State Historical Journal* 86 (1993).

———. "The Illinois Indian Tribe: From Autonomy and Self-Sufficiency to Dependency and Depopulation." *Journal of the Illinois State Historical Society* 69, no. 2 (May 1976).

Hechenberger, Dan. "The Cahokia Tribe." *M'Skutewe Awandiangwi* 1, no. 3 (1998).

———. "The Metchigamea Tribe." *M'Skutewe Awandiangwi* 1, no. 2 (1998).

———. "The Peoria Tribe." *M'Skutewe Awandiangwi* 1, no. 3 (1998).

———. "Towards Understanding the Illinewek View of the French at Cahokia." *Journal of the St. Clair County Historical Society* 5, no. 9 (1999).

Hey, Donald L., and Nancy S. Phillipi. "Reinventing a Flood Control Strategy." *Wetlands Initiative*, September 1994.

"A History of the Bridgeport Canal System." University of Illinois at Chicago. 1998. http://www.uic.edu/orgs/LockZero/II.html (accessed 2010).

Horsfall, William R., Robert J. Novak, and Forrest L. Johnson. "*Aedes vexans* as a Flood-Plain Mosquito." *Environmental Entomology* 4, no. 5 (October 1975).

Horsman, Reginald. "Great Britain and the Illinois Country, 1762–1800." *Journal of the Illinois State Historical Society* 49, no. 2 (May 1976).

Hunter, Andrea A., and Deborah M. Pearsall. "Paleoethnobotany of the Osage and Missouri Indians: Analysis of Plant Remains from Historic Village Sites." *Missouri Archaeologist* 47 (December 1986).

Illinois: Man and Resources, Past and Present: A Guide to the Exhibits in the Museummobile. Springfield: Illinois State Museum, n.d.

Jakle, John A. "The American Bison and the Occupance of the Ohio Valley." *Proceedings of the American Philosophical Society* 112, no. 4 (August 1968).

Jensen, Truls, Paul E. Kaiser, and Donald R. Barnard. "Adaptation to Intermittently Flooded Swamps by *Anopheles quadrimaculus* Species CI (Diptera Culicidae)." *Environmental Entomology* 23, no. 5 (1994).

Julio, Mary Antoine de. "Prairie du Chien and the Rediscovery of Its French Log Houses." In *French and Germans in the Mississippi Valley: Landscape and Cultural Traditions*, edited by Michael Roark. Cape Girardeau, Missouri: Center for Regional History and Cultural Heritage, 1988.

Kaplan, Lawrence. "Ethnobotany of the Apple Creek Archaeological Site, Southern Illinois." *American Journal of Botany* 60, no. 4 (supplement, April 1973).

Kay, Jeanne. "The Fur Trade and Native American Population Growth," *Ethnohistory* 31, no. 4 (autumn 1984).

———. "Wisconsin Indian Hunting Patterns." *Annals of the Association of American Geographers* 69, no. 3 (September 1979).

Keefe, James F. "The Inventory of Fort Des Chartres." *Muzzleloader* 18, no. 6 (January-February 1992).

Keene, David. "Fort de Chartres: Archaeology in the Illinois Country." In Walthall, *French Colonial Archaeology.*

Kellogg, Louise. "La Chapelle's Remarkable Retreat through the Mississippi Valley, 1760–61." *Mississippi Valley Historical Review* 22, no. 1 (June 1935).

Kimball, B. A., et al. "Effects of Thinning and Nitrogen Fertilization on Sugars and Terpenes in Douglas-Fir Vascular Tissues: Implications for Black Bear Foraging." *Forest Science* 44, no. 4 (1998).

Knapp, A. J., et al. "The Keystone Role of Bison in North American Tall-Grass Prairie." *Bioscience* 49 (1999).

Kunkel, K., and D. H. Pletscher. "Species-Specific Population Dynamics of Cervids in a Multipredator System." *Journal of Wildlife Management* 63, no. 4 (1999).

Leavelle, Tracy. "'Bad Things' and 'Good Hearts': Mediation, Meaning, and the Language of Illinois Christianity." *Church History* 76 (June 2007).

Lopinot, Neil H. "Spatial and Temporal Variability in Mississippian Subsistence: The Archaeobotanical Record." In *Late Prehistoric Agriculture: Observations from the Midwest*, edited by William I. Woods. Studies in Illinois Archaeology 8. Springfield: Illinois Historic Preservation Agency, 1992.

Lopinot, Neil H., and William I. Woods. "Wood Overexploitation and the Collapse of Cahokia." In C. Margaret Scarry, *Foraging and Farming in the Eastern Woodlands*. Gainesville: University Press of Florida, 1993.

Love, Kathy. "Save the Last Dance." *Missouri Conservationist*, February 2004.

Lunn, Jean. "The Illegal Fur Trade out of New France, 1713–1760." *Canadian Historical Association Annual Report*, 1939.

Manske, Llewellyn L., et al. "Spring-Seeded Winter Cereals Can Extend the Northern Plains Grazing Season." North Dakota State University, Dickinson Research Extension Center. www.grazinghandbook.com.

Martin, Terrance J. "Animal Remains from the Cahokia Wedge Site." In *Archaeology at French Colonial Cahokia*, edited by Bonnie L. Gums. Springfield: Illinois Historic Preservation Agency, 1988.

Martin, Terrance J., and Mary Carol Masulis. "Preliminary Report on Animal Remains from Fort de Chartres (11R127)." Appendix D in "Archaeological Excavations at Fort de Chartres: 1985–87," edited by David Keene. Unpublished technical report on file at the Illinois Historic Preservation Agency, Springfield.

Marysville, Kansas, Tourism Guide, 1997–98.

McCarthy, William P. "The Chevalier Macarty Mactigue." *Journal of the Illinois State Historical Society* 61, no. 1 (spring 1968).

McClure, James P. "The Ohio Valley's Deerskin Trade: Topics for Consideration." *Old Northwest* 15, no. 3 (fall 1990).

McDermott, John Francis, ed. *The French, the Indians, and George Rogers Clark in the Illinois: Proceedings of an Indiana American Revolution Bicentennial Symposium*. Indiana Historical Society, 1977.

McKinley, Daniel W. "The Carolina Parakeet in Pioneer Missouri." *Wilson Bulletin* 72, no. 3 (September 1980).

Messmer, Terry A., et al. "A Landowner's Guide to Common North American Predators of Upland-Nesting Birds." Berryman Institute publication no. 13, Utah State University, Logan, 1997.

Milner, George R., Eve Anderson, and Virginia G. Smith. "Warfare in Late Prehistoric West-Central Illinois." *American Antiquity* 56, no. 4 (October 1991).

Miquelon, Dale. "Envisioning the French Empire: Utrecht, 1711–1713." *French Historical Studies*, 24, no. 4 (autumn 2001).

Montague, E. J. "The History of Randolph County, Illinois, Including Old Kaskaskia Island." 1859. Copied by Elisabeth Pinkerton Leighty. Sparta, Ill., 1948.

Moodie, D. W. "Agriculture and the Fur Trade." In *Old Trails and New Directions: Papers of the Third North American Fur Trade Conference*, edited by Carol M. Judd and Arthur J. Ray. Toronto: University of Toronto Press, 1980.

Morgan, M. J. "Indians on Trial: Crime and Punishment in French Louisiana on the Eve of the Seven Years War." *Louisiana History* 50, no. 3 (summer 2009).

Morgan, Thomas D. "Purslane." *Prairie Falcon* 33, no. 1 (September 2004).

———. "Tree of the Month: Hop Hornbeam." *Prairie Falcon* 31, no. 4 (December 2002).

Morse, Dan F. "The Seventeenth-Century Michigamea Village Location in Arkansas." In Walthall and Emerson, *Calumet & Fleur-de-Lys*, 55–74.

Munson, Patrick J., Paul W. Parmalee, and Richard A. Yarnell. "Subsistence Ecology of Scovill, a Terminal Middle Woodland Village." *American Antiquity* 36, no. 4 (1971).

Naiman, Robert J., Carol A. Johnston, and James C. Kelley. "Alteration of North American Streams by Beaver." *Bioscience* 38 (December 1988): 753–62.

Nasatir, A. P. "The Anglo-Spanish Frontier in the Illinois Country during the American Revolution, 1779–1783." *Journal of the Illinois State Historical Society* 21, no. 3 (October 1928).

Nelson, Dennis C., and Roger C. Anderson. "Factors Related to the Distribution of Prairie Plants along a Moisture Gradient." *American Midland Naturalist* 109, no. 2 (April 1983).

Nelson, John C., Anjela Redmond, and Richard E. Sparks. "Impacts of Settlement on Floodplain Vegetation at the Confluence of the Illinois and Mississippi Rivers." *Transactions of the Illinois State Academy of Science* 87, nos. 3 and 4 (1994).

O'Malley, Claudia M. "*Aedes vexans* (Meigen): An Old Foe." *Proceedings of the New Jersey Mosquito Control Association*, 1990.

Osborn, Alan J. "Ecological Aspects of Equestrian Adaptation in Aboriginal North America." *American Anthropologist*, n.s., 85, no. 3 (September 1983).

Owens, Robert. "Jean-Baptiste Ducoigne, the Kaskaskia, and the Limits of Thomas Jefferson's Friendship." *Journal of Illinois History* 5, no. 2 (summer 2002).

Palm, Mary Borgias. "The First Illinois Wheat." *Mid-America* 13 (July 1930).

Pare, George. "The St. Joseph Mission." *Mississippi Valley Historical Review* 17, no. 1 (June 1930).

Parmalee, Paul W. "The Faunal Complex of the Fisher Site, Illinois." *American Midland-Naturalist* 68, no. 2 (1962).

Parmeter, Jon Williams. "Pontiac's War: Forging New Links in the Anglo-Illinois Covenant Chain, 1758–1766." *Ethnohistory* 44, no. 4 (autumn 1997).

Pechuman, L. L., Donald W. Webb, and H. J. Taskey. *The Diptera or True Flies of Illinois: I. Tabanidae.* Illinois Natural History Bulletin 33, no. 1. Champaign: Illinois Department of Energy and Natural Resources, 1983.

Piazza, Theresa J. "The Kaskaskia Manuscripts: French Traders in the Missouri Valley before Lewis and Clark." *Missouri Archaeologist* 53 (December 1992).

Post, E., et al. "Ecosystem Consequences of Wolf Behavioral Response to Climate." *Nature* 401, no. 6756 (1999).

Ray, Arthur J. "Indians as Consumers in the Eighteenth Century." In *Old Trails and New Directions: Papers of the Third North American Fur Trade Conference.* Toronto: University of Toronto Press, 1980.

Reichmas, O. J., et al. "Distinct Animal-Generated Edge Effects in a Tall-Grass Prairie Community." *Ecology* 74 (1993).

Robertson, Kenneth R., et al. "Fifty Years of Change in Illinois Hill Prairies." *Erigenia* 14 (November 1995).

Roney, Janet. "Kaskaskia Reflections: Where the Buffalo Roamed." *Community Record*, December 14, 2005.

Rose, Forrest. "Ring in the Old: Study of Tree Rings Brings Perspective to Human Life." *Focus* 21 (spring 1999).

Russell, Peter E. "Redcoats in the Wilderness: The British Officer and Irregular Warfare in Europe and America, 1740–1760." *William & Mary Quarterly*, 3rd ser., 35, no. 4 (October 1978).

Sampson, Homer C. "An Ecological Survey of the Prairie Vegetation of Illinois." *Bulletin of the Illinois Laboratory of Natural History* 13, no. 16 (1921).

"Sandhill Crane, *Grus canadensis*." Illinois Natural History Survey, Urbana-Champaign. http://www.inhs.uiuc.edu/animals–plants/birds/ifwis/birds/sandhill-crane.html.

"[Sandhill Crane] Occurrence in Illinois." Illinois Natural History Survey, Urbana-Champaign. http://www.inhs.uiuc.edu/chf/pub/ifwis/birds/sandhill–crane.html.

Saucier, Walter J., and Katherine Wagner Spineke, "François Saucier, Engineer of Fort de Chartres, Illinois." In McDermott, *Frenchmen and French Ways* (under Secondary Sources [Books and Monographs].

Schwartz, Mark W., et al. "The Biogeography of and Habitat Loss in Hill Prairies." In *Conservation in Highly Fragmented Landscapes*. New York: Chapman, 1997.

Seed, Patricia. "Taking Possession and Reading Texts: Establishing the Authority of Overseas Empires." *William & Mary Quarterly*, 3rd ser., 49 (1992).

Smith, Marian, et al. "Effect of the Flood of 1993 on *Boltonia decurrens*, a Rare Floodplain Plant." *Regulated Rivers Research & Management*, no. 14 (1998).

Smith, Winston P., et al. "A Comparison of Breeding Bird Communities and Habitat Features between Old-Growth and Second-Growth Bottomland Hardwood Forests." In *Bottomland Hardwoods*.

Smith, Winston P., and Patrick A. Zollner. "Seasonal Habitat Distribution of Swamp Rabbits, White-Tailed Deer, and Small Mammals in Old Growth and Managed Bottomland Hardwood Forests." In *Bottomland Hardwoods*.

Soper, J. Dewey. "History, Range, and Home Life of the Northern Bison." *Ecological Monographs* 11 (1941).

Sparks, Richard E. "Need for Ecosystem Management of Large Rivers and Their Floodplains." *Bioscience* 45, no. 3 (March 1995).

Stevens, Paul L. "'One of the Most Beautiful Regions of the World': Paul Des Ruisseaux's *Memoire* of the Wabash-Illinois Country in 1777." *Indiana Magazine of History* 83, no. 4 (1987).

Stickney, Gardener P. "Indian Use of Wild Rice." *American Anthropologist* 9, no. 4 (April 1986).

Stoecker, M. A. "Survival and Aerenchyma Development under Flooded Conditions of *Boltonia decurrens*, a Threatened Floodplain Species, and *Conyza canadensis*, a Widely Distributed Competitor." *American Midland Naturalist* 134, no. 1 (July 1995).

Storm, Colton. "The Notorious Colonel Wilkins." *Journal of the Illinois State Historical Society* 40 (March 1947).

Swank, Phillip J., James P. Geaghan, and Donna A. Dewhurst. "Foraging Differences between Native and Released Mississippi Sandhill Cranes: Implications for Conservation." *Conservation Biology* 2, no. 4 (December 1988).

Taylor, P. D., and S. M. Smith. "Activities and physiological states of male and female *Tabanus sackeni*." *Medical Veterinary Entomology* 3 (1989).

Trask, Kerry A. "To Cast Out the Devils: British Ideology and the French Canadians of the Northwest Interior, 1760–1774." *American Review of Canadian Studies* 15, no. 3 (1985).

Trewartha, Glenn T. "A Second Epoch of Destructive Occupance in the Driftless Hill Land (1760–1832: Period of British, Spanish, and Early American Control)." *Annals of the Association of American Geographers* 30, no. 2 (June 1940).

Turner, Lewis M. "Grassland in the Floodplain of Illinois Rivers." *American Midland Naturalist* 15 (1934).

Usner, Daniel H., Jr. "A Cycle of Lowland Forest Efficiency: The Late Archaic-Woodland Economy of the Lower Mississippi Valley." *Journal of Anthropological Research* 39, no. 4 (1983).

———. "The Deerskin Trade in French Louisiana." *Proceedings of the Meeting of the French Colonial Historical Society* 10 (1984).

Vetter, Craig. "Bloodsucker Zen." *Chicago Wilderness* 7, no. 3 (spring 2004).

Walthall, John A. "Aboriginal Pottery and the Eighteenth-Century Illini." In Walthall and Emerson, *Calumet & Fleur-de-Lys*, 155–76.

———, ed. *French Colonial Archaeology: The Illinois Country and the Western Great Lakes*. Urbana: University of Illinois Press, 1992.

———. "French Colonial Fort Massac: Architecture and Ceramic Patterning." In Walthall, *French Colonial Archaeology*.

Walthall, John A., F. Terry Norris, and Barbara D. Stafford. "Woman Chief's Village: An Illini Winter Hunting Camp." In Walthall and Emerson, *Calumet & Fleur-de-Lys*, 129–54.

Weymouth, John W., and William I. Woods. "Combined Magnetic and Chemical Surveys of Forts Kaskaskia and de Chartres Number 1, Illinois." *Historical Archaeology* 18, no. 2 (1984).

White, J., and Diane Tecic. "Proposal to Dedicate Storment Hauss Nature Preserve in Monroe County." Urbana: Illinois Department of Natural Resources, 2001.

White, John. "How the Terms *Savanna, Barrens,* and *Oak Openings* Were Used in Early Illinois." In J. S. Fralish, et al., *Living in the Edge: Proceedings of the North American Conference on Savannahs and Barrens*. Illinois State University, Normal, October 15–16, 1994. Great Lakes National Program Office: U.S. Environmental Protection Agency, 1994. Available online at http://www.epa.gov/glnpo/ecopage/upland/oak94/Proceedings/Index.html.

———. *A Review of the American Bison in Illinois, with an Emphasis on Historical Accounts*. Urbana, Illinois: Nature Conservancy, 1996.

———. *A Survey of Native Vegetation in the Big Rivers Blufflands of Calhoun, Greene, and Jersey Counties with Recommendations for Protection, Restoration, and Management.* Urbana: Illinois Department of Natural Resources, 2001.

White, John K. "Illinois." In *Encyclopedia of North American Indians*, edited by Fred E. Howe. New York: Houghton-Mifflin Company, 1996.

White, Richard. "The Cultural Landscape of the Pawnees." In *Kansas and the West: New Perspectives*, edited by Rita Napier. Lawrence: University of Kansas, 2003.

———. "The Winning of the West: the Expansion of the Sioux in the Eighteenth and Nineteenth Centuries." *Journal of American History* 65, no. 2 (September 1978).

"White-Tailed Deer: Seasonal Use of Forage Classes," in *Studies of the Cross Timbers Region of Oklahoma and Texas.* Samuel Roberts Noble Foundation. 1997–2009. www.noble.org/Ag/Wildlife/DeerFoods/habitatReq4.html.

Whitney, Ellen M. "Indian History and the Indians of Illinois." *Journal of the Illinois State Historical Society* 69, no. 2 (May 1976).

Williams, Chuck. "Lessons from Pigeon." *Natural Areas Journal* 22, no. 3 (2002).

Wilson, H. Clyde. "A New Interpretation of the Wild Rice District of Wisconsin." *American Anthropologist*, n.s., 58, no. 6 (December 1956).

Woods, William I. "Changes in the Landscape of the American Bottom—A.D. 1000 to Now." Paper presented in a roundtable symposium, *Changes in the Landscape: The Lower Valley and Elsewhere—A.D. 1000 to Now*, at the Joint Meetings of the Southern Archaeological Conference and the Midwest Archaeological Conference. Lexington, Kentucky, November 11, 1984.

———. "Maize Agriculture and the Late Prehistoric: A Characterization of Settlement Location Strategies." In *Emergent Horticultural Economies of the Eastern Woodlands,* edited by William F. Keegan. Center for Archaeological Investigations, Occasional Paper no. 7, Southern Illinois University, 1987.

———. "Population Nucleation, Intensive Agriculture, and Environmental Degradation: The Cahokia Example." *Agriculture and Human Values* 21 (2004).

———. "Soil Chemical Investigations in Illinois Archaeology: Two Example Studies." *American Chemical Society* (1984).

Woods, William I., and George R. Holley. "Upland Mississippian Settlement in the American Bottom Region." In *Cahokia and the Hinterlands: Middle Mississippian Cultures of the Midwest,* edited by Thomas E. Emerson and R. Barry Lewis. Urbana: University of Illinois Press, 1991.

Worcester, Donald E., and Thomas F. Schilz. "The Spread of Firearms among the Indians on the Anglo-French Frontier." *American Indian Quarterly* 8, no. 2 (spring 1984).

Yeager, A. F. "Root systems of certain trees and shrubs grown on prairie soils." *Journal of Agricultural Research* 51 (1935).

Secondary Sources (Dissertations, Theses, and Manuscripts)

Briggs, Winstanley. "The Forgotten Colony: Le Pays des Illinois." PhD diss., University of Chicago, 1985.

Caldwell, Norman W. *The French in the Mississippi Valley, 1740–1750.* Urbana: University of Illinois Press, 1941. PhD dissertation in the Newberry Library, Chicago.

Hauser, Raymond. "An Ethnohistory of the Illinois Indian Tribe, 1673–1832." PhD dissertation, Northern Illinois University, 1973; Ann Arbor, Mich.: University Microfilms, 1973.

Majors, Henry M. "Fort Ouiatanon and the Wabash River, 1700–1824." Unpublished manuscript, Lilly Library, Indiana University, Bloomington, 1970.

Rollings, Willard Hughes. "Prairie Hegemony: An Ethnohistorical Study of the Osage, from Early Times to 1840." PhD dissertation, Texas Tech University, 1983.

Sangunett, Brandi M. "Reference Conditions for Streams in the Grand Prairie Natural Division of Illinois." Masters thesis, Southern Illinois University Carbondale, 2000.

Index

Italicized page numbers indicate illustrations.

upland prairies: in 18th century, 24–25; of American Bottom, 19; archaeological studies of, 27; depleted state of, 139; documentation by American settlers, 5; faunal species of, 22; forest invasion, 23; migration from floodplain to, 6; movement of people through, 26; as north-south corridor, 39; parkland look, 33; settlement of, 4. *See also* prairies
upland sloughs, 33

Vaudreuil, Pierre Rigaud de, 95, 128, 237–38n. 8
vegetation: amaranth, 82; of Big Rivers area, 46; bulrushes, 35; bundleflower, 64; cattails, 35; cultigens, 51, 59–60, 65, 77–78, 85, 108; flood pulses and, 34; fruit, 35; fruit trees, 242n. 13; giant cane, 154; grasses, 28–29, 33, 85, 154, 192; horses and, 26; impact of grazing livestock on, 85; leadplant, 73, 224–25n. 6; oaks, 19, 33, 35–36, 85, 192; of prairies, 27–28, 31–32, 73; purslane, 30; scrubbing rush, 154–55; shifts in, among upland habitats, 25; spurge, 21; trees, 11, 34–36, 81–82, 113, 142, 175, 195, 235n. 35; water lily root, 82; wild rice (*Zizania aquatica*), 162–63
Vincennes, 122, *123* (map)
Vivier, Father, 22, 50, 64, 139

Wakeland soils, 78, 82
water: action of, and changes in settlement patterns, 141; and human lifeways, 17; in Illinois Country, 11–12; wells and springs, 14–15, 25; wetlands, 64, 102–3. *See also* marshes; *specific bodies of water*
waterfowl, 10, 26–27, 47, 61–62, 64, 163
Waterman Site (Mechigamea village), 109–10, 131
Western Intelligencer (*Illinois Intelligencer*), 32–33
wetlands, 64, 102–3
white-tailed deer (*Odocoileus virginianus*), 28, 64, 81, 86, 91, 195
Wilkins, John, 168–69, 180–81, 187, 196–97
wolves, 201–4
Woman Chief's Camp, 49
wood: depletion of, 113, 121, 221n. 24; uses for, 47–48, 81, 112–13, 142, 175, 192, 194. *See also individual tree species*
wooden breaking plows, 79–80
Woodland Indians, seasonal migrations of, 27
Wood River journals (Lewis and Clark), 204

yellow fever, 143–45

Zitomersky, Joseph, 65–66

M. J. Morgan teaches historical research at the Chapman Center for Rural Studies at Kansas State University. Her work on the environment and French in the Illinois Country has appeared in the *Journal of Illinois History* and *Louisiana History*, as well as in a historical geography essay collection (Rowman & Littlefield). She directs students in studies of lost towns, peoples, and landscapes.

 *Shawnee Books*

Also available in this series . . .

The Next New Madrid Earthquake: A Survival Guide for the Midwest
WILLIAM ATKINSON

Vicarious Thrills: A Championship Season of High School Basketball
PAUL E. BATES

Foothold on a Hillside: Memories of a Southern Illinoisan
CHARLESS CARAWAY

Growing Up in a Land Called Egypt: A Southern Illinois Family Biography
CLEO CARAWAY

Vernacular Architecture in Southern Illinois: The Ethnic Heritage
JOHN M. COGGESHALL AND JO ANNE NAST

The Flag on the Hilltop
MARY TRACY EARLE

A Nickel's Worth of Skim Milk: A Boy's View of the Great Depression
ROBERT J. HASTINGS

A Penny's Worth of Minced Ham: Another Look at the Great Depression
ROBERT J. HASTINGS

Southern Illinois Coal: A Portfolio
C. WILLIAM HORRELL

Always of Home: A Southern Illinois Childhood
EDGAR ALLEN IMHOFF

The Music Came First: The Memoirs of Theodore Paschedag
THEODORE PASCHEDAG
AS TOLD TO THOMAS J. HATTON

Escape Betwixt Two Suns: A True Tale of the Underground Railroad in Illinois
CAROL PIRTLE

Heartland Blacksmiths: Conversations at the Forge
RICHARD REICHELT

Fishing Southern Illinois
ART REID

All Anybody Ever Wanted of Me Was to Work: The Memoirs of Edith Bradley Rendleman
EDITH BRADLEY RENDLEMAN
EDITED BY JANE ADAMS

Giant City State Park and the Civilian Conservation Corps: A History in Words and Pictures
KAY RIPPELMEYER-TIPPY

A Southern Illinois Album: Farm Security Administration Photographs, 1936–1943
HERBERT K. RUSSELL

Yankin' and Liftin' Their Whole Lives: A Mississippi River Commercial Fisherman
RICHARD YOUNKER